Spinning Wheel

Complete Book of Dolls
volume two

Edited by Staff of Spinning Wheel

Gold Horse Publishing Inc.

SPINNING WHEEL'S COMPLETE BOOK OF DOLLS, VOL. II
Copyright © 1975, 1976, 1977, 1978, 1979, 1980, 1981,
1982, 1983 by Spinning Wheel Division, Gold Horse Publishing.

All rights reserved. No part of this book may be reproduced or utilized in any form or by any means, electric or mechanical, including photocopying, recording, or by any information storage and retrieval system, without permission in writing from the publisher, Gold Horse Publishing, Annapolis, Maryland 21401.

Library of Congress Catalog Card Number:
ISBN: 0-8119-0590-X

Prepared and Produced by Gold Horse Publishing.
Published by arrangement with Gold Horse Publishing.
Manufactured in the United States of America.

Distributed by:
Frederick Fell Publishers, Inc.
386 Park Avenue South, New York, N.Y. 10016 - 212 685-9017

Foreward

Since its inceptive days, **Spinning Wheel** has been concerned with collectible dolls. Many of the early articles, some written over 30 years ago, remain the solitary published works in their specialty area. Others continue to offer the curious collector a sure and ready reference for authenticating newly uncovered treasures. Angione's checklist of Simon and Halbig dolls, Bullard's early discourses on contemporary artist dolls, and the first published compendium of American doll trademarks by Luella Hart were among these landmark articles.

When **Spinning Wheel's Book of Dolls** was first published in 1975 the doll collecting world was far different than today. Many collectors were reluctant to discuss their seemingly eccentric interest, while the idly curious public had little notion of the serious intensity with which most collectors approached their subject. Museums relegated gifts of important dolls to the storage vaults—where sadly many were broken, forever lost to tomorrow's collectors—and no one, but no one, ever considered that seven years later a French doll, made about 1916, would sell at auction for $38,000! After all, fine quality German bisque dolls were then commonly sold for less than $200, a stunning and rare French bisque Bru bebe, all original, was "outrageous" at $4700 and nobody ever thought those upstart American dolls would be seriously collected.

In eight short years that picture is changed irretrievably. Serious full length treatises have been written; **Spinning Wheel Book of Dolls** alone has sold over 50,000 copies and a re-printing has just been issued. It is estimated that over a quarter million Americans collect dolls—a third of these are men. **Playthings** Magazine counts dolls the second most popular collectible. International conferences have attracted thousands of collectors worldwide, accredited colleges have held symposiums and the national media has hosted doll authorities with more than a passing interest.

Small wonder then that **Spinning Wheel** has seen fit to publish Volume II of the **Spinning Wheel Complete Book of Dolls.** This book is divided into seven major chapters each reflecting contemporay collector interest and emphasizing as a group the eclecticism with which collectors embrace their chosen subject. Finally in homage to the beauty of dolls a special new feature has been added—16 full color pages of antique and collectible dolls.

Enjoy our new volume. Browse, research or simply bask in the company of beautiful objects.

The staff of **Spinning Wheel.**

Table of

- **1** **Introduction to Antique & Collectible Dolls**
- **2** Poupees du Littoral *by Dorothy S. & Evelyn Jane Coleman*
- **5** Doll Messengers of Friendship *by Yolanda M. Simonelli*
- **10** Sicilian Marionettes *by Magdalena Byfield*
- **14** Pedlars & Pedlar Dolls *by Eleanor J. Mish*
- **20** Dolls Made By Joel Ellis *by Beverly S. Narkiewicz*
- **22** Lenci's Art Deco Dolls *by Dorothy S. Coleman*
- **25** The Sleeping Sand Baby *by Magda Byfield*
- **28** Collectible Cloth Dolls *by Magda Byfield*
- **31** The Versatile Dolls of Kathe Kruse *by Magda Byfield*
- **36** A Christmas Doll *by Yolanda M. Simonelli*
- **38** All Bisque Doll...French Style *by Magda Byfield*
- **40** Early American Folk Dolls *by Wendy Lavitt*
- **44** Emile Jumeau & His Beautiful Bebes *by Yolanda M. Simonelli*
- **49** For Whom Were You Made, Rowena-Rose? *by Magda Byfield*
- **51** A 19th Century Dolls Hospital *by Magda Byfield*
- **53** Politics Is Child's Play *by Judith Whorton*
- **56** Neapolitan Crib Figures *by Magda Byfield*
- **61** Photographs of Dolls in Carte de Visite Albums *by Evelyn Jane Coleman*
- **64** Doll Riding Tricycle *by Yolanda M. Simonelli*
- **66** He's A Real Doll *by Judith Whorton*
- **69** Happifat Collectibles *by Julie Masterson Child*
- **71** Enchanted Doll Museum—Mitchell, South Dakota
- **74** Rare Schoenhut Dolls *by John W. Clendenien*
- **76** **Introduction to Doll Costumes and Clothes**
- **77** Clothes Make The Doll *by Dorothy S. Coleman*
- **79** A Schoenhut Doll's Wardrobe *by Elizabeth Pullar*
- **83** Garment Samplers *by Dorothy S. & Evelyn Jane Coleman*
- **87** Doll Fashions—Plain & Fancy, Part I *by Judith Whorton*
- **89** Doll Fashions—Sports Clothes, Part II *by Judith Whorton*
- **91** Dressing Antique Dolls *by Dorothy Holloway Noell*
- **96** **Introduction to Doll Artist Dolls**
- **97** Madame Alexander Cloth Dolls *by Marsha Trentham Hunter*
- **100** Native American Indian Dolls *by Yolanda Simonelli*
- **105** The Manufactured Dolls of Magge Head Kane *by Helen Bullard*
- **109** Doll Museum in England *by Diane Hartlap*
- **110** Contemporary Japanese Doll Artists *by Helen Bullard*
- **114** Hand Carved Wooden Dolls—From Early Times *by Helen Bullard*
- **116** Hand Carved Wooden Dolls—From Modern Times *by Helen Bullard*
- **120** Dolly Dufour's Whimsical Dolls *by R. Lane Herron*
- **125** Suzanne Marks—Doll Artist *by R. Lane Herron*
- **129** Wee's "Weedidit" Dolls *by R. Lane Herron*
- **132** Martha Armstrong-Hand, N.I.A.D.A.—Mattel Doll Designer *by Helen Bullard*

Contents

- **136** Mme. Alexander Plastic Dolls—New Stars in the Doll World *by Judith Whorton*
- **140** Dolls Created by Emma Clear *by Ann S. Bland*
- **142** Edna Henderson—West Virginia's Gift to Dolldom *by R. Lane Herron*
- **146** Dolls Created by Xantos Kontis *by Judith Whorton w/Shirley Bucholz*
- **149** The Search for Alexanders *by Rhoda Shoemaker*
- **152** Doll Groups That Express American Culture *by Helen Bullard*
- **156** Effanbee's First Limited Edition Doll *by Judith Whorton*
- **158** **Introduction to Half Dolls & Novelties**
- **159** Marks on Half Figures *by Frieda Marion*
- **164** A Medley of Fine Porcelain Half-Dolls—A Picture Story *by Frieda Marion*
- **167** Pierrot & Pierette Half-Dolls *by Frieda Marion*
- **170** Parian Ware & Parian-Type Dolls *by Yolanda M. Simonelli*
- **174** Bisque Half Dolls *by Magda Byfield*
- **176** Collecting Little China Heads *by Frieda Marion*
- **180** The Wonderful Creeping Baby *by Yolanda M. Simonelli*
- **182** Continuing Research of the Snow Babies *by Jean H. Crowley*
- **185** The Mysterious Nodding Head Doll *by Jurgen & Marianne Cieslik*
- **187** **Introduction to Doll Houses & Furniture**
- **188** Doll's House Cradles, Cribs, Carriages & High Chairs *by Catherine Cook*
- **193** A Miniature Maryland Mansion *by Susan B. Howard*
- **194** The Farie Dolls' House At Auction *by Dorothy S. & Evelyn J. Coleman*
- **197** Mr. & Mrs. J.W. Elders—Miniature Furniture Makers *by Susan B. Howard*
- **198** Advertising Dolls' Houses & Miniatures *by Judith Whorton*
- **201** Advertising Dolls' Houses *by Judith Whorton*
- **202** Making Antique Furniture in Miniature-Part I *by Marjorie Congram*
- **205** Making Antique Furniture in Miniature-Part II *by Marjorie Congram*
- **208** Biedermeier Dolls' House Furniture *by Catherine Cook*
- **213** Banquets in Miniature *by Catherine Cook*
- **218** A History of Bathing in the Dolls' House *by Catherine Cook*
- **222** Dolls House Miniatures in Metal *by Catherine Cook*
- **226** Folding Dolls' Houses & Rooms—Made by McLoughlin Bros. *by Catherine Cook*
- **230** Dolls' House Furniture—in Red & Canary Yellow *by Catherine Cook*
- **234** Early American Miniatures—Made in the Orient *by Elizabeth Pullar*
- **238** Cast Iron Ranges—Child Size *by Emma Stiles*
- **240** **Introduction to Potpourri**
- **241** The Polemic Mother Goose *by Elizabeth Pullar*
- **244** Children's Old Cloth Books *by Elizabeth Pullar*
- **247** To Make A Cloth Book For A Favorite Child *by Elizabeth Pullar*
- **248** McLoughlin Bros.—The Prolific Publishing House for Children's Books *by Elizabeth Pullar*
- **251** Kewpies *by Inez B. McClintock*
- **256** The Lure of Automatons, Part I *by Mary Hillier*
- **260** The Lure of Automatons, Part II *by Mary Hillier*
- **264** **Index**

Antique and Collectible Dolls

Legally defined, few dolls collected today are antique. Antique, according to the United States Government, demands age of 100 years or more, and by far the majority of dolls collected today were made in the 20th century. Hence we add the word "collectible" when speaking of dolls that today's collectors seek.

What people collect—and why—is enigmatic to the layman. Is it beauty, nostalgia, a sense of history, a sense of whimsy, that speaks to the collector? The articles collected herein seem to reflect each of these. Who could deny the special fascination of Jumeau bebes with their haunting eyes? Yet the same collector could covet the realistic closed eye infant portrayed in the "Sleeping Sand Baby". Political dolls, crib figures and friendship messengers underscore the interconnecting role of the doll in the larger world. How peculiar it may seem to the uninitiated that the same collector who responds to the sophisticated charm of Lenci's Art Deco Ladies could also delight in the forlorn and winsome folk art doll.

Nevertheless to the collector they are all beautiful, all to be sought, all to be protected against the ravages of time and the uncaring. Today's collectible dolls are tomorrow's antiques.

Simon & Halbig's mold "1249" is made more intriguing by the additional green stamp mark "Old Glory A.W. Registered". An "Old Glory" silk banner also appears pinned to the dress. Made about 1900, the bisque doll has its original blonde mohair wig and gauze chemie.

Poupées du Littoral

by DOROTHY S. and CAROLYN JANE COLEMAN

Fig. 1. Boulogne fisherwoman in holiday attire as pictured in Mlle. Koenig's book showing dolls in the International Exhibition of 1900.

Boulonnaise

IN THE NOVEMBER 1898 issue of *Ladies Home Journal,* Annie Fields Alden, a doll collector, wrote: ". . . when my friends . . . visit foreign countries, I have always said: 'Bring me dolls of the people.' I have found that these dolls reveal more about their countries than one might at first suppose. I have expected them to show the differences of costume and of color, but they do much more than this—they show the airs, the spirit, the general trend of thought of the countries which they represent. One might say with a great deal of truth: 'Show me the dolls of a country and I will show you that country'."

Not everyone may agree completely with Annie Alden but the fact remains that dolls in foreign costume, especially those dressed in the locale represented, do provide a considerable amount of documented information. They show the local apparel of peasants, bourgoisie, nobility, and military as well as clothes related to religion, weddings, and occupations. Old dolls in regional costumes are more likely to be valid as historical artifacts than recently produced dolls which reflect modernization and changing customs.

One of the dolls in Annie Alden's collection represented a fisherwoman of Boulogne, France. She described it as a "peasant woman from Boulogne . . . an image giving such a good picture of the peasants that I added it to my collection although it is not really a doll to be played with."

Mlle. Marie Koenig of the Musée Pédagogique Paris in her book describing the museum's dolls exhibited at the

Fig. 2. Boulogne fisherwoman in holiday dress; bisque head marked "F.G." in a scroll; kid body; dressed with stiffly goffered lace cap, cream colored shawl with band of ornamentation and fringe, red wool overskirt, black and white cotton underskirt, blue silk apron, pendant earrings, and gold chain necklace with a cross. Ht. 26". *Virginia Dilliplane Collection.*

Fig. 3. Bisque head marked "F.G." in a scroll; kid body except for terra cotta arms; slippers and polka dot stockings on feet; pendant earrings are disproportionately large. Though in holiday attire, this doll carries a tray of fish and a net. Ht. 8". *Collection of the late E. J. Carter.*

Fig. 4. Head appears to be German bisque with black molded hair; cloth body, terra cotta arms; dressed in holiday clothes, stockings with circular stripes. Net is identical to the one shown in *Fig. 7*; wicker basket is proportionately larger than the ceramic baskets. Ht. 10". *Coleman Collection.*

1900 International Exposition, called these fisherfolk dolls from Boulogne "*Poupées du Littoral*" (dolls of the coast), and pictured a female doll dressed in holiday outfit.

These *poupées du littoral* of Boulogne were among the most popular tourist dolls. There were two female dolls—one in holiday attire, one in working garb—and a male doll in fisherman's work clothes.

According to Mlle. Koenig, the working women wore a bonnet of thick fabric with a flat brim and a large crown, while the holiday women wore a high goffered lace headdress, fastened with a large gold ball headed pin. High heeled sabots were used with the Sunday outfit; bare feet marked the working woman. Both outfits included long pendant earrings.

All three types of Boulogne fisherfolk dolls are shown in H. W. Canning's *Peeps at the Worlds Dolls* (London, 1922). He describes them as "real French dolls, dressed by the coast peasants in the ordinary everyday clothes . . . One is a typical fishwife in her holiday dress, with lace apron and handsomely embroidered shawl and lace cap. Another is wearing a striped skirt and knitted cardigan and carries a basket of fish and one of the nets. She is barefooted . . .

"The man has wooden-soled sea clogs, and oilskins rolled up in his hand . . . over one shoulder is a coil of rope

Fig. 5. Boulogne fisherman, mate to *Fig. 4* but in working clothes; cap missing; sea boots are molded. Ht. 10". *Coleman Collection.*

and on the other, his trawl with cork 'bobbers'... that float on the surface to show the position of the net in the sea. Everything is complete, just as you see the fishermen day after day in Brittany, with their stockinet caps, which at one time are worn with the bag flopping loose... and at others rolled over so that they fit closely down over the head.''

Léo Claretie in *Les Jouets* published in Paris, ca. 1894, shows a *poupée du littoral* with high goffered headdress, vertical striped skirt, and bare feet, and carrying a basket and triangular shaped net on a pole.

At least seven different types of dolls were dressed as *poupées du littoral:*

1. Bisque heads made in France (generally marked "F.G." in a scroll) on lady-shaped bodies of kid and/or cloth. These are usually fairly large dolls, dressed in holiday attire. *Fig. 2* is an example.

2. Bisque heads made in France (usually marked "F.G." in a scroll), kid and/or cloth bodies, limbs often of terra cotta. Example, *Figs. 7, 7a*.

3. Bisque heads made in Germany, cloth bodies, terra cotta limbs, with sea boots like those on fisherman in *Fig. 5*.

4. Composition heads, probably made in France, cloth bodies, kid arms, bisque legs. Example *Fig. 6*.

5. Composition heads on kid bodies without joints.

6. Composition heads probably made in Germany; cloth bodies with wooden arms; customary sea boots on men dolls.

7. Earthenware or terra cotta heads and limbs. A pair of these have been noted with a Christmas tag dated 1901.

Fig. 6. Pair of Boulogne fisherfolk with composition character faces, kid arms, and molded bisque legs; dressed in working garb. The woman doll may have lost her apron and scarf. Man's shirt is striped; he has a life preserver over his shoulder and carries a flat fish. Ht. 9''. *Coleman Collection.*

Fig. 7. Bisque heads with black painted hair. Woman's head is marked "F. G." in a scroll; man doll's clothes do not permit investigation of mark; terra cotta limbs. Man wears sea boots, carries fish in one hand, a small cask which may have held his oilskins in the other; and holds net and rope under his arm. Ht. 9-1/2''. *Coleman Collection.*

Most of these fisherfolk dolls were produced prior to World War I and except for the large sized dolls, they were often sold in pairs. The costumes show considerable variation but certain features do recur. The female dolls wear either the high goffered headdress or a heavy scarf around their heads. Long pendant earrings are characteristic as well as vertical striped black and white skirts. Male dolls wear stockinet caps and often carry a pipe. Dolls in working costumes are either barefooted or wear heavy sea boots. Many carry a fish or two; the women often carry fish baskets. Some fish are flat, some rotund; they are made in various materials—bisque, terra cotta, or papier mache. Many of the dolls carry some sort of net. Male dolls sometimes carry a life preserver, a rope, or a cask, the latter perhaps to hold his oilskins.

These *poupées du littoral* appeal to historians as well as collectors of dolls. They show in three dimensional form both a geographical and an occupational costume as well as the variations between holiday and workday dress. Of great interest are the many little accessories found with these dolls which so vividly portray the lifestyle of a bygone era in one specific locale.

A Japanese primary reader pictures a plump blonde child doll with a dark haired, dark eyed, kimono clad Japanese girl. The text tells about a blue-eyed doll, born in America, who arrived at a port in Japan with many tears. "I cannot understand the language. I don't know what to do when I become a lost child. Kind Japanese girls, please play with me friendly."

A Japanese song, by noted writer Ujo Noguchi, once a best-seller, now a nostalgic favorite, is about "honorable blue-eyed dolls." They cry because they can't understand a word of Japanese.

Blue-eyed dolls from America captured Japanese interest after the Committee on World Friendship Among Children (Federal Council of Churches of Christ in America) initiated a venture designed to promote affinity between the children of America and Japan.

In 1926 the World Friendship Committee circulated a bulletin around America. It pictured a Japanese child and an American girl, seated together conversing. Each held a doll. The bulletin discussed Japan's beautiful family custom, "The Hina Matsuri" (Festival of Dolls) celebrated on the third of March each year. "On that day each family brings out its ancestral treasure house, the dolls of mothers, grandmothers and preceding generations for a renewal of acquaintance." New dolls were sometimes added during the Festival.

The Committee on World Friendship Among Children proposed to children in the schools and families of America:

(please turn the page)

DOLL MESSENGERS OF FRIENDSHIP

by YOLANDA M. SIMONELLI

The National Museum of Natural History, Smithsonian Institution, Washington, D.C., received two Japanese Friendship Dolls in 1927. The one shown below is 30 inches tall; the other doll is of a smaller size. A large group of accessories accompanied the dolls.

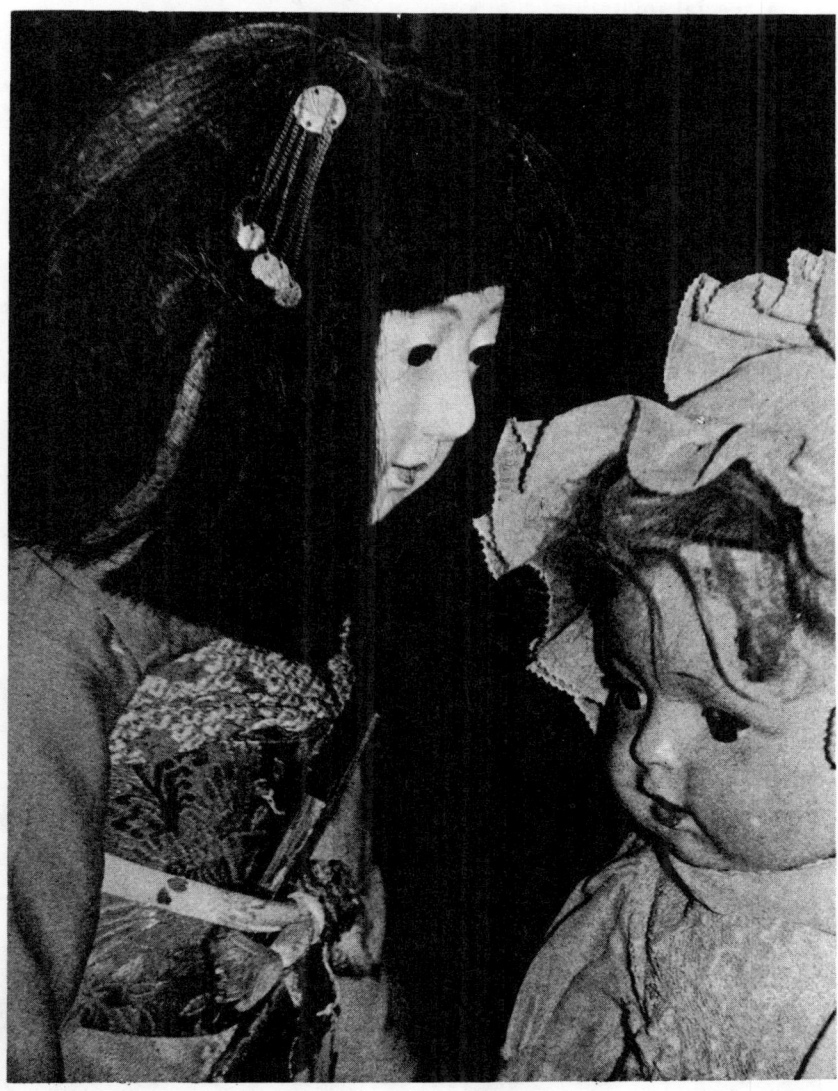

A dark-eyed Japanese doll of the 1920s comforts "honorable blue-eyed American Mama doll." The arrival of over 12,500 Ambassador Friendship Dolls sent by American children to the port city of Yokohama, March 1, 1927, inspired a song by noted Japanese writer Ujo Noguchi about the honorable blue-eyed dolls that cried because they couldn't understand a word of Japanese. The song became a bestseller, and is now a nostalgic favorite.

(1) That they get acquainted with this beautiful custom of Japan's doll festival, learn something of Japan's love for children and home, and begin to know Japan.

(2) That they send thousands of dolls to visit the doll families of Japan and to serve as "Messengers and Ambassadors of goodwill and friendship."

New dolls were solicited, clothed like typical attractive American girls. Extra garments and a "Mama Voice" were desirable. Costs of dolls, sizes 13 inches to 16 inches tall not to exceed $3. Each doll required a brief message, the donor's name and address, plus railway and steamer tickets and properly visaed passport to be obtained from Doll Travel Bureau, 289 Fourth Ave., New York, N.Y. Cost of tickets was ninety-nine cents. Passport fee was one cent. The bulletin cautioned, "Send dollar by postal order or by check. Do not send dollar bills in mail. It is dangerous."

A special invitation, composed in verse, urged dolls of America to go to Japan for the doll festival:

Come, Dolls of America, you're asked to go
To a Festival quaint, and you'd like it, I know;
So neatly and daintily dress in your best,
And start on your travels with gladness and zest.

O come by the hundreds and thousands and more,
And journey along to a far distant shore
Where dear little children, with joy and delight,
Will welcome and love you, their eyes shining bright;
The words they will speak—very strange they will be
To dolls who have travelled from over the Sea.

You'll sit as their guests and watch busy girls try
To learn how to keep their homes tidy—Oh my!—
To make dainty dishes that you've never seen
With bamboo and seaweed and sweet pasty bean;
To bow to their guests in a low, proper way,
And practice homemaking as though it were play.

And often the neighbors and guests who attend
The festivities gay, will all praise and commend
The lovely American dolls who have come
Over land, over sea, far away from their home.
And they'll ask why it is that you dolls have been sent,
Then for answer you'll say that your coming was meant
To tell of the friendship and interest true
Of children whose flag is the red, white and blue,
For those who are living in cherry-bloom land,
To whom they would hold out a child's friendly hand.

(Please turn the page)

A Yamato-ningyo Japanese doll purchased in Japan in 1929 for $100, plus duty. The doll came packed in a wooden box (called a casket by the seller). Its label carried the name "Shijo Sakimache, Kyoto, Japan. Heizo Iki Dealer in Manufacturer of Fine Art Dolls and Toys." The doll is dressed in fine silk garments decorated with hand embroidered floral designs. Colors include lavender, white, blue, red, orange and green. Birds, butterflies and fish are hand-painted in gold. A fan, comb, writing book and other personal articles are tucked in the doll's obi (sash). *Author's collection.*

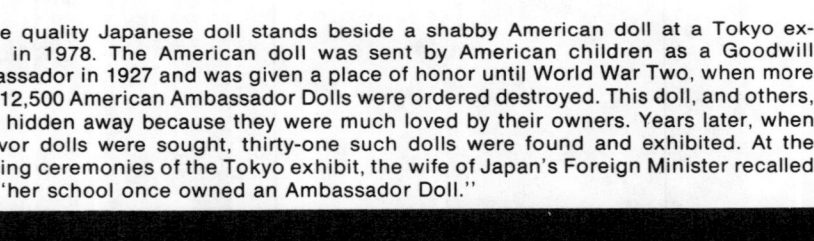

A fine quality Japanese doll stands beside a shabby American doll at a Tokyo exhibit, in 1978. The American doll was sent by American children as a Goodwill Ambassador in 1927 and was given a place of honor until World War Two, when more than 12,500 American Ambassador Dolls were ordered destroyed. This doll, and others, were hidden away because they were much loved by their owners. Years later, when survivor dolls were sought, thirty-one such dolls were found and exhibited. At the opening ceremonies of the Tokyo exhibit, the wife of Japan's Foreign Minister recalled that "her school once owned an Ambassador Doll."

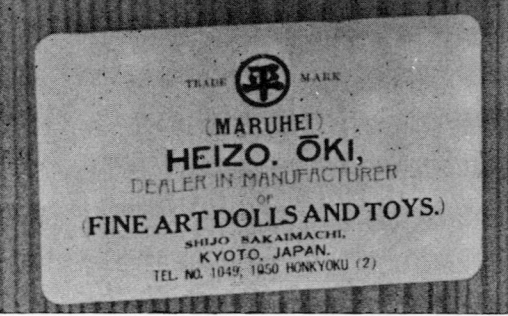

*And the spirit of childhood shall show us the way
To Friendship that lasts, and to Peace that shall stay.*

An Associated Press report, dated Tokyo, February 15, 1927, told that the doll messengers of peace from the children of America would be tendered a public reception, March 3rd. The Festival of Dolls was to be held at the Imperial Theater where U.S. Ambassador Charles MacVeagh and high Japanese officials would speak and present dolls to more than 3,000 Japanese children who, in honor of their American friends, would sing *The Star Spangled Banner*, which "they knew very well". On March 1, 1927, the port city of Yokohama would celebrate the arrival of more than 12,500 Ambassador dolls from the United States.

"Miss America," the finest doll, went to Princess Teruko, daughter of the Emperor. Many of the dolls went to schools where they were accorded places of honor. Some dolls were presented to favored children, chosen by teachers. The American dolls whose eyes opened and closed and said "Mama" were a marvel to the Japanese children, cementing a bond between children of the two nations.

When the liner *Tenyo Maru* docked in San Francisco, November 26, 1927, it brought a precious cargo of fifty-eight dolls from the hands of Japan's finest artists as expressions of gratitude and friendship from the children of Japan.

The most splendid doll, Miss Dai Nippon, gift of Princess Teruko, was valued at $350.00. The others, valued at $200 each, were paid for by 2,610,000 Japanese children who contributed one yen each (about one-half cent). The project was implemented by the Japanese Commission on International Friendship among Children, and the Department of Education.

The gift dolls represented Japan's forty-seven prefectures, the colonies of Korea and Formosa, and six of Japan's largest cities. Each carried a goodwill passport and first class ticket from Yokohama to San Francisco. Masa Matsudaira, daughter of the Japanese Ambassador, attired in full Japanese garb, presented the "Ambassadors of Good Will" to the children of America. The American dolls sent to Japan had made many little girls happy. "Japanese children are very anxious to be your friends. These fifty-eight dolls have come here to bring this with from two million and a half children in my country."

The dolls visited America's large cities in groups of six. Later, divided into smaller groups, they toured less populated areas. After six months of extensive travel and receptions, permanent homes were assigned. Miss Japan, gift of the Royal Princess, went to the Smithsonian Institution in Washington, D.C. The other dolls were mostly placed in children's museums.

Miss Akita from Akita Prefecture, northern Honshu Island, was awarded to the Children's Museum in Detroit. This choice doll represented a six year old girl. She was costumed in elegant formal garments including an outer garment of heavily padded aqua silk crepe decorated with hand-dyed designs of maple leaves, bamboo, and flowers of the seasons, worn over a red silk kimono and fine undergarments. Her obi of gold and silk brocade was hand embroidered with sixteen-petaled imperial chrysanthemums. Miss Akita wore the traditional tabi socks made of elegant silk with ivory fasteners. She brought with her a wealth of accessories including fan, colorful parasol, lacquer chests, vanity case, lamps, tea set, writing materials and personal ornaments. Beatrice Parsons, Director of the Detroit Children's Museum, describes every detail to be perfect miniatures and considers Miss Akita "an inspiration and reminder of the goals which we still seek in creating a world at peace."

(please turn the page)

"Miss Akita" is a Japanese Friendship Doll assigned to the Children's Museum, Detroit Public Schools, Detroit, Michigan. The doll is dressed in the formal costume of a young Japanese girl. Her heavy padded silk crepe furisoda (long-sleeved kimono) is in a lovely shade of aqua, decorated with hand-dyed designs of maple leaves, bamboo and flowers of the season. This is worn over a red silk kimono and underclothing. An obi (sash) of gold and red brocade embroidered with the sixteen-petaled Imperial chrysanthemum encircles her waist. She stands on a tatami mat, as she is indoors and so does not wear her zori or geta, as is the custom in Japan. On her feet are tradtional tabi socks made of elegant silk with ivory fasteners. Included in her luggage were several lacquer chests, a vanity case, a pair of lamps, tea set, writing materials and personal ornaments.
Photo and details courtesy Beatrice Parsons, Director, Children's Museum.

Miss Akita is a type of doll called "Yamato-ningyo," designed in Japan around 1910 as a play doll which represented children of that era. Dollmaking has been a serious expression of Japanese culture for many years. Expert artists concentrate on "doll art." Construction of Miss Akita and other superior dolls of her type require artistry and skill. To make such a doll, a master mold is carved of wood followed by preparation of resin molds for the casting of hollow body parts formed from a plastic-like substance made of kiri wood, sawdust and wheat paste. Pulverized oyster shells mixed with glue, called "Gofun," is applied in layers to face and body parts and sculptured with a knife. The hardened finish is carefully polished and delicately colored, leaving a smooth porcelain like finish. Girl dolls receive long dark human hair wigs with bangs. Boy dolls have hair trimmed round and short. Dark eyes are set into almond-shaped eye sockets.

A number of museums in Massachusetts showed great interest in the Japanese friendship dolls. One was assigned to the Boston Museum of Art and another to be shared by the Springfield Museum of Natural History and the Worcester Art Museum. Miss Oita, the shared doll, is presently at the Springfield Museum. Mr. John P. Pretola, Curator of Anthropology, notes: "There has always been an interest in Japanese culture at Springfield's Quadrangle Museums." Interest in dolls can be traced to 1926 when the Science Museum held an exhibit of Japanese dolls on loan from Miss Jessie Sherwood of Boston. While the exhibit was being set up, an executive of the Government of Formosa chanced to be visiting, and later arranged to send a Japanese Doll Festival Set to the museum.

Mr. Pretola describes their Miss Oita, the shared Friendship doll, as 33 inches tall with glass eyes and human hair. She wears a shirt of red silk with gold embroidery and white floral design, and three silken kimonos (orange, red, and green). The outer orange garment is handsomely decorated with chrysanthemums outlined with silver and gold threads. A green silk obi, tied high in the back, circles her waist, and is embroidered in gold. Miss Oita brought three trunks or chests, two chests of five drawers, a chest of four drawers, two lamps, one screen, one mirror, tea table with tea set accessories, parasol, two pairs of shoes and toy, together with a goodwill passport and steamship ticket aboard the *Tenyo Maru*, and eighteen letters written by Japanese children.

Another type of doll, "Mistuore," three bend, moveable at head, wrist, and knees, with joints at the waist, went to the Milwaukee Public Museum. Named Miss Kasumi Tsukubo, and created in the Ibarge Prefecture, this doll represents a six year-old girl, and can be placed in any position a child might assume.

The museums that received Friendship Dolls were asked to write to the Governor of the Province of origin so that he might inform children of his Province as to their doll's permanent home. The committee appointed to handle the distribution of the Doll Ambassadors of Goodwill issued the following statement:

> The dolls are of unusual size, being about thirty-one inches tall. They are dressed in superb silk kimonos and each are accompanied by quite an outfit of accessories, consisting of gold and silver inlaid lacquer articles.
>
> "The Committee on World Friendship among Children desires to have the dolls so located and treated as to convey their messages most effectively to the American children. With this in view, it wishes to make sure that each museum that receives one of the dolls fully understands the situation and will help to make their presence a continual reminder to our people, and especially to our children, of the goodwill gesture of the children of Japan."

The exchange dolls served successfully as symbols of friendship until the bond was shattered on Dec. 7, 1941, when the Japanese bombed Pearl Harbor, Hawaii, putting the American blue-eyed dolls into a perilous situation.

Aiyoshi Kawabata, Professor

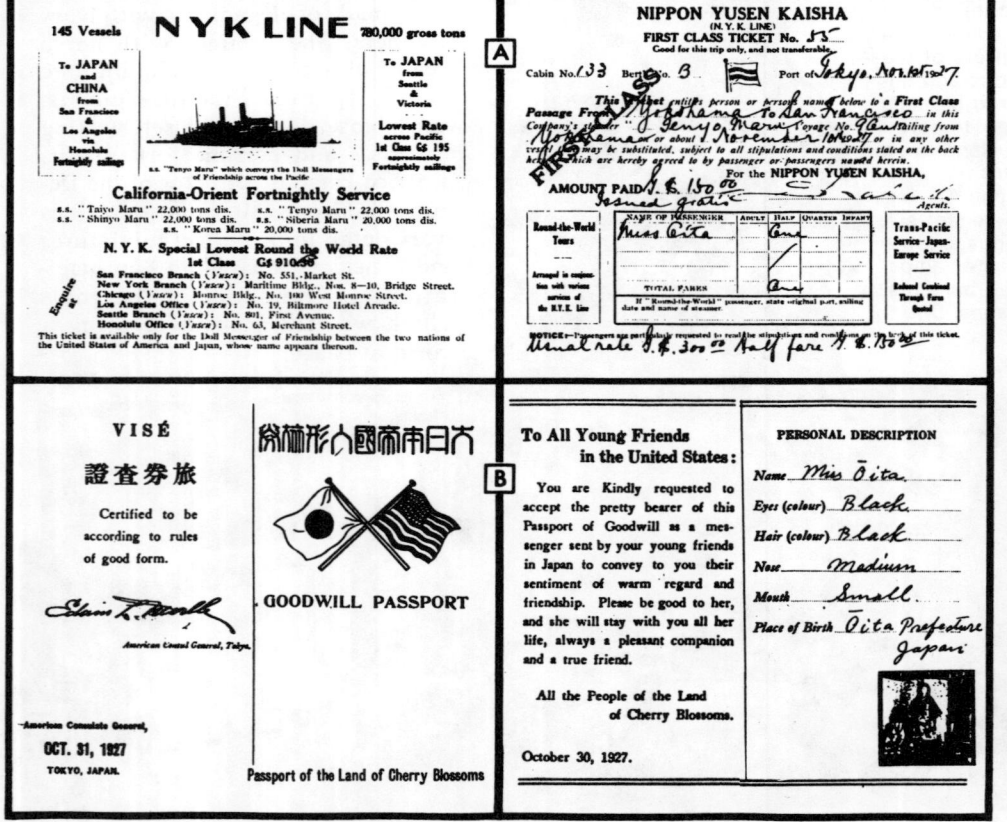

(A) This special half-fare ticket was issued to Miss Oita, the Japanese Friendship Doll assigned to the Springfield Science Museum and Worcester Art Museum, Massachusetts.
(B) Miss Oita's "Goodwill Passport" also accompanied her to America. Tickets like this were issued for each of the 12,500 American Friendship Dolls sent to Japan in 1926 as tokens of friendship. Each doll was also provided with a properly visaed passport.

Emeritus at Kyoto University remembers how the American dolls were treasured over the years, receiving places of honor in Japanese schools and homes. With the advent of war, they became victims of hate when hostility toward Americans was encouraged by local military groups and organizations of retired soldiers who feared affection for the dolls interfered with their efforts to cast Americans as the "enemy."

The American Friendship Ambassador Dolls were snatched from their places of honor at schools. They were pierced with bamboo spears and smashed, followed by gasoline baths and burnings in ritualistic displays on how to loathe the enemy. Miyuki Hoshi of Aizu-Wakamatsu recalls "the pain in my heart," when teachers at her school burned her doll. Chiyoko Ota of Yamagata was told to destroy her school's doll. I couldn't do it and sank it in a swamp after covering it with a red mantle," she said. Others secretly defied the orders to destroy the dolls. Professor Kawabata tells that some dolls disappeared, being hid away in dark places between ceilings and roofs, or in storage boxes buried under other items. Years later Ayako Ishimaru, a teacher, read a news report about an American doll treasured by a school in Kofu, 150 miles from Tokyo. The doll's name was "Ginella, 3 years old," donated by Dr. James Wilbur Hondrof, Rochester, N.Y. Miss Ayako determined to locate other dolls. A committee was formed which was able to assemble a group of thirty-one dolls for exhibit in Tokyo, in August 1978. Dresses were frayed, skins darkened with age. During a brief ceremony, the wife of Foreign Minister Sunao Sonoda recalled that her school once owned an Ambassador Friendship Doll. The Mitsukoshi department store which sponsored the resurrection ceremony planned to market copies of the original blue-eyed dolls to sell from $54 to $444.

Mrs. Helen Cullen, San Diego, California, who lived in Japan in 1973, tells another story which illustrates the love some of the American dolls received. Mrs. Cullen was watching television and saw a white haired Japanese cradling an American doll—"his doll." Because he could not destroy it, "she was hidden behind the Emperor's picture for a very long time." Mrs. Cullen contacted TV Station NHK through Mitzie Tanaka, a Japanese friend who spoke English. They learned the doll was one of the American Ambassador dolls, about 18" tall, with composition head and limbs, red hair and blue eyes, wearing her original beige dress, green cap and cape, shoes and stockings. Her name was "Mary." Mrs. Cullen researched the doll's markings, finding it to be a Madame Hendren doll made by the Averill Manufacturing Company. In her communications with the TV station she learned that after the telecast the station received many phone calls, telegrams, and letters saying, "We too have saved our dolls. We could not part with our beautiful Mama Doll. We have her still."

Mrs. Cullen's report helps make true the saying "The Japanese is born grown-up and remains a child all his life." Jiro Amano of Maebashi, a committee member who helped arrange the Tokyo exhibit of saved dolls, said: "I am confident that there are many others that lived through the war and hate." The plea of crying blue-eyed dolls from America, "Kind Japanese girls, please play with me friendly," was surely honored. One wonders how many American Friendship Ambassador Dolls reside in Japanese ancestral treasure houses waiting to be brought out again on the "Hina Matsuri," Festival of Dolls. ■

(A) "Miss Oita" is another Japanese Friendship Doll accessioned on October 16, 1928, to be shared by the Springfield Museum of Natural History and the Worcester Art Museum, both in Massachusetts. This doll wears three silk kimonos—orange, green and red. The outer orange robe is decorated with chrysanthemums outlined with silver and gold threads. Her obi (sash) is green silk embroidered in gold. She is pictured here with many of the personal items that accompanied her to America. *Photo and details courtesy to John P. Pretola, Curator of Anthropology, Springfield Science Museum.*
(B) Detail of the fabric used to make Miss Oita's outer robe.
(C) Detail of Miss Oita's obi (sash). The lower girdle is of green silk with gold thread embroidery. The upper portion, twisted around her waist, is red silk with white decoration. A knotted cord of white and gold silk embroidery separates the upper and lower portion of the obi.

Line drawing showing body construction of typical 19th century Sicilian marionette.

Early 19th century Catanian marionette depicting a Siren. Head has inset glass eyes and torso is cloth-covered with metal breast-plates and collar. Mythical "legs" are straw-filled fabric terminating in carved fins. This type was worked with four strings to convey a flying or swimming movement unlike walking figures which required only two. Length (without rod) 31".

Sicilian Marionettes

by MAGDALENA BYFIELD

THERE IS something about the Sicilian marionette which is halfway between carved puppet and classical portrait. This quality of refinement is just one of many aspects that sets them apart from the traditions of puppet-making. The role of the marionette was that of an actor; as such, he "wore" the equivalent of theatrical make-up. The feature carving and painting were necessarily overcharged in order that it would travel visually across the heads of large audiences to reach the back rows. In close-up, as with live performers, they appear intensely vivid; but not so with the Sicilian marionette. Their features are sensitively carved in a strange blend of delicacy and strength. The men are tall, slim and superbly masculine, and the women graceful, with hauntingly lovely faces. Evil characters are subtly imbued with sinister overtones, but are recognized more by their style of clothing than facial characteristics. The various chimerical animals are exquisitely whimsical, and only monsters are grotesque in the universal puppet tradition.

There is evidence that this refined approach was a conscious, peculiarly Sicilian manifestation. For instance, it is known that for a time during the early 19th century, a fine mesh screen was used in front of the stage to diffuse and soften the scene and temper even further the delicate outlines of the figures. It is probable that the main purpose of this was to deflect the eye from the heavy iron rods running through the heads (a design retained from the antique Roman marionette stage), but when tested today the effect can be seen to have been imaginative and fabulous. It is perhaps in the legendary Sicilian puppet plays that we find the key to their marionette's romantic concept. Although there are a variety of subsidiary themes, the chief and enduring subject remains based on Ludovico Oriosto's epic poem—*Orlando Furioso*.

A writer and courtier at the Ferrarese ducal house of Este, Ariosto began his great narrative poem in 1505 and took twenty-seven years and 38,736 lines to complete it. While the *Furioso* is deeply influenced by the author's own life and times, it is presented as a medieval legend of chivalry and heroics. Although an amalgam of innumerable sub-plots, the essential message is the defense of Christianity against Islam—represented by Charlemagne's paladins versus the infidels. The romantic exploits of these knights, their passions, intrigues, battles and duels, witchcraft and magic, unrequited love and noble death, is the fabric of which the Sicilian

Catanian marionette of a knight in armor. Emblems of lion rampant on shield and breastplate identify him as Rinaldo. Height to top of helmet: 36". 19th century.

marionette theater is woven and to which it still clings tenaciously. *The Paladin Cycle*, as the five hundred plays are called, are performed with the inevitable embellishments and improvisations of generations of puppet masters working for the main part in an oral tradition. By the very complex nature of the repertoire it would take three years of nightly theater-going to see every Orlando play in sequence.

A troupe of some four hundred figures was usual for the flourishing theaters of the 19th century, including the "stunt" figures required to stand-in for principal characters in scenes of violence, when the finely plumed and armored performers were replaced with more battered, but identical, specimens. Heads were interchanged where the part required aging or some form of feature alteration. There were double-sided or "metamorphose" marionettes which presented a front view only and were dramatically flipped to show their reverse (and usually horrific) side in scenes of sorcery or revelation. Other trick puppets had such contrivances as blood-spurting and fire-breathing mechanisms of great ingenuity. It was not unusual for a hundred figures to be on stage at the same time in battle scenes, and these could not all be manually supported by the puppeteers working the stage. Rails above the backdrop supported figures in a standing position in the scene, but the majority lay in slumped and disorderly heaps as slain knights, and such scenes of carnage required a long intermission to disentangle and clear the stage for the following act.

The principal characters are easily recognizable to spectators familiar with the Sicilian marionette theater. A few of the most leading figures are: Angelica, Princess of Cathay and object of Orlando's unrequited love; Astolfo, cousin of Orlando; Bradamante, warrior maid, sister of Rinaldo and destined bride of Ruggiero; Charlemagne, King of France and Emperor of Christendom; Ganelon, traitor Count of Mayence; Marfisa, warrior maid and sister of Ruggiero; Melissa, good sorceress; Milone, father of Orlando; Olivero, Marquis of Vienne; Orlando, paladin of France and nephew of Charlemagne; Rinaldo, Count of Montalbano; Ruggiero, King of Reggio.

The knights and warrior maids are identifiable by the emblems on their armor and this has been identical in all Sicilian theaters at all times. Other leading characters are recognizable by their coloring, garments and features which are again traditional and circumscribed. Good and Evil are divided in presentation as well as their organization on the stage: Christians, seen from the auditorium, are always on the left and Saracens on the right. Saracen knights wear Turkish trousers (and sometimes turbans) and Christians a short kilt. Marionettes representing the principal paladins are the largest figures (2'6"-4'6") and are extremely heavy. A knight is somewhat shorter than a prince, and foot soldiers, women and the supporting cast can be as much as 15" shorter than a paladin. Charlemagne is traditionally the tallest figure in the troupe and may be topped only by a giant.

Their method of articulation is as unique as their appearance. Puppets and marionettes technically differ only in their form of animation. The puppet is manipulated from inside while the marionette is controlled from above by strings or from below by fine rods. The puppet is the earlier of the two designs. Sicilian marionettes are by no means typical of this class usually having only two strings (with the exception of animal and transformation marionettes) and depending entirely for their walking action on the impetus from a central iron rod which combines with the figure's weight to result in a surprisingly realistic and majestic movement. A smaller control rod is looped to the right hand which is carved in a closed position with a large central holding-hole for swords or other objects. A string runs through the hole to the shaft of the interchangeable prop enabling the figure to reach for his sword, draw it from its sheath, replace it or let it fall to the ground. The left hand is flat and drilled through with a small hole for the second string which is knotted under the palm. Knights in armor have a third string to operate the visor, and their left-hand string is caught through loops in back of the shield. The marionette's torso is roughly carved from a single piece of wood. The legs are hinged into slots and secured by a wire passing horizontally through the trunk at hip level. Lower legs are jointed at the knees and painted. Lower arms are also painted and have turned grooves at the elbows for tying on the fabric upper arm sections which are secured at the shoulders with nails. A neck socket is carved out at the top and contains a strong iron loop into

Figure of a young woman from a Palermo marionette troupe, probably depicting Melissa. Elaborately carved hairstyle incorporates yellow circlet. Painted features. 19th century. Height (without rod) 28".

which the main control rod (holding the head) is hooked. The head has a central hole running up from the base of the neck through which the head is threaded onto the central rod. The bottom of the rod is hooked upwards and a second hole in the base of the neck provides the space to take up the hooked terminal and the neck then seats down on the shoulders.

A quick downward thrust of the central control rod will at once raise the head and disengage the hook from the loop, making "decapitation" a simple and popular maneuver—timed of course with a sword stroke from the victim's opponent. This is particularly useful in scenes of carnage where the headless bodies can lie on stage unencumbered by their lengthy rods. The severed heads are whisked away in a flying action at the moment of impact from the sword.

In carving, decoration and finish, the head is made with a consummate skill which is not employed in other sections of the marionette. The contrast, while striking, is not surprising if one considers that when the model was working and clothed, the body and limbs were all but entirely obscured. Where figures are semi-nude, such as with mermaids or devils, the entire body is carved in good detail or covered with a "skin" of painted fabric. Some figures have inset glass eyes (blue or brown) and a rare variant has sleeping eyes operated by a protruding wire. Painted eyes are more general. Hair is usually carved in one with the head, often with great detail, and sometimes incorporating hair ornaments and headdresses. Figures are also found with hair wigs; these are usually warrior maids whose gender is obscured by their suits of armor and their femininity only established by curled tresses emerging beneath their helmets.

The marionettes were dressed with a conscious effort to achieve a suitably archaic effect which, however, in no way resembled costumes of the medieval period. The style that evolved (and remains) is a hodge-podge of 15th-17th century fashions freely adapted from paintings and illustrations of the Renaissance and Baroque periods. Moors are presented as 17th century Spanish noblemen; magicians are dressed like Dr. Faust (the 16th century necromancer who claimed to have sold himself to the devil and met with a mysterious end). Christian knights wear Renaissance armor, and Saracens a more stylized version of the same basic design embellished with half-moons and stars. Marionettes representing women are dressed more consistently in High Baroque styles. There are some amusing discrepancies resulting from errors of interpretation: for instance in the portrayal of Angelica, princess of Cathay (West Indies), who is traditionally found dressed in a *red Indian* headdress of feathers!

Perhaps the most artistic and dramatic aspect in the costuming of Sicilian marionettes is the burnished metal armor worn by the knights and warrior maids. Their individual emblems are of great importance for identification, not only for the benefit of the audience but for the puppeteers working with such large numbers of armor-clad figures. If a knight was slain in battle the previous evening, he is stored away until the cycle comes round to include him again. The puppet master must know who was killed or merely wounded, because the audience will certainly remember!

Charlemagne's armor is traditionally decorated with the emblem of the Fleur-de-Lis; Orlando, an eagle and cross; Rinaldo, a lion rampant on a transversal bar; Ruggiero, an eagle argent; Olivero, the sun, etc. Personal coloring is also a fixed tradition: Bradamante is always a blue-eyed blonde and Marfisa a brunette.

Clothes are not removable, because of being nailed to the torso. Occasionally a petticoat is tied at the waist or a cape is hooked or buttoned on, but the intention was for the figures to remain unchanged until the clothes became worn out when they were simply ripped away. No attempt was made to extract the old nails and the various different types of nail-heads; together with trapped fragments of earlier fabrics, provide valuable clues to the figure's age which is otherwise difficult to assess. The regular repainting of heads and replacing of damaged limbs makes any attempt at precise dating from these aspects a virtual impossibility. Height and weight also vary, not (as might be supposed) according to the period in which the figure was carved, but by the size of the stage for which it was intended and the locality of the origin; Catanian marionettes are heavier than those made in Palermo.

Silver knight marionette with sun emblem on armor identifying him as Olivero. Kilt and white plume signify a Christian. Height to top of helmet: 36". Palermo, 19th century.

Late 19th century figure of a young woman from a Palermo marionette troupe. Hairstyle is drawn back into a coil with small red painted diadem in front. Iron staple in coil at back supports silk ribbon. Height (without rod) 28".

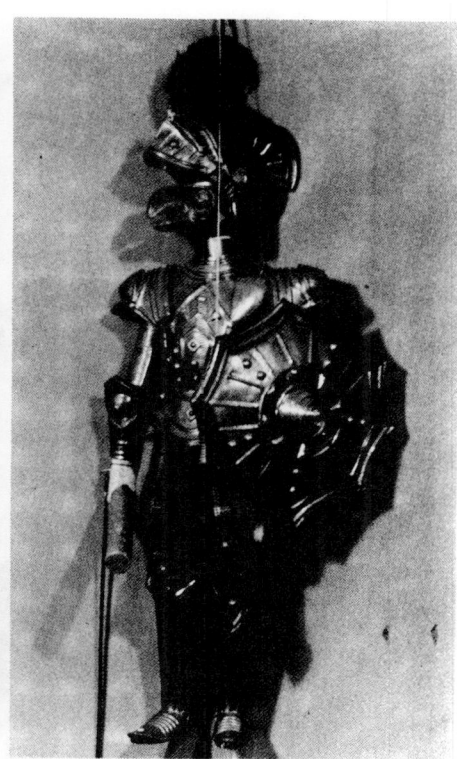
Monster knight marionette. Stylized armor, black plume and trousers (not kilt) denote a Saracen. From the same troupe as Rinaldo. Height to top of helmet: 34". Catania, 19th century.

Marionette of a Saracen with blood-flowing mechanism in head. Metal lined exit-hole is visible above right eye and enters beside central control rod. Rubber tube was inserted and ran parallel with rod. Manipulator released beetroot juice through tube to coincide with blow to figure's head. Height: 33". Catania, 19th century.

It is difficult to establish precisely when these marionettes were first evolved and perfected, or where the beginnings of the theater's present characteristics are to be sought, but records start to multiply after the first decade of the 19th century. Certainly the Orlando plays are considerably older than the Sicilian marionette theater, and in their original form pre-date Ariosto himself by some four hundred years. Historically, Orlando was Roland (Hruodland), a Frankish count in command of the rearguard of Charlemagne's army during the withdrawal into France through the Pyrenees, after an abortive campaign against the Saracens in Spain. Roland fell when the rearguard was attacked by Gascons in the pass of Roncesvalles on the 15th of August, 778. Stories carried by minstrels and troubadours of the disaster of Roncesvalles and the heroic death of Roland were gathered into one greath 11th century epic poem—*Le Chanson de Roland.* It was on this compound of history and legend that Ludovico Ariosto based his narrative of high fantasy—*The Orlando Furioso.*

Why this fabulous poem has enjoyed such a lasting influence on the Sicilian marionette theater in particular is difficult to define exactly. The Orlando plays were also popular with French and Belgian puppeteers, but in Sicily they found their most enduring hold. It is perhaps the continuing ability of local puppet masters to adapt and modify the plays that has kept the theater alive and topical. To some extent also the many facets of the repertoire can be seen to provide something for everyone. The violent battles, magical transformations, the cliffhanger endings to the evening's performance, the tragedy, comedy, romance and wit—and not least the artistry and elegance of the marionettes themselves, all combine to provide an entertainment for both the simplest and most sophisticated audiences. ■

Wax English pedlar doll, ca. 1845. Height 8¾ inches (22 cm). *Strong Museum Collection.*

PEDLARS

"The Irish Street-Seller," from Henry Mayhew's *London Labour and the London Poor*, 1849-1850.

PEDLAR DOLLS can portray any of a variety of different types of street-sellers. Usually, however, the notions or small wares pedlar is the kind represented. This type of pedlar sells a little bit of everything—thread, pins, ballads, and books—from a tray or basket slung around his neck.

Very little is known about pedlar dolls. Such secondary sources as doll encyclopedias and books on Victorian crafts tell us that pedlar dolls are most often British made, usually portray women pedlars wearing a "traditional" red-hooded cape, and are dated anywhere from 1750 to 1880. It is believed that they were yet another product of Victorian ladies' leisure crafts and were proudly displayed in the parlour or on a mantelpiece underneath a glass shade or dome. Many pedlar dolls have retained their glass shades but there is little else to testify to their popularity as an artistic recreation of the Victorian era.

While it is believed that the majority of pedlar dolls were homemade, there were a few commercial manufacturers. Several pedlar dolls in the Strong Museum collection bear the C. & H. White of Milton, Portsmouth (England) label, or can be attributed to that company. According to one source, the Whites began making the dolls in 1830; but virtually nothing else is known about them.

Because of the paucity of primary source information on pedlar dolls and their makers, studying pedlars in general may give us some clues as to why these dolls were made and why they were so popular. Furthermore, an occasional description or illustration may help to put the dolls into a more manageable time framework.

Before proceeding any further, a controversy over spelling should be resolved. Both spellings "peddler" and "pedlar" are acceptable. The latter is the British usage. Since the majority of pedlar dolls appear to be of British

AND PEDLAR DOLLS

by ELEANOR J. MISH, Intern Margaret Woodbury Strong Museum

"The Coster-Girl" from *London Labour and the London Poor*, by Henry Mayhew, 1849-1850.

Illustration from a story entitled "Roland Leigh, Or, The Story of a City Arab," which appeared in *The Leisure Hour, A Family Journal of Instruction and Recreation*, May 7, 1857. The disheveled looking pedlar is showing his wares to a young woman and a not-too-pleasant dog.

origin, they are most often referred to as *pedlars*. To avoid confusion in this report, this latter spelling has been retained.

Pedlars can also be called chapmen, hawkers, hucksters, colporteurs, and costermongers. The latter, however, is used only when referring to vendors of meat, vegetables, fruit, or fish. "Colporteur" is the French equivalent of "chapman" and more specifically, a seller of devotional or religious literature. The term "chapman" derives from the pedler's sale of cheaply printed story books called chapbooks which were popular in the late 18th and early 19th centuries. "Pedlar," "hawker," and "huckster" can be used interchangeably and usually are. Under British law, however, a hawker is someone who uses a horse and cart or van in his trade whereas a pedlar carries his merchandise unassisted. There is also a difference in the price of their licenses.

The best source of information for the study of pedlars is Henry Mayhew's *London Labour and the London Poor*.

15

Wooden 20th century pedlar doll, possibly made in America. Height 11½ inches (29 cm). *Strong Museum Collection.*

A pair of pedlar dolls with wax heads and leather bodies; England, ca. 1857. (The date "1857" was found inside one of the miniature books carried by the male pedlar doll.) Height: Man 10½ inches (27 cm); woman 11 inches (28 cm). *Strong Museum Collection.*

It was first published as a series of articles in a London periodical in 1849-50. This four volume work is an exhaustive exploration into the world of London streetlife and relates information on everything from clothing to religion to tricks of the trade for each sub-group studied.

From Mayhew we learn that the type of pedlar depicted by the pedlar doll existed in the London of his time. In addition, his illustrations, engravings made from daguerreotypes, show street-sellers in dress similar to that worn by the dolls.

Using costume as a clue for dating pedlar dolls is problematic. First of all, one cannot assume a pedlar's garb to be *haute couture* for any given decade, and secondly, a doll's costume is likely to be changed or altered for a variety of reasons. In placing a date on these artifacts, therefore, we have to take a number of different factors into consideration. Costume is a big factor but it cannot be used exclusively.

The second significant factor used to date pedlar dolls is what each carries in his tray or basket. Pedlars, however, sold just about everything and anything. Most of the articles cover too broad a time span to be of much help as dating clues. Furthermore, these items were frequently added to or replaced if damaged. A plastic article found in the pedlar's basket, therefore, does not immediately brand it a fake. It is conceivable that the pedlar's wares were added to in much the same way as charms to a charm bracelet. Examining each little object in the pedlar's basket thoroughly is important. Often there are trademarks and in some lucky instances even dates. On some newspaper filler in a tiny book on one of the pedlar's trays considered in this study an 1857 date was found clearly printed. Such things as ballad and book titles though often fanciful may also serve as clues in dating a collection of pedlar dolls.

The doll body itself is not a very reliable dating clue. When the doll became a pedlar and when it became a doll are not necessarily simultaneous. An old doll could have been used for a new craft. Furthermore, most pedlar dolls are wooden. Such dolls, having a long history of manufacture, are difficult to date exactly. An additional reason for not considering the doll body is the difficulty of getting at it. Many pedlar dolls have their clothing stitched on to them which makes a thorough examina-

Wax over composition pedlar doll, possibly German, ca. 1860. Height 13 inches (33 cm). *Strong Museum Collection.*

20th century cloth doll, possibly made in Russia. Height 26 inches (36 cm). *Strong Museum Collection.*

Papier mâché pedlar doll made in the United States by Elaine Cannon, ca. 1960. Height 6¾ inches (17 cm). *Strong Museum Collection.*

tion for possible maker's marks virtually impossible without damaging it.

Dating the doll body rather than the doll has been responsible in some cases for placing too early a date on pedlar dolls. Some have been dated as early as 1780. Some doll historians admit they know of no examples before 1800. In this study no well-documented examples were found prior to 1830. This date is based on the evidence of costume, clues gleaned from the pedlar's wares, and the fact that C & H White began production at this time as did Messrs. Evans and Cartwright of Wolverhampton, England.

This is also the period of time when the English poor received more attention from the upper classes. In part due to the effects of the Industrial Revolution, the hardships and lifestyle of the lower classes were simply more visible. There had always been poverty of course, but during this time of great industrial growth the numbers of poor reached frightening proportions, especially in the urban centers. This new visibility of the poor and the concern for their well-being that followed it may have some connection with the pedlar doll story.

The commercially made pedlar dolls may also have been connected in some way with advertising as a promotion for books about pedlars or the poor, or books *for* pedlars such as travel guides and maps. The dolls could also have served as signals to show those pedlars who were unable to read where to purchase the merchandise to fill their baskets. In Mayhew's time, establishments which sold pedlar's stock were called "swag shops." Although Mayhew does not mention any such advertising gimmicks, dolls were often used in this fashion. At any rate, the popularity of pedlar dolls may have started in this way and then caught on as a domestic amusement.

The best theory as to the popularity of pedlar dolls is the Victorian woman's love of miniatures. Pedlar dolls gave them the opportunity to admire and marvel over "the world of tiny things" if the doll was commercially made, or to labor over it themselves. The myriad examples of other Victorian fancy work collaborate this theory. At first, pedlars seem a vulgar topic for class conscious Victorian women of leisure, but they do make sense when seen in light of the aforementioned concern for the underprivileged and the Oxford Movement, a religious movement of the 1830's.

Bea Howe, author of *Antiques from the Victorian Home*, reports: "But the biggest incentive of all came with the Oxford Movement, when church restoration took place throughout England. For this praiseworthy effort, funds had to be raised and Fancy Fairs and Summer Fetes were

the order of the day. No one has described these fairs and fetes better in her novels than Miss Charlotte Yonge. Again and again, she tells us of the widespread and continuous demand for suitable articles to be sent to the nearest repository and sold there in the name of Charity. Amongst these articles were: 'Pincushions, watchguards, (knitted in beads or crocheted), leather pen-wipers, netted purses and the like. The making of these became a craze which entirely upset the schoolroom routine.... Even the governess descended so far as to countenance paste-board boxes being plastered with rice and sealing-wax, alum baskets, dressed dolls and every conceivable trumpery.'"

It is difficult to discern how Victorians actually viewed pedlars and the poor in general. As in any period there was probably a combination of emotions including sympathy and scorn. The dolls reflect this conflict to an extent. That they exist at all implies a certain degree of concern. That they are often quite romanticized connotes aloofness from the reality of poverty, the pedlar's problems, and his lifestyle.

The social attitude which most accurately explains the popularity of the pedlar motif is not scorn, indifference, sympathy, or nostalgia. Rather, the pedlar was an object of fascination closely allied to gypsies and witches. Indeed, often the three were interchangeable.

Many pedlar dolls have such witch-like features as wizened faces and leering eyes. One studied for this report had a pointed witch's hat and another was a doll originally marketed as a witch doll, complete with the warts and fang-like teeth, but re-dressed at some point in her career as a pedlar woman. A doll historian writing in 1968 reports:

"... It is still possible in country districts to meet an occasional gypsy woman with braided plaits and gold rings in her ears. She will offer to tell your fortune—'cross my hand with silver dear'—or sell you homemade clothes pegs, bunches of wild flowers or a card of lace from the basket on her arm."

That pedlars and gypsies were often one and the same is further testified to by an Englishwoman writing in the mid-19th century. Upon leaving her childhood home she was allowed to choose one parting gift:

"Sad to say we asked for some silly object of our childish imagination. I asked for a wax gypsy figure with a tray of tiny toys to sell, that lived under a glass case—I thought it rather like a doll...."

Finally, in my search for a period pedlar doll source, the closest approximation was instructions for a "witch pen-wiper" in an 1860 toy-making guide for young girls. Although ostensibly a witch figure, the instructions called for a small basket filled with "small pincushion

Left to right: Leather English pedlar doll labelled "C. & H. White, Milton, Portsmouth" (England), ca. 1830. Height 11 inches (28 cm). Leather pedlar doll attributed to C. & H. White, Milton, Portsmouth, England, ca. 1830. Height 9 inches (23 cm). Leather pedlar doll attributed to C. & H White, Milton, Portsmouth, England, ca. 1830. Height 9½ inches (24 cm). *Strong Museum Collection.*

&c." and even the red hooded cape!

The interchangeable aspects of these three types leads one to believe that fascination with the unknown was another factor in the popularity of the pedlar doll. Part of this fascination may have been based on an underlying distrust, for many pedlar characters portrayed in literature and song were of questionable reputation. Mayhew documents in detail certain tricks of the trade among street-sellers in general but gives the impression that the majority were honest businessmen. As for their occasional transgressions, he argues that the established London shopkeepers were not without their faults either.

The pedlar's motivation is not difficult to imagine. Though their income from small wares was miniscule, it kept them from starving or, worse, from the workhouse. Especially for the country pedlar, the illusion of freedom and mobility must surely have added to the attraction of such a trade. Initially, I doubted the appeal especially for women pedlars until a Dickens character, Betty Higden, in *Our Mutual Friend* outlined the compensations in this way:

" . . . I get numbed, thought and senses, till I start out of my seat, afeerd that I'm growing like the poor old people that they brick up in the Unions, as you may sometimes see when they let 'em out of the four walls to have a warm in the sun, crawling quite scared about the streets. I was a nimble girl, and I have always been an active body, as I told your lady, first time ever I see her good face. I can still walk twenty mile if I am put to it. I'd far better be a walking than a getting numbed and dreary. I'm a good fair knitter, and can make many little things to sell. The loan from your lady and gentleman of twenty shillings to fit out a basket with, would be a fortune for me. Trudging around the country and tiring of myself out, I shall keep the deadness off, and get my own bread by my own labor. And what more can I want?"

Initially, the whole idea of women pedlars was dubious to me. Would a woman of that time actually have braved the elements, highway robbers, and like hazards of the road? Mayhew does not mention itinerant women pedlars at all. In fact only one primary source surveyed for this study refers to them and then only one hardy soul. The women pedlar dolls resemble most the city vendors described by Mayhew as "street-sellers of small-ware, or tape, cotton, etc." who were "usually elderly females." The description of what one such pedlar had in her basket sounds exactly what pedlar dolls usually carry in theirs: " . . . tapes, cottons, combs, braces, nutmeg-graters, and shaving glasses, with which she strove to keep her old dying husband from the workhouse."

Another reason for doubting the country pedlar theory is the fact that the pedlar dolls do not look the part. A man or woman preparing to travel with his or her wares would more likely be carrying a pack or covered case. Some dolls had a wooden case with a lid which looks somewhat portable, but the majority carry an open basket or tray which looks all too vulnerable to loss of merchandise, damage from the elements, and thieves. Pedlar dolls depict city pedlars primarily and the majority of country pedlars were men not women. Women may have ventured into London suburbs or traveled on special occasions such as to country fairs. Mayhew calls this " 'tramping' the country."

The red-hooded cape which is worn by almost all women pedlar dolls has been a mystery to me since the start of this study. The similarity of dress on the pedlar dolls is probably due to a convention established among the various makers but also to the similarity existent in real life. Street-sellers did dress similarly according to the written descriptions and illustrations throughout Mayhew's work. As for the hooded cape, it is a practical street garmet. The significance of it being red was probably to attract the eye and attention of potential customers.

Although later examples exist, pedlar dolls were most popular between 1830 and 1870, a later time period than heretofore accepted. The latter date is based on photographs of street-sellers in an 1877 publication in which the costume, especially in headwear, is markedly different from that on most pedlar dolls. ■

FROM THE GREEN FORESTS OF VERMONT
DOLLS made by JOEL ELLIS

A beautifully preserved example of a Joel Ellis Wooden doll which came in three sizes—10″, 15″, and 18″. *Courtesy of Yesteryears Doll Museum, Sandwich, Mass. Photo by Paul F. Doble.*

Maple child's chair manufacturd at Ellis' Vermont Novelty Works. *Photo courtesy of Springfield (Vermont) Town Library.*

Four-wheeled model of the Ellis carriage or "cab." Painted blue, it boasted a red, white and blue fringed sun shade. *Courtesy of Yesteryears Doll Museum, Sandwich, Mass. Photo by Paul F. Doble.*

by BEVERLY S. NARKIEWICZ

TOY CAPITAL of the World was the impressive title bestowed on Springfield, Vermont, in the last half of the 19th century. There Joel Ellis, with his inventive genius, utilizing water power from the Black River and raw material from surrounding timberland, began a wooden toy industry whose impact is felt to this day. Wooden toys are no longer manufactured in Springfield, but examples made there in the 1860s and 1870s are now collector items; none are more prized than the doll which was made for a single year.

Joel Ellis had the reputation of being

able to do anything with his hands. At least 13 patents were taken out in his name for items ranging from baby carriages to road building equipment. Unfortunately, for him, his mechanical genius exceeded his business acumen for he never became the financial giant his inventiveness warranted.

He began his career in 1859 with the manufacture of toy wagons made of wood. Gradually he added other wooden toys to his line—tops, building blocks and logs, doll carriages, doll furniture, even toy musical instruments. He also made carriages for real babies. It is reported that Calvin Coolidge as an infant was perambulated about in a Joel Ellis "cab." Twice his factories were destroyed; the flood of 1869 wiped him out completely, and a fire in 1878 again leveled his shops. Both times he rebuilt

Two "much loved" Joel Ellis dolls; one on right shows patented friction joint at knees. *Photo courtesy of Springfield (Vermont) Town Library.*

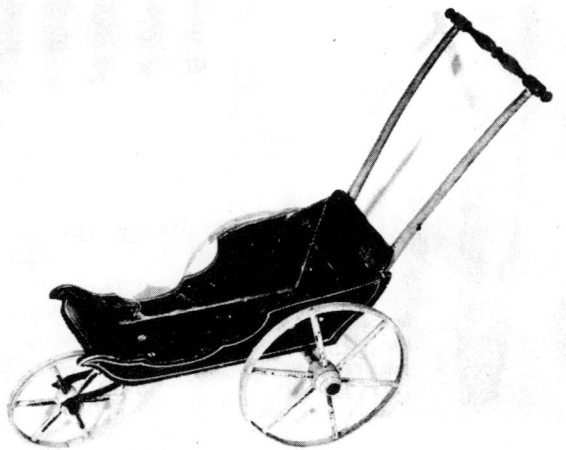

A Three-wheeled Ellis doll carriage, showing characteristic scroll work, striping, and turned handle. *Courtesy of Yesteryears Doll Museum, Sandwich, Mass. Photo by Paul F. Doble.*

of poses. Heads were hand-painted; hands and feet were of metal, painted black.

After one year of production, Ellis sold his patent and the manufacture of Springfield wooden dolls passed on to other toymakers, notably Mason and Taylor and George W. Sanders. The joint mechanism was improved and a neck joint was added so that the doll's head could be turned.

If, as has been said, the test of the success of a doll is in its condition—a poor specimen would be one in pristine condition, never having been played with—then Joel Ellis dolls must be judged successful; Little girls literally loved them to pieces. Today, Joel Ellis wooden dolls, in whatever condition, are rare and choice finds.

his toy factories, but his monetary losses were considerable.

Little girls had long played with wooden dolls, but until 1873 when Joel Ellis took out a patent for his double mortise-and-tenon arm and leg joints and began to mass produce them, wooden dolls were largely hand-carved or of the graceless pointy-nose variety so beloved by Queen Victoria in her girlhood. Joel Ellis dolls were a far cry from those early "penny woodens."

According to his designs, shapeless forms were replaced with turned bodies and limbs; heads were compressed under hydraulic pressure to form pretty facial features and molded hair; the patented friction joint for arms and legs allowed the doll to assume—aided by her young mistress—and hold a variety

Stamp on bottom of three-wheeled carriage indicates that it was patented in 1872. *Courtesy of Yesteryears Doll Museum, Sandwich, Mass. Photo by Paul F. Doble*

Lenci doll with felt head purchased in Italy 1936-40; original felt and cotton Italian peasant costume. Height 14½". *Courtesy of Mrs. Katherine Malcolm.*

Lenci's
The ART DECO DOLLS

by DOROTHY S. COLEMAN

DOLLS OF pressed felt usually dressed in colorful garments made of geometric-shaped patches, epitomize the Art Deco period. Up until now these artistic dolls have been more or less ignored by doll collectors. With the deluge of books on bisque-head dolls, collectors often overlook other dolls. There are several reasons for this neglect; first, very little has been written on other types of dolls and knowledge is the key to popularity in collecting. The first and finest of the felt dolls were made by the Scavinis in Turin, Italy, at the beginning of the Art Deco period, around 1920. They were soon known as Lenci dolls, Lenci being the nickname of Madame Elena di Scavini. The Lenci dolls were very artistic and well-made, thus placing them among the most expensive dolls on the market in the 1920s. For this reason, many imitations began to flood the market a few years after the Lencis appeared. Sometimes these Lenci-type dolls are difficult to distinguish from real Lencis unless labels are still on the dolls.

Access to three successive Lenci catalogs covering the period 1925-1930 provided the incentive for a new book titled *Lenci Dolls, Fabulous Figures of Felt*. These catalogs not only picture hundreds of Lenci dolls but also provide the series and model number for each doll pictured, thus making it possible to decipher the numerical Lenci code. Most early 20th century dolls were given a numerical code number. Thanks to several Kammer and Reinhardt catalogs their code was broken and interpreted in *My Darling Dolls*, edited by the author and published in 1972 by Pyne Press. Now for the first time the Lenci code is also deciphered. Not only does the code help us to date and identify a Lenci doll, but it also provides information that will help to separate Lenci-type dolls from real Lencis.

In the past, many Lenci-type dolls have been mistaken for Lenci dolls. This new book shows that the distinction is not always easy to discern and requires detailed study. Not all hollow-felt bodied dolls are Lencis, although most of them are. These hollow-felt bodies were made around 1930 and thus were not among the earliest Lencis as has been sometimes stated. The zigzag seam up the back of the neck was not used on Lenci dolls alone. Doll collectors and dealers are going to find it necessary to study this new Lenci book carefully in order to differentiate between true Lenci dolls and Lenci-type dolls.

The many different Lenci labels as well as some of the labels found on Lenci-type dolls are shown so that if only a partial or indistinct label or stamp remains it can be readily identified.

Lenci Harlequin, number 118, a model type shown in "Playthings" in 1920. The left arm and hand are replacements. Height 17½". *Courtesy of the Margaret Woodbury Strong Museum. Photography by Cherry Bou.*

Pair of Lenci dolls in practically identical costumes even to the string of glass beads. These French peasant clothes resemble those of the French World War I heroine, Bécassine. The large doll, number 300/43, shown in the 1930 catalog has a hollow felt body. This doll has lost her basket, cap and wooden shoes. The small doll, one of the Mascotte series, a type also shown in the 1930 Lenci catalog, is in mint condition. Heights, large doll 17½"; small doll 8½". *Coleman collection. Photograph by Cherry Bou.*

What makes Lenci dolls important to doll collectors? They are extremely artistic and typical of the popular Art Deco period. The painting and sculpturing on these dolls were done by fine Italian artists. There were many hundreds of different Lenci models made. Some appear to be rare while others must have been made in large quantities. A sizeable doll collection could be made of only Lenci dolls. Thanks to the information in *Playthings*, three Lenci catalogs, Kimport catalogs and the Laura Waters catalog (all summarized in the new Lenci book), collectors can now date their Lenci dolls and in many cases give them a tradename. Cloth dolls are more durable than most other types; they do not break like bisque and china dolls; the paint seldom peels off as on wooden and metal dolls and they do not crack like composition. A few moth flakes and protection from fading in strong sunlight will keep them in perfect condition. Lenci dolls were luxury dolls when new and therefore most of them were carefully preserved in their original clothes and even in their original boxes more often than most other types of dolls. Last but not least, Lenci dolls are still relatively inexpensive. When new, a Lenci child doll cost about the same as a Jumeau bébé, but today it can be purchased for a fraction of the cost of a Jumeau. Many Lencis can still be bought for less than a hundred dollars. When Lencis become fully appreciated, no doubt the prices will rise accordingly.

Appreciation comes with knowledge. Collectors will have to devote some real study to the new Lenci book in order to gain the necessary knowledge. The way the doll is seamed, the colorings used, the painting techniques, the methods of application of hair, the types of construction materials, the jointing of the dolls, the size and shape of the limbs, and many other details are important to recognize and know. The number code may seem bewildering at first, but after it is mastered, collectors will speak as glibly about a Lenci 300 or a Lenci 165 as they do about a Kammer and Reinhardt 101 or an S.F.B.J. 236. These code numbers provide an easy short-hand description of a given type of doll. The history of the Lenci dolls shows why the early ones are related to the fat little "Mama" dolls, while the dolls of the late twenties include such famous people as Rudolph Valentino and Shirley Temple. The history and social conditions of their time are reflected in Lenci dolls. It may come as a surprise to many collectors to learn that Lenci made many other items, such as hats and pocketbooks. Not all Lenci dolls were made of felt. There are records of bisque, composition, and vinyl Lenci dolls.

Although Madame Lenci died many years ago, the name "Lenci" has been carried on. Lenci dolls are still being made in Italy. The current owners apparently have no connection with their predecessors other than the name "Lenci." ■

Lenci doll of about 1940, one of the Miniature series, represents an urchin. The dog is marked "Steiff." Height 9 *Coleman collection. Photograph by Bettyanne Twigg.*

Lenci doll with felt face has glass or plastic movable flirting eyes. This type of doll could be as late as the 1940s. Height 20". *Courtesy of the Margaret Woodbury Strong Museum. Photograph by Bettyanne Twigg.*

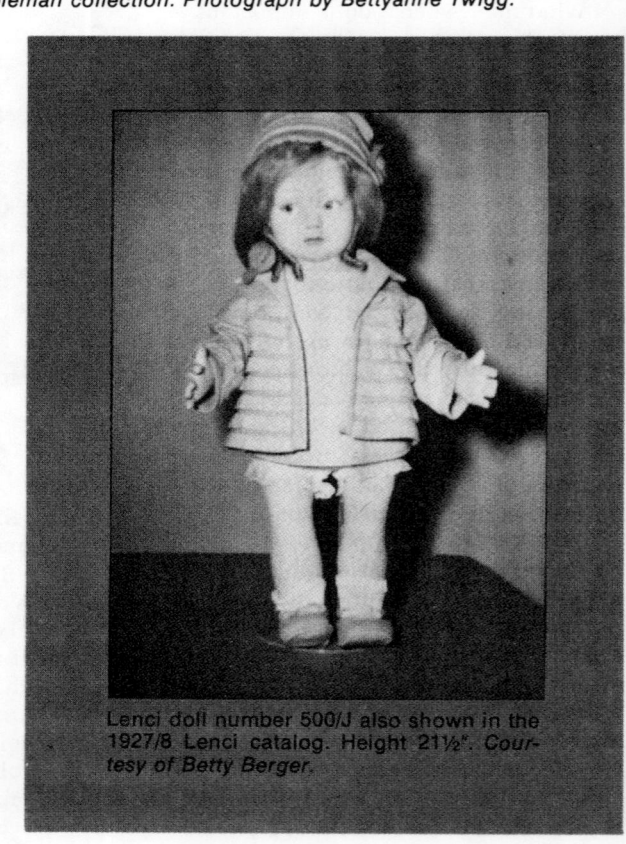

Lenci doll number 500/J also shown in the 1927/8 Lenci catalog. Height 21½". *Courtesy of Betty Berger.*

The Sleeping Sand Baby

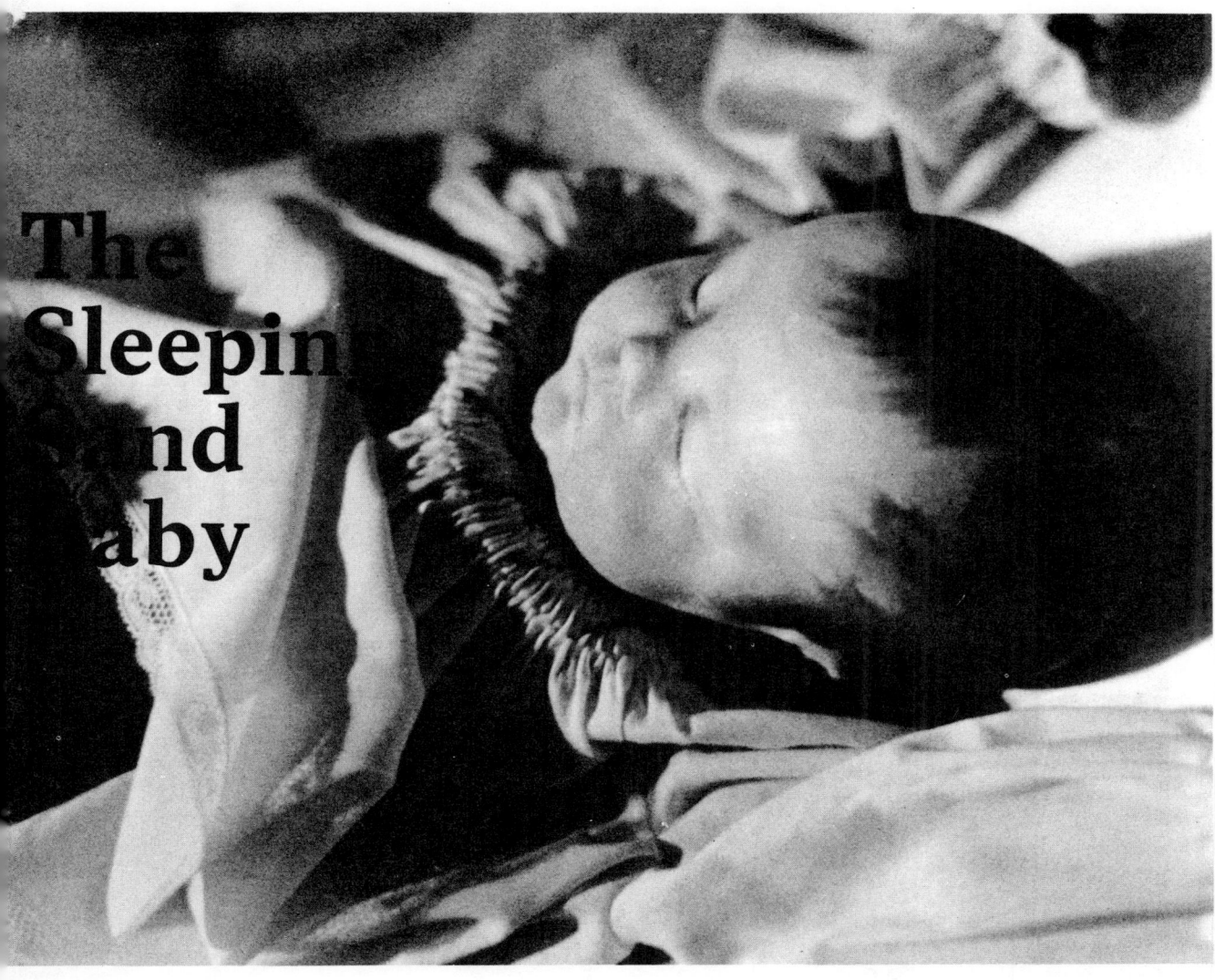

Illustration 1.

MAGDA BYFIELD

No one who has seen it can help but be moved by its sense of tranquility.

IF you think *Illustration 1* is a picture of a baby captured by the camera during the first sleepy days of its life you might well be forgiven for your conclusion. But the infant is a doll, and in this instance one made fifty-five years ago.

Marketed as "The Little Dreamer" it not only appears uncannily lifelike but when held also *feels* real. It is 19 inches long *(Illustration 2)* and weighs 7 lb—the bulk of the weight being sand lodged within the head. This is a handmade doll created out of stockinette with the head only painted in oils in a most fluid and masterly fashion. The designer and maker of this, one of the most emotive of all dolls, was the German artist Kathe Kruse (1883-1968).

We can guess by the dolls rarity that the design did not in its day meet with the acclaim bestowed on it by today's collector, though its production over many years suggests there were always those discerning few who saw it for the work of art it is. In an age when infant mortality was still comparitively high, a baby doll with closed eyes must have held morbid connotations and probably also forseeable frustrations for the child whose doll could not be made to "wake up." *Illustration 3* shows the open-eyed version; a doll of identical size and weight and today more easily obtainable suggesting this was the better seller. It must be said that both types are considered scarce as they were expensive toys in their day, and were not mass produced in the manner of some of Frau Kruse's smaller dolls.

No one who has seen a Sleeping Sand Baby can help but be moved by its sense of tranquility, its elfin-like daintiness and its amazingly sensitive reflection of the satiny perfection of a new born babe. Its very weight makes it sink into its clothing so that at all times it appears

25

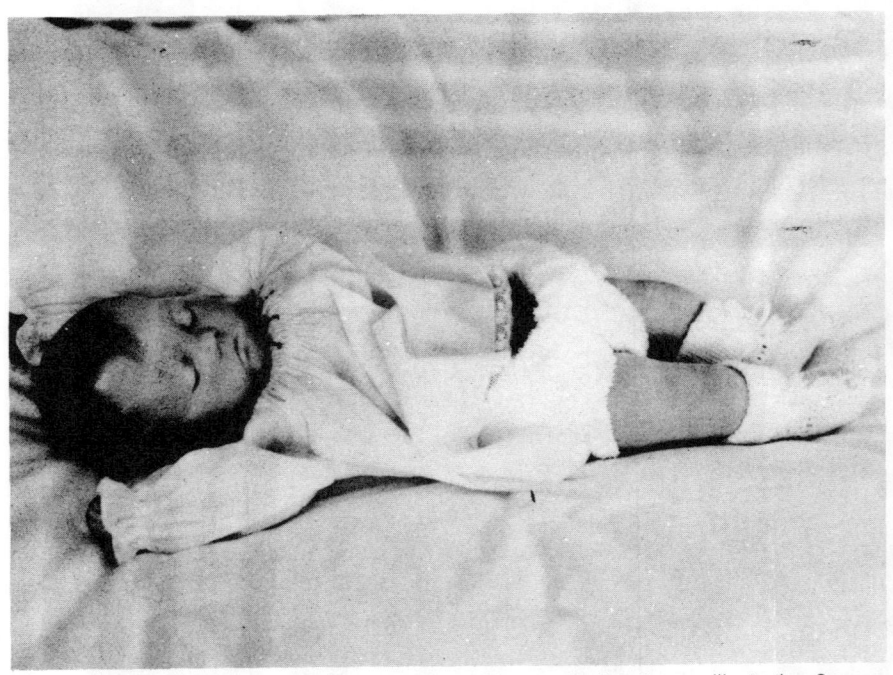
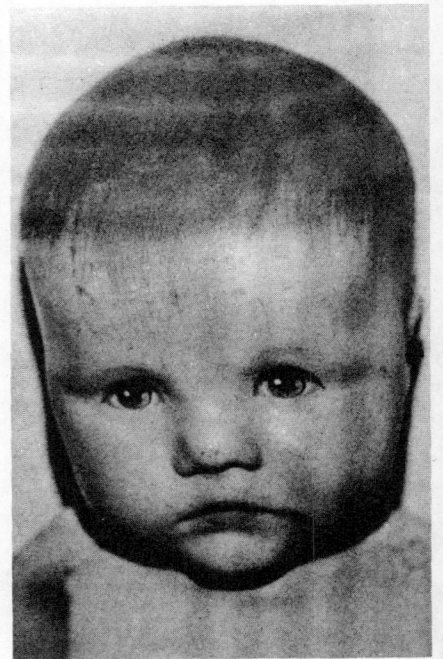

Illustration 2. Illustration 4 Illustration 3. Illustration 5

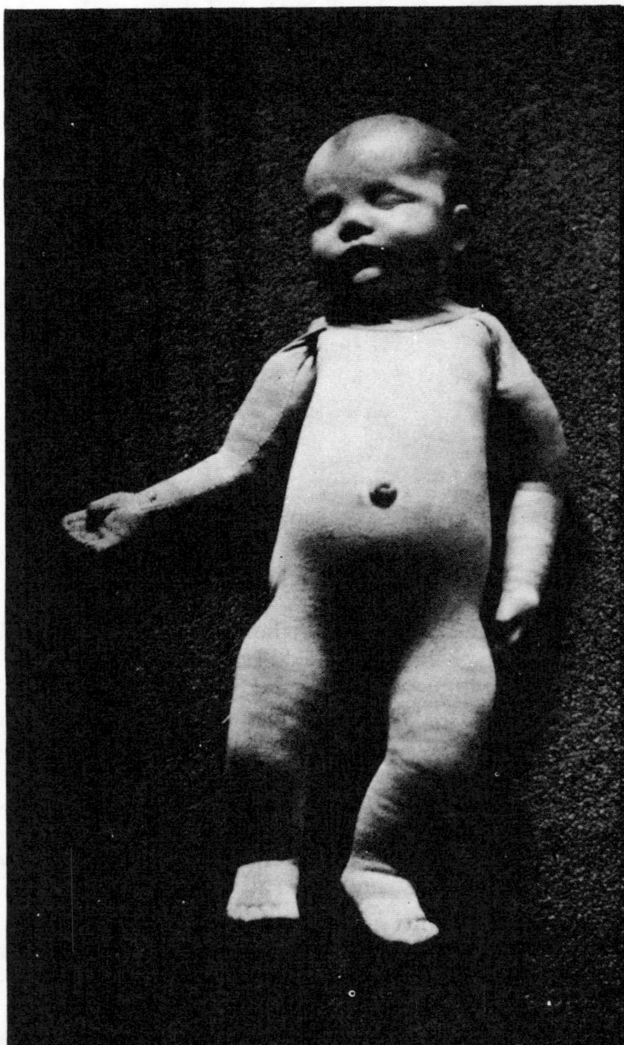

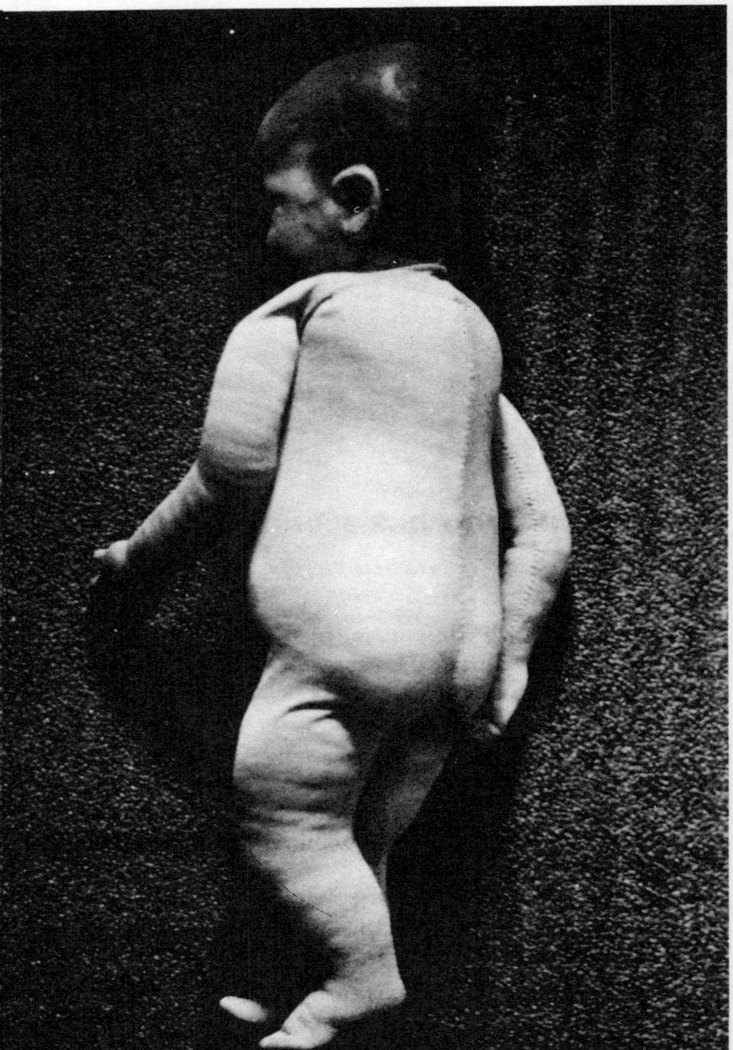

The captivating quality of the doll's face lies partly in its sculptural perfection.

snuggled down into whatever it is wearing or on whatever it is laid. Casually placed in a chair, cradle or on a rug, the remarkable sense of movement built into the doll's design ensures that it will come to rest in an attitude of perfect relaxation.

In *Illustrations 4 and 5* the simplicity of the body design can be clearly seen. The head, neck and collar are comprised of a single piece of material, the head somewhat obtrusively seam-stitched in a cross on top *(Illustration 6)* continuing down the back to the collar. Tucks in the neck are scattered at random, varying in the number and placing from doll to doll, but evidently even these did not hold the neck in shape and every Sand Baby is found with a stockinette loop round its neck—considered by many as a disturbing design flaw. The wadding-filled body and legs are of one piece of fabric appropriately seamed with remarkable ingenuity. The padded arms are each separate but linked by a strong tape running *inside* from one hand up the arm, through the body beneath the collar and down inside the other arm to the other hand. This gives added strength to the freely swinging arms that would otherwise be supported quite inadequately by the seams attaching them to the shoulders. Feet and hands are stitched, the latter with free-standing thumbs. On the dolls' tummy is the unique distinguishing mark of the Kruse Baby—a coiled navel of applied stockinette.

The captivating quality of the doll's face lies partly in its sculptural perfection. The ears *(Illustration 7)* tucked well into the head are a touching reminder of the true newborn look. But the paintwork on the mask with its subtle gradations of color from a milk-white forehead to the glowing tones around the cheeks, nose, chin and ears are truly the coloring of skin as yet unexposed to sunlight. The eyelashes resting on the cheeks are painted with unsurpassed delicacy and competence *(Illustration 8)*. The artist employed to paint the baby's hair with its sparse, whispey curls (always in a forward brushed style) was responsible only for the front portion of the head; the back part was painted by another less experienced painter and there are often slight variations in the two color batches.

The Sand Baby is said to portray one of Frau Kruse's seven children—Max. There is a sibling resemblance between all her dolls making even the most rarely found specimen easily recognizable, for her three daughters and four sons all posed as models for various designs.

The intense maternal sensitivity which Kathe Kruse brought to her dolls is undoubtedly the most notable aspect of her products, and in the Sleeping Baby more perhaps than in any other of her extensive and superb range, we see a design conceived of tenderness and a total awareness of the fragile beauty of newly born life. ■

Magda Byfield *is an English collector and writer. Her authoritative articles about collectible dolls, crib figures and marionettes have appeared frequently in* **Spinning Wheel** *and other antiques publications. Mrs. Byfield is the author of "Dolls' House Dolls." She lives in Surrey, England, with her husband and son.*

...there was always those discerning few who recognized it for the work of art it is.

Illustration 8.

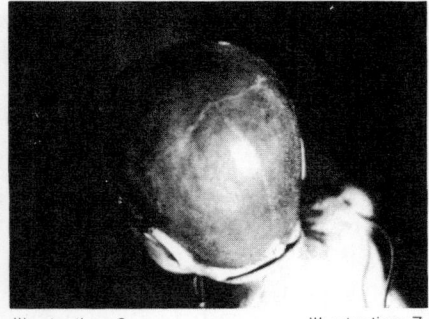

Illustration 6.   Illustration 7.

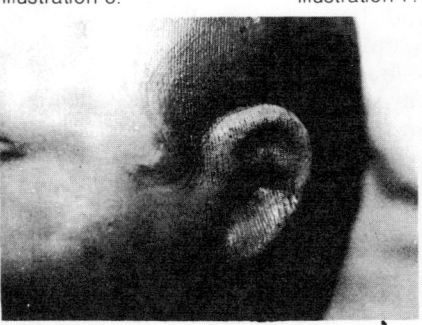

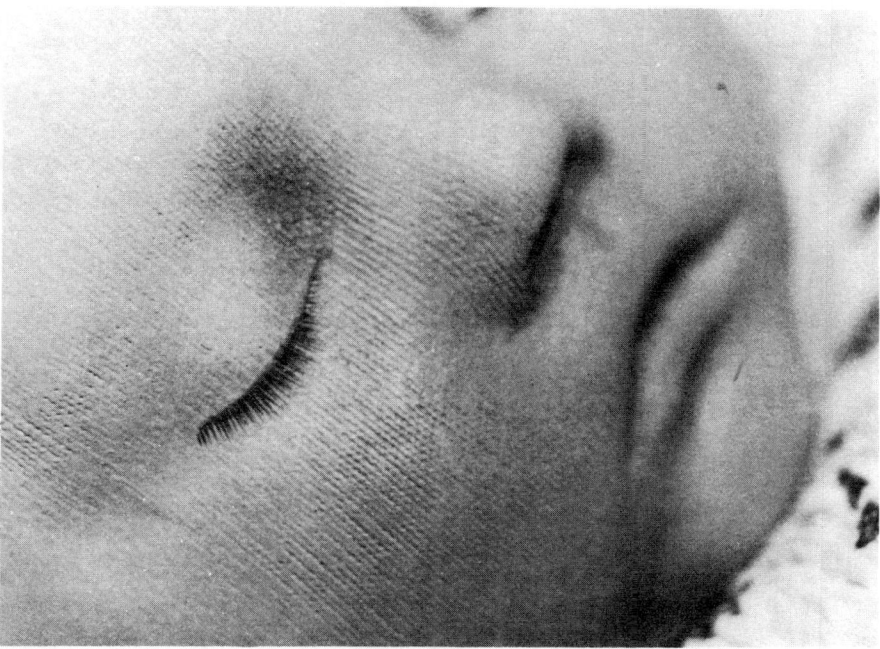

COLLECTIBLE CLOTH DOLLS

by MAGDA BYFIELD

YOU DON'T NEED a fortune to possess old dolls of outstanding merit. European rag dolls of the 1920s and 30s are some of the finest examples of their type. The concept of cloth dolls as being universally appealing to collectors is a recent one. An immense change of attitude has taken place in the last few years towards these formerly underrated specimens, due no doubt in part to the rapid price rise of more extant collectible dolls. In the past we have been too apt to think that a type as dissimilar in time and origin as the fabric doll would not complement those surrounding it and vice versa. But wax, bisque, wood, papier-mache, china and parian dolls of varying periods have long been displayed together, and the recent escalation in popularity of some very late bisque character dolls has paved the way towards an acceptance of the often very beautiful and gentle cloth doll.

Fig. 1 is a robust girl doll made by Dean's Rag Book Co. Like so many of the dolls from this factory, the face alone has been invested with realism and detail, inasmuch as the feature painting and modeling is confined to a mask. This is lithographed and varnished; the latter having darkened with age imbues the doll with

51 cm (20") cloth doll made by Dean's Rag Book Co. of London. Lithographed and varnished face with molded features. Mohair wig on gauze cap. Pink linen with articulation at neck, shoulders and hips. English. Late 1930s.

a bracing glow. All specimens of this model are found with this time-tint, though wigs vary, being applied either direct to the head or mounted on caps. Footwear also varies and the doll comes in small sizes with cotton socks and velvet slippers incorporated into the legs, while larger versions have removable hose and shoes. The once blue eyes have mellowed to green beneath the mature varnish. The face is rather feline in concept making this change strikingly appropriate. By contrast the rest of the doll is crude in design and finish. The front portion of the swivel neck is colored and varnished together with the face, thus bisecting it vertically with an obtrusive and somewhat disturbing seam. The back of the head and neck are largely ignored since this area was intended to be completely hidden by the wig and hat. There are no ears. The body is articulated at the shoulders and hips with metal pin-and-button joints, one of which is embossed with the manufacturer's mark. Fingers and toes are stitched. Its unquestionable success is all the more remarkable when one examines the naivete of the concept.

Kathe Kruse was a doll artist of exceptional insight and sensitivity. Her creations have a haunting innocence that has placed them among the most sought after of fabric dolls. It was this grave, slightly mournful quality that met with such reproof from Hitler, and ultimately forced her to close down her factory during his rule. Her dolls at this time had already enjoyed a long and successful run both in Germany and abroad, and had become synonymous with "the German child" ... a title she herself conferred on them. Through them she later reflected her personal sorrow and anxiety for her country's future. But such criticism, however subtly veiled, was unacceptable to Nazi Germany. After World War II production was resumed until her death in 1968. Her daughter, Hanne Kruse, continued the tradition at Donauworth, using some of the established molds together with her own new designs. The factory is still known as "Kathe Kruse Puppen."

Fig. 2 is a Kathe Kruse life-sized stockinette infant doll of astonishing realism. Its qualities are not only visual, for in movement and weight the design is also unexpected. The head is painted stockinette filled with sand. This gives the doll an overall weight of 7 lbs. so that the resultant top-heaviness makes it difficult to lift without initially supporting the head. Not surprisingly, many have been found in use as models at child care training centers although the doll was marketed as a toy. As such, Frau Kruse struck an ingenious balance between a human infant and a baby doll. The unpainted stockinette body is beautifully designed and padded to form all the creases and curves in the right places. The arms swing in the helpless fashion of the newly born. An inspired final touch is an applied tummy-button, a simple twist of stockinette to complete this novel and masterly concept.

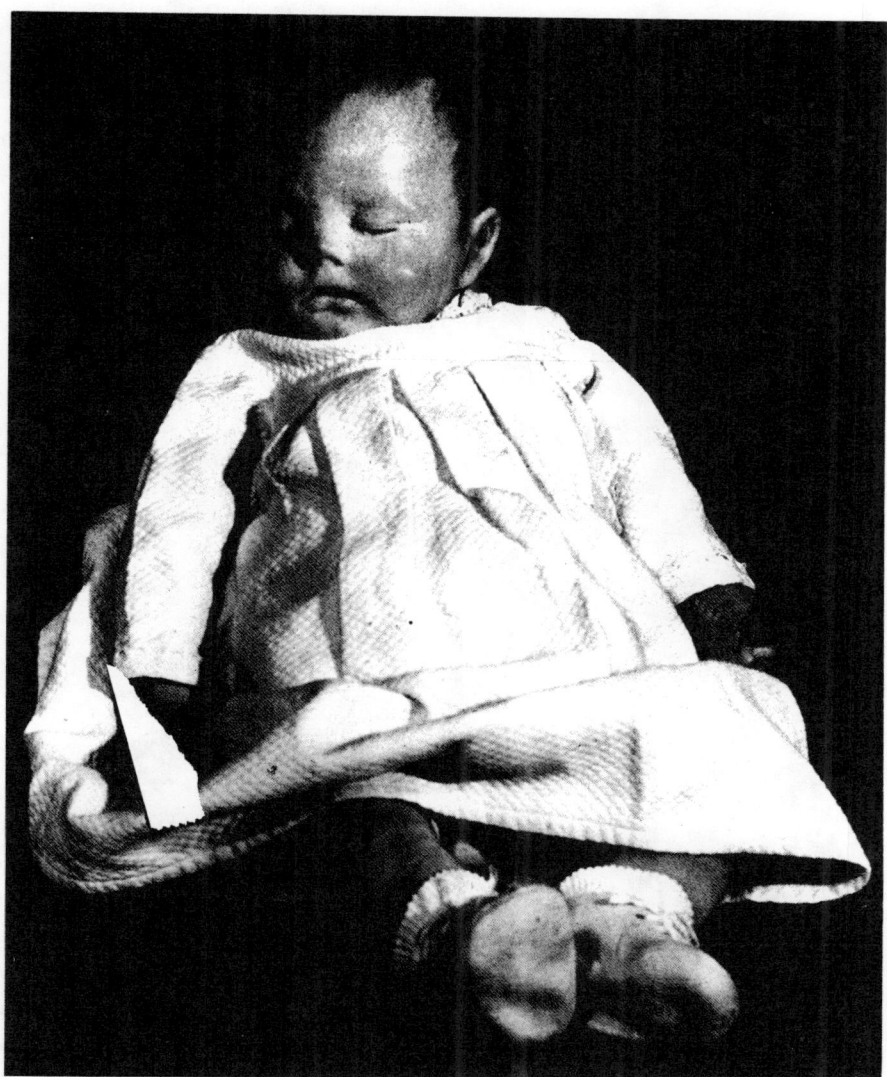

48 cm (19") stockinette baby doll by the Berlin artist Kathe Kruse. Head is painted and varnished and set turned slightly to the right. German, ca. 1920.

The English designer Norah Wellings made an immense and very personal contribution to cloth-dollmaking. A great exponent of humor, her dolls were worldly and factual with an ever-present overtone of comical vitality. As a professional artist, Norah Wellings joined the Chad Valley Company in 1919, but by the early 1920s had formed her own company with her brother, employing six girls. By the late 1930s employees numbered 300, and the firm had moved to a large garden factory with an office and showrooms in London's Regent Street. A creative and energetic woman, Miss Wellings personally supervised every stage in the creation of her designs. She continued in business until the death of her brother and partner in the late 1950s. She died in 1975 at the age of 82. Many of her creations were sold on luxury liners as souvenir dolls, with the ship's name embroidered on the doll's hat or headdress. These were often "costume dolls" dressed in the national garments of the countries of the

ships' origins or ports of call on the cruise.

Fig. 3. is a snappy young rider in hunting gear, all set to outfox the fox. Its jaunty stance and rotund features are typical of Norah Wellings' witty concepts. The doll is stuffed felt with applied ears and painted features, without any facial modeling. Clothes are machined felt except for the velvet "hard hat" and oilcloth boots. The hunting crop is stitched to the hand and is painted wood tied round with black cord. This model was one of Miss Wellings' "Norene" doll lines and appears in a pre-war trade catalog as model number 825. Other lines at this time were Jolly Toddlers, Novelty Dolls, Little Pixie People and Novelty Animals.

Products from the Turin-based firm of Lenci are extensive and well-known to collectors, though exceptional models are still turning up. The Lenci "stock head" was undoubtedly their best seller since this mold is the most frequently found, usually in a 16-inch size, in varying dress, coloring, hairstyles, and as boys and girls. But how many have seen this standard doll presented as a Red Indian?

Fig. 4 is a dusky Lenci child doll with applied black mohair wig and painted features. Side-glancing eyes are brown and nostril dots and lower lip are light red with a darker upper lip. Head and body are brown felt with swivel neck and articulation at shoulders and hips. Trousers are yellow felt with red trim and red, white, and blue machined felt insertion. Matching moccasins have white kid leather soles. Belt and bag are leather with green, brown, and red felt. Beads are blue and white strung on leather. A lovely and most decorative product from a manufactory renowned for its versatility. ■

38 cm (15") child doll by Norah Wellings. Stuffed felt with painted features, applied mohair wig and stand-out ears. Articulated at neck, shoulders and hips. Clothes are felt, velvet and oilcloth. Jacket and waistcoat have gold metal buttons and hat is trimmed with black ribbon band. English, ca. 1935.

41 cm (16") brown felt doll by Lenci representing a Red Indian child. Dressed in leather, felt and beadwork outfit. The wig was probably originally tied in bunches or braided. Headdress is now missing. Molded and painted features with applied ears. Articulated at neck, shoulders and hip. Italian, ca. 1930.

Fig. 1: Most frequently found toddler doll. Height 16 inches.

Fig. 3: Boy doll with finely knotted wig. One of the few made with a socket head. Height 19 inches.

Fig. 4: Girl doll with finely knotted wig and unusual leg articulation. Height 18 inches.

Fig. 8: Baby doll like Figure 7 but without a weighted head and with a wig. Length 19 inches.

Fig. 10: Store mannequin with rigid legs and lift-off composition head. Height 37 inches.

THE VERSATILE DOLLS OF KÄTHE KRUSE

by MAGDA BYFIELD

THE EMERGENCE of the handmade Art Doll took place in Germany in the period of World War I, and the most enduring products of those talented doll artists are without question the tender and imaginative dolls of Käthe Kruse. Her work is now known and sought by collectors the world over, but there are many examples among her creations that are extremely rare and very probably unknown to most. Because her dolls were such an immense success within her own lifetime, contemporary postcards showing one doll or several grouped together were marketed, and from these we know that many designs have yet to surface. Children's books were also published illustrated entirely with charmingly

Fig. 2: A pair of toddler dolls photographed in a setting. One of twelve color plates used to illustrate "The Katy Kruse Dolly Book" published in 1927.

Fig. 7: Infant doll with the eyes painted open. Otherwise identical to sleeping doll.

arranged groups of her dolls. There can be few individual dollmakers who have enjoyed a success of this magnitude or such appreciation from their own contemporaries.

Käthe Kruse first showed her dolls in Berlin at an exhibition of homemade toys and thereafter never looked back. Max Von Boehn writes of her in his book, *Dolls and Puppets:* "Since her discovery the dolls made by Käthe Kruse have been universal favorites, unrivalled by any competitor." In 1951 she published an autobiography entitled *Das Grosse Puppenspiel.* She died in 1968, but the factory continues to this day under one of Frau Kruse's daughters, Hanne, at Donauwörth.

It is unusual in the field of dollmaking for a designer to confine her models exclusively to likenesses of her own children, and it is this specialization and the narrow confines of the materials in which they were carried out that embues the Käthe Kruse doll with an insistent identity. They have expressive powers peculiar to her that makes them more instantly recognizable perhaps than any other maker's dolls. Facially, due to family resemblances, they do not differ much, but in the body construction Frau Kruse was continually exploring new avenues. These differences are significant because a successful formula produced without variety over a period of years could all too easily become stale, both for the dollmaker and the public. Käthe Kruse's dolls have always remained fresh and sensitive.

The oil paint work was applied by hand with unfailing skill to the doll's head only, the body always remaining in the natural fabric. This was invariably pink cotton or stockinette. The brushwork is the more remarkable as the molded facial surface on which it was worked in a most painterly manner imposes certain restrictions on an artist's freedom of approach. The women trained by Käthe Kruse in this work copied expertly her delicacy and fluidity of style. Her early doll heads were fabric stretched over a molded mask and stitch-seamed rather obtrusively. There can be little doubt that in these molds she was greatly influenced and guided by her sculptor husband, Max Kruse. The painted finish of the heads was, however, entirely her own gifted style. Her medium was the needle and the brush. The layers of pigment on the early dolls was very thin with the seams and the weave of the fabric showing through. Curiously this transparency in no way detracts from the charm or realism of the dolls, and there is a brightness and luminosity of color in these early specimens that became somewhat diminished later when a thicker surface was applied to mask the seams and fabric. Later still, the heavy impasto developed into a composition head and ultimately plastic took over, but the fabric bodies of varying construction have always remained.

One of the questions that often arises about Käthe Kruse's dolls is within what limit of function were they designed? Without doubt her creations were devoted chiefly to the toy industry, but not exclusively so. It is extremely difficult to attempt to draw a line between her dolls and her models and mannequins as in many instances the division was purely a matter of size. By their very nature, the dolls were utilized for purposes other than play. The life-sized sand weighted baby marketed as a toy often found its way into child care training centers. It not only looks but *feels* like a newborn baby. It weighs 7 pounds, and the head rolls in the manner of the newly born while the arms hang loosely from the shoulders and swing helplessly. It was in every respect the ideal candidate for training purposes. Her child-size "bendy" dolls were inevitably used as store mannequins and, though in later years she designed mannequins exclusively as shop display models, one wonders if these big dolls were her first real mannequins or accidentally opened up possibilities for another market. These wired dolls were made in all sizes, the majority of them very small. Few have survived because the continual twisting into different poses led to their eventual disintegration.

The best known of the Käthe Kruse dolls must be the 16-inch toddler, and by the numbers available for today's collectors, this model would seem to have been her best seller (*Fig. 1*). It has the usual oil painted

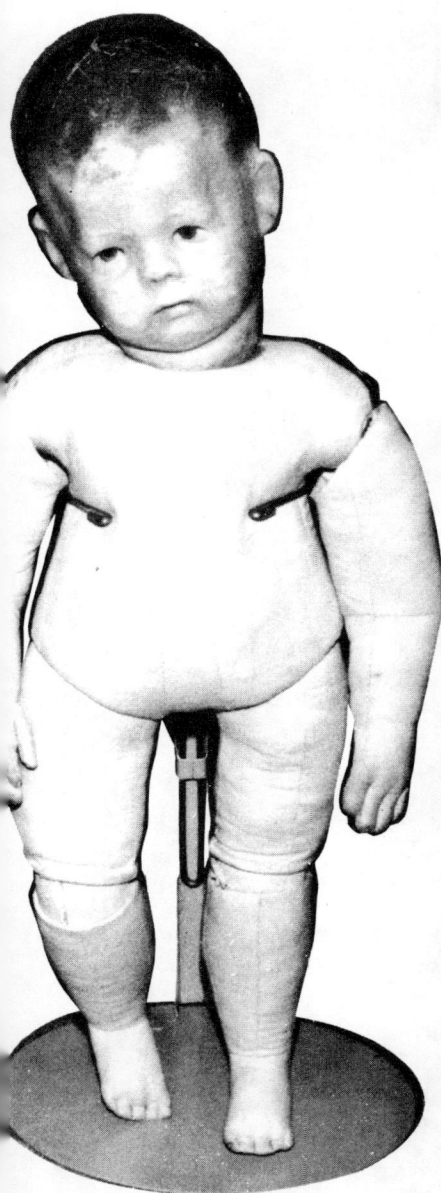

Fig. 9: Toddler doll with socket head, elastic strung and with ball joints at the knees. Height 19 inches.

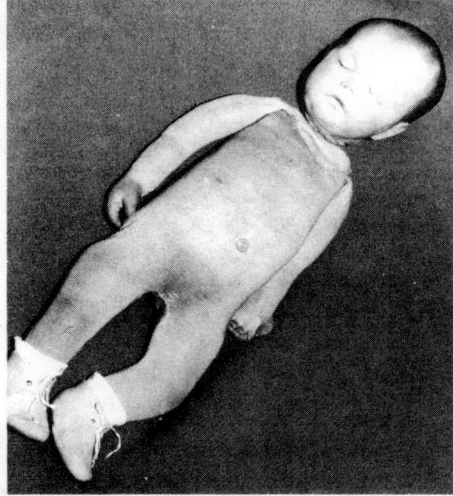

Fig. 5: Sleeping infant doll with a sand weighted head shown without clothes to illustrate simplicity of body design.

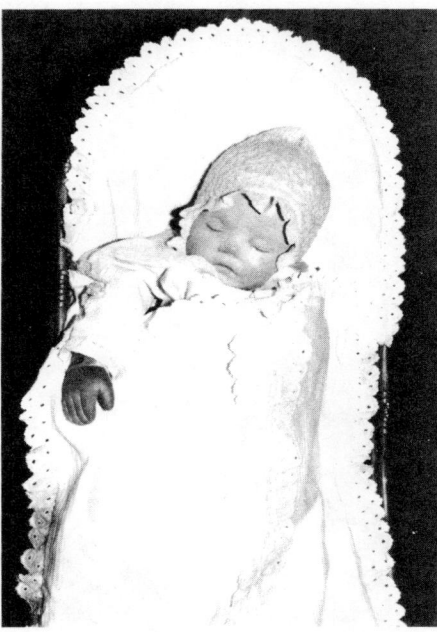

Fig. 6: Dressed sleeping infant doll tied into baby wrapper.

head with facial seams running downwards from the corners of the mouth. The painted hair serves well to disguise the obtrusive cross seams on the head. The cotton body and limbs are made in several intricate sections, resulting in a delightful chubby realism. The hips are swivel jointed, and the arms hang from stitch seams. The popularity of this doll is confirmed not only by the large numbers remaining but also by their frequent appearance on postcards. This model was also used to illustrate such children's books as *The Katy Kruse Dolly Book* published by George Harrap & Co. Ltd. in 1927, from which one of the plates is reproduced here (*Fig. 2*).

Almost equally familiar to collectors is the 19-inch boy doll with socket head and wig (*Fig. 3*). This is one of the very few models made by Käthe Kruse with a turning head, and was later produced also with a girl's wig. The specimen shown was found in his original box, the end label of which is too faded for photography but reads: "Käthe Kruse Doll/Boysie 11b/Made in Germany." The head and neck are painted in the usual manner and the cotton body is articulated with swivel hips and seam-stitched shoulders. The manner of construction of the body fabric is simple, with minimal seaming, but nevertheless achieves the usual standard of realism. The brown human hair wig is intricately knotted in small groups of hair through a shaped muslin cap and cropped in a disarming boyish style.

Less well known but available for the diligent searcher is the 18-inch wigged girl doll (*Fig. 4*). This model has an unusual leg design not found in other Kruse dolls. The leg tops are attached to the base of the cotton torso in the *front only* with slack tapes stitched to the backs of the legs and the seat. This enables the doll to hold a seated position without the possibility of tilting forward. When supported on a stand or laid flat, the tapes fold neatly into the space between the body and leg tops. There is no articulation at the neck or hips, and the arms swing from the standard stitch-seam design. The wig is made in the same professional way as that of *Figure 3*.

The most sought after and unquestionably the most emotive of all Käthe Kruse's dolls is the life-sized stockinette infant. Its visual effect of reality and its 7 lb. weight make it completely unparalleled. The sheer simplicity of the design is illustrated in the undressed doll shown in *Figure 5*. This 19-inch model was manufactured with the eyes painted sleeping (*Figs. 5 & 6*) and also painted open (*Fig. 7*). A feature unique to these dolls is an applied rosette navel. A similar but extremely rare variant is the stockinette "wigged" baby (*Fig. 8*). also 19-inch and constructed identically to its fellows, it is however without a weighted head and without the navel. The features are more pronounced and therefore the facial appearance is marginally more mature. The impasto of the head is considerably heavier than that of the infant dolls and this was necessary to achieve the more prominent nose and ears. The knotted hair wig is a masterpiece of baby-type sparsely distributed hair. All these baby dolls were conceived as toys for children, but there can be no doubt that several found their way into window displays for shops selling baby clothes.

The 18-inch boy doll with elastic strung articulation (*Fig. 9*) is a very rare type indeed. The head is the standard toddler model as shown in *Figure 1*, except that it is presented here with a socket neck. The stuffed cotton body has projecting shoulders, and the hip sockets are reinforced with carton cups. The hands have thumbs applied separately, and the arms are strung through the torso with carton cups at their top to fit over the shoulders. There is no articulation at the elbows. The legs have fabric covered ball joints at the knees, and the leg rubber passes up through the body to join the neck hook. The scarcity of this variant is likely in some measure to lie in its construction; the body and limbs are tightly padded and the rubber stringing has to pass through this morass of wadding. In the event of the rubber perishing (and the life of old stringing rubber was notoriously short) the stuffing would have to be removed before the doll could be restrung, after which it would be extremely difficult to refill again and would have been an impractical undertaking for a doll's hospital of the day. The model illustrated here has survived in mint condition and was clearly never played with. Even so, the rubber has lost its elasticity and the limbs now hang loosely.

The 37-inch stockinette model with lift-off composition head (*Fig. 10*) was designed and used as a store mannequin. In spite of this functional role, the figure has only scant articulation at the shoulders which will have posed considerable difficulties in getting it into and extracting it from the clothing it was designed to display. Holes in the base of the feet testify to the one time presence of a base stand. This mannequin has the familiar solemn Kruse face and the typical wig of hair knotted into a muslin cap. There are four large metal press stud cups in the head with corresponding studs attached to the wig which will have

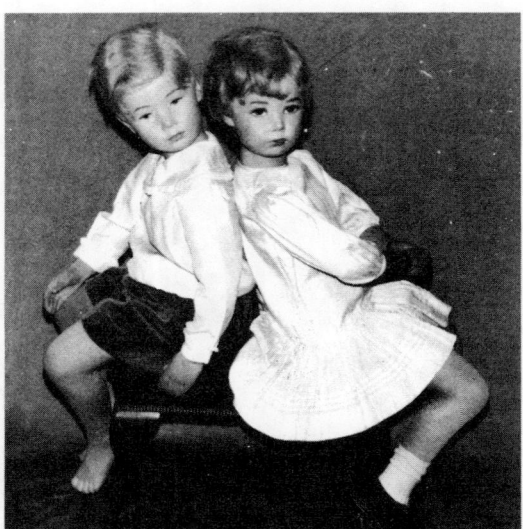

Fig. 11: Boy and girl store mannequins with wired "bendy" arms and swing leg articulation.

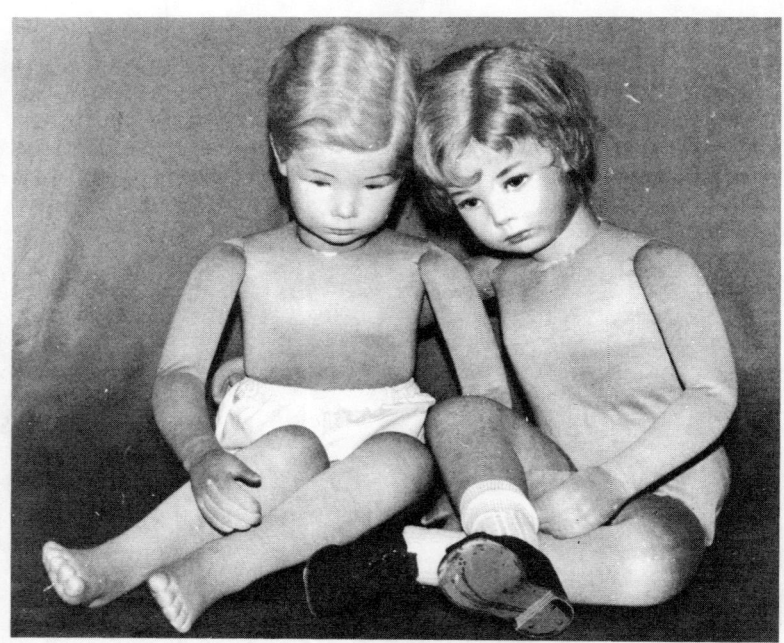

Fig. 12: These mannequins can only be posed in seated positions. Length 37 inches.

made this interchangeable. The body is both accurately and gracefully proportioned with only one seam along the entire trunk in the back. The effect of the child-like contours is achieved by the skillful distribution of the padding over which the stockinette is tightly drawn.

The 37-inch pair of mannequins (*Fig. 11*) are constructed in a slightly different manner and their design enables them only to be posed in a sitting position (*Fig. 12*). They, too,

(more on page 16)

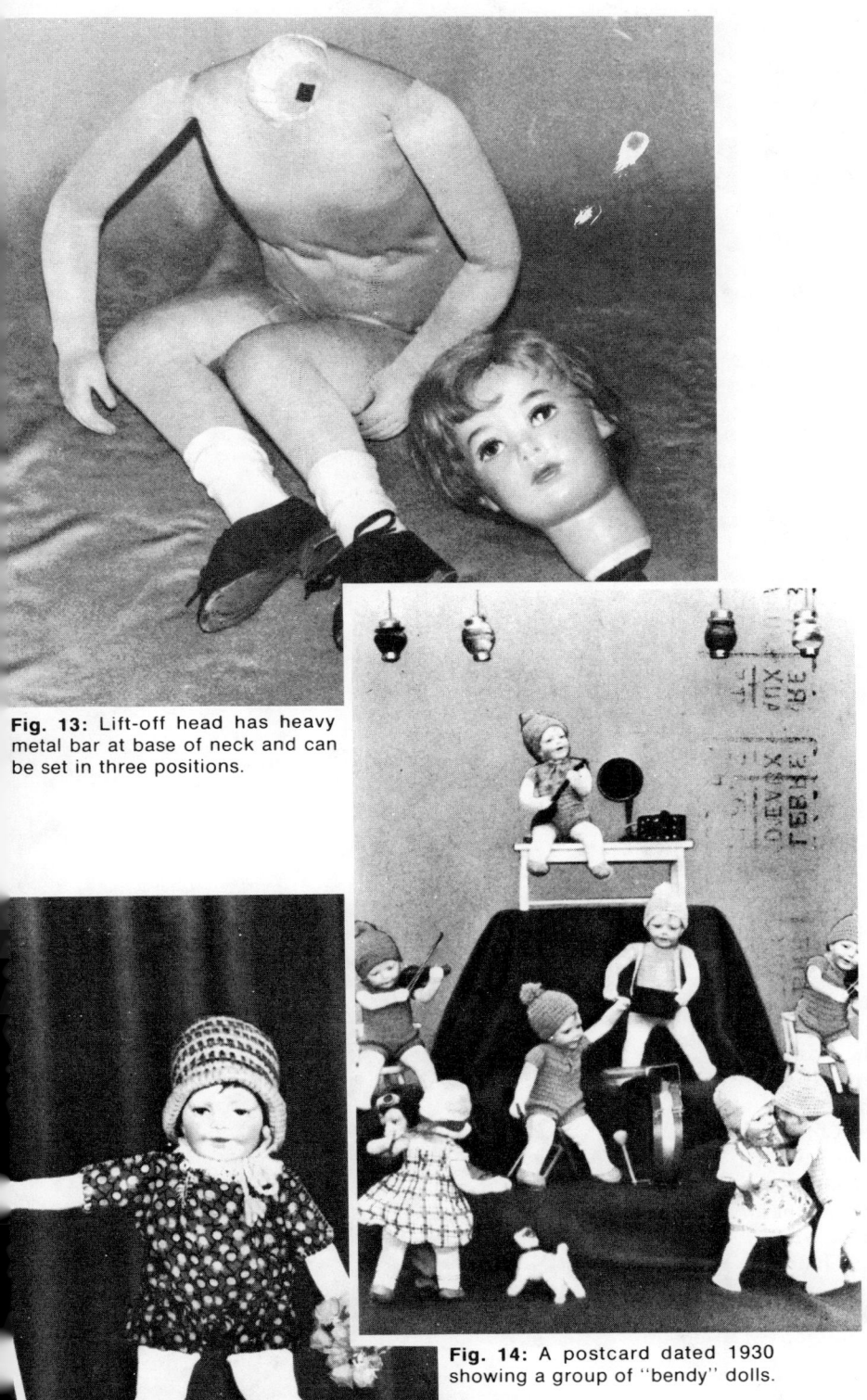

Fig. 13: Lift-off head has heavy metal bar at base of neck and can be set in three positions.

Fig. 14: A postcard dated 1930 showing a group of "bendy" dolls.

Fig. 15: Postcard showing a "bendy" doll with unusual smiling face.

have lift-off composition heads (*Fig. 13*) with wire armatures in the arms only, enabling these to be twisted into a variety of attitudes. The padding of the stockinette bodies terminates below the seat and an area of leg top is left hollow thus giving a swing-leg articulation. The legs are rigidly padded in a bent position which allows for a striking variety of seated poses. The wigs are press-studded to the heads as with *Figure 10*, and the faces have applied eyelashes. These are exceptionally fine and well preserved models with touchingly serious faces, exhibiting all the familiar slightly mournful qualities of the Kruse play dolls.

The Belgian postcard reproduced (*Fig. 14*) is postmarked 1930 and shows a number of the small Kruse "bendy" dolls. These had wire armatures in all four limbs and stood well unaided. Note the smiling character faces. From such post cards we know that Käthe Kruse made a variety of character heads. The card produced by The Alpha Publishing Company of London (*Fig. 15*) shows another "bendy" doll in good close-up with a distinctive and "different" face. As stated previously, very few of these wired dolls survived by the vulnerable nature of their design, and any such doll remaining today in good condition must be regarded as very rare.

From her work it can be seen that Frau Kruse was an exceptionally sensitive and feminine person. In her own words writing in 1923 she stated that: "A doll should be an education in maternal feelings." Through her dolls she has expressed her devotion to her own children. For most of us this is a private indulgence, but Käthe Kruse chose to share it with the whole world. ∎

This German Bisque open-mouth doll with long hair and teeth, dressed in a long baby's dress, is typical of the doll described in May Harrison's charming "Diary of a Doll." The Christmas tree is decorated with handmade decorations of the doll's era. Stars, bells, butterflies, a pitcher, and other shapes cut from cardboard, were covered with a soft fluffy substance in white, pink and gold, trimmed with gold metallic edging and brightly colored metallic stars. The wicker cradle is of a type seldom found, but certainly of the period.

A CHRISTMAS DOLL
Circa 1911

by YOLANDA M. SIMONELLI

LADY'S PICTORIAL, an English fashion and society magazine, gave prizes to children whose stories and poems appeared on their "Children's Pages." The November 18, 1911, issue, called the "Xmas Number," had a handsome colorful cover entitled "Children's Fete at the Savoy on Christmas Eve." An elegant interior festively decorated with bright garlands and Christmas trees was peopled with fashionably attired adults and children partying. In the rear of the picture, a Punch and Judy puppet show was in progress. The foreground of the cover showed two little girls teaching a golden haired doll to walk, a young miss hugging a little white dog, and a boy dangling a Golliwog (black-face male rag doll popular from the 1890s) by its shock of frizzy hair.

The cover illustration of this particular issue of *Lady's Pictorial* gives us a view of upper middle-class English society. On the "Children's Page," an article by May W. Harrison, "Diary of a Doll," takes us into an English household, affording a view of child life there and observations of the German dollmaking practices. What follows is little Miss Harrison's story as told by a doll:

DIARY OF A DOLL

November

I was made in Germany and packed in a box much too large for me, and sent over to England. When I crossed *die Nordsee* (bother, when I'm in England I must not talk German!) I feared I should be seasick, but I was not a bit.

By the end of the month I was getting quite settled down in a London toy shop, where I hoped to live always, for there were so many other toys for me to be with.

My name was just "Doll," and I was dressed as a baby, in spite of possessing quite long curly brown hair.

December

It was about the eighteenth day of the month, and the toy shop was looking very gay, when a lady and a pretty little girl walked in. The lady—Mrs. Gibson as I afterwards learned—asked to see some dolls, and consequently I was shown to her. Lily took a fancy to me, so Mrs. Gibson said I should be taken to her home, and would you believe it, she actually paid for me; I thought slavery had been abolished long ago! I was packed securely in my box and given to a man, with many other friends of mine, to be delivered at various houses. When the man got outside the shop, he dropped me and gave me a bad headache.

For a week I remained in a dark drawer, and then on Christmas Day I was placed with many other things on the nursery table. There were boxes of chocolates, bad-tempered noisy crackers, a teddy bear, a paint box, and a sailor boy doll. Lily came to look at her presents, and gave a shriek of joy when she saw me. "Oh, you darling," she said, "you shall be called Esseldweda Marwy Lily Murwiel" (which I afterwards found to be Ethelreda Mary Lily Muriel, a most horrible muddle—*ent setzlich!* (That's the worst of being made in Germany, one never knows which language one is speaking!) All that day I was treated kindly; the next day Lily had a party, and I was shown with great pride. Tommy Holmes asked if I was called Jemina or Maria, and Lily said indignantly that I was called Esseldweda Marwy Lily Murwiel, but she was going to call me "Dweda." When tea-time came I was given some bread and butter with jam on it; but of course the jam went all over my face and the bread pushed one of my teeth out of place. (I should not have had any teeth seeing that I was a baby, but that is the fault of the German who made me!) Nurse was angry and took me away to be washed, and I fear Lily did not miss me a bit.

January

I had been in the toy cupboard ever since Christmas, and I felt very sad. However, one day Lily took me out of the cupboard and began to play with me. She found something which she had not noticed before—the something was a string which when pulled made me cry "Mutter" whether I wished to or not. Lily pulled the string too hard, and now I shall never say "Mutter" again!

Lily had been sewing, and she brought some wonderful garments which she called "coatand-twowsers" and began to undress me. *Schrecklich!* She made me into a boy and dressed me in miserable things made of dark blue serge sewn with white cotton. I thought I made just as silly a boy as I made a baby, with my long hair.

March

I remained a boy all this time, for Lily went to school, and had not time to undress me. But one day when she was at home with a cold she undressed me and dressed me again as a woman. Then she took a hair brush and brushed my hair. Now, my hair was never meant to be treated like this, and about half of it came off, while the remaining half came out of curl; so Lily wetted it and plaited it. The next morning all my hair came off with being wet, and I looked like an old woman! Lily was so astonished, she dropped me, and my leg broke off and fell on the carpet. Lily was so disgusted that she shut me up in a drawer, where I remained for many, many long dark months.

December

My leg has been mended and my hair glued on, and I am to be given to a poor little girl as a Christmas present, so I hope I shall be happy with her. I am going to try to make her happy for I heard Mrs. Gibson say that Daisy Walker—my new mistress—was a cripple, and had not many toys, so I suppose I shall be of some use in the world after all! ∎

ALL BISQUE DOLL

...FRENCH STYLE

by MAGDA BYFIELD

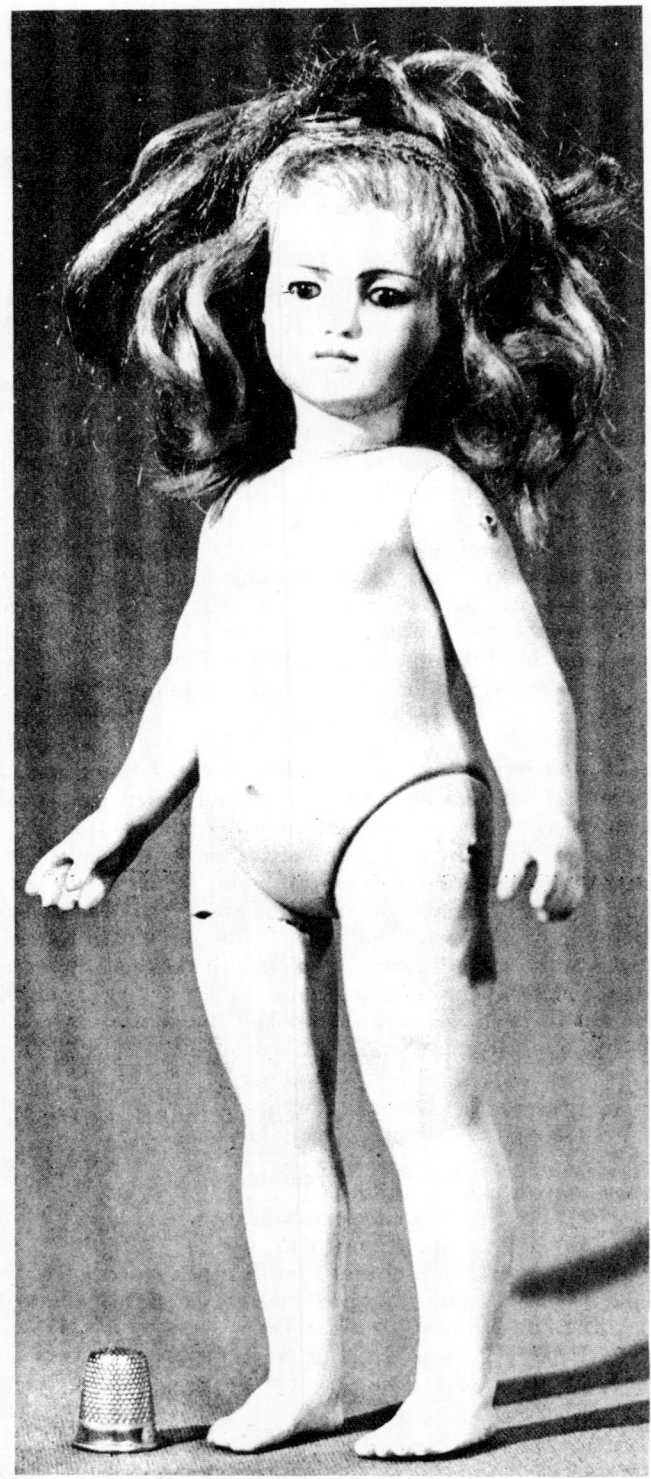

FOR THE DOLL researcher working with unmarked 19th century specimens and virtually no contemporary records, the vexing fact emerges that the distinction between dolls produced in France and those made in Germany is rather more hazy than previously thought. French attributions to enigmatic doll types must ever be regarded as conjectural and collectors should be cautious to draw a line between French and French-style... the latter usually being of German origin.

The collector's vision has been somewhat clouded by the longstanding reputation of the French doll being superior to the German. This is true only up to a point. This concept was in many instances formed on the exquisite dolls that French manufacturers had in fact contracted for with German porcelain factories.

France entered the field of dollmaking on a commercial scale at some point in the mid-19th century, not so much in a spirit of rivalry, but rather with a fresh approach and sophistication unique to that country. Their ideas on dollmaking were loudly acclaimed and the high standards adhered to throughout the latter half of the 19th century. But all industries must capture a wide market to earn good profits, and the cheaper doll lines had to be produced without any apparent sacrifice to the excellence of the product; wherever possible, this was done by buying good German doll heads.

When one considers that a wholly self-sufficient organization such as Maison Jumeau (producing their own heads, bodies, eyes, wigs, clothing, shoes and even boxes) also on occasion using German heads, this inescapable fact casts an interesting slant on the whole French doll industry! Their manufacturing costs were high compared with German factories and the importation of doll parts was doubtless an economic necessity which the French neither liked nor readily conceded. It is also probable that Germany's long tradition in dollmaking made that country more capable of handling complex casting problems and commissioned work was undoubtedly contracted to German factories by French dollmakers. Maison Jumeau cannot have been an isolated example of this interchange, nor is it now seen to have applied only to cheaper "French" dolls. The picture becomes even more confusing when German dollmakers deliberately began to pirate the intrinsic French styles. Manufacturers who are quite unalike react in much the same way when confronted with shifting demands in fashionable taste.

The mystery surrounding the Franco-Germanic doll is probably the direct result of longstanding political tensions between those two countries. This has rarely affected commerce directly for long, but in sensitive postwar situations diplomacy becomes a necessary expedient. The Franco-Prussian War undoubtedly contributed greatly to veiling the doll-interchange-system for many years to follow, and this period poses some of the knottiest puzzles for us now.

Fortunately for the researcher, manufacturers who remained in business over long periods were in the habit of re-issuing models which after 1891 were (if for export) required by international law to display the country of origin, and by this time incised marks and mold numbers were general on doll heads. Such later specimens are recognizable by the quality of the bisque, type of eyes used and methods of facial decoration. Also body construction and clothing styles are helpful where the doll is in its original state.

Such specimens make invaluable comparative material and the recording of these often less attractive later types is a vital factor in arriving at attributions with some measure of confidence. I stress the phrase "some measure of confidence" because even in the event of a perfect cross-matching between a marked and unmarked specimen there are pitfalls! Seemingly master molds were sold or leased from one manufacturer to another and identical heads have been found, one marked by a French maker and the other by a German! Never has the saying "The more you know, the more you know you don't know!" been more truly applicable than to doll research.

The all-bisque doll illustrating this article can be regarded as the classic type to confuse even the most experienced collector. When the doll came on the market again in 1975 she was regarded as a complete maverick. Offered for sale as "French ca. 1875" she in fact predates this age slightly, judging by the quality, weight and white color of her bisque, and evidence has come to light which strongly suggests that she was made in Germany. By a happy coincidence the writer had access to an identical later cast presented on a leather body with the swivel head on a shoulder plate and with bisque lower arms and legs with bare feet . . . marked S & H. Unless German dollmakers purchased French heads and doll parts—and there is no evidence to support such a theory—the all-bisque is from the Simon & Halbig factory. This identification posed a further question: Was the head imported from Germany and mounted on a shapely French body? Or was it perhaps a replacement marriage? The answer to both these questions was quickly seen to be NO. The parian-type bisque of the doll's head exactly matches the tone and texture of the trunk and limbs, and all parts share the type and age of dirt stains. The damage to her right leg occurred many years ago when brown fishbone glue was used to fuse the break.

This all-bisque child of fine early quality has stationary threadless blue glass eyes, with black pupils a closed mouth and unpierced ears. Her swivel neck is strung from a wooden crossbar balanced inside the baldhead which is not smooth but modeled with cranial accuracy. The silky golden-brown mohair wig appears to be original and is mounted on a gauze cap of the same color. She is hip and shoulder peg-strung with kid washers lining the five points of articulation. Blush marks are delicately applied to breasts, knees and elbows. Arm and leg tops are flat to fit the flat shoulder and hip design of the adolescent body, which is closed except for stringing exit holes. Fingernails and toenails are molded and tinted pink. Her right wrist is turned outwards and free-standing thumbs are situated under the palms. The lovely oval face is beautifully decorated with very fine dark blonde two-tone feathered eyebrows, upper and lower lashes and eyelines. The deeply molded eyelids give a unusual downward glancing dreamy expression. Rosy lips are outlined in a darker tone with a dark central line. The cheeks are lightly tinted and nose and inner eye dots match the lighter lip shade. All the brushwork decoration is delicate and sure-handed and the whole results in a completely graceful little doll, perfectly balanced to stand unaided (if one dares) despite the anatomical modeling on the base of her feet.

The experienced doll collector will be using the term "French-Style" more and more. Fruitless as it may seem at times to even try and analyze the complexity of early dolls and their origin, serious research continues hopefully. But the simpler and perhaps more important approach should never be overlooked or blinded by study; it is better and easier to emphasize the beauty of these artifacts, their own kind of truth and their lasting power to delight us. These are the qualities that caused them to be preserved through generations and to remain for us today as collector's items. Insofar as we have all experienced childhood, they are a part of us. ∎

Early American Folk Dolls

WENDY LAVITT

HANDCRAFTED DOLLS have been part of American history from the days of the early settlers. Children have always wanted dolls to play with and fashioned dolls from whatever material was at hand. Parents, too, created dolls, often as Christmas gifts when store-bought dolls were too expensive or unavailable. Letters and diaries of pioneer women fondly relate the stories, imagination, and love behind these dolls. In Utah in the 19th century, Minnie Brown recalled a special Christmas present:

"It was a pretty doll, about twelve inches high. The body was made of cream-colored factory cloth, and it was stuffed with wool. It had a pretty shaped head and arms and legs. Its hair was made of fine gray yarn which had been unraveled from a child's sweater. The yarn was very curly. My mother was well trained in hand-sewing, and the face of my doll was a piece of art: the eyes, nose, and mouth, were perfect in shape. My doll was completely dressed. Its underwear was made of white material. The panties were trimmed with homemade lace and came down to its ankles in length. The little white chemise was also trimmed with lace. The pretty petticoat was tucked and lace adorned its edges. The pink calico dress and bonnet to match made this doll the most beautiful doll in the world...."[1]

Many handmade dolls accompanied their owners across the plains in covered wagons. These silent eyewitnesses to history were born in isolation and hardship but reflected the triumph of spirit and creativity. By far the most popular homemade dolls were the beloved rag dolls. Many were crudely made by children, but others testified to the needlework skills of pioneer women. Occasionally a man made a rag doll — especially if a woman's presence was lacking as in the case of Dan Tibbot one New England Christmas in the 1890s.

"... on the top of the tree, overlooking all this splendor, sat a rag baby Dan had made himself. It had a round flat head made out of a piece of Dan's shirt, and charcoal eyes and mouth. It had arms that stuck out like a pair of sore thumbs, and legs that crooked so many ways you couldn't count the turns. Over it all was a dress that Dan made out of a piece of white cloth."[2]

A homemade rag doll that once belonged to Jane Mower of New Hampshire, who played with her until her death at age five years, in 1832. Her homespun body was stuffed with wool. Facial features were penciled on. Her now tattered lavender dress and rose underskirt were made of fine muslin. Height 10 inches. *Courtesy Shelburne Museum, Shelburne, VT.*

Wendy Lavitt is co-owner of "Made in America," a shop that sells antique quilts and Americana. She is a contributor of articles to various magazines, and has lectured to museum groups. Ms. Lavitt will be a guest curator for an exhibit entitled **Children's Children: American Folk Dolls,** to be held at the Museum of American Folk Art in 1983. Her book, **American Folk Dolls,** will be published in November 1982.

Cloth doll, ca. 1840, with real hair held in place by a black lace hairnet. The doll's dress is characteristic of the period. *Collection Nancy and Gary Stass. Photo by Schecter Me Sun Lee.*

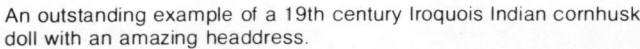

An outstanding example of a 19th century Iroquois Indian cornhusk doll with an amazing headdress.

Most rag dolls were made of muslin or linen stuffed with sawdust, bran or straw. Features were painted or inked on with fruit and vegetable dyes or embroidered. Yarn, thread, animal fur and human hair served as hair. Carefully made dolls enjoyed articulated fingers and bendable arms and legs. When a doll's face grew soiled, parents often replaced it by adding a new layer of cloth. Although children might yearn for the more sophisticated commercial doll, they still treasured their rag babies. A 1902 *Harper's Bazaar* article noted this phenomenon:

"Even to the small girl, who cannot understand why or argue it out, there is a flavor of old-time charm about a good rag doll that the finest miniature lady or baby from Paris does not possess."

Paper soldier doll made by an unknown child as part of a vast army of soldiers and their steeds. *Museum of American Folk Art, New York City.*

After cloth dolls, the homemade doll a 19th century child was most likely to own was a wooden doll. While the cloth doll was the provence of the frontier mother, the wooden doll was carved by men who enjoyed whittling. Out of the readily available woodpile, fathers and brothers created gifts of dolls. Even discarded household items could be turned into dolls. Doll were made from clothespins, potato mashers, spoons and even bedposts. Carving wooden dolls proved to be a popular pastime in the Southern Highlands. These simple dolls, called "poppets," were whittled from native woods and often portrayed elderly hardworking mountain people.

Any representative grouping of American folk dolls

Black cloth fisherman doll with sewn features. This doll is the product of a cottage industry. It, and others like it, was made by hand and sold throughout the United States. *Collection Brooklyn Children's Museum.*

This lively band of applehead figures includes a guitarist, banjo player, drummer and two horn players. All have gray human hair and were made in Maine about 1930. *Author's collection. Photo by Schecter Me Sun Lee.*

In a constantly changing society, people still found time to make dolls out of whatever material was available.

would include corn dolls. Corn figures were part of the English settlers' harvest tradition and cornhusk dolls were also made by many Eastern Indian tribes in the New World. Before long, corn dolls moved westward across the United States. At Christmas they would appear under Christmas trees from the Atlantic throughout the prairies as noted in some fond remembrances
"And there would usually be a cornhusk doll, perhaps with a prune or walnut for a face, and a gay dress of an old corset-cover scrap with ribbons still bright."[3]

Many dolls included unusual combinations of materials such as the above mentioned prunehead or walnut doll with its cornhusk body. The fruit and nut dolls, unlike the corn dolls, were primarily indigenous to American culture. As children gathered acorns, pecans, walnuts and hickory nuts, they saved some for tiny dolls that often portrayed various members of their community. Applehead dolls with their wrinkled faces were particularly suited for grandmother and grandfather types. Nut dolls were often painted black and turned into "plantation" figures. Many of these Black dolls express the poignancy of their place in American history. Few pre-Civil War Black homemade dolls survived and even fewer were documented. Cloth and nut dolls did portray the well-known "Mammy," and dolls of this type continued to be made through the 1930s.

Indian children like children all over wanted dolls, and their parents responded with miniature versions of themselves. Most Indian dolls are adult dolls instead of "baby" dolls and were often used to teach the customs and traditions of the tribe. Indian dolls are as different as the tribes themselves. They present an accurate record of Indian life and reflect the encroachment of the White man's culture. Dolls of bone, antler, ivory, cloth, skins and wood represent the Arctic regions. The isolation of Eskimo life contributed to a well-established craft heritage that inspired creative dollmaking. The Indians of the Northeast were known for their corn and apple dolls, while the Indians of the plains made buckskin dolls adorned with quills and beads. The Hopis and Zunis of the Southwest were famous for their Kachina dolls made from cottonwood, while the Mohaves and Yumas fashioned their dolls from clay. Little girls everywhere are eager to emulate their mothers, and a child of any tribe could have echoed the same feelings as did Pretty-Shield, a Crow Indian:

"I tried to be like my mother.... I carried my doll on my back just as mothers carry their babies; and besides this I had a little tepee (lodge) that I pitched whenever my aunt pitched hers."[4]

Dollmakers have collected wishbones, seeds, dried moss and any number of other found objects and turned them into imaginative dolls. Some were so fragile and fleeting that they lasted but a day. Dolls from flowers and cakes enjoyed short lives. Wishbone dolls made from the Sunday turkey fared better with some of them serving as penwipers. Penwiper dolls could also be made from clay pipes; the bowls forming pointed little faces with prominent noses. Often the stems of clay pipe dolls fit into spools of thread while skirts and aprons carried sewing implements. These "sewing" dolls were especially popular in Victorian times when skilled needlework was a prized accomplishment.

Children spent countless hours playing with the most basic doll—the paper doll. With paper, ink or pencil and some paints a child could create a rudimentary figure or a detailed doll with elaborate wardrobes and accessories. In pioneer homes paper, like cloth, was a treasured commodity. Paper dolls were carefully stored. At times the clothes were sewn onto pieces of cardboard for added protection. Tiny drops of sealing wax attached clothes to dolls. Sometimes the clothing became three-dimensional with layers of tissue, lace and rich materials added to the flat surface. Whether cut from old cards, newspapers or magazines, paper dolls reflected the styles of their era.

Most homemade dolls allow a glimpse into a changing America. In a society that was meeting the challenges of expansion and the industrial revolution, people still found time to make dolls out of whatever material was available. Little did they dream that some of their finest examples were destined to be admired in museums and great collections as masterpieces of folk art. ∎

Footnotes

(1) *Heart Throbs of the West* (Vol. 9): Compiled by Kate B. Carter; Daughters of the Utah Pioneers; Salt Lake City, Utah; 1940-1951.

(2) "The Story of Dan Tibbor," *New England Magazine;* Dec. 1903.

(3) *Prairie Christmas:* Paul Engle; Longmans Green; New Yok; 1960.

(4) *PRETTY-SHIELD.* Medicine Woman of the Crows: Frank B. Linderman; University of Nebraska Press; Lincoln, Nebraska; 1972.

EMILE JUMEAU and his BEAUTIFUL BÉBÉ'S

Emile Jumeau Boy Bébé—13" tall—incised 3 at nape of neck. Body has blue stamp "Jumeau Mdaille D'or 1878". Body is composition with ball joints at elbows, thighs and knees. Wrists are straight. Original cork is intact on head covered by a blonde mohair wig attached to the original skin. Mouth is open-closed and ears are pierced. Eyes are blue with black pupils and outlines. Expertly painted eyelashes and eyebrows accentuate the beautiful eyes that bulge forward at the centers.
Doll was found in a Vermont attic carefully wrapped and protected by camphor, wearing a complete outfit consisting of loden green wool jacket and trousers trimmed with tiny brass buttons. There is also a finely tucked white cotton long sleeve shirt which buttons down the back. Long stockings are black cotton and high shoes are black leather with brass buttons that match suit.
This doll won a blue ribbon in the National Competition of the United Federation of Doll Clubs held in New Orleans in 1969, competing against a grouping of French Male Dolls. *Author's Collection.*

by YOLANDA M. SIMONELLI

A TWIST of fate thrust Emile Jumeau into the unwanted role of dollmaker during the mid-19th century.

Acceptance of the task and his efforts thereafter earned him recognition as a leading innovative industrialist. The dolls he produced were among the finest of an era now called the "Golden Age of Dolls." They were awarded many medals of excellence at expositions around the world. Those that remain today are costly coveted collectors' prizes.

Jumeau specialized in the development of child-type dolls called Bébés whose beauty was exemplified by satin smooth delicately tinted bisque heads, finely painted eyelashes, and distinctive broad eyebrows accentuating large inset eyes of blown glass, which were amazingly naturalistic in form and color. Heads were capped with cork and quality mohair or human hair stylish wigs. Originally, stuffed kid bodies were used, and then wood, until satisfactory techniques were developed to produce sturdy composition bodies with ball-jointed limbs. Ultimately, the dolls were meticulously costumed in high fashions by professional dressmakers and milliners.

The combined skills of many artisans were necessary to complete each beautiful bébé to meet the critical requirements and satisfaction of Emile Jumeau, the ex-architect turned dollmaker.

History of the Jumeau firm originated with Pierre F. Jumeau who first gained recognition in the doll business in 1844, when he and his associate, a man named Belton, were accorded "Mentio Honorable" at the Paris Exposition of French Industry.

Thereafter, Belton and Jumeau parted. Pierre continued teaching the trade to his eldest son, Georges. Emile, the second son, was intent on a career in architecture. The untimely death of his brother propelled him into the doll business in order to sustain an aging parent.

Georges had tried to slowly up-date some of Pierre's old-fashioned methods, but since the business was already profitable, he met with much resistance from his father. However, Emile's active participation and involvement set a "modernization revolution" into motion.

During the 1870s, when he gained full control, smoky, dark, dust-filled shops and antiquated equipment had been replaced with new buildings bright with windows, modern gas lights and equipment for full production, including heads which had been previously imported from Germany. An attractive courtyard with trees and an ornamental fountain was surrounded by brick walls and decorative iron work. Signs carried the name, BEBE JUMEAU, in large letters and showed facsimiles of medals awarded at major world exhibitions.

The dolls of the father's era were slim-bodied lady types, called Poupée Parisiennes. The French concentration was on body construction and display for the latest French fashions, while Germany supplied the majority of doll heads for Jumeau and his competitors.

These earlier dolls, in essence, were playthings for the rich. Dolls of this type are now called "French Fashions" and can be found with variations of bodies; all kid or with bisque or wood arms, cloth, wooden bodies, blown kid, kid with brass joints, kid over wood, etc., indicating that the manufacturers of the era were competitive, as today, in trying to present something new or different.

14" unmarked except for incised 4 on head. However has unmistakable Jumeau characteristics. Eyes are deep blue with black pupils and outlines with bulging centers. Eyelashes are finely painted with dark paint while eyebrows are the golden color. Ears are pierced and top of head is cut low in the Jumeau fashion and filled in with a cork cap. The brown human hair wig is as found. The composition ball jointed body is unmarked.
Most Jumeaus have closed mouths but this doll has an open mouth with tiny teeth. However, this may have been produced in the 1890s when Jumeau began releasing dolls at cheaper prices. Their advertisement of 1892 quoted in Coleman's *Encyclopedia* stated: "NOTICE OF CHANGE: The Maison makes two new models of indestructible jointed bébés undressed and dressed with some differences of 20% and 40% but with the same irreproachable quality remaining and NOT CARRYING THE JUMEAU NAME." In 1895, further reductions in prices were advertised, "WITHOUT MARK with a difference of 40% to 60%".
While these ads did not include mouth types, *Youth's Companion*, October 1888, described their premium doll as follows: "Our new doll differs from those previously offered by us. It is made after the celebrated Jumeau model, having the ball and socket joints at the elbows, shoulders, knees, also joint at the neck, so that the head can be turned naturally. It has a beautiful bisque head with 'natural' eyes and flowing hair of a most luxurious growth. This doll is unlike others with simply a painted mouth. *Its lips are beautifully moulded and slightly parted, showing pearly porcelain teeth which have been naturally inserted.*" The premium doll was available to subscribers for one new name and $1.25. It seems likely then that this doll could have been produced during the period of reduced price unmarked dolls. It is costumed in a lovely old fine quality yellow silk dress with matching hat trimmed in peach color velvet. *Author's Collection.*

24" Jumeau—head red marked "Depose—Tete Jumeau—Bte SDG 11 H 111" with a check mark in black as shown in photo. Pierced applied ears. Bulging eyes are deep blue with black pupils and outlines. Eyelashes are accentuated in black but eyebrows are golden. Mouth is open-closed type and ears are pierced. Was found with original cork and a sparse mohair blonde wig nailed thereon. Wig in photo is old and matches the original. Doll was purchased (from original owner) wearing white cotton lace trimmed undergarments (short chemise with petticoat and drawers). There were also black patent shoes with ankle ties and long black silk stockings with tops an ivory color.

The body of this doll is heavy composition with ball-jointed arms and legs. This was one of the more expensive models because it was a "talking doll". The photographs show how the doll was fabricated in two sections. The lower section contained a metal voice (at left in picture) box which was incised "Tete Jumeau". Two cords were attached to the box and extended through two small holes at the waistline. When the child pulled one string, the doll said "Ma Ma". A tug at the other string produced a call for "Pa Pa". The doll has been costumed in a handsome red dress with matching beret; both trimmed in red satin ribbon and fine feather stitching. (Outfit was found in an old doll's trunk and its detailed construction is worthy of a Jumeau Bébé. *Author's collection.*

Emile Jumeau turned gradually from expensive lady-type dolls, concentrating instead on the development of quality, realistic child-type dolls at a price more available to a mass market.

His new factory proved an important asset, being equipped for the production of fine quality artist designed bisque heads. Carrier-Belleuse, a gifted sculptor who also worked at the Sevres porcelain works, is believed to be one of the artists who worked for Jumeau.

Admiration and respect for Emile Jumeau's efforts is shown in the French report of the 1873 Vienna Exhibition, quoted in the Colemans' *The Collector's Encyclopedia of Dolls.* "M. Jumeau has established at Montreuil, near Paris, a factory where he makes doll heads of enameled porcelain with the greatest perfection. He has surpassed in beauty the products that we used to buy

19" Jumeau Bébé—head bears red mark "Depose Tete Jumeau Bte SDG 8Vvv." The composition ball jointed body has a paper label—"BÉBÉ JUMEAU DIPLOME DE HONNEUR". This doll has the deep blue eyes, with black pupil and outline, which in profile protrude forward, giving a wide-eyed look characteristic of the Jumeaus. Dark finely painted lashes and golden color feathered eyebrows also distinguish the Jumeaus. Complexion is delicately tinted with deeper color cheeks and softly painted mouth. This doll has applied ears, and its original cork with long golden color human hair and a faded pink ribbon. Doll is wearing a simple white cotton lawn dress with handmade lace and old pink leather high button boots have been added as well as the lavish blue silk lace bonnet lavishly trimmed with flowers and silk ribbons, befitting to a beautiful Jumeau Bebe. She carries a tiny mesh metal purse. *Author's collection.*

from Saxony. The Exhibit of M. Juneau at Vienna was splendid, and Viennese merchants were impressed by the good prices at which they could purchase his products." The report also stated, "M. Jumeau of Paris, the first and most important doll-making house, has freed us from former obligation to have the foreigner furnish us with porcelain doll heads."

At the Vienna Exhibition, Jumeau was unanimously awarded "Medal of Progress" as well as a Gold Medal. A Medal of Cooperation also went to four representatives of the "Maison P. F. Jumeau", one being Emile Jumeau.

The French report hinted at tension with German dollmakers. Feelings were fierce, and passed on to the children of the era, illustrated in a little sixteen-page booklet found in an old Jumeau doll box, which was translated and printed in *Spinning Wheel's Complete Book of Dolls.*

The little booklet was titled "Lettre d'un Bébé Jumeau a sa Petite Mere"; a letter written by a "Jumeau Baby to her little Mother." The doll as well as its maker were exalted. "I am unbreakable, a priceless quality I inherit from my father, M. Jumeau, the best of fathers and the most famous of manufacturers.

"Woe to the unhappy one which does not answer to his expectations; it is pitilessly sent back to the factory with these terrible words: 'Destroy this camelot! [Trash] What an insult for a well-born baby's self respect! It is good only for those frightful German babies, that word. They are ugly and ridiculous.

"If I find myself one day face to face with one of them I will break it like glass, this cardboard baby which smells of tallow and wax."

To further exemplify French scorn for the German product, the cover of the booklet pictured the "Baby Jumeau" jumping on the body of a rival.

It is interesting to note also that the so-called "unbreakable" Jumeau adds a postscript. "If after some too violent shock, my head should happen to break, do not weep. Go find my father, M. Jumeau. Clever doll surgeon that he is, we will put another on me."

Another French publication, printed in 1885, by a J. Cusset, was found by Nina S. Davies, and her translation in the book, *The Jumeau Doll Story* (Hobby House Press 1957 and 1959), also illustrates French-German hostility.

"Profoundly patriotic M. Jumeau tries, to the best of his ability to prevent the importation of German goods which infest our Bazaars. Nothing is equal to the French toy. Its only disadvantage is that it is a little more expensive."

Mrs. Davies pointed out, in her introduction, that while German dolls did not compare with the "finesse and beauty of the Jumeau, the extreme bitterness can be comprehended when it is realized that this writing was done at a time when the German defeat of France in the War of 1870 was still a keen memory."

The mark of Emile Jumeau continued as he competed for excellence and won awards at expositions around the world. He was extolled as a philanthropist as well as a

16" Jumeau—marked in red on neck, "Depose Tete Jumeau o HD". The number 6 is incised at the nape. The composition ball-jointed body has the blue BÉBÉ JUMEAU mark and other faded words. The doll is fitted with a cork cap and lovely blonde mohair wig. Ears are pierced. Bulging eyes are deep brown with black pupils and are accentuated by dark finely painted eyelashes and golden brush marked eyebrows. The delicately painted mouth is closed. The bisque is satin smooth, delicately tinted in soft natural color.
The doll wears a peach color fine cotton dress, lavishly trimmed with delicate beige lace and red silk ribbons. The bonnet matches the hat. Slippers are of red leather tied at the ankle. *Author's collection.*

dollmaker, being awarded "Chevalier de la Legion d'Honneur" in 1886.

His manner of conducting his business and his acts of charity intertwined. Skilled artists and craftsmen were necessary for a quality product, and Jumeau depended on the apprentice system for many of his workers.

Taking pity on orphaned and destitute young ladies, he took them under his wing, teaching the delicate procedures necessary to effect the brilliant naturalistic blown glass eyes, for which the Jumeau dolls are famous. He paid no salary for five years, the time necessary to acquire the needed skills. He provided for their needs during the learning period, and later paid adequate salaries to make them independent. At the time of the Cusset writing, twenty girls were so employed, and none but orphans were privileged to make the eyes. Jumeau also provided little orphans with Jumeau Bébés to love and cherish, as well as warm clothing at Christmas.

Jumeau became known as a fair employer of women. Many worked in his factory and others, unable to work away from home, were trained to mold specific parts of the "unbreakable" Bébé bodies. Once proficient, these women could work at home.

M. Cusset praised the dollmaker for not taking advantage of female workers as others sometimes did. "One cannot accuse M. Jumeau of having thought to find cheap labor by employing mostly women. He has given himself the unrewarding task of employing as many women as possible. He pays them a very good salary, as thanks to him, the women have learned to do work which previously was only done by men. It is much more a profound humanity and charitableness which has guided him."

The factory at Montreuil employed over 300 workers. In addition to the bodymakers in homes, numerous seamstresses and milliners worked through the Jumeau Shop, Rue Pastourelle, Paris, the domain of Mme. Emile Jumeau.

The shop displayed a wonderland of Jumeau dolls costumed in the latest fashions as well as many special costumes. Mme. Jumeau supervised the production of fine quality high fashion wardrobes for the dolls. Her shop was described as "a kingdom where clothes wave the sceptre." Mme. Jumeau held court each morning, when her workers brought her their latest models in hats and clothes. "It is a task to which the workers, with fairy fingers, put all their energy. Many children of millionaires do not have more beautiful clothes than the Bébés Jumeau. The colors are artistically blended, the silks and satins of the clothes and the laces and ribbons are skillfully blended to form an artistic whole."

The various writings provide a portrait of a man and his influence on industry and labor. M. Cusset obviously admired Jumeau. "I can assure that M. Jumeau is not one of those industrialists who puts his trust in the more or less conscientious outsiders. He directs everything himself. This is one of the principal causes of his success. Today his reputation, founded on a solid basis, need fear no competitors, and the Bébé Jumeau goes to every country, with its irresistible smile and the elegance of its toilettes, that 'je ne sais quoi' which betrays its origin as being Paris."

It is to the credit of Emile Jumeau, would-be architect, that the Bébés Jumeau were acclaimed in their time, and today are coveted artifacts for collectors. Jumeau built an industry instead of buildings, and his beautiful Bébés remain an exquisite tribute to his memory. ∎

FOR WHOM WERE YOU MADE, Rowena-Rose?

by MAGDA BYFIELD

ROWENA-ROSE has been so named in deference to her mysterious incised head marking: R.R. She is not the first of these enigmas to have come to light, but may well be alone in that she has survived in her original state and box, the end-label of which is also illustrated.

Her bisque socket head is the typical French Bébé type associated with Emile Jumeau. The stationary striated eyes are an unusual light amber color with dark blonde eyebrows. The mouth is closed and the ears pierced. Head has a cork crown and is incised at the base of the neck: "R.8.R." The jointed wood and maché body is unmarked. Wrists are jointed.

Rowena-Rose is dressed in a high-necked ivory silk blouse, cherry colored skirt and matching jacket with lace trim at the sleeves. Her two-strand necklace is of black wooden beads tinted with a gunmetal finish. The velvet hat is trimmed with an ivory colored bow and matches the cerise of the doll's outfit and socks. Her dark brown leather shoes are impressed on the soles with a honeybee and "8 // Paris // Depose." On the right shoe the store ticket and price remains: "Au Bon Marche // 9.75." Beneath the chic outergarments the doll wears a factory-made shift of starched muslin threaded with cerise ribbon. This is a typical example of cheap commercial clothing hastily run up yet achieving a maximum effect from minimal materials and labor. Her long blonde mohair wig is mounted on a linen cap stamped in green on the underside: "8." Box end-label reads: "1878 - MÉDAILLE D'OR - 1878 // Bébé Articulé // Fabrication 8 Supérieur." Height 49 cms (appr. 19").

It is surprising that the name of Jumeau does not appear anywhere about this doll—not even on the box. She is so patently Jumeauesque in type, closely resembling

Rowena-Rose in her original box.

The end-label of Rowena-Rose's original box.

Rowena-Rose shown wearing the factory-made chemise found beneath her silk top outfit.

the E.J.'s of the late 1890s where, as if to emphasize the point, her dress style also places her. Such self-concealment is uncharacteristic of this firm to say the least, renowned as they were for quite unconcerned self-adulation throughout their history of intensive advertising! As the doll's shop label remains to testify that she was sold at the Paris store Au Bon Marché, the incised initials R.R. cannot relate to this retailer as in the case of the Bébé Louvre (B.L.) which is found on a Jumeau-marked body and was patently a model produced exclusively for this fashionable emporium.

Maison Jumeau claimed and marked as their own many German heads as well as those made by other French manufactories on commission. They also used dual markings with S.F.B.J. after the merger . . . the apparent reluctance to show their hand in this particular product. The weight of evidence about this doll points heavily to a Jumeau origin. E.J. won the Gold Medal in 1878, a fact recorded on the box label. The size number 8 fits the Jumeau sizing pattern for her 19 inches and the honeybee impressed on the soles of her shoes was a trademark registered by them in 1896.

If we ignore the fact that one F. E. Winkler of Germany registered BÉBÉ ARTICULÉ as a trademark in 1899 (see Coleman's Encyclopedia) we can place this doll fairly, squarely and solely at the gates of Emile Jumeau. But in the business of researching, no student can afford to ignore records of a patentee however unlikely or even absurd the connection may seem! Friedrich Edmund Winkler of Sonneberg was one of a group of Grand Prize winners at the 1900 Paris Exposition (see Coleman's Encyclopedia) and the previous year Emile Jumeau sat on the jury of this exposition. These facts could be the link between the two dollmakers. They are more likely than not to have met during this or previous trade fairs and when manufacturers in the same line of business get together, ideas are exchanged and deals may be clinched. Such exhibitions—then as now—were arranged with an eye to making new contacts and expanding trade as well as providing publicity and kudos for prizewinners. If some arrangement was made between these persons, a third party was almost certainly involved. This may have been a wholesaler or a distributor with French and German outlets. Whoever he was, the enigmatic initials R.R. must surely relate to him. Whatever the arrangements between Jumeau and person or persons unknown, the order seems to have been a limited one, for dolls thus marked are very scarce.

It cannot be entirely ruled out that "Bébé Articulé" was used on this doll's box purely as a descriptive term indicating a "jointed child doll," but this seems improbable in the light of its late date; by this time this type was general, and would hardly justify headline lettering.

It is ironic that such an all-original specimen with incised initials, box label and store ticket should pose so many questions where one could reasonably expect all this information to provide a complete set of answers! Had the doll not been found in a dusty state, with live and dead parasites firmly entrenched, and with her right hand horizontally broken off, but lying in the box, (a common weakness in French dolls' feet and hands) it could have been argued that some water-soluble head stamp or body label may have been removed. No trace of such types of marking exists.

This brings me to a word of advice to collectors concerned with preserving information for future studies. The type of dirt stains and the insect life found between layers of clothing on undisturbed dolls, plays a vital part in ascertaining the originality of the clothing and wig and pinpointing any marriages of parts and later additions. While such soiled specimens are unacceptable in the long term, their condition should not be remedied with too much haste. Original clothing leaves "tide marks" on the neck, arms and legs and there is time-tinting on the clothes themselves. Within the light-protected folds and creases of outergarments, lies the true color tone which can often be otherwise faded beyond recognition. Time should be taken to observe and record these findings in detail and, whenever possible, to photograph the doll "as found" before soap, insecticides and dry cleaners are enlisted. Such data will ensure for today's collector the inestimable gratitude of tomorrow's researcher.

Page from an "Au Bon Marché" catalog showing several examples of Bébé Articulé dolls available from this large department store in Paris. *Collection Bibliothique Nationale. Photo courtesy Dorothy S. Coleman.*

A 19th Century Dolls Hospital

by MAGDA BYFIELD

Fig. 1: The Gypsy Jumeau doll

IN 1972 the owners of an English Doll Museum purchased a "Tete Jumeau" marked doll of the type dubbed by collectors as the Gypsy Jumeau (Fig. 1). The type is so-called because of its heavy black eyebrows, black wig and invariable brass hoop earrings. The original clothing was always red. In the process of cleaning and re-stringing the doll, its cork pate was removed revealing a neatly folded tissue paper leaflet 9" x 5½" inside the head. After ironing, the paper was seen to publicize the services, stock and prices of A. Gesland. Both sides of this leaflet are reproduced here (Figs. 2 & 3) together with an English translation (Figs. 4 & 5) by courtesy of Dolls in Wonderland, Brighton, England, where the document and doll are on permanent exhibition. It is thought that the paper was inserted when the doll was taken in for a repair or replacement head. (Note that the advertisement states that any head can be fitted to any body.) This Jumeau Be'be', and therefore the leaflet, are dated by the museum around 1895.

The discovery of this leaflet confirms several points of interest. In the present day light of doll values it is amusing to see that a fixed-wrist Be'Be' of 12½" was fifty centimes *cheaper* that a jointed wrist doll of the same height. Also the price differential of dressed and undressed dolls establishes (for anyone of those people who might still

Fig. 2: First side of A. Gesland's leaflet.

Fig. 3: Other side of A. Gesland's leaflet.

A. GESLAND

5 bis, Rue Béranger—PARIS

MANUFACTURERS AND RETAILERS

REPAIRS IN TEN MINUTES
of Bébés and Poupées of all makes

WE SUBSTITUTE DAMAGED HEADS

Open: Every day 8 hours of the morning and 8 hours of the night. From the 15th of November to 15th January, every day Sunday & holidays. Christmas Eve and New Year's Day 8 hours in the morning & 11 hours at night.

Nearby to the Temple Market and the Rue Charlot

THE BEST MARKET IN ALL PARIS

HEADS OF INDESTRUCTABLE BÉBÉS, Patented (without the governments guarantee) Manufactured by our Establishment.

PLEASE—NOTE
The establishment has no branches elsewhere

Fig. 4: English translation of Fig. 2.

 This article is not sold in any other shop or bazaar in Paris

A. GESLAND
HIGH QUALITY NOVELTIES
MANUFACTURERS OF BÉBÉS
AND INDESTRUCTABLE HEADS

Patented without the governments guarantee

MANUFACTURERS OF PARIS
Establishment founded in 1860—Bronze medal Paris

The most durable Bébés with metal joints, stringing rubber replaced and hands, arms and shoulder plates of hard wood. Curly wigs, the Bébé sits, and can kneel. Can be easily dressed.

LIST of UNDRESSED BÉBÉS Bisque Heads		LIST of DRESSED BÉBÉS Richly attired in removable clothes Bisque Heads		LIST of BISQUE HEADS Stationary with collars & ribbons	
Height	Price			Height (incl. head)	
FIXED HAND		Sleep eyes with lashes		25cm	0 40
32cm	3 95fr	Height	Price	29	0 50
JOINTED HAND		32cm	11 50	32	0 60
32cm	4 45fr	35	13	35	0 70
35	4 95	38	14 50	38	0 80
38	5 95	42	16 50	42	1 ..
42	7 25	47	19	47	1 25
47	8 50	52	24	52	1 50
52	10 25	57	29	57	1 90
57	12 45	62	34	62	2 35
62	14 45	67	40	67	2 85
67	16 75	73	45	73	3 50
75	19 95	78	55	78	4 25
78	23 75				

We sell separately: Heads, wigs, Tibetan mohair or human hair, drawers, petticoats, shoes, gowns, hats, pelisses, down trimmed, Christening bonnets and robes, pinafores, corsets, berets, Maillot Bébés, Talking Bébés, sleeping and negro, Walking Bébés.

N. B.—Indestructable heads of all sizes are adapted for all Bébés

RETAILER OF EVERYTHING FOR A BÉBÉ

NOTE: The establishment repaints wooden heads and renovates old dolls.

PRICES FIXED

Fig. 5: English translation of Fig. 3.

be in doubt) that the clothes *were* more expensive than the dolls themselves. The same 12½" jointed wrist Bébé retailed undressed at 4.45F but its clothes were an extra 7.05F totaling 11.50F for the dressed specimen. The cost margin differs at much the same ratio up through to 31", the outfit always being more highly priced than the Bébé itself.

For the perfectionist collector seeking all-original dolls such documents strike a chill note. Rarely indeed can one be quite free of doubts about a doll's absolute originality if one concedes that with the advent of the mass produced porcelain headed doll came the Dolls Hospital, a most necessary service which Gesland clearly supplied to the last detail. Their listings of substitute parts—heads, shoulder-plates, hands, arms, legs, wigs plus every conceivable item of clothing (all apparently available for a "switch" within ten minutes) causes one to reconsider the criteria of all-original dolls.

It is regrettable that the somewhat arbitrary issue of originality has assumed such significance in recent years, particularly in the light of well-researched material confirming that many dolls were a compendium of parts manufactured in widely separated areas and frequently even in different countries. By this token the doll can be seen as a union of composites, the combinations varying slightly or greatly according to a number of factors not the least of which was how many and which manufacturers were involved in the end product. These artifacts were designed as playthings which a flourishing industry of repairers helped to preserve with a hoard of spares and a great deal of skill. If their work (which probably goes undetected much of the time) now poses some knotty problems for researchers, we also owe them a very real debt of gratitude. Without the dolls hospital to replace a damaged part in the melée of components that comprised the doll, surviving specimens would indeed be few and far between.

The services of Gesland and countless others can be seen as integral to the conservation of many dolls. And how discreetly far-sighted of this establishment to seal their leaflet within the "patient's" head against the day when a nursery catastrophe would expose its presence, thus directing the owner to the Maison Gesland at the hour of need. ∎

POLITICS IS CHILD'S PLAY

by JUDITH WHORTON

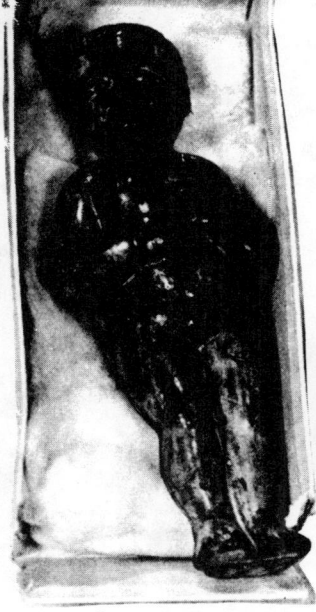

Rare black campaign soap doll with original box. Produced by the Monarch Soap Company of Lancaster, Pennsylvania. The lid of the box identifies the doll as being made for the McKinley 1896 campaign. The legend on the box top reads: "Papa Will Vote For McKinley, Gold Standard, Protection, Reciprocity and Good Times."

The story about the Teddy Bear having been inspired by President Theodore Roosevelt is well known, but less known is the fact that other political personalities have also inspired dolls. In some cases dolls have even created a controversial political storm.

Some of the most intriguing are the political soap dolls of the 19th century. These dolls were not only associated with politicians, but they were actually used as a conscious part of political campaigns. The 1896 presidential race was a heated campaign. The Democratic candidate, William Jennings Bryan, made more than 600 speeches in 27 states. The burning issue of the day was whether gold or silver would be used as the basis of our money. The dolls for both parties reflect this issue. A doll representing William McKinley's campaign was produced with a picture of the candidate. It also had the following slogan: "My Papa will vote for McKinley, gold standard, protection, reciprocity, and good times."

The box was also interesting in that it illustrates the social condi-

Rare papier mâché Hindu doll produced for the W. P. A. in Birmingham, Alabama, under the supervision of Hattie Hayes Whorton.

Campaign soap doll made from a mold similar to the one used to make the McKinley soap doll, but produced by Andrew Jergens & Company, Cincinnati, Ohio. The "16 to 1" slogan refers to the ratio of coinage of silver to gold promised by the Democrats. Bryan ran for president three times—1896, 1900 and 1908.

Paper Play figure from the Sunday Supplement of the "Boston Globe." By attaching the separate suits to the head, the figure was changed from McKinley to Bryan and their respective running mates.

This paper doll book is highly prized because it features detailed information on each first lady from Martha Washington to Eleanor Roosevelt, and accurately describes the inaugural dresses displayed at The Smithsonian Institute.

Paper doll inaugural dresses of First Ladies—Julia Gardinier Tyler, Sarah Angelica Van Buren and Ida Saxton McKinley. This set was produced in 1937 by Saalfield and originally sold for 39¢

tions of the time. Inasmuch as women's suffrage was years away, the box mentions only "papa" voting. However, the doll was made in both a white and a black version. Even in the 19th century the value of minority votes was recognized.

The box for the Bryan doll was a bright silver, suggestive of a bar of silver. The doll had a tag around its neck which said: "I'm for Bryan and Silver. 16 to 1 for me. Ain't you?" The "Ain't you?" was a subtle effort to appeal to the less educated. A note of warning—identical dolls to these have been found in non-political boxes. A doll without a political box should not be classified as a political doll.

In our own century, the dolls and puppets created under the Works Progress Administration were part of the controversy surrounding this New Deal agency of the Depression Era. But now the dolls made by the WPA are recognized as worthwhile collector's items. At a recent national

McLoughlin Bros., Inc., of Springfield, Mass., published this set of paper dolls in the early 1930s. One of the costumes for the paper doll is draped with a sash stating "Votes for Women," and holds a "Votes for Women" document in her hand; a strange costume choice since women had the voting right some twn years earlier, in 1920. *Collection Barbara Whitton Jendrick.*

The controversial Kelly Girl cloth doll.

convention of the United Federation of Doll Clubs, Inc., these government sponsored dolls were included in competition for ribbons. The dolls were made in many parts of the country, often by unemployed artists and seamstresses. Most of the time the dolls were given to schools or libraries. The majority of the dolls found have been made of cloth.

The First Ladies have long held a fascination for collectors. The dolls produced ranged from paper dolls, inexpensive at the time of issue, to the vinyl dolls made by Madame Alexander which sold for an original price of several hundred dollars.

Recently there has been a number of politically inspired dolls. Effanbee offered Susan B. Anthony in its limited edition series for 1980. Peggy Nesbitt designed a Prime Minister Margaret Thatcher doll. The Toy Factory produced an Amy paper doll.

One of the most politically controversial dolls was made in 1976. The innocent looking little girl was designed by Knickerbocker for the Kelly Girl Company. Fifty thousand of the dolls were issued to be used in an advertising campaign. Company executives were sent the dolls with a reminder that if they needed temporary secretarial help, hire one of "our dolls." Many women's groups objected to the skilled professionals being classified as dolls. The wire services carried the news of the protest. The doll was quickly withdrawn. Collectors liked this doll, especially since the ad campaign came to such a quick and unsuccessful end, thus proving in collecting political dolls even losers can be winners. ■

Tricia and Julie Nixon paper dolls from LIFE magazine. Julie holds a needlework presidential seal presented to her father the night of his re-election. Mrs. Pat Nixon was also part of this set of paper dolls.

Neapolitan

Fig. 1: A complete Neapolitan crib scene. Height 21'; depth 16'; width 22'. *Photo courtesy The National Museum of Naples.*

THE CHRISTMAS CRIB has probably been known in some form for as long as the festival itself; established in the year 354 by Pope Liberius. Cribs in the "modern" sense date from the mid-16th century and were a progression from the high relief altar pieces of the ancient church. A tendency to detach figures from others in the same scene led to the gradual development of the "assembled" crib, which came into usage during the 17th century throughout Catholic Europe.

Figures were executed in varied materials: wax, paper, pewter, ivory, coral, bronze, wood, lead and terra cotta. Some were carved, or cast in molds as whole figures, while others were wired dolls with modeled or carved extremities. Many were made with sophisticated joints at their points of articulation and animated musical puppet cribs are also recorded.

In 18th century Naples, crib art had its firmest and most passionate hold, and here it grew into a highly or-

Crib Figures

by MAGDA BYFIELD

Fig. 2: *Photo courtesy The National Museum of Naples.*

Fig. 5: Group by Giusseppe Sammartino. *Photo courtesy Bavarian National Museum.*

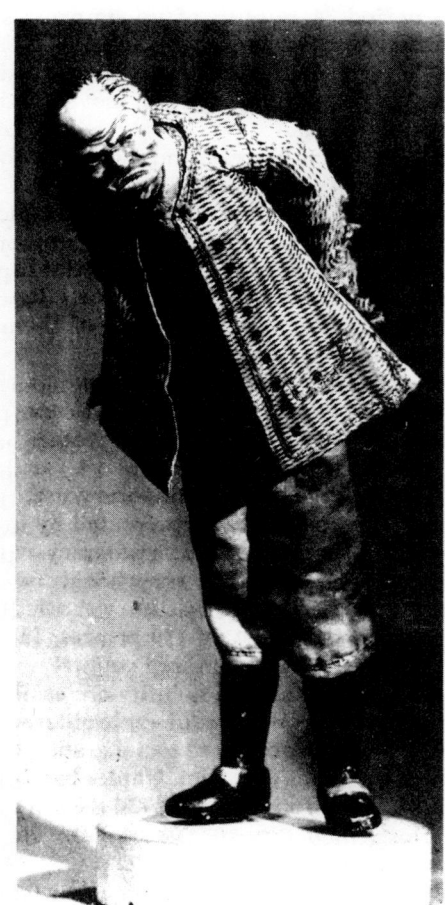

Fig. 4: Height without stand 9". *Private collection.*

Fig. 3: *Photo courtesy The National Museum of Naples.*

ganized industry of considerable proportions. So we find the Christmas Crib (Presepio) a firmly established and flourishing craft in the Gulf of Naples by the 17th century, with The Nativity represented by figures of The Holy Family, kings, shepherds and animals of the stable. From these narrow confines the humble scene gradually grew in scale, scenery, attendant figures and animals, until by the second half of the 18th century the crib had developed into an immense tableau with its theme, the

Fig. 6: *Photo courtesy The National Museum of Naples.*

birth of Christ, almost entirely submerged by a wealth of paraphernalia. (*Fig. 1*)

At this time when crib art had attained its fullest development, the innumerable subsidiary themes provoked reproof from the Church which viewed the multitude of lay figures as subordinating the mystical subject and as serving merely a decorative and frivolous function rather than the desired religious propaganda.

It is among these portrait sculptures of real people that we can best see crib art at its highest level of excellence and an intimate and reliable picture of contemporary life in 18th century Naples. Crib artists and craftsmen freely transplanted themes of their own era, making use of local scenery (carved in wood and cork) comprising houses, inns, markets, rivers, bridges and whole streets. Modes of dress, footwear, hairstyles and headdress displayed on the figures give an added observation of current fashions at every social level.

The fantasy of a fair being held in Bethlehem at the time of Christ's birth is the essence of the 18th century Neapolitan crib. The legend declared that there was not a soul on earth who was not presented at the festivities. This concept afforded the crib artists an infinite variety of possibilities and gave added impulse for those who specialized in the modeling of animals (*Fig. 2*), for every species was added to the pulsating scene, from domestic pets to exotic and performing beasts. Foodstuffs were also modeled and carved for display in the shops, inns and market stalls, and give an accurate account of contemporary diet. Craftsmen in precious stones and metals were employed for gold and silverplate and the embellishments adorning the figures themselves: swords, crowns, halos, earrings, necklaces, etc.

And so the crib developed at its evolutionary peak into a luscious spectacle of an ebullient folk scene; a kind of dumb theater with a cast of several hundreds! The Holy Family, placed high and to the rear of the tableau (usually against a classical ruin) still retained some measure of devotional stylistic treatment, but the angels and winged cherubs suspended above them in great proliferation were fashioned without sentiment or markedly religious connotations. (*Fig. 3*)

It is the superabundance of lay figures relating one to another through attitude and expression, fusing the prodigious whole into one three-dimensional exhibition, which provides the most charming and spirited testimony of the period. A quality of uncompromising realism and vitality pervades even the humblest and smallest figures (*Fig. 4*) which were arranged according to the rule of perspective, with the largest (not exceeding 20 inches) in the foreground.

Cribs were added to year by year, and those who could afford it donated figures sculpted in their own likeness to their church as an act of attonement or simply for kudos. In such cases the donor and his entire family were sometimes introduced. People with deformities had their portraits modeled with gruesome accuracy in the hope of facilitating a cure by the inclusion of their disfigured image in the holy tableau.

An extensive crib would display numbers of shepherds accompanied by their flocks, the three kings with prodigious entourages, noblemen and women, merchants, tradespeople, townfolk, villagers and a variety of ethnic groups. Every object in contemporary use, whether decorative or functional, was represented by its miniature counterpart. Members of the aristocracy were particularly well-represented—not surprisingly when one reflects that a mid-17th century survey showed Neapolitan territories to be the home of 119 princes, 156 dukes, 173 marquesses and several hundred counts!

Figures representing the nobility are easily recognizable by their sumptuous gold embroidered garments. Here, as in all the represented social grades, the influence of Spanish fashion is apparent. Naples had been ruled by Spanish viceroys from 1503. In 1734 the son of Philip V of Spain, Don Carlos (titled Charles III), established the Bourbon dynasty in Naples.

The Neapolitan crib figure is generally composed of a terra cotta shoulder-head with inset glass eyes. These are comparable in design to our present-day contact lenses, with the painting of the iris, pupils and whites of eyes

Fig. 7: Height without stand 16''. *Private collection.*

Fig. 8: Peasant women with infant. *Photo courtesy Bavarian National Museum.*

executed on the obverse of the glass. After firing and before painting, these were applied to the head and secured with gesso eyelids. The head was painted with tempera and a final coat of oil varnish resulted in a delicate satiny finish. The body and upper limb sections are constructed of wire padded and bound with tow string. The head is attached to the body through sew holes on the front and back of the shoulders. The carved and painted lower limbs are fixed to the protruding wire forming the upper limbs. Figures are also found with terra cotta lower arms and legs, and less usual, with carved wooden heads. Holes in the base of the feet fitted onto protruding pegs fixed in the figure's appointed place within the crib scene.

Clothed and nude figures are also found made wholly of terra cotta or carved wood. The naked variants were designed for display in scanty clothing such as beggars and children in sparse rags (*Fig. 5*). Cherubs and angels are also represented unclothed, but whether the figure is a child or adult, nudity in crib art was strictly confined to males (*Fig. 6*).

Great attention was lavished on the costumes. Needlewomen engaged in this final stage of the figure's construction displayed their skill with imagination. Every type of available cloth was used from simple home-spun linens to rich velvets and exotic silks. Gold and silver embroidery was a notable feature of embellishment (*Fig. 7*). This difficult art was practiced only by professionals; a five-year apprenticeship being deemed necessary. Much use was made of braids, blown glass beads, lace trim and ornamental buttons. Paper linings were used for additional support and occasionally the insertion of fine wire stitched into hems was twisted to form a sweeping distension which complemented the figure's attitude.

Headdress was often modeled as part of the head, but where specimens are found wearing hats, veils or kerchiefs of textile (*Fig. 8*), adhesive was used to secure these head coverings. Footwear, too, was carved in one piece with the legs, sometimes with great elaboration and detail, but here also cloth, braid and leather were used to cover or partially cover beautifully carved bare feet. Where the figure was portrayed wearing sandals, the soles would be carved and strips of leather, string or braid, were added and laced up the leg. Shepherds are usually found with their legs bound in rags and tied to mid-calf level (*Fig. 9*).

Saints bearing no relation to the nativity were sometimes included in the crib according to the locality where he or she may have been venerated as a patron of that region. These are sometimes difficult to identify, except for the certain clue provided by the hole in the back of the head into which a halo was fixed. They are often unexalted in dress, and unspiritualized in concept. Where saints are distinguishable through dress and symbols associated with a particular saint or archangel, the figure will have served a dual role; it will also have been a shrine figure. Methods of securing the feet onto pegs in cribs were also used for mounting figures onto individual pedestals. The presence of linen underwear provides the evidence; figures used purely for cribs are traditionally without undergarments.

The word "crib" ultimately became designated as a descriptive term for groups of figures set up at varying times of year depicting scenes other than the Nativity. Hence the Lenten-Cribs displayed events from The Passion. Figures have been found bearing witness to "cribs" of Adam and Eve and the Finding of Moses in the Bulrushes. The principal theme, however, was scenes from the Nativity cycle: The Annunciation, The Visitation, The Search for Lodgings, The Birth of Christ, The Adoration of the Angels and of the Shepherds, The Procession and Adoration of the Magi, The Flight to Egypt, The Massacre of the Innocents, Christ's Visit to the Temple, and The Marriage at Cana.

The influence of Neapolitan techniques in crib-making had spread rapidly northward throughout Italy and across the Alps into southern Germany and Austria, both through the export of figures and Neapolitan-trained artists. Schools are known to have been established in Rome, Venice, Florence and Genoa. By the 19th century, Spanish, German and French crib figures all bear witness to the influence of Naples. Sicily alone retained her own unique approach both in the construction of figures and a taste for the gruesome, the Massacre of the Innocents being a favorite Sicilian theme. Figures from Sicily were carved from limewood draped in glaze-soaked cloth and finally painted in tempera. The result was a strikingly sculptural effect of substance and fluidity.

Legions of Neapolitan sculptors were engaged to work on church and family Presepios. Many of these were also designers of the Capo di Monte porcelainware. Among the most notable were: Matteo Bottiglieri, Giuseppe Sammartino, Francesco Gallo, Salvatore di Franco, Guiseppe Gori, Francesco Celebrano, Nicolo Somma, Guiseppe Sarno, Lorenzo Mosca, Giovanni Batista-Polidoro, Domenico Antonio Vaccaro and Nicolo Vassalo.

Crib figures were occasionally signed and those that are bear the artist's initials (and sometimes the date) *inside* the head—a virtually inaccessible place, unless one is prepared to unpick the fragile clothing, dismantle the figure and then reassemble it with all the accompanying risks, plus the possibility of the absence of a signature! Research and the assiduous study of figures in collections for which the sculptor was known provide the necessary comparative material for identification of isolated specimens. Attributions arrived at through such studies must, however, be regarded as conjectural despite personal stylistic peculiarities and specifically recognizable qualities of any given artist, for the circumscribed nature of crib art and the personal links between the artists inevitably resulted in close similarities.

When the luxurious and sophicated Presepio fell from favor with The Church in the 19th century, a gradual decline in the enthusiasm of the sculptors, and by degrees in the quality and craftsmanship of this art form followed. Happily, these curious and often beautiful artifacts were never entirely discarded and large numbers have survived. For today's collector, the chances of finding examples with their removable embellishments intact are slim, particularly those of precious metal and stones. With the decline of this fabulous tradition, accessories of value were the first to be salvaged (and pillaged) from the banned displays which encumbered innumerable churches and religious institutions.

Of course, there had always been hazards in the storage of the objects which were laid away annually between Candlemas and Christmas. Figures could all too easily become separated from their accessories and headdress appears to have been the chief victim. Crib animals are almost impossible to find, although huge

Fig. 10: Length 6¼". *Private collection.*

Fig. 11: Heights without stands 13¼" and 13"; made by Lorenzo Mosca. *Private collection.*

Fig. 9: Heights without stands 14" and 10¼". *Private collection.*

numbers were made. Scarce, too, is the Holy Family, the Bambino in particular (*Fig. 10*). This group was retained together with oxen, asses, and sheep and continues to be used at the Christmas festival to the present day. Of the lay figures, the rarest are the "Deformi" . . . those macabre unfortunates woven into the scriptural tapestry of the most sizable Christmas cribs. Always depicted in cheerful and alert appreciation of the scene about them, their scarcity today is hardly surprising; their disturbing condition found little acceptance when these figures assumed their later role as individual decorative objects. Freak crib figures are to be found only when entire cribs have been donated intact to museums.

A once costly and passionately collected "devotional toy," the hobby of royalty and the aristocracy, today it is left to the collector to bring together these long disbanded members of the Christmas crib. With their vein of exhibitionism and their features often recorded with such felicity as to verge on caricature (*Fig. 11*), and the observation in depth of each as an individual portrait, they remain as a scriptural and legendary combination with the third historical dimension, and as a reflective testimony of the skill and artistry of a dynamic school of sculptors, painters, architects and craftsmen.

For the benefit of collectors it may be useful to present the descriptive terminology in current use for crib figures. The French term *Creche* is used in America as well as France. In England, Italy and German-speaking countries the direct translation of "manger" is again used, hence *crib*, *presepio* or *krippe*, respectively. In Spain and Latin America the term *Santos* covers shrine and crib figures. The Christ Child alone carries the international term of *Bambino*.

Bibliography

Denkmaler Der Krippenkunst. Rudolf Berliner. B. Filser. Augsburg.
Die Weihnachtskrippe. Rudolf Berliner. 1955. Prestel Verlag. Munich.
Krippen. Luciano Zeppegno. 1970. Sudwest Verlag. Munich.
Dolls & Dollmakers. Mary Hillier 1968. Weidenfeld and Nicholson. G.B.
Dolls and Puppets. Max von Boehn. 1966. Cooper Square Inc. U.S.A.
Bavarian National Museum Guide. 1971 Dr. C. Wolf & Son. University Press. Munich.

Photographs of Dolls in Carte de Visite Albums

by EVELYN JANE COLEMAN

ONE OF the peripheral areas of interest for many doll collectors is searching for pictorial images of children with dolls. Such pieces can be excellent sources for documentation, or can be complimentary decorative accents in the collector's home. There is special delight in procuring such works, for frequently they were created at the same time as when the doll portrayed was first made. Through such mediums we may glimpse the doll in its original form, and often in the atmosphere in which it was played with when new.

Until the mid-19th century man created images, which by the very fact of their creation were the artist's own interpretation of the scene that he was trying to portray. All such works, in whatever medium, reflect the artist's attitude and his vision toward his subject matter, to say nothing about his ability to create a work of art. However, in the 19th century with the invention of the camera, images could be captured by mechanical means without the interference of the artist's attitude and visions toward his subject. People and objects were thus recorded by photographic means without the prejudice of the artist, though the composition, subject matter, and method of developing the picture were still under the control of man. Sometimes areas in the photographs are out of focus because of movement, or because the camera was not equipped to take a close detail. During the early days of photography the camera did not take pictures in color, which meant that the colors were transformed into

Fig. 1: Cromolithograph of the mid-19th century showing a sleeping girl with her doll. The delineation in this picture gives no clues as to the type of doll shown.

shades of light and dark sepia tones, or black and white tones. To enhance such photographs, some were hand-tinted with water colors, in the same manner as many of the prints of that time.

Even taking these drawbacks into consideration, today's collectors can get a more precise visual message of how the doll looked from early photographs, in most instances, than they can from the details of the doll found in a drawing or sculpture created at the same period. Too often when a doll is included in such a work, all one can see is that the thing with the child has two arms, two legs and a head, if that. An example of this nebulous portrayal is seen in *Figure 1*. Even in catalogs and other advertisements that show drawings of dolls for sale, today's viewer has difficulty discovering important details. Frequently it is impossible to determine the type of material

61

used for the head or body. In fact, it is not certain whether the picture really showed the doll then currently for sale, because distributors often continued to use the same cut (drawn advertising illustration) year after year. But with a photograph one can usually discern if the doll has a bisque head, or if the head resembles the now much coveted Bru, or is of the German-type manufacture. If the photograph was taken when the doll was new, the viewer can see the kind of clothing the doll originally wore.

In a way these early photographs provide a vehicle which enables the modern viewer to be transported back in time to when the doll was new, and see it in its comtemporary surroundings. One of the best documents that can be transferred with an antique doll to its present owner is a photograph showing the doll with its first owner.

Another advantage with photographs occurs when several dolls are seen in the same contemporary picture, which of course indicates all of the dolls shown were played with at the same time. *Figure 2* shows a little girl dressed to portray the "Old Woman in the Shoe" who had too many children. This little girl had 19 doll children. Most of the dolls are either the so-called parian type with the flat-top hair style, or china heads with cork-screw hair arrangements. There are two wax-over composition headed dolls, one wearing a snood over the back of its hair. Most of the dolls dressed as females have the large circular skirts popular in the 1860s. These dresses do not appear to be of contrasting colors, a style that was in vogue in the 1850s. This photograph can be dated fairly accurately because on the back is a two-cent excise

Fig. 3: Cabinet size photograph, ca. 1900. Young child standing on a Renaissance style chair. In the hand of the child is a bisque-headed doll on a composition body. It is probably of German manufacture. The doll appears to be wearing commercial clothes. Under the photograph is stamped "Mueller/Owatonna, Minn." The size is 6-¾ inches high and 4-½ inches wide.

Fig. 2: Carte de Visite size photograph, ca. 1865, of a little girl with spectacles on her nose pretending to be the "Old Woman in the Shoe" with 19 doll children. On the back is J. C. Moulton/Photographic Artist/Fitchburg, Mass. The size is 4 inches high and 2-⅜ inches wide.

tax stamp. Photographers were required to collect this tax between 1864 and 1866, as a way to raise funds for the Union side in the Civil War, according to records in the International Museum of Photography. (Fortunately in some cases the photographer has even penned in the date when the excise stamp for the photograph was sold.) It is not surprising the only male doll shown in *Figure 2* is dressed in military garb, though unlike the uniforms associated with the American Civil War. This doll appears to be helping the "Old Woman." He looks directly at the frolicking children, and his stance is such that he appears to be keeping them under control while one arm supports the back of the shoe.

In the 19th century, photographs took many forms. First there were those produced under the invention of Mr. Daguerre, who perfected his technique in 1839. Only one picture could be had from each shot, and the finished product had to be kept in a case to protect it from abrasion and light. This meant that such photographs were expensive and only available for the personal use of people who presumed that they could afford them. In the early 1850s the collodion process was developed, whereby a number of photographs could be had from a single negative. On the back of the photographs shown in *Figure 2* it states: "Additional copies from the plate from which this picture was taken, can be had if desired." Apparently the collodium process allowed photographs to be produced in a variety of forms, such as the Ambertype, the tin-type and photographs on paper, which were then supported by a stiffer cardboard. The latter group was available chiefly in two sizes, at first the Carte de Visite size and then the larger Cabinet size. According to a late 19th century dictionary, the term "Carte de Visite" is described as "A photograph mounted on a small card, originally intended to be used as a visiting card." In the past when people paid formal social visits to their friends they frequently left behind a card which is referred to as a visiting or calling card.

The Cartes de Visite served as remembrances of friends and family members. These photographs were placed in an ornate album which kept the family's collection in a form that became a treasured keepsake. In a colored fashion plate of 1863, a pair of elegantly dressed ladies are posed leafing through just such an album. Today when going through such albums, one often finds a child holding a toy. In fact, occasionally toys were used as props by the studio just as they used background drops and potted plants. In the Cartes de Visite a child often holds a wax-over composition headed doll, a china headed doll, or a doll that resembles the papier-mache Greiner-type. In the later and larger photographs called "Cabinet," the majority of the dolls have bisque heads (*Figure 3*).

In the same year that H. W. Diamond, an Englishman, introduced the Carte de Visite, 1852, George P. Putman of New York published a book, *Homes of American Authors*, which included photographic views. With this new tool, namely the camera, people could promote anything from important persons of historical note to the latest circus curiosity. Today one is more likely to find a Carte de Visite showing Tom Thumb than Abraham Lincoln. Even merchants saw the advantages of this new process. As an example, toy shops realizing the possibilities had Cartes de Visite albums produced that showed their wares. These pictures are indeed some of the earliest photo-

Fig. 4: Carte de Visite from the *Album de la Poupee*, ca. 1870, shows a doll with a bisque swivel head and glass eyes. This type of doll is referred to as a fashion-type doll according to the recently published *Glossary* for the United Federation of Doll Clubs. The doll wears a regional costume of Brittany and carries a bag hanging from its hand. The size of the Carte de Visite is 1-¾ inches high by 1 inch wide.

Recently an album entitled "Dolly's Album/Arranged for Little Ladies by W. H. Cremer/Toy Warehouse 27 New Bond Street" came up for sale at Christie's auction in London. It contained eight photographs of dolls. Great interest was shown in the album for it brought 105 pounds (approximately $200). The picture from the album that is in the catalog for the sale shows a lady doll with a bisque swivel head, and wearing a promenade dress. Most of these Carte de Visite albums for dolls were produced in the 1860s and 1870s, when the lady dolls were most popular. A facsimile of a similar miniature album containing photographs of dolls in a Paris store has recently become available to collectors. This "Album de la Poupee" was originally distributed by Au Paradis des Enfants, which was advertised in 1867 as the largest store in Paris specializing in childrens' toys. The store was operated by Perreau Fils. This little doll-size album contains thirteen photographs showing a variety of dolls. The majority of them are bisque-headed lady dolls attired in assorted outfits, including a doll in a swishy taffeta ball gown; a doll dressed in a walking ensemble and holding a walking stick; a doll preparing her toilette at her draped boudoir mirror, while another provides the finishing touches to her outfit. One doll is dressed in the provincial garb of Brittany (*Figure 4*), and one wears elaborate baby clothes, perhaps representing a christening gown. This, the only infant in the group, resembles a Motschmann-type doll. On a clock-work tricycle toy rides a young lady doll with questionable decorum, as we associate it with the mid-Victorian period. Her dress is pulled way above her knees, and her hair is loose to fly in the breeze which would be created when the clock-work mechanism is activated. Decorum, however, is reinstated with the spectacles on her nose and the properly placed pill-box hat on her head. There are two dolls dressed as men, one of them is a horse-groom tending a horse on wheels, while the other male doll is a soldier who strikes a comical pose with his large nose and slightly old fashioned clothes. Existing examples of this type of doll are virtually unknown to this author.

Fig. 5: The larger Cabinet size photographs gained in popularity over the smaller Carte de Visite towards the end of the 19th century for it gave the viewer a larger image as seen in this early (5½" by 3 ⅞") photograph of a little girl posed with her beautiful new doll.

graphs of items that graced the shelves of toy stores. Fortunately for the doll collector, these advertising albums containing pictures of dolls could be used as one of the accessories for the then popular Lady Dolls. In an article written in the December 1865 issue of the *Englishwoman's Domestic Magazine* about the famous Toy Shop in London belonging to Mr. Cremer Jr., the necessity for having a doll-size Carte de Visite album was confirmed: "(He) kindly showed us the trousseaux of many miniature ladies all containing everything that a lady can require and many of them everything a lady might desire. She has her carte de visite book...."

A doll's Carte de Visite Album such as this one of about 1870 from Au Paradis des Enfants, with actual photographs of their finest dolls becomes today not only a valuable accessory for a fashionable doll, but also an important historical document. We can actually see through the camera's eye the dolls that tempted little girls over a century ago. In fact, any early photograph of dolls shows collectors exactly how their dolls looked when new. As better techniques in photography have been developed, photographic records of dolls and other objects become even more precise. The doll historian of the future will have an infinite number of colored photographs to show exactly how the dolls in the 1970s looked. ■

An American Mechanical Toy, Ca. 1870

DOLL RIDING TRICYCLE

by YOLANDA M. SIMONELLI

PATENTS for American clockwork toys began to appear around 1860 and thereafter followed an era of toy manufacture which exemplified American ingenuity and fine craftsmanship, evidenced by surviving toys.

Clockwork toys are set into motion by the gradual release of tension in a coiled spring that has been key wound. One such toy is a doll riding a tricycle; a three-wheeled design; the rear wheels being larger in diameter than the front wheel. The toy measures 9" at the highest point and is 11" long.

The doll has a shoulder head of hardened cloth which is sometimes misreported to be papier-mache. This is nailed to a woody body. Hair is molded with deep comb marks and is painted a mustard color; eyes are painted blue; long molded earrings cling to the ears. Brass colored metal hands are pierced to fit the handlebars of the tricycle. High button shoes of the same metal fasten to the pedals. The dolls wears an original red cotton coat with a white embroidered collar, and trousers of a blue and white striped cotton.

Doll Riding Tricycle by George H. Hawkins and William F. Godwin, American toy designers of the late 19th century. The doll head was patented in 1868 and the tricycle in 1870. This rare mechanical toy still operates a century after it was made. *Simonelli collection.*

The tricycle has wheels of cast metal and is painted dark green. The spring mechanism is housed on the axle between the larger back wheels. A separate key operates the spring. Metal housing for the works is painted green and decorated in gold. Gold lettering reads, "Patented Jan. 25th & Feb. 1st 1870".

Coleman's *Collectors' Encyclopedia of Dolls* and other sources attribute the tricycle design to William Farr Goodwin, a Washington, D.C. inventor who patented mechanical toys in France, Britain, and the United States.

The shoulder head doll is credited to George H. Hawkins of New York who received the following patents:

USA #81999—Doll of textile fabric, stiffened with glue and pressed between heated dies (1868).
F #83285—Molded Doll (1868).
USA #85589—Manufacturer of dolls' heads (1869).

The pictured doll is unmarked but *Handbook of Collectible Dolls* by Merrill & Perkins reports the patent dated tricycle with the same doll, except for the addition of a black hairband and gilt touched earrings, marked "X.L.C.R. DOLL HEAD Sept. 8, 1868". This information is on a label tacked to the doll's shoulder. The Colemans report the same marking, explaining the letters are the phonetic equivalent of the word, "Excelsior."

Thus it appears the doll riding tricycle toy was contrived through the combined ingenuity of two Americans. To date, the writer could find no record of the manufacturer who may have produced this well-constructed mechanical.

True, the doll head is scuffed, its clothing tattered, and the bike's paint is faded and chipped. Yet, the original key slips easily into the spring and smoothly turns it. The shabby little bike rider circles along any smooth surface as well as it did a century ago.

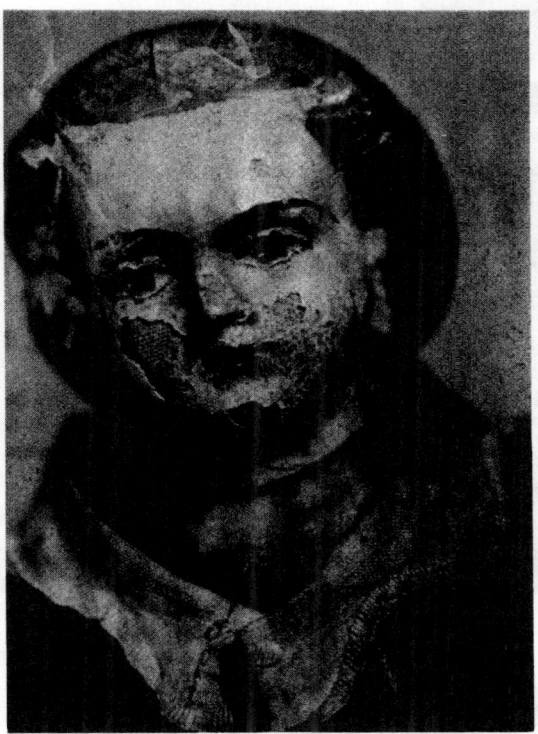

Close-up of doll's head made by George H. Hawkin's patented process of saturating fabric with sizing or glue and pressing between heated dies. Buckram-type fabric can be seen beneath peeling paint. This doll shoulder head was attached to a wooden body with metal hands and feet.

POSTSCRIPT:

Toys generally imitate and illustrate the times from which they originate and the writer began to wonder why the little rider was female and why the three-wheeled toy was described as a tricycle instead of velocipede, a similar three-wheeled vehicle for children.

Checking for clues to see what differences there might be, I found information from old advertisements.

F. A. O. Schwarz Spring Circular of 1870 pictured a three-wheeled version having one large wheel in the front and two smaller in the rear, called, "boy's foot velocipede".

In an advertisement of 1897 showing tricycles and velocipedes, the velocipede had a wheel design similar to the Schwarz picture and was described as a "Boys' All Steel Velocipede". On the other hand, the tricycle illustrated had a front wheel of smaller dimension than the two rear wheels. This vehicle was listed as being available in various sizes to fit girls of ages two to fifteen.

Further, an 1881 advertisement by W. J. Bowen & Co., Norwalk, Ohio, showed, "The American TRICYCLE, invented and manufactured for girls".

Again in 1911, F. A. O. Schwarz advertised velocipedes having the large front wheel design. They also showed a three-wheeled vehicle having the smaller front wheel, for girls from under four years to ten years of age, described as, "FAIRY" BALL BEARING TRICYCLES.

One might then conclude that toymakers designated large front wheel models, called velocipedes, for boys and small front wheel models, called tricycles, for girls. The tricycles also seemed to have the added comfort of upholstered seats. ■

REFERENCES

Colemans'—*The Collectors' Encyclopedia of Dolls*
Kimport—*Doll Talk*—March-April 1970
Merrill & Perkins—*Handbook of Collectible Dolls*
Gwen White—*European and American Dolls*
Ruth & Larry Freeman—*Cavalcade of Toys*
Louis H. Hertz—*The Handbook of Old American Toys*

Fig. 1: French male doll with fashion face and kid body. *Eunie Collection. Photo by Joe Aloia, III.*

Fig. 2: Candy box boy, popular in France for christening parties. *Photo by Joe Aloia, III.*

Fig. 3: Bru boy doll. *Author's collection. Photo by Joe Aloia, III.*

HE's a REAL DOLL

by JUDITH WHORTON

Fig. 4: French gentleman doll with intaglio eyes and molded grey hair. *Eunie collection. Photo by Joe Aloia, III.*

Fig. 5: Armand Marseilles Mexican doll with frowning eyebrows. This is similar to the style used for Indian dolls. *Mrs. J. R. Sims collection. Photo by Joe Aloia, III.*

Fig. 6: Dolls' house man and "Chubby." *Author's collection. Photo by Mrs. J. R. Sims.*

IN TODAY'S MARKET, male dolls are responsible for a large proportion of sales. In 1975, the year the doll called the Million Dollar Man was introduced, over two million were sold. It became the most successful toy of the year.

The scarcity of earlier male dolls is hard to visualize when looking at today's store shelves filled with soldiers and male celebrity dolls. In 1888 Butler Brothers, a nation-wide wholesale order firm, offered two pages of dolls, yet not a single boy was listed. Over forty years later, in the liberated twenties, Montgomery Ward advertised only four. A doll should only be classified as a male if the original costume or face is definitely masculine. A doll face example redressed and wearing a cropped wig should not be included as such.

Figure 1. This elegant gentleman, a blue ribbon winner at a national doll convention, has a face typical of many of the so-called French fashions. His difference lies in his original costume which includes satin britches, coat with tails, and tricornered hat.

Figure 2. Jacque, with his name printed on his costume, serves as both a doll and a candy box. He divides into two parts at the waist, with the hollow lower section containing the sweets made by the Bonnet Company. He also has a swivel neck and glass eyes. His solid dome bisque head is marked with the initials "F.G." Luella Hart reported a patent granted in 1865 for a box doll to Felix Egrefeuil. He suggested the doll could be used to serve the sweets at christening ceremonies. The doll pictured, although made by another firm and at a later date, closely resembles the Egrefeuil patent illustration for the first christening doll to be made in France.

Figure 3. Another French lad wearing a factory-made sailor costume of red faille, was made by the prestigious Bru Company. His head is incised "Bru Jne R. 7." The "R" is a good clue to his age, since in 1892 Paul Girard added the letter to the Jne mark. The sailor also wears leather high-topped shoes which bear the mark "Bru Jne Paris."

Figure 4. A later French example, complete with a molded mustache, was made in 1917 by (Edmond) Hieulle, a firm which specialized in historical men dolls. His original

Fig. 10: General Douglas MacArthur doll. *Author's collection. Photo by Joe Aloia, III.*

Fig. 7: China doll dressed as a boy. *Mrs. J. R. Sims collection. Photo by Joe Aloia, III.*

Fig. 8: Walking papier-mâché boy doll. *Veradell Bryant collection. Photo by Mrs. J. R. Sims.*

Fig. 9: Charlie Chaplin has been found in many materials. At the present time, the composition version is a favorite with collectors. *Author's collection. Photo by Joe Aloia, III.*

Fig. 11: This realistic version of an Indian doll is an unmarked German bisque of excellent quality. *Mrs. J. R. Sims collection. Photo by Mrs. J. R. Sims.*

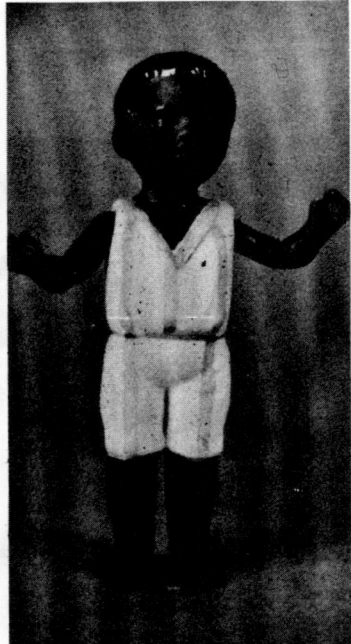

Fig. 12: Well modelled black all-bisque boy doll. *Mrs. J. R. Sims collection. Photo by Mrs. J. R. Sims.*

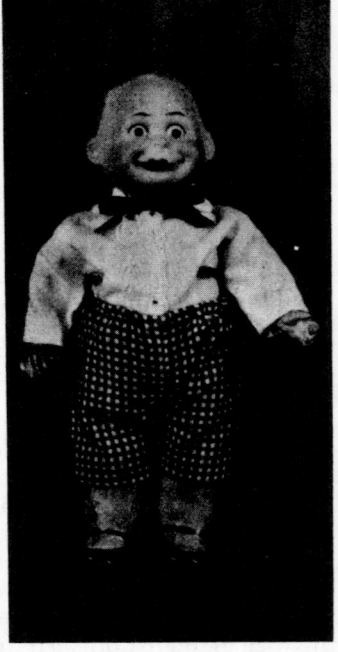

Fig. 13: "Googlie," with German mark "R.A." *Mrs. J. R. Sims collection. Photo by Mrs. J. R. Sims.*

Fig. 14: Modern examples often show humor and imagination. This celluloid tramp doll even needs a shave. *Collection Mrs. A. Christian Revi. Photo by Joe Aloia, III.*

clothes represent the era of 1871. He carries a portrait of his lady in his hat.

Figure 5. Various German firms also produced some intriguing examples of male dolls. Many of the boy dolls were made to represent ethnic groups or military subjects. In 1895, Butler Brothers' catalog offered an "assorted Wild West" group which consisted of an Indian brave, a squaw and a Mexican cowboy. These dolls, 13½ inches tall, with jointed wrists and knees, sold for $8.35 a dozen. The price seems low today, but a 12-inch girl doll with jointed wrists and neck in the same catalog sold for $1.72 a dozen. This 7½ inch doll made by the prolific Armand Marseille firm matches the costume illustration for the Mexican cowboy.

Uncle Sam, another German character (see cover), is owned by Myron Briley.

Figure 6. Although the all-bisque boy and the dolls' house men were produced in greater numbers than the bisque ball-jointed variety, collectors prize them. "Chubby," made by the Lewis Wolf Company, is a quality all-bisque. This doll, which first appeared around 1915, must have been a good seller. Ten years later Butler Brothers was advertising Japanese celluloid dolls seemingly inspired by "Chubby."

The dolls' house dolls had a variety of males, including fathers, grandfathers, butlers and boys. In the 20th century, even chauffeurs became available.

Figure 7. Bisque is not the only medium in which male dolls have appeared. Chinas with short hair and molded ears are regarded by many collectors as male.

Figure 8. A late papier-mâché boy with molded hair has the "g e g e" trademark (registered in 1943 by Giroud, and renewed in 1958). His handmade clothing has some imaginative accessories. In one pocket he carries a passport with his name and date of birth (1947), and a tiny black-and-white picture of a little boy. One hip pocket contains a leather bag filled with tobacco; the other has two French coins.

Figures 9 and 10. Charlie Chaplin, made of composition by Louis Amberg & Son, Cincinnati, Ohio, in 1915, is one of the first celebrity dolls in this material. General MacArthur *(Fig. 10)* made in the 1940s, is one of the last; it was produced by the Freundlich Novelty Corporation of New York City.

The rest of the male dolls pictured here *(Figures 11 through 14)* are described in their respective captions. ∎

Happifat Collectibles

by JULIE MASTERSON CHILD

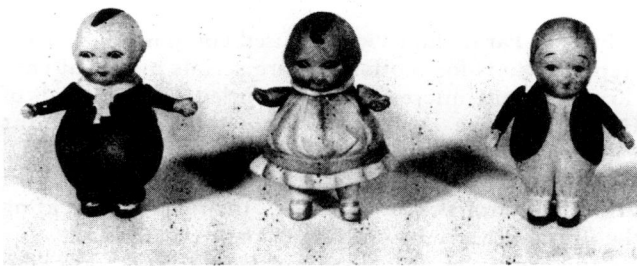

Left to right: Japanese Happifat boy and girl; these carefully duplicate the colors of the original German dolls. Japanese Happifat boy as described in the text of this article.

Back view of the three Happifat dolls shown above.

WHILE COLLECTORS have been long aware of the existence of Happifat dolls, chinaware, and novelty items, reference to them has been conspicuously absent in early books about dolls and antiques. Then, in 1969, the Coleman's *Collector's Encyclopedia of Dolls* provided a clue to their origin.

"Happifat. 1913-1921. Registered as a trademark by Borgfeldt in the U.S. and Germany in 1914. Dolls based on the drawings by Kate Jordan which appeared in *John Martin's Book*. The rotund little boy in molded suit or underwear and the little girl in molded dress both had molded hair and rubber elastic-jointed arms. They were made in 1914 in Germany of all-bisque or all-composition."

Books and Paper Material

At a recent antiques show, several doll collectors gathered about a booth featuring Paper Americana where the dealer was showing them prints of dolls and toys. They paid little attention when a client interrupted, asking for the "pictogram flip-book" about which he had written her. The terms were unfamiliar to them and the thick little 2 by 2 ¼-inch book he handed her was in no way impressive. But they took a closer look as she rolled her thumb across the fore-edge and the figures printed on the pages appeared to be moving—each had been drawn in a slightly advanced position to create the illusion of animation. Suddenly there was "instant bedlam."

The reason for excitement was not so much the animation as the title on the red paper cover—*Another Happifat Pictogram*, above a line drawing of an exceedingly chubby little boy. On the inside title page appeared, "*The Happifats and the Kite*, by Kate Jordan," and although the page was torn, a 1911 date was visible as well as part of the publisher's address: " . . . 9 W. 37th Street . . . ork, N.Y."

To the doll collectors this proved the Happifats had been drawn as early as 1911, at least two years prior to their first credited appearance in *John Martin's Book*.

Who was John Martin and what was his *Book*? A search in a large city public library led first to the *Ladies Home Journal* for 1911, where "John Martin's Letters to Very Little Boys & Girls" appeared as a full-page feature in the September, October, and November issues. Each page was illustrated with black and white drawings; none were of Happifats. The series seems not to have been continued beyond 1911.

Further library research of early publication listings revealed that in 1912, Morgan Shepard, who had been writing under the John Martin pseudonym, was operating John Martin's House Publishers. Credits for items in print were brief: "John Martin's Letters to Children. Two subscription series, each 13 letters a year $2.50; 13 letters $4. Letters from fairies, birds, animals, giants, and characters in history mailed and delivered by the Postman."

John Martin's Book was listed as a 1912 juvenile magazine, not an actual book. The June 1915 issue, the only copy available for inspection, showed no illustrations of Happifats, but did give the John Martin address—5 West 39th Street, N.Y.

Other John Martin Books listed, some with prices, were:

1913 —*Jolly Big Alphabet*/ 50 cents/ John Martin's House.

1917 —*John Martin's Big Book for Little Folks*/ $1.25/

John Martin's House, Garden City, N.Y., for sale by Doubleday.

1917 —*John Martin's Big Book for Little Folk, No. 3/* $2.50/ Houghton

? —*John Martin's Big Book for Little Folk, No. 4/* $3.50/ Houghton

1921-3—*John Martin's Big Book for Little Folk, Nos. 5-7/* No. 6, $3/ No. 7, $2.50/ John Martin's Bookhouse; for sale by Dodd.

1922 —*A Chubby Book for Chubby Children/* $1.50/ Dodd

1929 —*John Martin's Book: Stories for Little Men & Women Selected from John Martin's Book/* Platt & Munk

1932 —*John Martin's Book: Tell Me A Story Selected from John Martin's Book/* Platt & Munk.

A notation elsewhere stated that the *John Martin Annuals* progressed through No. 16, but that the titles varied. No information was given as to dates, publishers, or price.

Any of these books may have contained stories and pictures of the Happifats.

The only applicable reference found to Kate Jordan was: "Kate Vermilye (Jordan), Mrs. Frederic, *Happifats and the Grouch: Pictures by the Author.*" This was published by Dutton in 1917 and sold at $2.

An interested librarian volunteered the information that sometime between 1914 and 1916, her mother had been given a Japanese-made dresser set decorated with Happifats. It consisted of an oval porcelain dresser tray, round powder box, round hair receiver, and tall hatpin holder.

Happifat Dolls and Tea Sets

In 1915, Geo. Borgfeldt & Co. advertised 3½ inch and 4½ inch bisque Happifat dolls. They were marked with oval-shaped stickers, showing they had been made in Germany. The boy's coat and shoes were hunter green, his pants light brown. The girls' molded dresses were either pale blue with pink shoes and sashes or pink with blue shoes and sashes. Borgfeldt also introduced a variation with cloth body and composition head and hands.

Happifats were offered in Butler Bros. "Our Drummer" catalog dated 1915. Wholesale prices for the Happifats listed at $2.25 per dozen pairs; single pairs, boxed, were offered at 35 cents per pair. *Courtesy Mildred Vealey Hardcastle.*

In 1916 Paramount Pictures used composition-headed Happifat dolls for motion picture serials aimed at capturing juvenile interest. Although titled "The Hazards of Happifat," the series was known as "Paramount Pictographs—The Animated Magazine of the Screen." The dolls were manipulated by a series of wires which projected through the floor into their bodies, creating the illusion they were moving of their own accord.

Stills from the serials may be seen in the book *Film Flashes* (Leslie-Judge Co. 1915). In addition to the Happifat children and baby, the Happifat dog was pictured—the same spotted dog shown caught in the tail of the kite in the flip-book.

During 1919 and 1920, Louis Amberg & Son advertised 10-inch Happifat dolls with composition heads and cloth bodies. The following year, this firm introduced "Freshie" as a new addition to the Happifat group.

Japanese versions of the original all-bisque pair of Happifat dolls carefully duplicated German colors and sizes. From their markings, it appears possible they were manufactured at different times or were made by more than one manufacturer. On some, "Nippon" is incised in small straight letters of uniform size in the center of the

German child's tea set with red over-glaze mark of Beyer & Bock, Volkstedt, Germany. (Decorated china from 1853; manufactured from 1890.) Set is banded in bright blue; Happifat children, baby and dog are in orange, blue, yellow and green. The strawberry cluster appears on all pieces, but otherwise no two pieces are alike. "H" appears on sweaters of Happifat boys. Dog depicted on this set is orange—not the black and white spotted Happifat dog shown in Paramount Pictures' pictograph or pictogram flip-book.

When Westmoreland reissued the Happifat glass candy container, they called it "Boy on a Drum." *Drawing courtesy of C. Smith, Westmoreland Glass Co.*

back. On others, also marked on the back, the lettering is larger, slanted to the right in varying degrees, and is not the same on all dolls; dolls with this marking tend to have more facial coloring.

A Japanese version of the Happifat boy, apparently a later model, has the same small, neat lettering on his back, but instead of the "Mohawk-Indian" hair style, his blond hair is molded in a typical boyish-cut, and his eyes are not brown, but blue. His molded garments consist of a black coat with tails, black shoes, pale blue pants. Like the others, his slender arms are attached to the hollow bisque body with elastic.

There were also Japanese versions of Happifat tea sets for children. Both German and Japanese tea sets used underglaze as well as overglaze markings in more than one color. German sets usually bring higher prices, but any good Happifat tea set, because of its scarcity, will fall in the high price range of the better Sunbonnet Baby chinaware.

Candy Container and Bank

The Happifat boy appeared as a glass candy container. According to G. Smith of the Westmoreland Glass Company, the original Happifat glass candy container was brought out in clear crystal between 1900 and 1910. In 1973, the original mold was reactivated in clear plum-colored glass and called "Boy on Drum." Production has already been discontinued.

In their comprehensive *American Candy Containers*, George Eikelberner and George Agadjanian list the original as 4⅜ inches high with a 2⅛ inch base diameter. They describe the Happifat boy as having painted brown hair and pants, gold face and tie, white hands, white drum top and straps, and a red band at top of drum. The closure was a tin slip-on lid, painted brown and slotted for a bank.

Sketches of the original Happifat candy containers are to be found as marginal drawings in *Toys Through The Ages*, by Dan Foley (1962).

The crenelated towers and iron gates of The Enchanted World Doll Museum greet hundreds of visiting doll enthusiasts daily.

Mitchell, South Dakota
Enchanted World Doll Museum

Mabel Gurney's "Old Country Store" depicts America's pioneers in miniature.

THE Enchanted World Doll Museum, with its turrets, stone walls, drawbridge and moat and stained glass windows, was built in 1981 to house the thousands of dolls in the museum's collection. It first opened its doors in May 1982 in Mitchell, South Dakota, and has already been enthusiastically received by more than 5,000 visitors who flock to this small Midwestern town during the summer months, from May through September.

The birth of this large and rare collection of dolls actually took place many years ago, in 1936, when Dr. Sheldon Reese was traveling around the world and buying ethnic dolls for his doll-collecting sister. This beginning blossomed into an even greater interest to include earlier dolls made in France, England, Germany and the United States. Today the collection numbers over 5,000 dolls and boasts a bevy of beautiful Brus, Jumeaus, Simon & Halbigs, Kammer & Reinhardts and other well-known dollmakers of the 19th and 20th centuries.

The more than 5,000 dolls of all types and periods are artfully displayed against nearly 400 scenic backgrounds and in dioramas relating to Mother Goose fairy tales, story-book characters and real-life situations.

The 9,000 square foot interior of the museum was skillfully laid out by Mrs. Eunice Reese, who also supervised the arrangements in the many showcases — though she insists she had a great deal of help from local artists.

Special features of the museum include a hospitality room available to groups needing a place to meet, show their slides or view those owned by the museum. A small library of doll reference books is at the disposal of

(cont'd on page 52)

The Schoenhut Circus performs daily at The Enchanted World Doll Museum.

The museum collection numbers over 5,000 dolls.

researchers and students, too. And a gift shop specializing in high quality gifts (including modern and antique dolls) is also housed in this fire-proof complex.

Among the many interesting and amusing displays are "Rooming House Saturday Night" in which are arranged Frozen Charlies all lined up in front of the communal bathroom, dressed in robes, awaiting their turn to use the facilities. Cinderella "At Home" and "At the Ball" is realistically set up with dolls playing their parts and includes an amusing Fairy Godmother. Mrs. Tom Thumb dressed in her wedding finery closely resembles the real-life Mrs. Thumb made famous by P.T. Barnum. And the large display of baby dolls dressed in early embroidered and lacetrimmed Christening Gowns is a treat every doll collector should experience.

Dioramas of a Frontier Barroom and Country Store peopled with miniature dolls and furnishings are true-to-life stories of America's past. In other dioramas, Dr. Dafoe and a nurse attend to the infant Dionne quintuplets, and Hansel and Gretel once again overcome the Wicked Witch. Japanese geisha girls, samurai and members of the Imperial Court arrayed in their colorful costumes constantly delight the young visitors to this fascinating museum.

The museum is open seven days a week from May 1st through Labor Day, from 8 a.m. to 8 p.m. It is also open the third week in September when the world-famous Corn Palace, across the street from the museum, holds its annual celebration and show. (See *Observations* in this issue.)■

Top: Mrs. Eunice Reese rearranges some of the many ethnic dolls on display in The Enchanted World Doll Museum.
Bottom: Cinderella "At Home" (top) and at "At The Ball" (bottom) is played out with dolls in feature roles. Note the Fairy Godmother in the "At Home" setting.

Rare Schoenhut Dolls

by JOHN W. CLENDENIEN

ALBERT SCHOENHUT, the son of a German toymaker, migrated to the United States in 1866, when he was 17 years old. He settled in Philadelphia where he was employed by the John Wanamaker store to repair broken glass keys on imported German toy pianos. Six years later young Albert (Fig. 1) was in business for himself, making wooden toys which would not break. His first toys were wooden pianos which utilized steel chime-like plates instead of glass keys.

In 1903, the circus clown became the first human figure to be created by the Albert Schoenhut Company. With the clown came a chair, barrel, and ladder. The popularity of these circus characters led to the development of complete circuses. These would include a tent, many animals, and various circus personalities, such as a ringmaster, a hobo, a strongman, trapeze artists, bareback riders, even a Chinaman with a queue down the back of his neck. The circuses were packaged as small units or as entire sets, ranging in price from $1 to $35. Thus, Schoenhut circus characters were available to people of all means.

It seems only natural that Albert Schoenhut would see the possibilities of creating dolls from wood. His grandfather had made primitive wood dolls in Germany as early as 1796, and his father created less primitive ones in the mid-19th century. Following in their footsteps, Albert applied for a patent for a spring-jointed doll on July 3, 1909. The patent was finally granted 18 months later on January 17, 1911.

Schoenhut dolls were made entirely of wood, and came either with molded hair or with mohair wigs. Ribbons, bows, and braids were often featured on molded hair girls. Occasionally top knots were also used. Molded hair boys were given the short hair characteristic of little boys of the early 20th century.

Only two Schoenhut dolls were issued patents with trade names, "Tootsie Wootsie" and "Schnickel-Fritz". Both were patented June 6, 1911. Both are extremely rare and are desired by doll collectors everywhere.

"Tootsie Wootsie" (Fig. 2) is a 15-½ inch tall boy whose sober face is aged beyond his toddler years. His original suit consists of a blue cotton jacket and knickers. The jacket has pleated sleeves, and a sailor collar. His white linen dickey is trimmed with a red embroidered six-pointed star. Brown leather shoes and brown cotton stockings complete his all original outfit. The shoes have two holes in the sole which made it possible to pose Schoenhut dolls on a stand.

"Schnickel-Fritz" (Fig. 3) is a smiling child, also 15-½ inches tall. He is dressed in an original white linen sailor suit. The blue sailor collar and cuffs are trimmed with white braid. Seated on a Schoenhut piano, he is able to show his original black leather tie shoes which are also

The Schoenhut Factory in 1872.

Fig. 1: Young Albert Schoenhut and the first Schoenhut factory; reprinted from "Forty Years of Toy Making," Schoenhut's 40th anniversary booklet.

Fig. 2: "Tootsie Wootsie." *Collection Mrs. John Neumyer.*

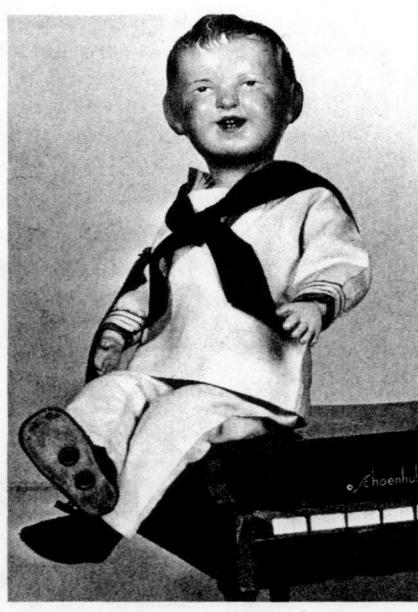

Fig. 3: "Schnickel-Fritz." *Collection Miss Margaret Dowling.*

Fig. 4: Albert Schoenhut and his six sons. Reprinted from "Forty Years of Toy Making."

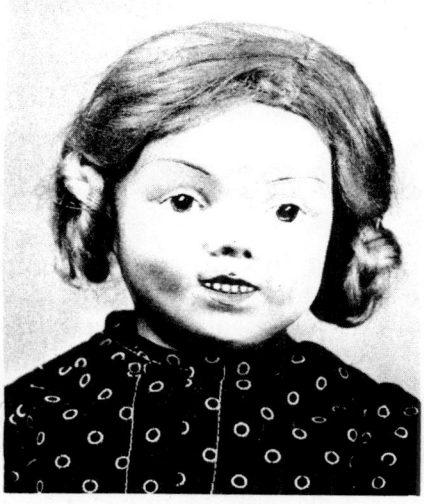

Fig. 6: Smiling Schoenhut girl. *Roberts collection.*

Fig. 8: Girl with molded hair bow. *Roberts collection.*

Fig. 5: Schoenhut "Pouty" modelled after the Kammer and Reinhardt No. 114 doll, holds a "Felix the Cat." *Author's collection.*

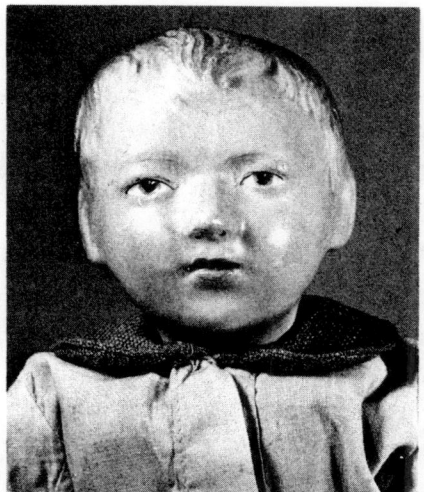

Fig. 7: Sober-faced Schoenhut boy. *Roberts collection.*

Schoenhut shoes with the holes in the bottom. Schnickel-Fritz wears black stockings. He also has an original navy blue wool suit with white silk braid on the sailor collar and around the sleeves; his bell-bottom sailor trousers are flared.

Albert Schoenhut's six sons became a part of the Albert Schoenhut Company. Each had a specific responsiblity *(Fig. 4)*. Following their father's death in 1912, A. F. Schoenhut became president of the company; T. C. Schoenhut was manager of the mechanical department; H. E. Schoenhut managed the art department and designed many of the dolls; O. F. Schoenhut was assistant manager of the sales department which was managed by W. G. Schoenhut; the treasurer of the company was G. A. Schoenhut.

The girl with a closed pouting mouth *(Fig. 5)* is actually a copy of the German bisque Kammer and Reinhardt doll, mold no. 114. She has blue intaglio eyes. Her white cotton lawn dress with inserted lace and lace trim is original. Her white leather shoes are also original, as is her brown mohair wig. She is 16-½ inches tall. Standing on an original Schoenhut stand, she holds a 4-inch Schoenhut "Felix the Cat". The cat has a decal on his left foot which reads:

Copyright 1922, 1924
by Pat Sullivan
Pat. June 23, 1925

The smiling Schoenhut girl *(Fig. 6)* features carved teeth, dimples, and intaglio eyes. The blonde mohair wig on this 16-½ inch lass is original. She wears a blue cotton dress and black leather shoes. She is incised Jan. 17, '11.

Seventeen inches is the height of the sober-faced boy with carved blonde painted hair and blue intaglio eyes *(Fig. 7)*. His white cotton shirt is trimmed with blue coarse linen collar and cuffs that match his pants. He also wears original tan leather button shoes.

Molded bows in the hair of carved haired Schoenhut girls usually appear on the back of the head. The bows may be either blue or pink and are generally accompanied by molded ribbons of the same color. More unusual is the little girl with the bow on the side of her head *(Fig. 8)*. Her bow is blue and has no matching ribbon. This 15-inch girl has blonde hair and blue intaglio eyes. Her smile features four painted teeth. She is identified by a decal on her back. Her white cotton blouse is trimmed with Irish lace around the neck and sleeves. Her wool skirt is a red, green, gray and white plaid. She also wears black leather shoes and white cotton knee socks.

Doll Costumes and Clothes

A growing connoisseurship in any collecting area makes new demands upon the collector who would be exact. For exacting doll collectors these new demands are properly in the area of costume. These connoisseurs seek originality of costume—period clothes of proper fit and style—or lacking that, seek to learn the principles of correct re-costuming. In this following chapter, a small but exacting group of authors has added to collector's knowledge. The information they share not only aids the would-be doll costumer, but reflects the changing societal mores and trends during the late Victorian and early 20th century. Clothes, it seems, not only "make the doll", as Coleman explains, but also help us understand the society that created that doll.

A typical American child, as modelled by Dewees Cochran and produced by Effanbee, circa 1940, stands near her wardrobe and trunk. The dolls owns six cotton school dresses, navy blue coat, two flannel bathrobes, sweater and cap, blue plaid snowsuit, two playsuits and pairs of shoes and gloves.

Clothes Make The Doll

by DOROTHY S. COLEMAN

A COLLECTOR'S dream is to discover a whole new area in his field. To be among the first to enter an untapped area where demand has not yet sent prices soaring is surely a collector's vision of Utopia.

Doll collecting in recent years has become extremely popular with resultant astronomical rise in prices. Here in America the collector has been interested primarily in the head and body of the doll with little, if any, attention paid to the clothes on the doll. Yet original clothes, that is, the clothes that belonged to the doll when the original child owner played with it, are a most important and vital part of the doll.

Originally the clothes cost as much and often many times more than the doll itself. Besides the original monetary value, clothes have much to commend them. A naked doll's body is certainly not a thing of beauty; clothes often transform it into an artistic artifact.

The historical value of a doll lies largely in its original clothes. Seldom does one find any naked or redressed dolls in accredited museums, and dressed dolls are generally included in the costume collections. The original function of dolls as educational tools was based primarily on their clothes. These taught children not only how to dress properly, but the art of sewing in an age when making one's own clothes was a necessary accomplishment for most women.

For the collector today, the original

Papier-mache head, kid body, homemade clothes of the 1840s. Blue and white print cotton dress, white chemise and drawers for underwear. Height 19½". *Courtesy Wenham Museum*.

Wax doll purchased in London in 1873. Commercially dressed in a white muslin dress with coral colored silk ribbons. Underwear consists of petticoat, chemise, and drawers. Height 23". *Courtesy of Magdalena Byfield*.

clothes tell a great deal about the doll. In most cases they provide clues as to its chronological age, the age and sex represented, and often the geographical origin. The latter is not necessarily dependent on a provincial costume; certain characteristics of ordinary clothes can often determine whether a doll was dressed in France, Germany, or an English speaking country.

Why have such valuable artifacts as original clothes on dolls been neglected and often even discarded? The reason, of course, is ignorance. We cannot appreciate things about which we have little or no knowledge. Few collectors and even some dealers are unable to recognize original clothes. It is not always easy to do so. Frequently dealers strip original clothes from a doll and redress it in a modern version of an antique style because their customers demand it. Concepts of costume beauty in the past differed from those today and the old clothes appear strange and unfamiliar to those who have little knowledge of them.

But why does this ignorance and wanton destruction persist? The reason is that source materials for study and comparison are difficult to find. Fashion plates are of relatively little value because they are influenced by artistic license and seldom portray what either dolls or people actually wore. Portraits are also influenced by artistic license and usually show only the best clothes; not what people wore everyday or what the less affluent wore. Dolls' clothes show, more accurately than any other source, clothes commonly worn.

Photographs of dolls prior to the 20th century are rare and often of poor quality. Extant people's costumes are generally best clothes, and many of these have been altered through the years. There are innumerable books on costumes but, alas, most of them are based on the above sources and thus compound the errors. The best series of costume books are those written by the Cunningtons, whose collection forms a large part of the people's clothes and dolls in original clothes in Platt Hall, Manchester, England. Many other museums, especially in Europe, include dolls in their costume departments, but few doll collectors can visit a sizable number of these museums to see and study dolls in original clothes.

If it is difficult to find dolls that one can be certain are in original clothes, it is also difficult to find other primary source material on original clothes. The commercial dolls' clothes appear in catalogs and a few of these have been reprinted, but original catalogs are rare; even large libraries seldom have more than a few. The one exception is the Bibliotheque Nationale in Paris. But not many American collectors have the opportunity of spending endless hours in a Paris library.

Beginning around 1860, patterns for making dolls' clothes began to be published; like the catalogs, some of these have been reprinted recently. The original copies of these patterns are extremely rare, but they are of great value in learning about and identifying original home-made dolls' clothes.

The problems outlined above explain the lack of understanding and appreciation of dolls' clothes. But with the publication of our new book, *The Collector's Book of Dolls' Clothes, Costumes in Miniature, 1700-1929*, a whole new world of interest should be opened to collectors. This is a pioneer effort and the first study in depth of dolls' costumes. It took seven years for three people to complete and many trips to museums and large collections in both America and Europe. Tens of thousands of dolls in original clothes were studied, hundreds of catalogs showing dolls in original clothes were examined, as well as countless contemporary patterns for dolls' clothes.

As this mass of information was sifted and analyzed, certain significant features were evident in every part of a doll's outfit in each era. One day collectors should be as excited over finding with their doll an aumoniere (purse to hold alms for the poor) or a zouave jacket (an adaptation of the Algerian zouave jacket worn in the Italian War of 1859), as they are today in finding a Bru or Kestner mark on their doll.

Dealers should always seek the original clothes for the dolls they purchase. Often a family doll has more than one outfit and sometimes there may be some second generation clothes that must be identified as such. Although not original clothes, the second generation garments are part of the doll's history and should be preserved with it. Frequently family tradition will date a doll a generation earlier than it really is. Fuller understanding of original clothes will usually clarify this misconception. If any alteration or replacement was required to the original clothes, records should be kept and passed along with the doll.

Some people are interested only in collecting doll-size clothes, but dolls and their clothes went together originally and should remain together. The dressed doll shows a complete costume and how it was worn.

Bebe Jumeau with clothes made from Butterick patterns about 1895. The dress on the doll and the dress on the right behind her were both made from the Butterick "French Dress" pattern. A Kestner doll belonging to the same little girl, who lived on Staten Island, N.Y., had clothes made from the same patterns. Height 18". *Courtesy Staten Island Historical Society.*

A SCHOENHUT DOLL'S WARDROBE

by ELIZABETH PULLAR

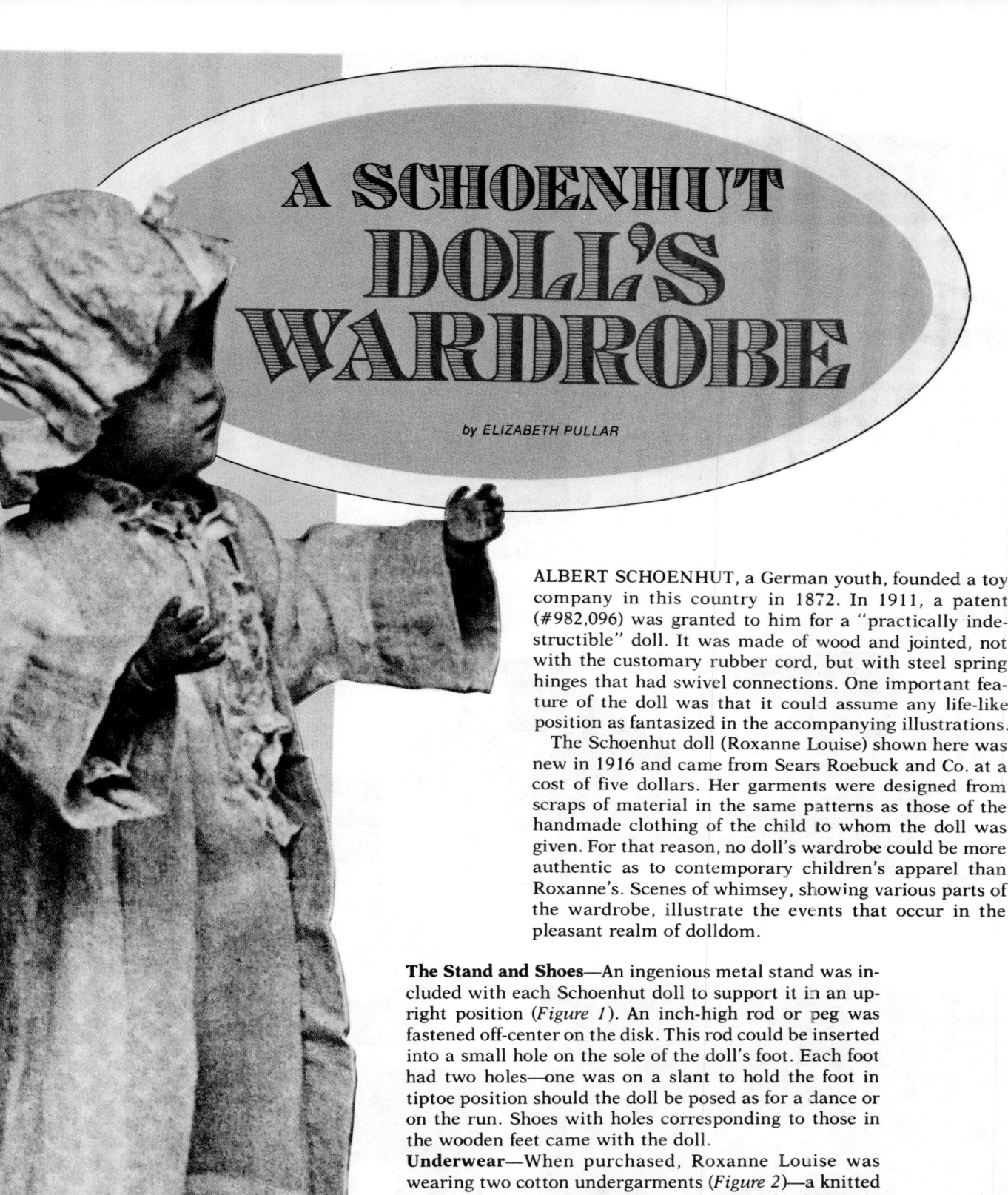

ALBERT SCHOENHUT, a German youth, founded a toy company in this country in 1872. In 1911, a patent (#982,096) was granted to him for a "practically indestructible" doll. It was made of wood and jointed, not with the customary rubber cord, but with steel spring hinges that had swivel connections. One important feature of the doll was that it could assume any life-like position as fantasized in the accompanying illustrations.

The Schoenhut doll (Roxanne Louise) shown here was new in 1916 and came from Sears Roebuck and Co. at a cost of five dollars. Her garments were designed from scraps of material in the same patterns as those of the handmade clothing of the child to whom the doll was given. For that reason, no doll's wardrobe could be more authentic as to contemporary children's apparel than Roxanne's. Scenes of whimsey, showing various parts of the wardrobe, illustrate the events that occur in the pleasant realm of dolldom.

The Stand and Shoes—An ingenious metal stand was included with each Schoenhut doll to support it in an upright position (*Figure 1*). An inch-high rod or peg was fastened off-center on the disk. This rod could be inserted into a small hole on the sole of the doll's foot. Each foot had two holes—one was on a slant to hold the foot in tiptoe position should the doll be posed as for a dance or on the run. Shoes with holes corresponding to those in the wooden feet came with the doll.

Underwear—When purchased, Roxanne Louise was wearing two cotton undergarments (*Figure 2*)—a knitted union suit trimmed with lace and a slip with ribbon ties on each shoulder. *Figure 3* shows the doll in the union suit searching through her packed trunk for the slip which has escaped notice under the table.

An Every Day Costume—Green and white checked gingham was the material used in making the doll's play dress (*Figure 4*). It consisted of three pieces—a blouse, skirt and bloomers. In *Figure 5*, the blouse is seen at the bee skep with long sleeves common to the era. *Figure 6* shows the pleated skirt hanging below the long blouse. The skirt, attached to an upper vest, hides the bloomers that in 1916 were a part of everyday dresses. Bloomers

Fig. 1: This metal stand came with Roxanne Louise as did the tie-on black leather shoes. The sole of each shoe had two holes, into one of which the prong was inserted to enable the doll to stand. The doll will remain upright with either foot supported on the rod.

Fig. 5: Right—As the doll sniffs a sprig of mint in the herb garden, her long sleeved blouse is pretty with its cross stitched embroidered belt. (Obviously Roxanne Louise is a country doll).

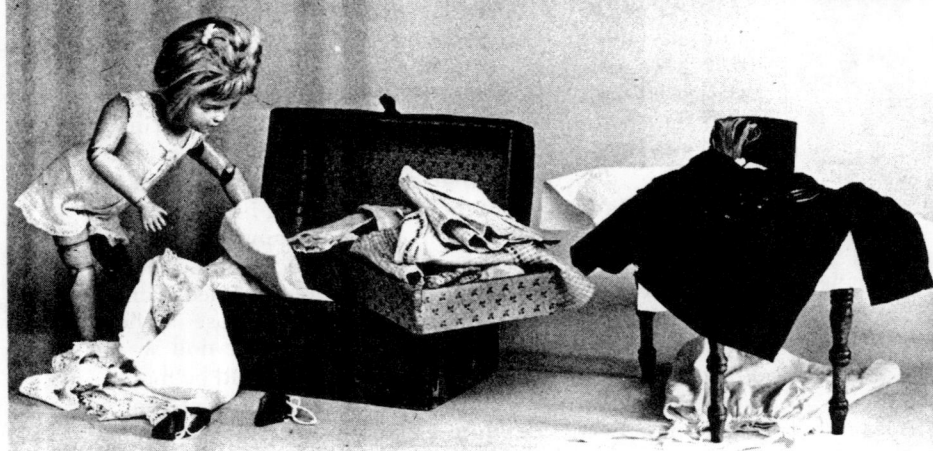

Fig. 3: Left—Roxanne Louise, wearing her union suit, is rummaging in vain through the little French trunk trying to find her slip that has fallen under the table.

Fig. 2: Below—Schoenhut dolls were sold with this lace-trimmed union suit and a sturdy cotton slip, both of which are still in good condition after sixty years of "putting on and off" by three generations of children.

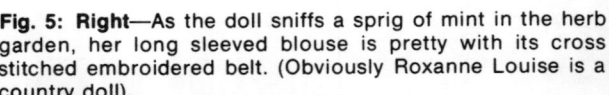

All Photos by T. Budney.

Fig. 4: A three-piece gingham outfit served as a play or school dress for children of the 1916 era.

Fig. 7: On a Fourth of July picnic, Roxanne is climbing the rocky cliff to the Top of the World. As a protection from scratches, she has pulled her bloomer legs down over her knees.

Fig. 9: **Below**—An old-time Valentine box is the feature at Roxanne's party for her friends where she is wearing her very best dress.

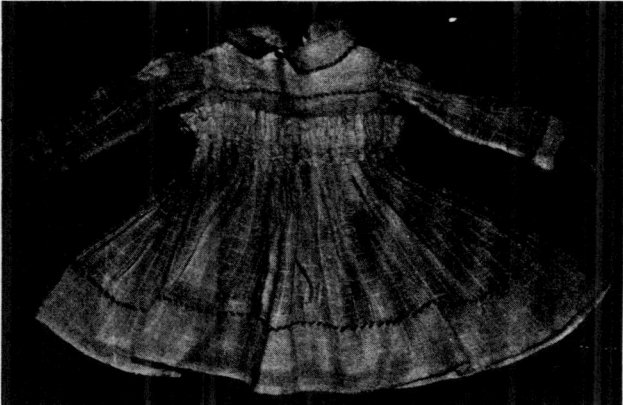

Fig. 8: The doll's party frock was of white dimity with pale blue borders.

(*Figure 7*) served to conceal lace-trimmed undies while the child hung from a trapeze, fell while running or climbed an apple tree. They were, in a way, predecessors of today's denim jeans.

Party Dress—Roxanne Louise's best dress (*Figure 8*) was a high waisted frock made of sheer white dimity. A pale blue fabric, now faded and worn, edged the hem and lower bodice and was used for the collar and cuffs. Black and white outline stitching marked the space where the blue trim met the white. A small pearl button decorated the center of the collar. The full skirt was gathered to the high bodice with rows of white smocking. In *Figure 9*, the dress is being worn at a Valentine party for Roxanne's friends.

Negligee—When Roxanne Louise was new, it was the custom for little girls to wear kimonos and boudoir caps together with dainty nightgowns (*Figure 10*). Lace and satin ribbon trim the neck and sleeves of the doll's nightgown. The kimono or dressing gown was white bordered with wide bands of pink. It fit smoothly over the nightie without buttons, snaps or ties. The boudoir cap was of pink cloth covered with white lace and trimmed with a blue bow in front. It was worn over the head in the morning before the hair had been brushed and combed. In *Figure 11*, Roxanne, dressed in her nightgown, is ready for retirement after putting her dolls to bed. On Christmas morning (*Figure 12*), when there is no time to waste on dressing, Roxanne can look fetching in her three piece negligee.

Millinery—Wearing apparel for the Schoenhut doll boasted a best hat of black satin trimmed with pink ribbon and feathers (*Figure 13*). It included, too, a cap and scarf set knit from navy yarn with red stripes. The latter set is ideal for venturing outdoors (*Figure 14*) to gather snow for making maple wax. Pure maple syrup is boiled a few minutes and then spread over a pan of snow. The syrup hardens on the cold surface to form a chewy, taffy-like confection which is enjoyed apparently by dolls as well as children.

Coat—The coat for Roxanne's outerwear (*Figure 15*) was, of course, navy blue serge, the conventional fabric for children's coats in 1916. The lining was a blue and white silk. Gold buttons adorned the front closing and cuffs. In *Figure 16*, the doll wears her best hat and the serge coat on a trip to the market stand to select her Easter baskets and plants.

Wedding Gown—Second generation children in the 1940s dressed Roxanne Louise in a wedding gown made from old linen napkins and curtains (*Figure 17*). ∎

Fig. 12: Impatient to see her tree on Christmas morning, Roxanne quickly dons her pink and white kimono with the lacy cap to hide her disheveled hair.

Fig. 16: The doll displays her feather trimmed hat and warm coat as she shops for Easter plants and baskets.

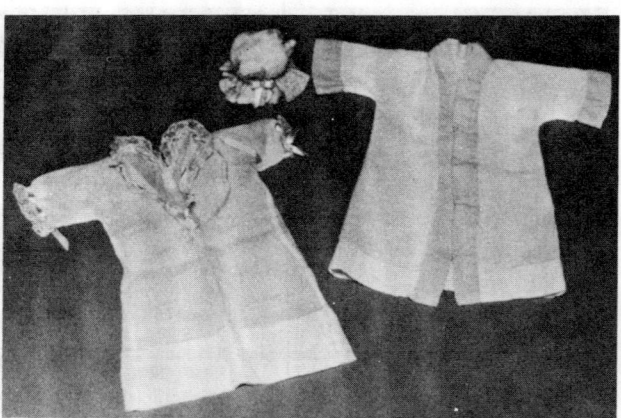

Fig. 10: During the first quarter of the century, sets of negligee for little girls comprised a kimono and boudoir cap in addition to a nightgown.

Fig. 17: Roxanne Louise is pleased to dress up as a bride. While she poses in the garden, she can hear the bluebells over her head ringing out a wedding song.

Fig. 14: The doll is warmly dressed with cap and scarf as she gathers pans of snow for making maple wax indoors.

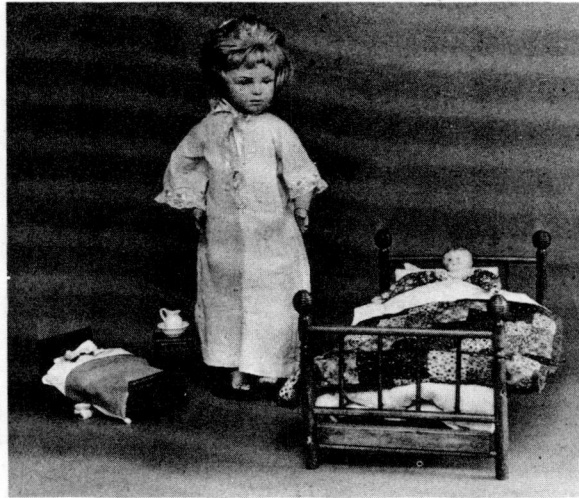

Fig. 11: Dainty lace and ribbons trim the nightgown of Roxanne Louise as she supervised bedtime for her dolls.

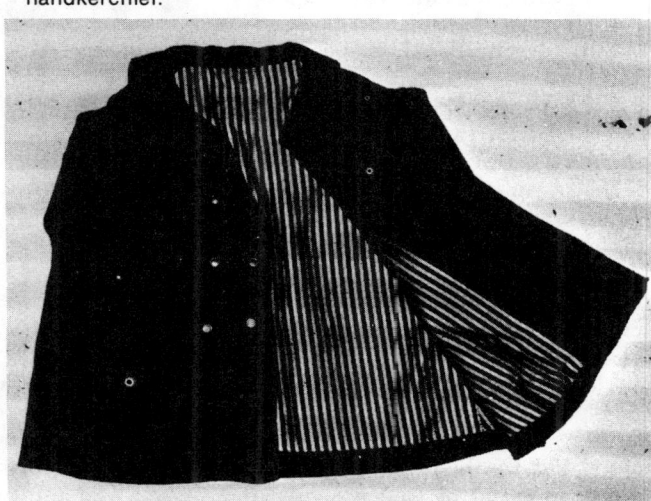

Fig. 15: Roxanne's navy blue serge coat was lined with striped silk that concealed an inside pocket for the inevitable handkerchief.

Fig. 13: Roxanne Louise's best hat was a shiny satin pillbox adorned with ribbon and feathers. The knitted wool cap and scarf set was a common combination for little girls of long ago.

Garment SAMPLERS

by DOROTHY S. and EVELYN JANE COLEMAN

ACCORDING to *Webster's Dictionary* a sampler is "A piece of fancy sewed or embroidered work done by girls for practice, an example."

There are many types of samplers but probably the most practical were the miniature clothes made by schoolgirls which taught them how to make garments that they and their families would eventually need. Fancy stitches in embroidery samplers or in knitting samplers were desirable to learn for decorative purposes and for the identification of clothes and linens, a practice followed by our ancestors. However, the knowledge of how to sew attractive and comfortable underclothes and how to knit stockings, shawls and so forth was far more useful and practical.

During the 19th century most girls' schools must have included courses in making garments as part of their curriculum. One can only guess at the pride with which the young lady took home her garment sampler to show off her skill with sewing or knitting needles. Probably there was a class competition and a certificate of merit was given for the sampler that showed the finest and best workmanship.

Some of these apparel or garment samplers have survived, but the majority have either disappeared or been used as clothes for dolls. Their miniature size made them useful for the dolly's trousseau of a younger sister or friend.

Care must be taken in the identification of garments made as samplers when found not sewed on the cardboard sheets and they must not be confused with clothes made by skilled seamstresses or commercially produced garments. Sometimes a collector today finds a single knitted

Fig. 1. Cover of the garment sewing sampler made by Edith Whiles in 1881. Page size 9¾ inches by 12 inches (24.5 cm. by 30.5 cm.).

doll-size stocking made with tiny stitches and perfect shaping that could indicate it was originally made as a sample by a schoolgirl.

Not every young girl was fortunate enough to attend a school where she could learn to become proficient in sewing and knitting. Sometimes the family lived in too remote an area and more often the family finances did not permit the luxury of an expensive school. For one shilling eight pence (about 40 cents) one could have purchased *The Ladies Knitting Book* by Miss F. G. Kelly published in Dublin without a date. This book was available "At the different book sellers and Berlin wool shops." Miss Kelly "being in the habit of teaching knitting has [explained] the various styles of knitting so much in use amongst ladies of taste....this has been the first Knitting Book published in Ireland." Among the knitted garments for which instructions were given were the following: Prudence cap or necktie, opera cap, demi (cap) and baby's cap; ermine cuffs, Russian cuffs and lace cuffs; knitted bustle; Moscow shawl, Saxe-Coburgh shawl (probably named after Saxe-Coburg, one of the Duchies of Germany and the birthplace of Prince Albert, husband of Queen Victoria), Shetland shawls, and scarfs; five patterns for muffs; nine patterns for purses; carriage shoes and baby's socks.

The inclusion of a bustle indicates that this book was probably published in the 1870s or 1880s.

Examples of the knitting directions were as follows:

Knitted Bustle

"Cast on eighty stitches with white fleecy wool and No. 6 needles. Knit forty-four rows; then with larger needles, knit one row; then knit twenty-two rows more on the No. 6 needles; cast off and draw a string through the row that you knit with the large needle."

Carriage Shoes

"No. 14 needles and four-thread fleecy wool. Cast on forty-five stitches on each of two needles, and forty-eight on the third needle, knit a round of three stitches plain and three pearled alternately; knit every round in the same manner, of three stitches plain and three pearled until you have two inches and a half knit; then join on a lighter colour and knit four rows, then three more stripes of

Fig. 2. White cotton chemise and drawers made by Edith Whiles in 1881.

four rows each alternately dark and light; then six rows light; now one row making a hole in the centre of each rib by bringing the wool forward, and knit two together; knit six rows more, and then cast off; join the commenced edges together rib to rib; plait about three threads of the wool together to make a string half a yard long for each shoe, draw it through the holes which you have made in the ribs."

In addition to the clothes in the Irish knitting book there were seven patterns for quilts, a square cushion and round pillow and "Four Receipts for Fringes." A previous owner of this book had made samples of various fancy knitting stitches which are still placed in the book by sewing them to the pertinent pages.

Heather and Clifford Bond of London found two samplers, one a garment sewing sampler and the other a garment knitting sampler. These miniature garments were mounted by sewing them onto cardboard sheets through which holes were punched and narrow pink ribbon was inserted to tie them together; thus forming books. The front covers of the two books were similarly decorated with elaborate calligraphy. The writing on the cover on the sewed garment sampler was "WESTGATE HOUSE/PETERBORO/Edith Whiles, July/81/Conducted by/Mrs. and Miss WILLOUGHBY" (*Figure 1*). The writing on the cover of the knitted-garment sampler was "Westgate House/Peterborough/Specimens of Knitting/Lillaly Whiles. July 1880" (*Figure 5*). Edith and Lillaly were probably sisters. It appears that Lillaly spelled Peterborough in the more accepted manner but the spacing of the letters in this place name may have required a shorter form by Edith.

Edith Whiles' garment sampler contains the following items:

Page 1: A white cotton nightgown trimmed with lace around the high neckline, the panel down the front, and the bottom of the sleeves. The white cotton drawers shown with the nightgown are partially slit and the long legs have three tucks. There is no lace trimming on the drawers. (See figure 2.)

Page 2: A greenish-white flannel undershirt and petticoat. The pet-

Fig. 3. Greenish-white flannel underskirt and petticoat; also a white on white embroidery strip made by Edith Whiles in 1881.

Garment SAMPLERS

Fig. 4. White cotton under-bodice and petticoat made by Edith Whiles in 1881.

Fig. 5. Cover of the knitted garment sampler made by Lillaly Whiles in 1880. Page size 9½ by 12 inches (24 cm. by 30.5 cm.).

Fig. 6. Blue fringed cape, gray mitt and a pink and white bootie made by Lillaly Whiles in 1880.

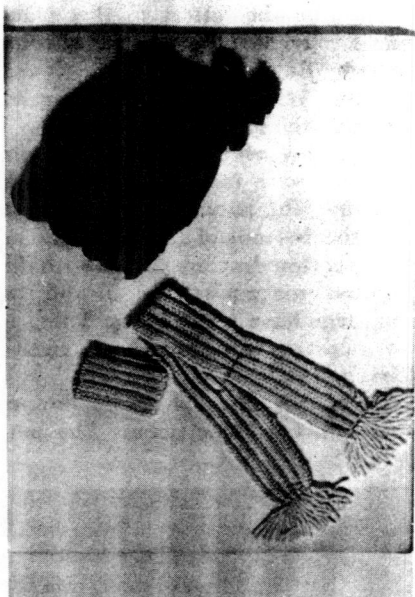

Fig. 7. Knitted red petticoat and white tippet and muff set made by Lillaly Whiles in 1880.

ticoat has a wide tuck and is scalloped around the bottom. Besides the white embroidery of the scalloped area there is a line of feather stitching above the tucks. A sample edging of white on white punch-work embroidery was also stitched to this page. (*See figure 3.*)

Page 3: A white cotton under-bodice that opens down the front with three tiny buttons. The bodice is shaped with six vertical tucks. It has a low neckline and short sleeves edged with lace. Each sleeve has two circular tucks. Below the bodice is a white cotton petticoat with four tucks and a tightly gathered waistband. There is no trimming on this garment. (*See figure 4.*)

All of the above garments have covered buttons with the exception of the flannel undershirt.

Lillaly Whiles' woolen knitted garment sampler contains the following items:

Page 1: A turquoise-blue shawl made in a square edge with a long fringe. The square is folded so that one corner extends down the back and the opposite corner forms the back point of the collar. The other two corners are folded to form the arm coverings. A gray mitt is simply a tube with a tubular thumb attached. Black bands were placed below the thumb and near the top of the mitt. A sock or bootie has a pink foot and white top with a wide cuff. White ribbon woven around the ankle is tied in front. (*See figure 6.*)

Page 2: A red petticoat has various knitting stitches with a scalloped edge at the bottom and a crocheted drawstring around the top. The drawstring has tasseled ends. A white tippet (scarf) and muff set was made with simple knitting and purling. The scarf has long fringed ends. (*See figure 7.*)

Page 3: A white ribbed undershirt has a drawstring around the neckline. The drawstring is crocheted and has tasseled ends like that on the petticoat on page two of this sampler. The short sleeves have triangular sections under the armpits. Two stockings, one in gray with a straight leg and a larger one in dark blue with a shaped leg, are also sewn to this page. (*See figure 8.*)

All of the garments mentioned so far have tiny stitches both in the sewing and in the knitting samplers. They would fit a doll that was approximately twelve to fourteen inches tall.

Research by Heather Bond has provided information about the school conducted by Mrs. Ellen Willoughby and Miss Sophia Willoughby in Peterborough. The Willoughbys came to Peterborough from London in 1862. The school moved into Westgate House in 1865 and it was later described as "a fine roomy house of the type of an old English mansion, with comfortable modern arrangements for the health, relaxation and education of pupils." A picture of Westgate shows it to have been a large two-story ivy covered house situated on a corner and surrounded on the two sides shown in the picture by trees, a garden and an iron fence. The costumes in this picture suggest a date of the 1890s and the following description of the

Fig. 8. White knitted undershirt, a dark blue and a gray knitted stocking made by Lillaly Whiles in 1880.

Fig. 9. French folder showing miniature clothes, a bed quilt, bolster and pillow cover. The stocking is knitted and the clothes have white on white embroidery. The size of this folder, when opened as shown, is 11¾ inches by 17¾ inches (30 cm. by 45 cm.).

school published in a Peterborough illustrated paper is probably from the same period:

"Miss Willoughby is very popular with her scholars and their parents, and she has sufficiently solved the difficulties of combining the ordinary strictness of school discipline with the familiarity of a kind-hearted preceptress to ensure that love of school in the minds of her proteges shall only be second to their affectionate regard for home. A sound education, including writing, arithmetic, English grammar, history, geography, needlework, etc., combined with the privileges and refinements of a cultured home, are offered on terms which will be approved by those desiring to secure such for their daughters. There are extras, for which special arrangements are made and professors engaged, French, drawing, German, music, singing, violin, calisthenics, etc., coming under this head. A Parisian and German governess resides in the house, and Miss Willoughby herself takes part in the special lessons in music and singing. Pupils are prepared for the Oxford Local, College of Preceptors, and Musical International College Examinations if required. Westgate House is not far from the Cathedral. It is situated on the higher ground above Long Causeway. The sanitary conditions are perfect, with lofty dormitories and very large class and diningrooms."

Mrs. Ellen Willoughby was Head Mistress at one time but probably had retired or died by the time this article was written. In 1896 the school was moved from Peterborough to Hastings.

Grace Dyar found a similar sampler with the garments and other items labeled in French which suggests that it was probably made by a young lady in a French school (*Figure 9*). These garments are sewed onto a folder without any information as to their origin. The styles suggest that this group might be a little earlier than those made for the English garment samplers. There are the following articles: A white cotton chemisette with feather-stitching and lace edging around the neckline and bottom of the sleeves; there is a feather-stitched band across the front of a high gathered waistline to which tie strings are attached. The garment is labeled a "Jaquette." A white cotton baby bonnet is trimmed with five parallel rows of lace edging, around the face and around the head. The back of the bonnet is outlined with a tiny cording. White silk ribbons form the ties. A larger white organdy bonnet has embroidered scallops all around the edges including the ties. The bonnet is turned back around the face and is gathered into a ruffle around the bottom. A white knitted stocking has a lacy stitch for the leg and a shaped foot. This stocking is about the same size as the dark blue British stocking but the leg part is not as long. It probably was knee-length.

A quilted silk bed set which included the bolster cover, the pillow cover, the night clothes container and the quilted coverlet comprised the rest of the items. These are all in white silk, quilted with blue thread and bound around the edges with blue and white striped silk fabric. At the corners are white silk tassels with blue trim. The night-clothes envelope is fastened with a button covered with the blue and white striped fabric. A lace edging surrounds the pillow cover as well as the bottom and sides of the white protector over the top edge of the quilt.

When one is fortunate enough to find these garment samplers they should be preserved as a part of our history and not torn apart to bedeck some doll or dolls' house. They are important for many reasons. They show period clothes in original condition. They are an example of school work a century or more ago. They illustrate the sewing and knitting skills of our ancestors. They seem to encompass considerably more than Webster's definition of a sampler indicates. ■

Doll Fashions — Plain and Fancy

Part 1

by JUDITH WHORTON

Nurse doll's costume.

Costumes for a little girl and her doll from the "Delineator," January 1878. Between 1878 and 1881 the magazine offered more than fifty patterns for doll costumes in seven sizes. The pattern prices ranged from 15¢ to 25¢ each.

Lady doll's "Reception Toilette."

JUST AS precious metals are appropriate as settings for jewels, so are authentic costumes for old dolls. The *Delineator*, a monthly magazine about American and European fashions, sold patterns for dolls in a variety that could rival the clothes of a teen-age doll of today. The patterns included outfits for all seasons and activities, some made of inexpensive materials which are still available today. The following designs are from the *Delineators* and were in resource material of the respected doll author, Genevieve Angione.

Although not difficult for the modern collector to recreate, few outfits will equal the charm of the nursemaid's uniform.

"Little dolls, like little girls, often require a nurse to go out with them when they take their airing and watch over them when they are playing house," states the December 1881 issue in which directions for the essentials of a nursemaid's uniform are described. "A nurse doll must have a plain dress, a nurse cap and apron." The dress can be made out of a print, gingham, linen or wool. The waist top has a standing collar with an optional bow for decoration. The top is fitted with bust darts and fastened by buttons. If the dress is made out of solid material the long sleeves may be decorated with striped facings. This uniform should have little trim. The skirt, which is slightly gathered at the waist, has four gores, two on the side, one front and back. On the side is a placket, or slit, to aid in dressing.

The one-piece apron can be made

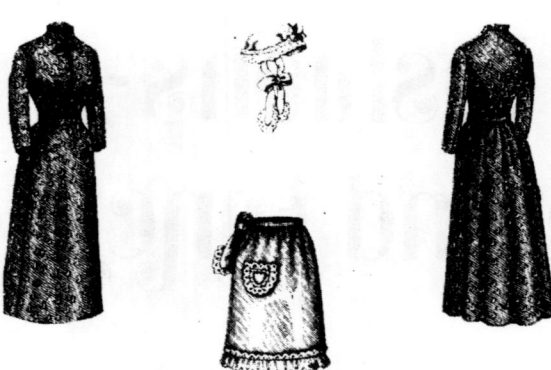  

Nurse doll's set No. 71, consisting of a dress, cap and apron.

Girl doll's set No. 60, consisting of a Princess dress.

out of any cotton goods. It is gathered at the top of the band which is long enough to tie in a large bow at the back of the dress. The "cunning" oval jacket on the side of the apron, and the hem and ends of the tie may be trimmed with narrow lace or scallops.

The cap, also cut from one piece, can be made of any thin white material, such as dotted Swiss. Tiny pleats and shirring help shape it to fit the head. It may have a narrow "standing and deeper falling frill of torchon lace" as decoration. The narrow ties are trimmed with lace. A bow made of ribbon at the front of the cap makes a nice touch.

A pattern of a Lady Doll's Reception Toilette appearing in the same issue is quite a contrast to the modest uniform. "Of all Miss Dolly's beautiful costumes, there is none more elegant . . . She wears the costume only when receiving her lady doll and gentlemen doll friends or when attending a full dress party."

Contrasting material such as white dotted swiss with blue silk or cream colored brocade with pale blue plush are suggested. The skirt is deeply shirred in back to form full puffs. There are eight rows of shirring with an inch between every two rows. The skirt beneath the puffs falls in a long square train. Two tapes are sewed under the side seams, tied together to keep the train in place. An oriental front gore is made of a contrasting material for best results. Above the slightly gathered drapery on the side are darts to insure a smooth fit. The drapery can be bordered with lace and the front end is fastened under the side panel. Box plaits (pleats) are used at the bottom of the skirt from the oriental gore to the train.

The basque or fitted top falls in double points at the center. In back the matching notches are quite deep. There is a choice of either a heart shape or square neck which can be decorated with two frills of lace, one standing and one falling. The sleeves, as in the case of those found in the ladies' evening dresses, reach only to a little below the elbow, and are finished with lace in the same manner as the neck.

Slippers, possibly of the same material as the dress, should be worn with this outfit.

One of the earliest patterns, a girl doll's night dress and cap, appeared in the January 1880 issue. Although simple it does have appeal. The sack-shaped night dress is fastened down the front with small white buttons. It is shaped by seams on the shoulders and under the arms. The collar falls in a Piccadilly style in front. Cotton edging may be used for decoration.

The cap, made of the same material as the gown, is divided in three parts, one forms the top and the others the two sides. It fits the head and neck as a close hood. The tapes are sewed to the sides to tie under the chin. The *Delineator* recommended any washable material for this costume.

In December 1880, a princess style party dress was offered for girl dolls. The dress has a long dart at each side of the front. It is fastened half way down the back with pearl buttons.

Girl doll's set No. 50, consisting of a night-dress and night-cap.

"Around the bottom of the skirt is a row of Italian lace headed by a row of Swiss and one of lace insertion; above these are another row of lace and two of insertion." A drapery with a lace border is gathered through the center under ribbons and is sloped off at the ends. The ends of the drapery are laid up in plaits and then fall in a sash style.

As in the case of the Lady's Reception Toilette, the sleeves are decorated in a similar style. The standing collar is concealed by a double ruffle. Lace insertion decorates the front.

The little girls were warned that they must sew very neatly for this dress to look well. Since these doll styles were designed for young girls to make, surely today's adult collector can make them also. ∎

Lady doll's set No. 67, consisting of a basque and trained skirt.

Doll Fashions—Sport Clothes

Part 2

by JUDITH WHORTON

Lady doll's bathing costume.

Lady doll's riding habit.

Girl doll's street costume consisting of a walking skirt and shooting jacket.

WHEN CONFRONTED with making clothes for the almost antique dolls—those slightly less than 100 years old—collectors often decide that only a party frock is suitable. As a result, dolls of the 1880s in a collection appear far too similar. Another problem many face is that the materials of the party clothes are today quite expensive. Instead of concentrating only on the elegant clothes, the *Delineator* magazine in the late 1870s and 1880s offered imaginative styles for dolls. The clothes for various activities ranged from breakfast caps and wrappers to capes for rainwear. Since the women and dolls of this era are sometimes stereotyped as leading sedate lives, the doll patterns for year-round sporting activities from skating to bathing are a delightful surprise to collectors.

The following designs are from copies of the *Delineator* in the research files of the noted doll authority, Genevieve Angione.

The lady doll's riding habit illustrated in the January 1880 *Delineator* would be an authentic yet unusual choice of costume. Any woolen or flannel material in black, navy, lighter blue, brown or dark green would be fashionable. The hat should be made of silk with a gauze veil wrapped around it. The ends fall at the back in long streamers as illustrated. The riding skirt is long and wide and caught up at one side so that "Miss Dolly can walk to horse without treading on it." The *Delineator* advises that ladies put weights–shot or lead–in the hems

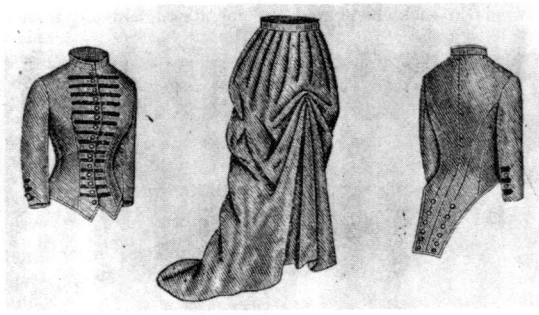

Lady doll's riding habit showing front and back of jacket and skirt.

Girl doll's walking skirt in two views, front and side.

Lady doll's bathing suit consisting of a blouse, drawers and cap.

of the skirt to keep them from flying up. "But probably dolly's habit will stay down all right if she only rides a rocking horse." The little girls are warned if dolly rides a dog or cat "she might not have any riding habit at all."

The skirt has an opening in the back with two plaits (pleats) on either side. In the front are two plaits turning backwards on each side of the center of the skirt. The belt or waistband is fastened in the back with a hook or button.

The basque top with a fitted waist has darts at the bust and is short in front with a notched or Van Dyke style. The side gores extend into long coat-tails at the back.

The coat-shaped sleeve is decorated with piping (bias trim) or rows of buttons and braids. Narrow braid is arranged between every two buttons on the front of the basque. "A little round standing collar edged with piping completes the neck very prettily."

The *Delineator* states that dolls even in ball costume "fail to look as bewitching as when dressed in a lady doll's bathing costume." It warns that only rubber or painted wood dolls's will not be spoiled by "acquatic sports," but dolls of other varieties could go through a "dry bath operation."

The wide drawers which are put on first have legs which are drawn closely about the knees by shirring made about half an inch above the bottom. The lower edges of the legs are "neatly bound with white braid." There are openings on each side at the top to aid in dressing. The front and back are closely gathered and sewed separately to bands which close at the side.

In contrast to the full legs of the drawers, the blouse is "snugly shaped." It has a high neck and is decorated with a sailor's collar. The blouse comes to the knees and has box plaits front and back. The front is closed with eleven porcelain buttons. Braid, scallops or striped bands can be used on the sash collar, sleeve and bottom of the skirt. "The effect is very pretty when white braid is used on blue or scarlet flannel, or blue or scarlet braid is used on white flannel. Serge or bunting would also be appropriate materials."

The cap is decribed as resembling a clown's with rolled brim and a tassel that falls "over the side." Tapes (tees) are sewn to the underside of the cap to hold it in place.

Sport clothing for dolls with childlike figures were not neglected. A doll with a youthful shape does not need to appear as a little girl trying to wear her elder's finery. In the December 1881 issue of *Delineator*, a 15 cent pattern described how to make a shooting jacket and walking skirt for a girl doll.

This costume can be made out of "any kind of dress goods." However, the *Delineator* advises that "shooting jackets are usually made of soft woolen material so you would not want to make your dolly's of anything more expensive."

"The jacket is first fitted very much like a basque with a dart in each side of the front and a seam at the center of the back. The front is closed by means of small hooks and loops. Then a double box plait is sewed to overlap and cover the closing. Small steel buttons are placed on the front just for decoration. The back of the jacket has the same box plait but without an opening. This gives the garment a 'loose' look that is very pretty for the house. But when Miss Dolly goes upon the street she should always wear the belt and bag which accompany it."

The bag can be made of the dress material, discarded leather gloves or silk. It is pointed at the center and each lower corner. The folding flap which can be trimmed by braid is fastened by a button. The long narrow strap loop fits over the belt before it is fastened.

The walking skirt has an apron style drapery which covers two-thirds of length of the gored skirt. The apron is cut in three tabs which can be decorated with three points of braid. The middle piece of braid is the longest. The drapery can be made of different material than the skirt for contrast. The drapery may also be trimmed with a contrasting ruffle or braid.

At last dolls can be liberated from stiff clothing to be worn only at formal occasions. A doll dressed in these charming sport clothes will attract attention even in a large collection.■

DRESSING ANTIQUE DOLLS

by DOROTHY HOLLOWAY NOELL

THE HOBBY of collecting antique dolls is growing rapidly. Because of the large number of new collectors, it is increasingly difficult to find (and afford) an all-original doll. If the original outfit is missing, and a contemporary one is not available, the next best thing is an authentic, well-made, new costume. Many patterns and books of authentic styles are available to collectors and dealers, but often there is uncertainty about authentic fabrics and trimmings.

Your choice of fabrics for your doll's outfit is a major consideration. Select them carefully. Be particular about the weight, look, feel, and fiber content.

The importance of the fabric weight cannot be overstressed. The draping ability of your material is extremely important. Styles that require gathering need material which will flow and drape well.

If you plan to use a pattern that utilizes pleating as part of the style, try to obtain a fabric which will iron into a crisp pleat, although this is not strictly necessary. Starch will help with cottons. Silk and wool may be improved with the addition of a lining which will iron well.

When using a sheer fabric on a larger doll, it is advisable to line the dress. It is a good idea to line all clothing, with the exception of miniatures, some baby doll clothing, and certain types of average weight cotton.

When lining a stiff fabric, choose a thin material. Medium-weight fabrics are generally lined with materials of slightly lighter weight. Wools should be lined with sheer silk or light-weight cotton, except when you wish to give the garment more body, i.e., collars, cuffs, hats, etc. Silks were usually lined with cottons of various weights.

Lining a costume gives it more body, is extremely authentic, and creates a neater finish on the interior.

Always consider the material's color, pattern, and weave. Make an effort to find goods which resemble the antique fabrics. Choose a fabric that looks old.

Bright, garish colors should be avoided, unless you are striving for a particular effect. When the dolls were originally marketed, the colors were bright and new-looking. However, our basic concept of an antique doll's dress is one where colors have been muted by age. Try to find unusual "off" shades of green, rose, lavender, and blue. It seems that the favorite stereotyped colors are pale pink and baby blue. Why not try to capture an effect which is different and unusual? It would be well worth the effort!

The design in the fabric you choose should depend upon the size and type of doll to be dressed. Keep the scale in mind. Use a tiny pattern rather than a larger design, if you are doubtful. Huge, splashy flower prints, large plaids, and thick stripes should be avoided. Select a design which will enhance your doll, not overpower it.

Another consideration when selecting the fabric is

Fig. 1: German bisque doll, early 1900s. Dress is of antique (ca. 1890s) blue and white striped silkaline trimmed with Val lace at the neckline and cuffs, and with two decorative buttons at the throat. Pinafore of cotton organdy trimmed at the hem with French knots and two tucks; waistline of pinafore is formed of Swiss embroidery beading through which blue silk baby ribbon has been drawn; ruffles along pinafore bodice are formed of Swiss embroidery edging; closure in back with worked loops and tiny 2-hole pearl buttons. Jacket of blue pima cotton (pima is a type of very fine broadcloth) lined with white lightweight cambric; raw edges of inside armholes are bound with silk baby ribbon; fastens in front with hooks and worked loops; the four antique carved pearl buttons are purely decorative. Handmade leather shoes have silk baby ribbon ties and rosettes. Height 14 inches. *Author's collection.*

whether the design *looks* old. Materials with wild designs, modern prints, and a generally "new" look are not suitable, because they do not resemble antique fabrics.

The weave of the fabric must be one that was in existence when your doll was manufactured. As a general rule, shun fabrics which have novel and unusual weaves, unless you are quite positive that the matieral is like that which was manufactured in your doll's era.

Modern synthetics such as polyester, rayon, and nylon should be avoided. They weren't in existence when the dolls were made. The exception might be rayon, since it was invented in the 1880s, and was known as artificial silk. Rayon did not come into common use, however, until about 1910. Artificial silk was considered a poor substitute for the real thing.

It is sometimes difficult to distinguish between natural and synthetic fibers, particularly when the two are blended. A reliable test is applying a hot iron to the fabric. If it really sticks, you can safely assume it is synthetic. The exception can be highly sized or finished cotton, which will sometimes catch slightly, but not to the degree that a synthetic will.

When testing for silk, unravel a thread from an edge and apply a lighted match. If silk, the thread will leave a small, easily crushed black bead at the end, which will have an acrid odor. Heavily weighted silks will burn, yet retain their shape. Rayon and cotton will burn like a flash, leaving no remains. Acetate rayon melts and leaves a dark bead that resembles plastic. Nylon will shrink away from fire and leave a plastic *tan* bead. With experience, you can identify real silk simply by touch.

The "feel" of your material should be soft and fine, not scratchy and rough. Again, remember the scale, and use a fabric that will give a professional finished appearance.

To aid in identification, some authentic fabrics are listed by name, (with a short definition of each) on the Fabric Chart. *(See page 12)*

Not to be forgotten are goods that were used for the underclothing. The basic five, listed in order of strength, were muslin, cambric, lawn, nainsook, and batiste. The question that comes to mind is, "How can I tell them apart?" Refer to the chart for a brief description of each.

These fabrics are sometimes hard to identify, because the quality may be confusing. As noted, a fine nainsook may resemble a coarse batiste, etc. One way to become an "expert" is to continually compare fabrics of which you are certain.

Lace, ribbon, braid, beads, sequins, embroidery, buttons, feathers, and artificial flowers are the main types of trimming. Self-fabric binding and piping are also authentic for many types of clothing.

The first lace considered for doll clothing is Val (or Valenciennes) lace from France. It is still made in the very narrow widths that are beautiful and in perfect scale for doll clothing. The quality ranges from absolutely exquisite to rather coarse.

Hand-crocheted lace was often used on baby clothing, particularly on flannel. It can also be used as adorable edging on petticoats, drawers, chemises, and cotton dresses. Hand-crocheted Irish lace is heavier, but it is good-looking and authentic, especially on collars and cuffs.

Irish Limerick would be more aptly described as embroidered net since this is what it appears to be. This type of delicate lace was often used on antique doll dresses. It can be extremely airy-looking and dainty.

Torchon lace can either be very fine, or crude and coarse. Most of the antique Torchon I have found has been of the latter type, although I have seen some that was very delicate. There are three or four different types of Torchon. Most patterns are geometric in shape; not too many are florals, or swirly, like the Val.

Honiton braids and edges are also found on antique dolls clothing. Much was made in narrow edgings, which is helpful in keeping a costume in correct proportion.

Always consider the scale of the doll's costume when selecting a lace trimming; it should be fine and lightweight.

Embroidered and eyelet trim was so widely used that it can't be ignored. Embroideries ranged in quality from

Fig. 2: Same doll as in **Fig. 1**, shown here to display the hat which is formed of buckram and wire covered with three layers of aqua-colored silk crepe de chine. Lining under brim is ruffled pure silk grosgrain moire which dates from the 1890s, as does the crepe de chine, pre-ruffled organdy trim around the brim, and ruffled net next to the ruffled organdy. Around the crown is a circlet of artificial flowers which are still obtainable today. A large aqua-colored silk satin bow adorns the lower back edge of the hat. Under garments on this doll consist of soft white lawn trimmed with Val lace, feather stitching, and French knots; closures are with buttons or hooks with worked loops.

exquisite to very crude, sloppy work. Old embroidery was often of such high quality that it can be difficult to determine if it is hand- or machine-made. You will most often find the finest embroideries on antique baby clothing, petticoats, and drawers. Lengths of unused eyelet were often saved by the thrifty housewife. Today it is not uncommon to find bits of eyelet (or lace) wrapped neatly around a piece of cardboard. It frequently turns up in a forgotten box or trunk in an attic. Embroidered eyelet edgings were gathered and sewn as ruffles on pinafores, bretelles on dresses, trimmings on sleeves, petticoats, drawers, etc. It was one of the most popular methods of trimming.

Another type of embroidery was narrow entre-deux (also known as veining). This was used when attaching a bodice to a skirt, particularly when both were gathered. Entre-deux was also used as an insertion to decorate a seam, around armholes, insertion down a sleeve, in a yoke, etc.

Ribbons of all kinds and types were used to trim a doll's costume. Refer to the Fabric Chart for a list of the most common types, with suggestions for their use.

Braid was used as decoration on sailor suits, for both boy and girl dolls. It was also used extensively on wool dresses, to outline the cut of the garment and to add needed detail. Braid usually looks best when sewn in rows, close together.

Beads and sequins were also used as decoration. Sometimes they were sewn into the center of a rosette; the type used to decorate the toes of shoes. They were also used in certain styles and periods for decoration on bodices. Beads work wonderfully well as buttons for miniature dolls, and were used in a variety of combinations as doll jewelry; strung on wire, they make dainty earrings.

Decorative buttons add an extra touch to an outfit, making it appealing to the eye. Several types were typically used on doll clothing: first, the small pearl buttons. This type can have a design carved or etched on the surface. These look especially quaint on baby dolls. Pearl buttons were also dyed different colors, which is helpful when matching the colors in an outfit.

Tiny glass buttons, often decorated with gilt are especially lovely on velvets and other rich fabrics.

Bone buttons covered with crocheting are suitable for baby dolls' clothes, certain types of cotton frocks, and sometimes wool or silk, depending upon the style and era of the clothing.

Brass buttons were very widely used, and are perhaps the most difficult to find. They must be ¼" or smaller, preferably ⅛", with a smooth, shiny surface. (Occasionally the surface was machine-engraved.) Unfortunately, they are no longer made. Dome-shaped nautical buttons are still available, but usually are unsuitable.

Jet buttons, ivory buttons, and the scarce (and expensive) handpainted porcelain buttons, are also authentic.

The size of a button is very important. A too-large button can ruin an otherwise attractive ensemble. Use tiny buttons that will add a note of piquancy to Mademoiselle Dolly's costume.

Hats, bonnets, and caps were commonly trimmed with feathers. Ostrich tips, quail feathers, pheasant feathers, aigrettes, chicken feathers, and peacock feathers were among the types used. On home-made doll clothing, a little girl would use whatever she could find. If the family

Fig. 3: China head doll, late 1870s. Dress of aqua-colored pure silk taffeta lined with cambric; bound along neckline, hem, and sleeve edges with black silk broadcloth; ruffled black Val lace under ruffle in back; top edge of ruffle bound with antique black silk velvet ribbon; black silk moire ribbon bow at lower waistline in back of doll helps to achieve a bustle effect; closure in front has fourteen worked loops and hooks. Decorative flat back black beads add the finishing touch. Under garments are of soft nainsook trimmed with Val lace, French knots, and feather stitching; closure of chemise with a drawstring neckline; petticoat and drawers fastened with tiny pearl buttons. Height 15 inches. *Collection Dr. Cecil Connelly.*

Photos by Leon Photography.

raised chickens, then of course chicken feathers were used! Sometimes a child would be even more imaginative. Here is an account in *Youth's Companion*, April 21, 1887, of: "...a white lace bonnet, with a wreath of green leaves about it, drooping gracefully at the side, being considered most stylish."

One note of caution: if you use an ostrich feather, curl it up very tightly before attaching. Since the fronds can be much too long, trim them and curl them up tightly to the spine, then curl the spine into a curved position. Spray lightly with hairspray to hold the feather in the desired shape.

Tiny, delicate artificial flowers add a lovely detail to hats and bonnets. When using flowers, choose the smallest available. Combining two or three types is charming. Flowers are basically made of either paper or fabric, and sometimes the two are combined. Be cautious when using new flowers made of fabric. Quite frequently these are made of rayon. As noted previously, it is not, in most instances, authentic to use rayon, because very little was used in antique doll costuming. Rarely, if ever, were flowers composed of it.

Nothing, of course, can take the place of exquisite hand embroidery. Feather stitching, french knots, and scalloped

Fig. 6: China head doll with elaborate hair-do. Costume of green and white striped silk taffeta; skirt trimmed with antique Val lace, antique black velvet ribbon, and very fine antique crocheted lace. Overskirt trimmed with antique black Val lace; antique black silk moire ribbon with a white picot edge, and black velvet ribbon, are made into bows at the top back edge of the overskirt. Sleeves are trimmed with black Val lace and crocheted lace. Bodice fastens down front with antique black buttons made of opaque glass. Hemline of skirt, sleeve edges and neckline are bound with antique black silk broadcloth. A beautiful antique black lace fichu crosses in the back and front where it hangs down to about hip level; this is made of the finest handmade Val lace that feels like silk. Armholes are corded with broadcloth. Under garments are made of nainsook and consist of drawers, chemise, petticoat and a corset, trimmed with tucks, Val lace and embroidery. Height 22 inches. *Collection Amy Tanaka.*

edges are perhaps the most common. Many lovely results can be achieved by combining these stitches on yokes, collars, cuffs, hemlines, and bodices. A row of feather stitching along a hemline is perhaps the most typical, and would give your costume an authentic touch. For certain periods only, it was used, not on the very early dolls, but in the late 1800s and early 1900s. Make your embroidery as dainty as possible and the finished product will more than reward you for your extra effort.

Underclothing is considerably enhanced by embroidery. Cotton dresses lend themselves to it very well. Use silk thread for wool and silk dresses. Buttonhole twist is a good substitute for silk floss, which is no longer made.

Several items were used for trimming which are very difficult to locate today. Among them are: miniature wax bridal flowers (so many of the old flowers have melted), decorative shoe buckles, real jewelry made espcially for dolls, silk millinery flowers, etc. Certain supplies for doll sewing are also scarce or non-existent: silk covered millinery wire, extremely fine thread, extremely fine needles, silk embroidery floss, minute hooks and eyes, etc. When we can't locate these items, we have to make do, but it can be quite exasperating! Who hasn't ever dreamed of walking into a sewing shop and requesting silk ribbon (a *full* selection!) or size 100 cotton thread, or size 14 needles?

In conclusion, a fabric may be suitable for one doll, but not for another. The same rule applies to lace and trimming. There are exceptions to the rule in every period in which we try to classify dolls' costumes. Generally speaking, the boundary lines for a certain period of time and its corresponding authentic fabrics, etc., are not rigid. Life was not so harried and changing as today, but more stable. Hence, a woman could wear the same "best" dress for many years; and so it was with dolls.

It is difficult to determine definite guidelines for each period. "A certain style, fabric, etc., is authentic within this period, but unheard of in any other . . ." does not apply. With some styles this may be true, but it is usually necessary to give or take a few years, unless the time span is long.

To discuss and define every type of fabric and its corresponding peak of popularity is not within the scope of this article. But it is possible to speak in general terms of the *types* of fabrics popular during certain periods.

Satins, velvets, and luxurious brocades were popular approximately 1860-1890. (Excluding Queen Anne dolls, etc.) Taffeta silk was used extensively from 1850-1880. Calico prints, tiny geometric patterned cotton, dark florals: 1840-1890. Sheer fabrics such as voile, gauze, thin cottons: early 1800-1840, and 1890-1920. Sheers, such as chiffon, china silk, batiste, crepe de Chine: 1890-1920. Wool was used in all periods. Various types white cotton: early 1800-1920; cotton was most popular during early 1800-1840 and 1890-1920.

Most laces discussed in this article were used widely from 1870 on. Embroideries were very common in the 1860s. (Machine-made eyelet had just been invented; it had been a luxury trim previously.) Braid trimming was always popular. Sequins were especially popular in the 1890s.

Feathers for hats were always used. Artificial flowers ranked second in popularity.

Colors, also, enjoyed periods of special interest. Before 1856, when aniline dyes were discovered, pale pastel colors were the most popular, although of course there were also bright colors, which did not tend to retain their true color. From the 1860s-1880s, harsh, bright colors predominated. From the 1890s on, there was an increasing trend towards pastels and white.

It is difficult to find antique fabric for doll clothing. A prime source is antique clothing, which can be cut up. Ribbons, laces, etc., are wherever you find them—estate sales, flea markets, antique stores, garage sales—and occasionally through answering an ad of a fellow collector or dealer.

Finding new fabrics which are non-synthetic and appropriate requires searching. If you look constantly, everywhere, you will accumulate a good supply. Never pass by a fabric store without checking. Designer fabric stores in the larger cities ususally stock four or five pure silks, a variety of imported 100% cotton, and a wide selection of woolens.

Costuming an antique doll will be rewarding if you start with the goal of perfection. Strive always to do your best. Patience, skill, and knowledge acquired by study, trial, and error are required, but the results are richly rewarding.

■

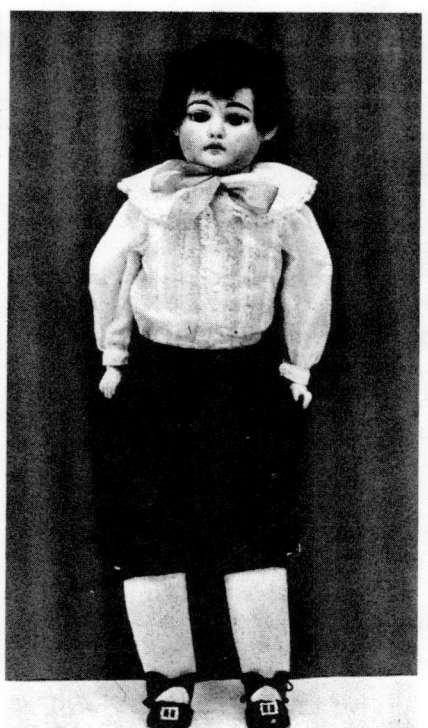

Fig. 4: Early 1900s German bisque doll with kid body and bisque hands. Blouse is formed of crisp white cotton lawn; front bodice trimmed with tucks and lace; cuffs and collar also trimmed with Val lace; front closure is a placket fastened with tiny 2-hole pearl buttons; drawstring at waist helps to achieve a slight puffy effect in the blouse. Knickers of pinstripe dark grey wool serge trimmed at knees with two brass buttons; back closure fastens with hook and worked loop, with another brass button as a decorative touch. Bow at collar is mint green soft satin ribbon of the early 1900s. Height 20 inches.

Fig. 5: Simon & Halbig bisque doll of the early 1900s. Dress of champagne-colored silk crepe-back satin from the 1920s, trimmed on sleeves and down the front of the dress with antique Irish Limerick lace; Irish Limerick lace also forms a ruffle at the neckline; wine-colored silk velvet ribbon trims sleeve edges, neckline, and gathered sash; closure in back with two antique pearl buttons. Hat is formed of antique pink silk taffeta for the ruffled brim, and antique pink silk velvet for the crown, lined with antique white silk surrah; fluffy pink ostrich feather trims front brim, and antique silk satin ribbon graces the back. Under garments on this doll are all original. Height 24 inches. *Author's Collection.*

FABRIC CHART

Cotton Fabrics
Batiste: lightweight, fine, plain weave.
Bedford Cord: resembles pique, lengthwise cords.
Broadcloth: closely woven, extremely fine, plain weave.
Calico: small flower prints, plain weave.
Cambric: woven closely, one side polished, plain weave.
Chambray: solid colored gingham, can be very fine.
Corduroy: cotton velvet with ridging in it, pinwale suitable.
Dimity: lightweight, woven stripes or plaids.
Gingham: very popular fabric, plaids, checks, stripes.
Lawn: usually white, from coarse to fine, plain weave.
Muslin: strong, slightly coarse thread, plain weave.
Nainsook: stronger than batiste, lighter than cambric.
Organdy: crisp, transparent, better grades treated to retain body.
Poplin: slightly ribbed.
Silkaline: glazed, shine lost after washing.
Pique: waffle, corded weave.
Velveteen: used extensively, various qualities.
Voile: similar to lawn, soft, sheer.

Wool Fabrics
Batiste: drapes well, fine, smooth.
Cashmere: made from hair of cashmere goat, soft, fine.
Challis: soft, always printed, plain weave.
Flannel: soft, thinner than serge, plain or twilled weave.
Merino: made from hair of Merino goat, very fine.
Serge: most common wool, plain weave.
Viyella: 50% wool, 50% cotton, prints or solids, twilled weave.

Silk Fabrics
Broadcloth: woven closely, very fine.
Chiffon: thin, sheer.
China silk: lightweight, soft, plain weave.
Crepe de Chine: lightweight, sheer, crinkly.
Faille: ribbed, soft.
Maline: thin stiff net, sticky when wet, unless chemically treated.
Moire: watered effect.
Mousseline de Soie: silk muslin.
Ottoman: heavily corded, ribs heavier than faille.
Peau de Soie: heavy, dull, lightly twilled.
Pongee: strong, slightly rough.
Satin: lustrous, shiny, smooth.
Surah: soft, shimmery, twilled.
Taffeta: crisp, closely woven, plain weave.
Tulle: silk net.
Velvet: pure silk or silk and cotton, many types and weights.

Linen
Handkerchief: very soft, for underclothing on smaller dolls.
Cambric: fine, smooth, closely woven.

The above fabrics were also made in a combination of fibers, i.e., silk and wool, wool and cotton, etc.

Fabrics for Underclothing
Muslin: strongest of all, bleached or unbleached, slightly coarse thread.
Cambric: strong, less coarse than muslin, polished on one side.
Lawn: from coarse to *extremely* fine and sheer.
Batiste: soft, thin, highest quality has mercerized thread.
Nainsook: fine, softly finished, fine nainsook is similar to coarse batiste.

Ribbons
Grosgrain: hat bands, hair bows, drawn through beading.
Silk satin: sashes, hair bows, drawn through beading, rosettes, hat bows, decorative bows on a skirt, etc.
Silk Organdy: crisp, full rosettes.
Silk baby ribbon: hair bows, shoe ties, drawn through beading, bows for underclothing, rosettes.
Velvets: hat bows, drawn through beading, stitched in rows along a hem, etc.
Colored embroidered tape: stitch down on both sides, decorative.

Bibliography and Sources:
Fabrics and How to Know Them, by Grace Goldena Denny; copyright 1923.
Fabrics, by Grace Goldena Denny; copyright 1962.
Youth's Companion, April 21, 1887.
Doll Making and Collecting, by Catherine Christopher; copyright 1971.
World Book Encyclopedia.
How to Dress an Old-Fashioned Doll, by Mary H. Morgan; copyright 1908.
Sears Roebuck Catalog (1902).
My grandmother, Dorothy Hart Evans, who answered many of my questions concerning lace and fabric.

Doll Artist Dolls

A special challenge confronts the collector of contemporary artist dolls. Unhampered by prejudice of past collectors—but also, unguided by judgements of proper critics—this collector is often alone in choosing works of art. What is a good doll? What qualities define it? How can the trendy fad be distinguished from the classic work of art? Where among the chaff lies that special gem?

The challenge is similiar to that confronting the collector of contemporary paintings. Searching the Paris or New York galleries, the collector hopes to find tomorrow's Picasso. Among thousands of ill-considered or poorly executed paintings may linger a work of art. The hope of the collector—and of course, the artist—is the discovery and public recognition of that work.

With public recognition may come new problems. Commercial success may demand sublimation of private goals. Mass production and cost accounting can diminish the original design. For the "discovered" doll artist, as with all artists, the challenge must be the proper balance between public appreciation and private achievement. The articles in this chapter, covering both newly discovered artists and commercial success stories, present this challenge well.

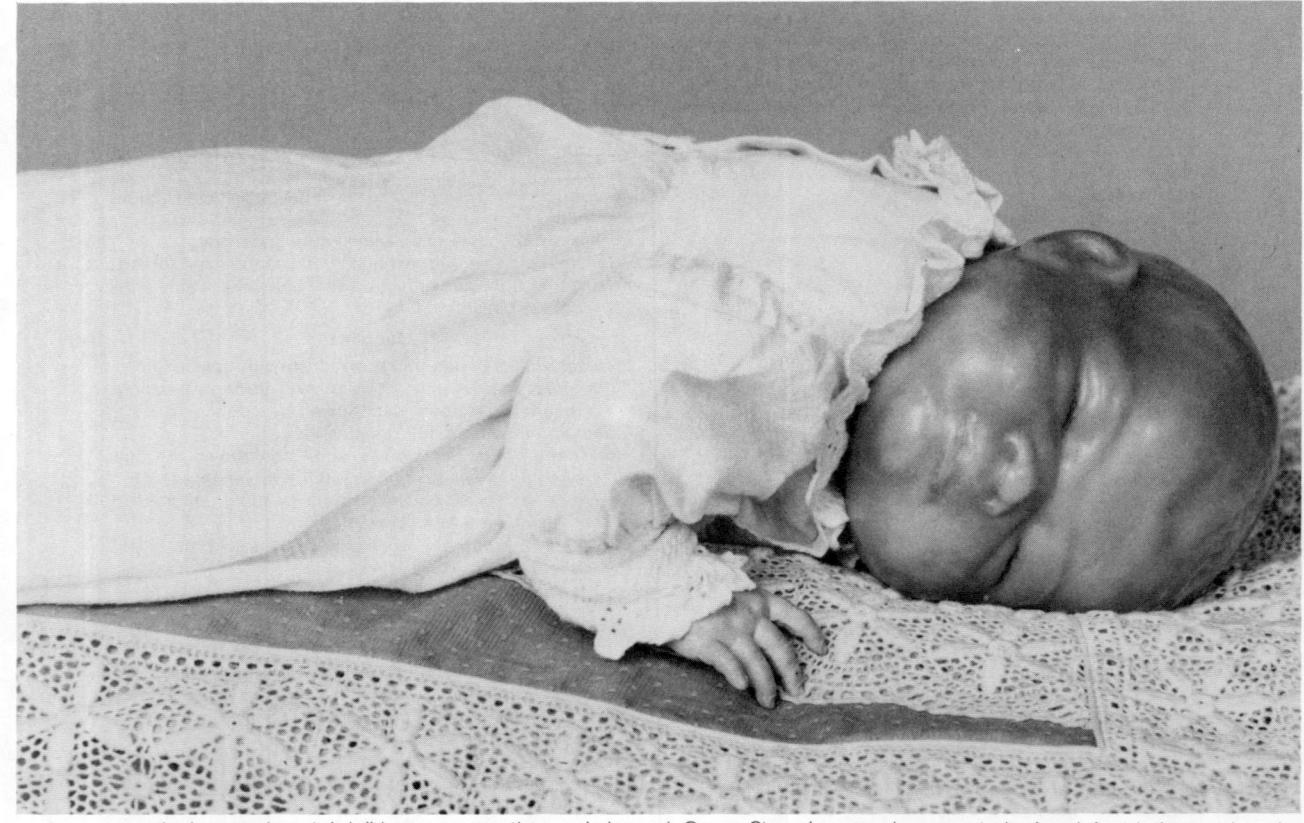

One generation's experimental doll becomes another era's legend. Grace Storey's poured wax portrait of an infant baby, produced about 1923, was a very limited edition of her popular bisque "Bye-Lo". Hauntingly lifelike, its' current value is several thousand dollars. In the 1920's it sold for a then expensive $25.

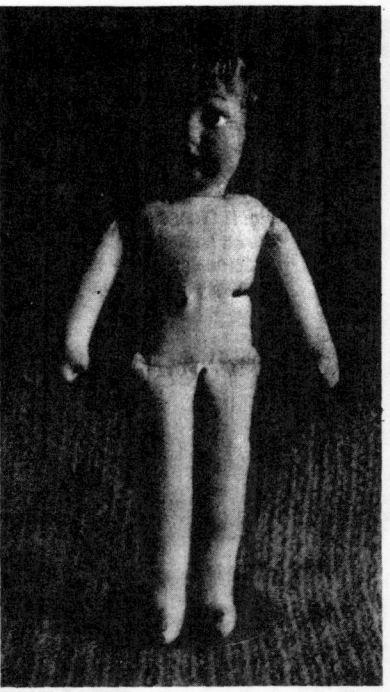

Fig. 1: David Copperfield — Unclothed to show basic body construction of the 1930s. Note the center seams in each limb, the masked face with painted-on features and blond mohair wig; 14 inches tall.

Fig. 2: Alice in Wonderland (1930) — All original with early flat face of polished cotton, yellow yarn hair. Tag reads "Alice in Wonderland/Trademark registered U.S. Patent Office/ Madame Alexander NY;" 22 inches tall.

Madame Alexander Cloth Dolls

MARSHA TRENTHAM HUNTER

COLLECTING Madame Alexander dolls for the past eight years has been a pure joy. It all began with the gift of twenty-five modern dolls given to me by my parents. The dolls had been part of a collection my parents had purchased, and only three or four were Alexander dolls. From that point on I was fascinated with Madame Alexander dolls and began collecting and researching them with diligence.

It was the gathering of information — or rather the lack of it — that lead to my book *Alexander's Rag Dolls*. Information, particularly descriptions and photographs of Alexander cloth dolls, was as difficult to find as the dolls themselves. Little was known about the cloth dolls, and company records had not been kept. A few pictures and lists of Alexander cloth dolls were found in trade advertisements. The first Alexander catalog was issued in 1942-43, and only four cloth dolls appeared in it along with twenty-one stuffed animals. But cloth dolls had been produced by the Alexander company for at least fifteen years prior to that time.

From 1930 (the year the first trademark for "Alice in Wonderland" was issued) to 1942, the Alexander Doll Company produced a variety of *continued*

Fig. 4: Little Shaver (1942) — All original with pink stockinette body and black velvet feet; pink muslin masked face with yellow floss hair; 20 inches tall.

97

Fig. 3: Posey Pet (Rabbit) — All original with white fur hands, feet and head; purple flower petal eyes; purple felt hat and plaid dress of purple and green. 1930s and 1940s; 19 inches tall.

Fig. 7: Dionne Marie (1936) — All original with pink stockinette body, felt masked face and brown human hair wig. Her pink taffeta coat was removed to show the pink organdy dress underneath. Also wears a pink taffeta bonnet and gold "Marie" necklace. All the cloth Dionnes were dressed in pink; only the necklace distinguished one from another. 24 inches tall.

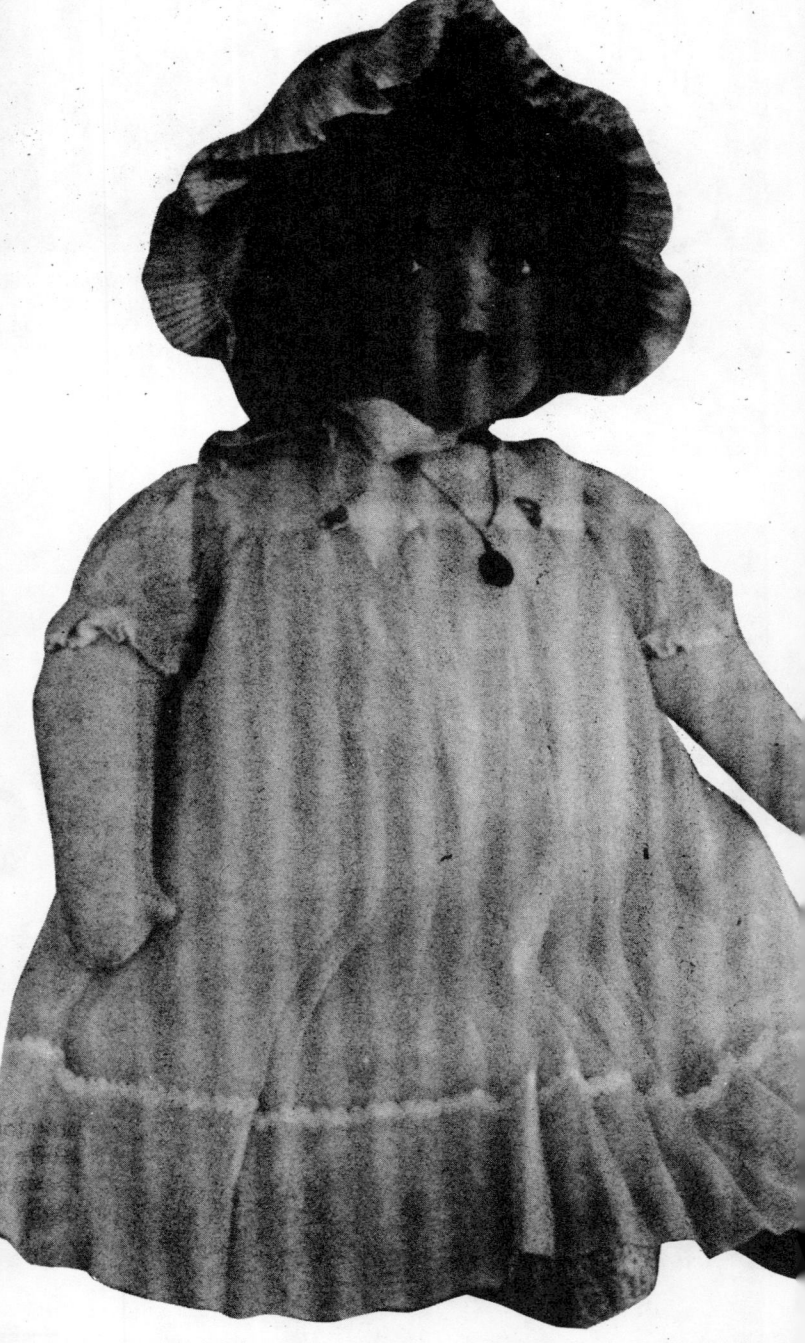

Fig. 5: Amy of the Little Women (1930) — All original with felt masked face, blond mohair, yellow flower-print dress. Tag reads "Little Women/Amy/Copyright Pending/Madame Alexander N.Y." 14 inches tall.

cloth dolls from "Little Women" to "Dickens Characters" to "Dionne Quintuplets" to a whole family of rabbits and many more.

The first basic doll body (Fig. 1) appears to have been pink cotton or muslin with separately stuffed limbs sewn to the torso. This body design was used for characters as well as animals — the only difference being the head. The first faces were flat (Fig. 2) with painted-on features. Then came the masked face — made of suede-like felt pressed over a stiff form in the shape of the face (Fig. 1). For an animal, the basic body design added a head shaped like the animal desired (Fig. 3).

At all times, Madame Alexander's "Rag Line" was top-notch.

Variations on the basic body appeared during the mid- to late 1930s. To make it possible for the cloth doll to stand, the legs were attached to the torso before stuffing and then stuffed firmly. The legs did not bend, but the doll stood. Also, printed fabrics were used for the limbs to create a stocking or clothed effect. For instance, the "Bobby-Q" and "Suzy-Q" dolls all had striped legs of blue and red respectively. Baby bodies were often made of a pink stocking fabric that made them softer to hold. The Dionnes were of pink stockinette with the felt masked face and human hair wig. The "Little Shavers" also used this body material but were firmly stuffed to stand and had black velvet feet (Fig. 4).

During the 1940s the Alexander cloth animals were constructed and dressed the same as the character dolls; only the animal head identified it as an animal. The oil skin animals of

Marsha Trentham Hunter has been collecting Madame Alexander rag dolls for more than eight years. During this time she has made a concerted effort at researching this particular type of Alexander doll. What she has learned is related in her recently published book, **Alexander's Rag Line**.

Fig. 8: French Poodle (1950s) — Grey fur with darker grey yarn hair, black button eyes with felt lids and black velvet collar; tag glued to bottom. 16 inches tall.

Top— Fig. 6: Bobby Q (1938) — All original with auburn hair, blue striped legs, pink muslin masked face. Note the black umbrella and the Fourth Grade Reader tied to the wrist. 13 inches tall. Fig. 9: Clarabelle Clown (1952) — All original with flower petal eyes, felt facial features, orange yarn hair, grey and yellow satin suit with bell on each wrist and white net ruffle collar. Note the "Clarabelle" box belt to his front and the Fashion Award Tag that cannot be seen. 15 inches tall.

the 1942-43 catalog represent the first dolls where the pattern pieces, once sewn together and stuffed, became the shape of a specific beast — such as an elephant, dog or horse. The poodles of the 1950s followed this same type of construction and were shaped like sitting French poodles.

The first Alexander cloth dolls had facial features painted on by Madame Alexander or by one of her three sisters. Most of the mouths were bowshaped; the eyes were side-glancing with a white highlight at the center of the black pupil and a red dot at the inside corners. The eyebrows were single stroke; the wigs were mohair, yarn and occasionally human hair. As the company grew and production increased, facial features became applied pieces, such as flower petals, buttons, felt pieces, lashes and heavy thread. These took less time and skill to apply. Quality, however, was not sacrificed. At all times, Madame Alexander's "Rag Line" was topnotch. ■

e Lunsford Goodnow, N.I.A.D.A., Creates—

NATIVE AMERICAN INDIAN DOLLS

by YOLANDA M. SIMONELLI

JUNE LUNSFORD GOODNOW, who considers herself a genuine "country girl," marvels that in 1976 she was invited to join the prestigious group known as the National Institute of American Doll Artists, Incorporated. A "barefoot, blue-jeaned farmer's wife with no formal art training" (as she describes herself), she spent her childhood in the sand hills of Oklahoma among farm people who "made do" with what the land could provide. Her mother used to fashion "clay babies" from the red mud found along the banks of the Washita River, and carved, modeled and stitched toys from whatever material was available, much as the early pioneers did. "With sticks, pebbles and handmade dolls, five little farm girls had a marvelous time playing in the shade of a big, old cottonwood tree."

Years later, June married a farm boy from South Dakota who took her to live in the heart of pheasant country where she became the mother of a little girl of her own. June Goodnow discovered that she, too, had artistic talent. While playing with a piece of modeling clay she created a miniature face of an elderly uncle. Thereafter, whenever farm chores allowed, she created little doll people as a pastime hobby.

In 1972, a friend suggested that Mrs. Goodnow attend the United Federation of Doll Clubs' National Convention in Omaha, Nebraska, to explore the possibility of interesting collectors in her dolls. She took along a group of dolls she dubbed "Campaign Trail," which consisted of portrait dolls representing President Nixon, Senator McGovern, Hubert Humphrey and Shirley Chisholm.

"When I viewed the marvelous creations exhibited by members of N.I.A.D.A" she said, "I decided I had a lot to learn!" However, Hilda Geuther of Eureka Springs, Arkansas, saw Mrs. Goodnow's creations, was impressed by the natural talent of this fledgling doll artist, and commissioned her to create an Indian doll for her museum.

Mrs. Geuther offered helpful ideas for costume designs, and her constructive criticism and correspondence gave Mrs. Goodnow the courage and desire to continue making new dolls, each one always a little better than the last. June Goodnow purchased several books describing and illustrating the costumes of native American Indian tribes and studied them diligently. She learned to cast plaster-of-Paris molds, fire greenware, paint features, construct bodies, do beadwork, and make doll wigs. All of her dollmaking processes were learned by trial and error. With each new process mastered, a better doll emerged because she wanted "each doll as right as possible."

The determined young artist furthered her self-education by attending local Pow Wow Indian celebrations, communicating with Indians and photographing all who would pose for her. To have suitable buckskin for her costumes, she learned tanning. Intricate floral and geometric bead designs were studied and scaled down to doll size using

"Whispering Leaves," 12 inches tall, represents a Plains pre-teen girl. She is dressed in white buckskin with leggings and moccasins decorated with tiny blue, yellow and white seed beads. She carries a three-inch leather doll dressed in a similar costume. The doll's features are outlined with beads. *Author's Collection.*

← "Sarah" represents a Kiowa woman dressed for the Anadarko, Oklahoma, Pow Wow. She is a robust Indian woman dressed in colorful beaded white buckskin moccasins trimmed with bells that reach to her knees. Her calico dress is sprinkled with tiny flowers, and she wears a beaded red and white pendant with strings of colorful beads that encircle her plump neck. Sarah's head and arms are bisque, and her body is polyester knit stuffed with fibre filling. Height 17 inches. Mrs. Goodnow modeled this doll from photographs of Agatha Bates, a Kiowa woman living in Anadarko, Oklahoma. Compare the doll's features with an actual photograph of Mrs. Bates.

tiny seed beads. Fashioning ceremonial feather warbonnets in miniature, and little clay peace pipes that actually smoked became a part of her art. Whatever costume accessories were needed, she made herself so that her dolls would be properly fitted out.

When she isn't busy being a mother, helping her husband haul bales of hay, driving a tractor, feeding cattle, caring for lambs, serving huge meals to crews of men who arrive at harvest time and cattle drives, and assisting her husband in their feed business which supplies and delivers commercial feed to dairy cow, cattle and hog farmers, she is constantly experimenting to improve her doll work and methods of production.

Her first dolls had heads and hands made of U.S. Gypsum Hydrocal, formed by using flexible rubber molds. Seeking improvements, she acquired a small kiln and switched to using plaster-of-Paris molds to make low-fire bisque doll parts which she painted with water-based acrylic paints. Her latest efforts feature fired porcelain doll parts and china paints to color facial features. The clothing and accessories for each doll are all made and designed by the artist after thoroughly researching authentic costumes.

Within a very short time, June Goodnow's concentration, study, and artistic endeavors brought recognition. In April 1973, she was awarded first place for her portrait doll of Mary Barnes, a local Sioux Indian, which she had entered in the Modern Doll Artist Competition at a U.F.D.C. Regional Doll Meeting in Lincoln, Nebraska. At the 1973 U.F.D.C. Convention, Louisville, Kentucky, her "Lame Bull" portrait doll of a Sarsi tribesman won first place in the Aspiring Doll Artist Class.

The sensitivity of Mrs. Goodnow's art was such that Mrs. Red Hawk, an eighty-four-year old Sioux Indian, shed tears upon seeing herself depicted as a doll. She offered Mrs. Goodnow one of her handmade star quilts in exchange for a portrait doll to leave to her children. This artist's strong desire to portray native American Indians, showing their pride, joy, suffering and heritage, is manifested in every portrait doll she creates.

Top: June Lunsford Goodnow is a member of the National Institute of American Doll Artists, Inc. (N.I.A.D.A.). She is shown here with her Plains grandmother and grandfather dolls and her Eskimo doll child dressed in a fur trimmed costume.

Bottom: June Lunsford Goodnow's talented hands can produce one square inch of lazy-squaw style beadwork in about one hour. She uses the tiniest seed beads available for this work.

Left: Eskimo child doll. **Right:** "Daughter of the Plains" doll.

"Mandeh Pahchu" represents a young Mandan Indian and is 17 inches tall. His fierce countenance is highlighted by red face painting and pierced ears that sport hanging bead earrings. Ermine tails and beadwork decorate his fringed white buckskin costume and hang from the back of his head. This doll was limited to an edition of thirty. *Author's Collection.*

June Goodnow takes orders for her portrait dolls, or will do special request portraits, usually giving a delivery date of about one year. Her adult dolls stand between sixteen and eighteen inches tall; children dolls are about eight inches tall. Doll bodies are usually made of a knit fabric stuffed over a wire armature.

A partial listing of Indian portrait dolls by June Goodnow includes:

Mary Barnes: A Sioux woman with full bosom and stout figure dressed in a soft buckskin dress, the yoke decorated with beads to represent elk teeth, and wearing a miniature "Hairpipe" necklace and beaded leggings and moccasins.

Napa: A Sioux man dressed as a fur trader and wearing buckskin coat, beaded moccasins and "stroud cloth" leggings decorated with simulated silver spots. His hair is dressed in Sioux style braids and scalplock with miniature feathers tied in back. Napa carries his winter's "fur catch," ready to trade.

Old Plains Indian Woman: A mature-faced woman wearing an elaborately beaded costume (illustrated).

Black Hawk: A chief and distinguished warrior of the Sauk and Fox tribes who was best known as the leader of his people during the Black Hawk War of 1832. His costume is a miniature woodsland style buckskin. "Roach" and "trade beads" adorn his ears which are pierced all around the edge. He sports a fur cape with bear claws and a finger-woven sash around his waist. Black Hawk carries a wooden "gunstock"-shaped tomahawk which was popular with woodland tribes.

Drummer of the Sioux Tribe: This doll wears an old style feather warbonnet. His hair shirt is ornamented with scalp trophies to attest to his bravery in combat. The shirt, leggings and moccasins are beaded in geometric designs typical of the Sioux tribe, and are constructed of real "brain tanned" buckskin. He holds a rawhide drum decorated with a painted buffalo effigy.

(please turn the page)

"Old Plains Indian Woman," 17 inches tall, dressed in an elaborate beaded yoke, leggings and moccasins. Her fringed white buckskin costume required approximately fifty square inches of lazy-squaw style beadwork. This doll was one of a limited edition of twenty and is now in a Florida museum's collection.

"Saltwater" represents an elderly Plains Indian dressed in a white buckskin shirt, leggings and moccasins. His colorful ceremonial feather warbonnet and shirt are trimmed with elaborate beadwork, and he carries a beaded tobacco pouch. Height 18 inches.

White Eagle—Pawnee Indian Man: The costume for this doll is a completely beaded vest, old calico shirt, beaded leggings, moccasins and breachcloth. He holds a miniature "catlinite" pipe and "strike-a-light pouch" filled with tobacco. White Eagle is seated in a wooden rocking chair.

Cuna Indian Woman: Representing a tribe from Panama's San Blas Islands, this doll is dressed in a "mola" blouse (see SW oct '75), a colorful skirt and scarf. A gold nose ring and a black stripe painted vertically from her nose to her forehead complete her image.

Papago Indian Woman: Barefoot and dressed in a long cotton dress and calico apron, this doll carries a miniature burden basket filled with basketmaking supplies.

Star: Life-size Indian baby in a beaded cradle board. (The doll comes without the cradle board which can be ordered from an Indian supply house.)

Saltwater: A wrinkled old Indian man (illustrated).

Sarah: A Kiowa Indian woman (illustrated).

Crow Woman: This doll wears an "elk teeth" dress, beaded yoke, belt, possible bag, knife case, leggings and moccasins. The many elk teeth on her dress proves she has a mighty hunter as her mate.

Susie Stockings: An elderly Eskimo woman dressed in parka, calico dress and mukluks.

She Steals the Fire: An Indian matron of the Blackfeet tribe wearing a beaded buckskin dress with old style U-shaped beading on the yoke. She wears a "white man" hat made of black felt and a necklace of glass beads set in a geometric pattern.

Mandeh Pahchu: Young Mandan Indian (illustrated).

Navajo Grandmother: She is dressed in the traditional velvet shirt, gathered skirt and leather moccasins.

Whispering Leaves: Pre-teen Plains Indian girl (illustrated).

Other portrait dolls include Chief Ouray (diplomat, statesman, warrior and recognized head of the Ute Nation) and his wife, Chipeta; Lame Bull, a Sioux tribesman; Red Cloud, Sioux chief; Sitting Bull, a Hunkpapa Sioux leader; Two Moons, a 19th century Cheyenne leader; Ben Black Elk, a modern Sioux leader; Bessie Red Hawk, an aged Sioux woman; Eskimo and Indian children (illustrated); and two character ladies, "She Smiles" and "Tattooed Susie" (illustrated). ■

Oshkosh Indian portrait doll dressed in a fringed and beaded white buckskin costume with elaborate feather and bead trimmed warbonnet.

"She Smiles" **(left)** and "Tattooed Susie" **(right)** are character Indian dolls designed and executed by June Lunsford Goodnow. "Tattooed Susie," one tooth missing and the rest worn down, wears the traditional tribal tattoo on her face.

1967–The baby called "G.W." was finished either as a boy or a girl. Photo by Bell Ceramics, Inc.

THE MANUFACTURED DOLLS
of Magge Head Kane

by HELEN BULLARD

ALTHOUGH Magge Head Kane is widely known for her handmade original dolls, others were designed to order. The complete identification and listing of all of these designs is now made available to collectors for the first time.

Commercial Designs Under Various Arrangements

Reproduction rights only: In 1954, the Mark Farmer Company of California leased the reproduction rights to a few of Kane's designs. "Adam and Ima," an early comic couple, were among them. After a short period of production and promotion during which the dolls did not sell well, Kane recalled the rights and terminated the connection with Farmer. Exact number of dolls sold is unknown.

Sale of rights to specific designs: In 1958, while designing dolls and props for their new museum in Carlos, Indiana, Kane sold the rights to about thirty of her designs to Wayne and Pauline Tharp. This was an outright sale of

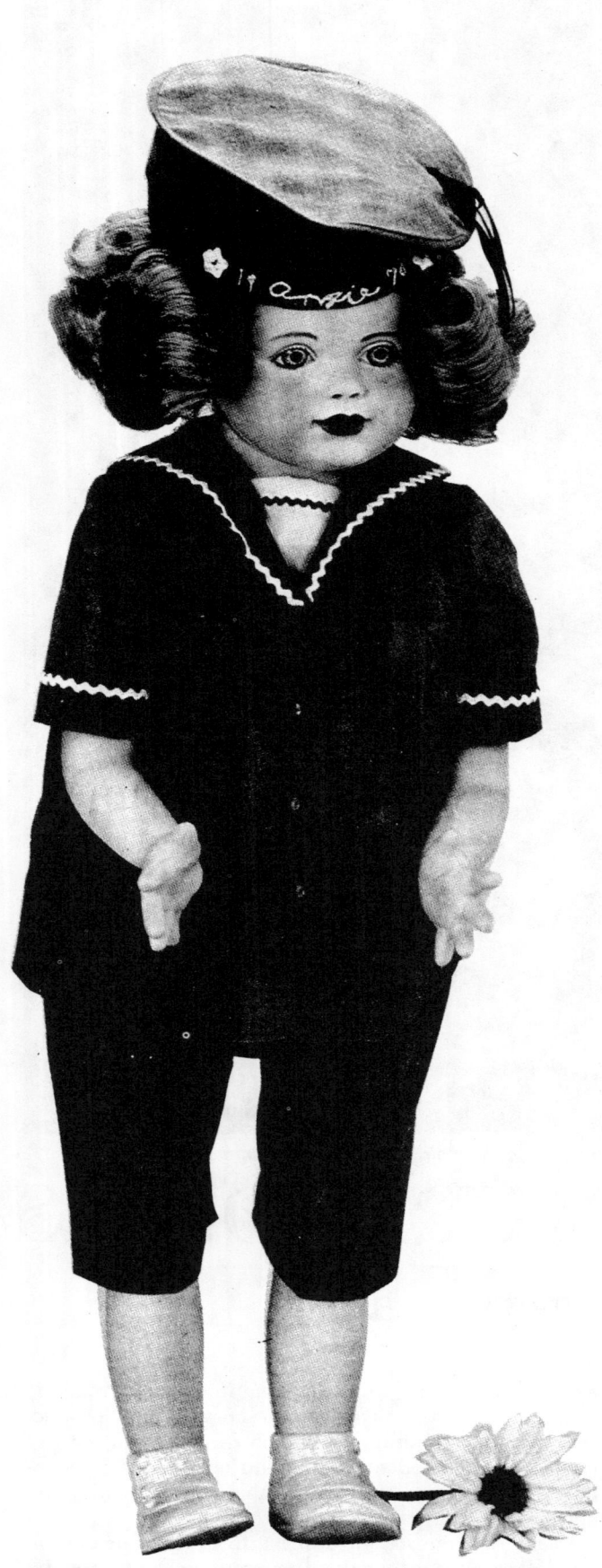

"Angie," 19 inches high, was featured in color on "Bell's Dolls" 1976 catalog. This was Magge Head Kane's last doll design for Bell Ceramics, Inc.

unrestricted rights. The Tharps have so far reproduced only a few dolls from these designs, some in several different sizes.

Molds designed for the mold market: In 1977, Magge Head Kane created three dolls to be sold on the mold market. Keith Kane, Magge's husband, is a mold maker and they wanted to try something different. The molds sold so quickly that the work of making and shipping them overwhelmed the couple. They withdrew all advertising after deciding to leave mold making on this scale to the big mold manufacturers. The three dolls are still for sale, but only in limited editions. These molds for commercial use have been identified by Mrs. Kane as:

1. "Sheila," 20¼ inches. No. HK100-HAF. Mold for head, hands and feet. Pattern for a soft body. High fashion hair style, circa 1850; legs just above knee with ballet slippers; arms to elbow with graceful fingers. Marked "©1977/Magge Head/Kane."

2. "Linda," 19¼ inches. No. HK101 HAF. Molds for head, hands and feet. Pattern for cloth body. Gibson Girl type with hair softly combed upward, gathered into a loose bun on top. Legs are just above the knee, shoes molded in high boot style with many tiny buttons, medium heel and slightly rounded toe. "The shoes are a source of pride to me," said Magge. "I enjoy creating shoes more than heads." This doll's arms are about elbow length, with nicely shaped hands. Marked "© 1977/Magge Head/Kane."

3. "Alberta," 18 inches. No. HK200 HAF. Alberta is a plump black woman made to wear a wig. Mouth open in wide smile, top teeth showing. Her elbow-length arms have plump hands; feet have black strap slippers with low heels. Legs are below knee length. Body pattern is included and is correct for a figure which is not skinny. Marked "© 1977/Magge Head/Kane."

All three molds were priced at $125.00 postpaid (for three). Kane personally made twelve reproductions from the original Alberta mold and sold them to collectors. These dolls were 21 inches tall. The purchasers were told that the smaller size Alberta was on the mold market. It did not seem to matter to them at all. She then made one sample from each of the three commercial molds and used them to demonstrate the dressed dolls. These samples remain in her prototype collection.

In 1967, Kane began working as a designer of dolls for Bell Ceramics, Incorporated, a firm dealing in porcelain, molds and paints. Bell has more than 140 distributors throughout the United States, Canada, Central and South America, and Australia. The company has expanded as interest in hobby ceramics has grown, promoting acceptance of its products through audio-visual devices and traveling teachers who demonstrate how molds are used. Its molds are used by commercial ceramicists who market heads or complete dolls.

Under contract with Bell from 1964 to 1976, Magge still receives a royalty check every month, and will continue to receive them as long as the molds from her designs are being sold.

In order to copyright all of these designs, Magge had to mark them with her name (at first Magge Head, latter Magge Head Kane) and the copyright sign, just as she must do for her original dolls which she makes herself and sells to collectors. This has led to some confusion which is hard to clear up, although she has tried to do so through articles in doll and ceramic magazines. More and more dolls are now showing up with the repro-

1967—Left to right: Nick, Nick as a girl, and Jake. All have the same body. *Photo by Bell Ceramics, Inc.*

ducer's name incised below the Magge Head Kane copyright mark. The first designs commissioned by Bell were:

1967. G.W., a baby, 16 inches. Mold No. 648. Jointed head, hands and feet on a ceramic body. Used as either a boy or a girl. In Bell's advertisement the baby has an open mouth, large eyes, and short modeled-on hair with a bang falling in a long strand to just above the nose. Those who own and use the mold have sometimes applied wigs of real hair, or carved two little teeth in the mouth. Others make no changes.

1967. Santa Claus, 17 inches. Mold No. 601. Jointed arms and legs with boots modeled on the feet. Jointed at the shoulders with modeled-on gloved hands. Hips and knees jointed for sitting. Large ceramic chair was made for him, 18 inches high.

1967. Mrs. Claus, 17 inches. Mold No. 663. Jointed like Santa, Mrs. Claus had upswept hair ending in a bun on top. Plump smiling face. Hands appear to be sewing.

1967. Jake, 12½ inches. Mold No. 698. Ceramic body with arms joined to shoulders, legs jointed at the hips, and head attached to the body by a socket. All parts are ceramic. The doll has bare feet and a straw hat modeled on his head. Nick, a 12½ inch black boy with bald head and four teeth showing in his wide smile, has the same ceramic body as Jake. One mold number is used for both dolls. Heads for both Jake and Nick were created by Magge to be placed on cloth bodies, with arms modeled to elbow, and legs to knee. Nick, known as "Lil Nickodemus," was created in 1957. Jake's head, originally created for one of "Kane's Rebels," was designed in 1963.

The only changes made in these two heads were the removal of the shoulder plates and the addition of neck parts which would fit into the ceramic body of the Bell doll. This was done because sometimes there is as much as 18% shrinkage in porcelain when it is fired, and a bit less shrinkage when an item is poured in low-fired ceramic liquid clays. As the clay dries, the water evaporates and the piece gets even smaller when it is fired. Shrinkage thus becomes a prime clue to identification. The original doll in this case is 15 inches tall; those cast by ceramicists from the Bell molds are 12½ inches tall. This difference alone is enough to distinguish the original from the commercial mold dolls. Also, Magge's dolls have always been made with soft cloth bodies, while the commercial dolls have ceramic bodies. "I can state for the record," says Mrs. Kane, "that I have never made dolls from Bell molds and sold them. I do, however, have a sample which I cast for my own collection of commercial dolls made from my designs."

1971. Pearl, 11 inches. Mold No. 980. Black pre-teen girl with a jointed ceramic body, arms jointed at the shoulders, legs jointed at the hips. The head fits into a neck which is modeled on the body; head moves several ways; definite black features. Short hair, modeled with center part and curled ends. Feet are modeled with ballet slippers.

1971. Becky, 11 inches. Molds No's. 581 and 973. Becky has the same body and arms as Pearl. Her shoes are high-buttoned on long legs joined at the hips. This doll head was taken from a mold of the Becky which Bell sold as part of a Mark Twain series. The shoulder plate was removed to enable the neck to fit into the ceramic body. The first Becky had a soft body, legs to the knee, and arms to the elbow. Both have long curly hair falling from beneath a modeled-on fancy straw hat which is decoated with a bow on top of the brim, and bows on the underside of the brim near the hair. A ribbon from these bows is tied under the chin. In its original mold, this doll was about 17 inches tall. Magge called her "Margaret Ann" and made twelve of them, keeping two for her own collection.

1972. Mark Twain, 18 inches. Mold No. 972. Modeled to represent the character of that name, it has a soft body with hands modeled to the wrist, legs to below the knee. "From the original molds," states Magge, "I personally made six dolls and kept two. They measured about 20 inches. No more will be made from this mold. I have no sample from the Bell mold."

1972. Sidney, 13 inches. Mold No. 975. Long boyish-bob hair style with bangs. He is used in the mark Twain series. Arms are elbow-length, legs below the knee with slipper-type shoes. Cloth body patterns were designed by Magge and sold by Bell.

1972. Aunt Polly, 18 inches. Mold No. 977. This larger size made from Bell's Mrs. Claus, designed by Magge Kane. Head is designed for cloth body; arms to elbow, and legs just below the knee.

1972. Garett, 9 inches. Mold No. 947. This laughing baby wears modeled-on mittens and modeled-on winter cap; legs are above the knee and shoes are ankle-high.

1972. Judge Thatcher, 18 inches. Mold No. 976. Made with shoulders to fit a cloth body. Arms are wrist length, legs below the knee. Hobbyists have used him in the Twain series as well as costuming him as part of a bicentennial scene for Bell advertisements.

1972. Miss Nanny, 18 inches. Mold No. 978. Elderly black woman with cloth body, arms to elbow, legs to below the knee. Made to wear a wig. Mouth open, as if

Magge Head Kane's commercial work for Bell Ceramics, Incorporated, included this group of Mark Twain characters: Top, left to right—Aunt Polly and Judge Thatcher. Middle row—Becky, Mark Twain, and Injun Joe. Bottom row—Sidney, Tom Sawyer, and Huck Finn. Photo by Bell Ceramics, Inc.

singing. Pictured in Bell's catalog holding a tiny baby which Magge Kane designed early in her contract with Bell. Baby is 4½ inches, and made from *Mold No. 253.* Head and body are molded together. Arms and legs are joined at shoulders and hips.

1974. Huck Finn, 13½ inches. Molds No. 992. Cloth body, bare legs to knees, arms to elbow; mouth puckered in a whistle and hair a ragged long tangle.

1974. Tom Sawyer, 13½ inches. Mold No. 991. Cloth body with same type limbs as Huck Finn doll. Hair is molded in a wind-blown style, mouth open in a wide grin with top teeth showing.

1975. Angie, 19 inches. Mold No. 2087. A toddler with a sweet, plump face; wears a wig; arms to elbow; feet with modeled baby shoes, one of which is turned inward. Shoes have four buttons and ceramic legs go to just above the knee. Angie is on Bell's 1976 catalog cover in color. This is Kane's last design for Bell to date.

Figurines Designed For Bell Ceramics, Inc.

These figurines, especially designed for Bell Ceramics, Inc., were made into plaster molds and sold to distributors of ceramic supplies.

1964. Ivan Aufulitch, 8 inches. Mold No. 611. A scarecrow, and part of a group of pixies designed from drawings in Magge Head's book *They're Pixies* (1963). A figurine in ragged overalls, patched shirt and hat with bird on top. Tic tac toe marks on nose.

1964. Ivan the Clown, 8 inches. Mold No. 611. Same as above in clown suit.

1964. Four Pixies, 8 inches. Molds No. 616 and 614A. Alvin, Gertrudy and Mabel with distinctive hair; Starwinkle is a black baby with curl on top of head. All four have the same arms and bodies, with legs modeled as part of the body. These heads are also used on another body, which is modeled with realistic arms and legs and jointed to resemble a doll.

Another modification of these figures includes the following:

Starwinkle, Mold No. 612. Dressed in bra and bikini with a morning glory blossom for a hat.

Rinkle. Mold No. 615-626. Santa's mailman, asleep, leaning on his mail pouch.

Jeanmarlyn. Seated figure with legs dangling, hair combed down from a topknot, jacket modeled on, pixie shoes.

Squidgen. Molds No. 623 and 624. Seated figure wearing pixie jacket and shoes, and painting a large leaf on her lap.

Q-Ball Charlie. Standing figure with bald head, bossy, wide open mouth.

1968. Funny Bunnies. All of these figures have the same faces as three of the pixies: *Alvin, 12 inches. Mold No. 693.* Kneeling figure dressed in bunny suit, holding hands to ears. *Gertrudy, 10 inches. Mold No. 692.* Figure dressed in bunny suit, smiling face, squatting, with right hand on knee. *Mabel, 8 inches. Mold No. 694.* Figure dressed in bunny suit, crawling, face in a pout. These three bunnies are looking down into a cracked egg at a crying and a sleeping bunny, each of which is 3 inches long. *Mold No. 689 (egg) and 690 and 691 (bunnies).*

Other Figures from "They're Pixies!"

P. U. Winkle, 6 inches. Mold No. 627. Little skunk wearing hat and jacket.

Myrtle, the turtle, 10 inches. Mold No. 633H and 633. Dressed in hat and fancy collar.

Buzzaz, the bee, 4 inches. Mold No. 625. A smart, lazy-looking fellow smoking a cigar as he lies on his back. He wears a visored cap, swallow-tail coat and spats.

The Singing Mice (three), 3 inches. Mold No. 966. Oscar, Ollie and Oly have no moving parts, very large ears, fat bellies, skinny legs and open mouths. Oscar wears white tie and tails; Ollie is dressed in a ski sweater; and Oly wears overalls. Six hats were created for this group. The three mice were a part of a scene entitled "Sing along with Santa."

Santa, 7 inches. This figure is sitting at a colorful piano, directing the singing mice.

New designs for "Sing along with Santa." Molds No. 925 and 925A.

Brandon, 8 inches. Mold No. 924. Toddler dressed in a snow suit, long scarf.

Mabel, 8¼ inches. Mold No. 955. Figure kneeling to pray, holding a rag doll in her arms.

Santa riding a hobby horse,? inches, Mold No. 961.

Alvin's Rag Tag Band (four figures), 10 inches. Mold No. 923. Alvin, directing the band, wears stocking cap with long tassel, big jacket laced in front, and round-toed boots.

Monkey, 10 inches. Dressed in ragged clothes and cap, and carrying a drum.

Mouse, 10 inches. Large ears, mouth open to toot horn.

Owl, 10 inches. Wearing leather jacket with fringe on sleeves.

Doll Museum in England

by DIANE HARTLAP

Mrs. Vera Kramer with her "Secret Comfort" doll, a French bisque, marked "A. Marque."

AT THE DOLLS of Wonderland Museum, located in Kings Road in Brighton, one of England's most famous watering places, more than 500 dolls of all sizes and types are displayed in eye-level settings based on well-loved children's stories and nursery rhymes.

Vera Kramer, director and owner, was from a large family of children to whom toys were a luxury. She was eight years old when she was given her first "boughten" doll. She called it her "Secret Comfort" and did her best to keep it hidden from prying brothers and sisters. But alas, a brother found the hiding place, and in the ensuing tug-of-war, the doll was completely demolished.

She never forgot her treasure, and in grown-up years she began to search for a doll that resembled her Secret Comfort. She found it eventually, a French bisque, marked "A Marque," but by that time she had become a dedicated doll collector. The museum, which she opened in 1973, is her way of sharing her collection with children and adults alike.

Some of the dolls in the 56 tableaux are rare, others more common. Bisques, both French and German, are in abundance, but there are wooden and wax dolls, too, and an occasional composition. Each doll wears a clearly visible number; a corresponding number in a printed catalog gives its full description. Dolls not retained by the museum are offered for sale.

Alice in Wonderland is a Simon Halbig 1079, ca. 1900; her friend with book, a long faced Jumeau.

Left to right: Pinocchio, by Knickerbocker Toy Co., U.S.A. composition, ca. 1955; poured wax head portrait-type, shoulder plate, English, ca. 1880; French SFBJ 225, character, ca. 1908, original boy's dress.

Little Jack Horner, SFEJ 252, character type, French, ca. 1910.

CONTEMPORARY JAPANESE DOLL ARTISTS

by HELEN BULLARD

An original carved wooden doll dressed in fabrics by Mr. Goyo Hirata, Japan's most important doll artist. Mr. Hirata is a "Living National Treasure" in his own country. His child dolls are incomparable interpretations of quiet play or gleeful antics.

Editor's note: Helen Bullard and Miyoko Ishikawa have corresponded about Japanese dolls for two years while planning a meeting of Japanese and American doll artists in Tokyo last September 1978. (See *Observations*, page 2, SW September 1978.) Unfortunately, unexpected problems caused a cancellation of this meeting. What follows is a brief report on the contemporary doll artists of Japan compiled from Mrs. Bullard's notes and exchange of letters with Miss Ishikawa.

A modelled porcelain doll made by artists of the Hakata District in Japan. These are considered production dolls and not on a par with the carved or sculpted originals.

JAPANESE DOLLS are as varied, one from another, as the American or German dolls with which we are more familiar. They are elegant original creations of artists, expertly cast replicas of excellent or less distinguished designs produced in small factories or—more often—in small cottage-industry type operations, and an endless number of figures produced in many different materials. Until the author's friend, Miyoko Ishikawa of Tokyo, Japan, sent her a recently published catalog of dolls, she had no idea how vast the doll business was in Japan.

This 190-page catalog (book is published by the KODANSHA, as a part of their LIFE CULTURE SERIES.) is sold in bookstores—and quickly sold out, necessitating additional printings. An average page measuring nine by twelve inches has from five to ten photographs of dolls, most of them in color. The works of leading doll artists are featured, as well as many regional dolls made in only one area of the country, and an endless variety of play dolls and production dolls. Also illustrated are many splendid photographs of Brus and other important antique dolls. Miss Ishikawa informed us that many of the Japanese people who travel abroad are big buyers of antique dolls in Paris.

A pair of wooden dolls with kimekomi fabric costumes carved by Mrs. Eiko Serikawa, a famous Japanese doll artist and a student of Mr. Goyo Hirata.

This unfinished carved wooden doll made by Miss Miyoko Ishikawa will eventually be dressed in a black kimono decorated with appliques of the embroidered butterflies shown to the left of the model. The doll portrays her niece, aged five years, playing the part of a boy Kabuki dancer named "Goro."

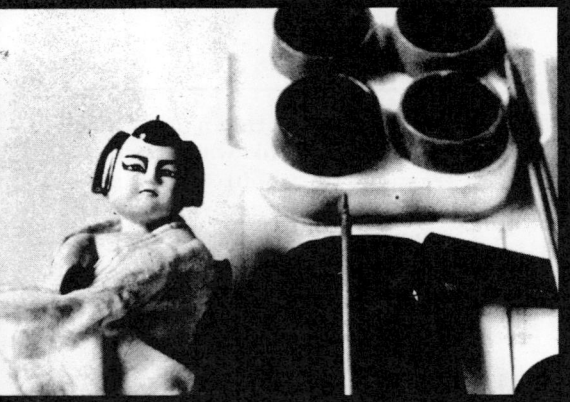

"Goro" receiving his final paint job.

"Goro" ready to be dressed in his costume.

"Goro" completed by Miyoko Ishikawa in 1979 stands 8½ inches high.

Front and back view of a "Sakura" doll in fabric costume made by Miss Miyoko Ishikawa, a student of Mrs. Serikawa. Sakura dolls are formed out of excelsior and wire with a cloth covering. The body and limbs are bent into form.

Scarcely distinguishable from the antique dolls are the growing number of fine reproductions. The long experience of the Japanese in casting porcelain and other materials makes possible the most accurate reproductions.

In Japan, dolls included in the top echelon are original creations painstakingly made by hand (no two are alike), and either carved from wood or sculpted, using a wood base (wood particles mixed with paste) or a paper base (papier mâché). Some dolls are carved or sculpted in the final image, then finished with a covering of fabric, rice paper, or paint. ("Kimekomi" is the term used to describe dolls finished with fabrics.) The mode of these figures varies from realism to greatly simplified artistry. The early dolls of all artists tend to be realistic. Porcelain, clay and other cast dolls are considered production dolls.

The earliest doll artists' organiza-

"Girl with Bean Bag" by Mrs. Serikawa. Made of carved wood and dressed in various fabrics, it stands 6½ inches tall.

"Oomi No O-Kane" in the rough stages of being carved, and before her Kimekomi fabric costume has been glued to the body.

"Oomi No O-Kane" completely costumed in the Kimekomi style by Miyoko Ishikawa in 1978. Height 9½ inches.

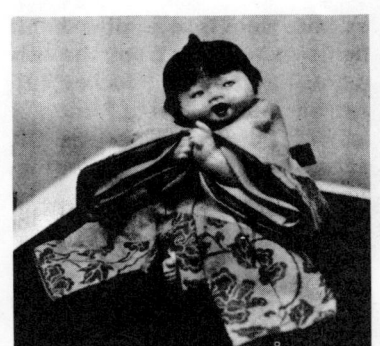
A child doll carved and costumed by Mr. Hirata. Note the expressive hands and toes.

tion, called *Hakutaku-kai* (a group of dollmakers), was organized in 1928 for the purpose of studying and creating original dolls and exhibiting them. The members did some commercial dollmaking until about 1935 when the group was dissolved. The new Japanese Doll Association which was then set up, devoted its efforts to the study and development of artistic dolls. The *Teiten*, the leading art exhibit in Japan, was being reorganized at this time and the Japanese Doll Association made a concerted effort to have artists' dolls included in the exhibit. Six doll artists were successful in having their dolls accepted for this exhibition, including Mr. Goyo Hirata, who was soon recognized as Japan's number one doll artist. Doll artists grew steadily in importance after this exhibition. The lively controversy between dolls realistic and dolls artistic has continued to rage ever since.

Leading artists and one-man shows, and a new organization known as the Doll Art Institute followed. In 1948, the *Nitten*, a national art show with awards for excellence, accepted dolls, and became an important showcase for artists' dolls. The comments of a noted doll critic and collector can bring serious criticism to the field of artists' dolls, and commands the attention of art collectors.

At present the leading artists exhibit with the Japanese Arts & Crafts Association whose annual exhibition—a very prestigious one—is held every autumn in Tokyo. The dates vary from year to year, but travel agents can supply the dates on request. Americans interested in dolls will find this exhibition not only rewarding but amazing as well.

The acceptance of dollmaking as a serious expression of Japanese culture has long been firmly established, and doll artists receive public recognition of their works. ■

"Kamuro" (a hand maiden to a courtesan), a carved wooden doll made and costumed by Miyoko Ishikawa in 1975. height 7¾ inches.

Hand-Carved Wooden Dolls
~From Early Times

by HELEN BULLARD

HAND-CARVED WOODEN dolls may not have been the first dolls to be made, but they had survival qualities greater than cloth, wax, or any other simple material except clay. The oldest known dolls, which were probably votive objects, were clay and date around 2500 B.C.

Encountered nowadays in posh exhibitions of antique dolls, the "Queen Anne-type" woodens are the earliest type of dressed wooden doll which appears in modern collections. They are also known as "Queen Anne-Georgians" because they were made in both those English periods, from about 1690 to 1740. Each differed from all others in details.

With a knife and a few pieces of wood a creative and skillful carver can produce practically anything he has in mind; of that the distance between funny old "Aunt Thirza Cantrell," a country doll carved by a hunter for his little girl, and the earlier Queen Anne lovelies is proof enough. "Aunt Thirza" may not be elegant, but she has worlds more personality than the elegantes.

"Queen Anne" dolls were all wood, hand-carved, with human hair wigs, extra fancy court costumes, and rather vacant expressions. A surprising number of them exist. Probably because of their expensive, "worth-saving" costumes, they were cared for, passed down to heirs, and finally sold to collectors or, as with those in the photographs here, given to the Victoria and Albert Museum in London.

Another very old wooden, now preserved in the museum at Salisbury, England, is not a Queen Anne-type, but a French doll which Queen Marie Antoinette dressed while she was in prison in 1793.

Penny woodens were produced by the tens of thousands in many sizes and were very cheap. Also called "Dutch," a

Group of penny woodens celebrating May Day.

corruption of "Deutsch," they were made in cottage industries in Germany's Black Forest during the 15th to the 19th centuries, with whole families working on dolls. Of simple construction, they were jointed and fastened together with wooden pegs. Faces were flattish with sharp little carved noses protruding from the simple round faces. Hands were spoon-type; legs were usually sticks, sometimes with slippers indicated on a slightly swelled stick-end by painting. Later bodies, legs, and arms were lathe-turned. The dolls in Queen Victoria's famous collection, which she is said to have costumed when she was a very young girl, are penny woodens.

The pattern of the penny wooden varied little over the centuries. Modern copies were produced for a time in England, and good reproductions were made in this country by the House of Seven Gables in Marblehead, Mass. Few American hand-carved dolls owe anything to these penny woodens except for the jointing, which is so simple and functional that almost anyone could have figured it out.

The earliest hand-carved wooden doll in the collection of water color renderings in the Index of American Design, located in the National Gallery of Art, Washington, D.C., is a ball-jointed wooden with over-large head and hands, and fat legs, whose date of 1800 is unverifiable. The carved wooden heads of a Cree Indian pair, also from the Index, are artistically stylized, especially that of the man.

"Queen Anne" woodens. The smallest is 12", tallest, at far right, 24". 1690-1800.

Wooden doll (not Queen Anne type), dressed by Queen Marie Antoinette while in prison in Paris in 1793.

"Aunt Thirza Cantrell" ("Old Bullet Eyes"), carved by a hunter for his daughter, is a real country doll.

An 1800 American wooden, 16" tall; owned by the Society for the Preservation of New England Antiquities.

"School for Scandal" detail. The hair on the oversize head is human, dressed with flowers made of velvet, beadwork, pearls, shells, wax berries, etc.

Penny wooden doll, English, early 19th century, costumed as an English peddler by Mrs. Clive S. Hinckley.

"School for Scandal" dolls, made completely of wood with jointed arms and legs; hands crudely carved where visible, with leather gloves. Tallest is 23". Late 17th and early 18th centuries.

Cree Indian dolls have carved heads and stuffed fabric bodies. Designed and made by Marie Rose of the Montana Cree Reservation late in the 19th century. 10" tall. Now at the Wenham (Mass.) Historical Society.

Hand-Carved Wooden Dolls

Part Two - From Modern Carvers

by HELEN BULLARD

Among members of the National Institute of American Artists, only a few work with wood as their medium. One is Helen Bullard, a charter member and first president of that prestigious organization, who began carving dolls in 1949. Here she writes intimately of her own hand-carved creations and others that are being produced today.

THE KENTUCKY "Poppets" (*Fig. 1*) are the only true hand-carved primitives I have ever found. While there must be others, they are probably one-of-a-kind and not in museums. A few Poppets were made for sale and I bought a pair in 1952, probably for $4.

Their characteristics are those of most primitive dolls: large heads, round eyes, anus-like mouth, short arms, tiny hands and feet. Allen Eaton in his *Handicrafts of the Southern Highlands* (Russell Sage Foundation, 1937) mentions their makers, Mrs. Anne Green Williams of Ary, Kentucky, and her sister, Mrs. Orlenia Ritchie of Viper, who had learned to make them from their mother. The head, arms, and legs were carved from buckeye and the cheeks made pink with pokeberry juice. Features were indicated with ink.

The Willy Smith pair (*Fig. 2*) is modern, made in Asheville, N.C., until about 1965, with bodies carved in one piece. Also modern is the old mountain couple, "Aunt Jenny and Uncle Pink" (*Fig. 3*), still being carved and dressed in old calicoes and denims by Polly Page of Pleasant Hill, Tenn. They were designed by Margaret Campbell and Tom Brown of Pleasant Hill Academy about 1938 when Miss Campbell was crafts teacher and Tom was a budding sculptor. The two set out to design the dolls in the manner of primitives, and the unfailing popularity of the cedar Uncle and Auntie for over 35 years is a testimonial to their success. Mrs. Page maintains the original

Cherokee women carved in Cherokee, N. C., the smaller in white suede tribal dress, the taller in the kind of clothes worn ca. 1920 by older women. Basket is of honeysuckle in a Cherokee design.

quality with stubborn dedication. Other Southern Appalachian wooden dolls are the two Cherokee women shown in *Fig. 4*.

Modern hand-carved dolls of foreign origin include the Greenland Eskimo (*Fig. 5*), carved of driftwood and elegantly costumed in fur and leather; the Hilda Ege (a famous Danish dollmaker) grandmother (*Fig. 6*); and the primitive Pitcairn Island doll (*Fig. 7*).

I came along in 1949 with "Miss Holly" (*Figs. 8, 9*), Barb'ry Allen (*Fig. 10*), a peddler, Hitty, and a modern creche. By 1954, I had carved Caroline, (*Fig. 11*); she was the first Bullard doll. Gradually, as my helpers developed problems, Holly Dolls, as I called my group effort, was phased out; Bullard dolls remain.

My dolls depend for their effectiveness on simple modern planes, control of detail, and understatement. I work in horse chestnut wood and use water colors only to define the features and paint the shoes, if any. Each figure is an original (technically known as a "primary"), carved from small blanks of wood except for the upper arms which are usually wrapped wire for easy positioning.

My principal work is "American Family," a procession of nine generations of a Puritan family from Massachusetts in 1632 to the Midwest in 1900, caught at their "blooming," the

"Uncle Pink and Aunt Jenny," a neo-primitive pair still being made. Ht. 10".

Kentucky "Poppets," made by Mrs. Anne Williams.

Old mountain couple carved by Willy Smith of Asheville, N. C., and dressed by Mrs. Smith. Ht. 6".

Greenland Eskimo woman has jointed wrists and a simple but clever jointing in the ankles to permit putting on and taking off the boots. Chignon at back of head holds up parka for warmth and circulation of air. Ht. 12".

A group of 1950 "Miss Hollys," Helen Bullard's "group effort" dolls.

Maimiti, Pitcairn Island doll, carved in one piece, except for arms, of local booron wood, which is very soft. Inked features. Ht. 5".

Helen Bullard and three of the nine couples of "American Family 1630-1900." *Left to right:* 1840, 1875, and 1900. Tallest men are 18".

"Miss Holly" after the design had "jelled."

Bullard dolls: "Three Rebels", Caroline, center, was the first of the Bullard dolls. Constance, at left, 1800, carries Mary Wollstonecraft's *Vindication of the Rights of Women;* Caroline, 1889, holds Ibsen's *A Doll House,* and Margie, the flapper of 1928, a copy of *Freud.*

Bringloe dolls, often used by schools and museums, portrays everday people of historical periods, scaled 1½" to a foot (adult male 9" tall); of Alaskan cedar, jointed throughout with springs and swivels; hands and faces hand-carved.

Barbr'y Allen, the last of Helen Bullard's real mountain girls, 1920 style. Ht. 18" Scale model dulcimer by Jean Horner.

Cobbler, by Fred Thompson, is one of a series of craftsmen figures, each complete with tools of his trade. All wood, 24" tall, ball-jointed.

Grandmother with hand-carved head, remainder of stuffed fabric, by Hilda Ege, famous Danish dollmaker. Ht. 11"

time of their marriage. Three of the couples are shown in *Fig. 12*. My usual subjects are regional or American, such as Davy Crockett, the 1970 College Rebels or Hippies, and Gertrude Stein. Three mountain children are currently in work.

During the 1945-60 period, Avis Lee (who graduated from Carl Schurz High School in Chicago, as I did, and from which neither of us received an iota of inspiration for carving dolls) carved active and charming figures with cloth bodies. Groups of her children were photographed in color for several covers of the magazine *Junior Activities*.

Frances Bringloe of Seattle has brilliantly solved the problem of producing bodies quickly and at a reasonable cost. With the help of her architect husband, she designed body parts which are automatically turned, then strung together with tiny springs and swivels, making elegant and substantial bodies. Heads and hands are hand-carved; costuming is meticulously in scale and in period. Bringloe dolls are authentic historical figures: pioneers, explorers, Indians, and famous personages. (*Fig. 13*)

"The Prophet," (*Fig. 14*), a cobbler (*Fig. 15*) complete with bench and tiny carved tools, and other oldtime craftsmen are Fred Thompson's most popular figures. A wood carver who turned to making dolls a few years ago, Fred carves intricate detail, especially in the aging faces and hands which he loves to do. Frances, Fred, and I are members of the National Institute of American Doll Artists.

It is a surprisingly short list of fine modern hand-carved people figures. The work is slow; material has to be searched for; and there are no teachers. But to those who work with it, wood, more than any other material, provides deeply satisfying qualities; it can be handled simply or in great detail and made to say almost anything the artist desires.

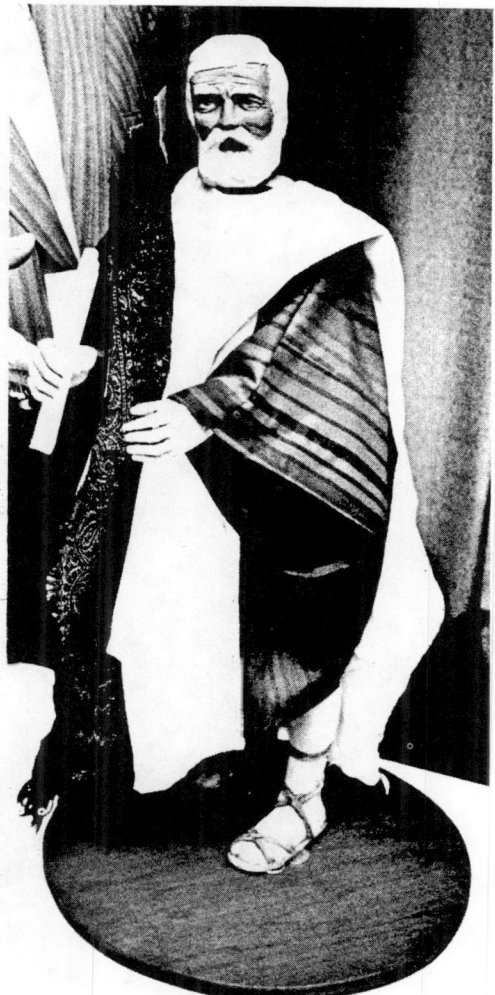
Fred Thompson's "Prophet" is 24" tall, all wood, ball-jointed; dressed by Mrs. Thompson.

Maid from Victorian Family (for St. Louis U.F.D.C. Convention).

Dolly's Uncle, the Riverboat Captain, made of cloth and clay.

Dolly Dufour's WHIMSICAL DOLLS

by R. LANE HERRON

All clay sachet doll inspired by the poem, "My Secret," ca. 1800.

STE. GENEVIEVE, MISSOURI (named after the patron saint of Paris), is a microcosm of American history, the only town in the state with so many surviving vestiges of French culture. It is also Missouri's oldest existing town; the second oldest town west of the Mississippi River. The ancient structures that dot the historic sites like so many artistic postcards, are not reconstructions—thirty of the buildings being built before 1800; the majority standing precisely where they stood two centuries ago. What better surroundings then for a painter—or a dollmaker?

If you turn right on Merchant Street and amble eastward you stumble upon the DUFOUR house, a log cabin built in 1795 by pioneer scout, Parfait Dufour. It now houses the studio of Dolly Dufour, resident artist and dollmaker in this picturesque river town.

Meeting Dolly Dufour is an experience unto itself, for here is an artist who lives and breathes her craft; small wonder the dolls she creates are beholden with such joyous facial expressions. Her home and studio was open to the public as a tour house until the illness of her 86 year old mother and 83 year old uncle. Both are now in her care, which has considerably slowed down her doll work.

But taking care of her loved ones has not deterred her completely. She has shown her dolls in California and they are sold in prestigious gift shops throughout the United States. In the years when her doors were open to the public, many of her early doll contacts were made right on the premises. People from all over the world passed through her portals. She wanted to join the U.F.D.C., and it was even a tourist who made that dream come true. The tourist admired Dolly's dolls and sponsored her. The tourist? Mrs. Carolyn Munson of Sedona, Arizona Verde Valley Doll Club and Prescott Doll Club). Joann Williams, the current President of ODACA, then made it possible for her to be a member of that organization.

Born and reared in St. Louis, Dolly was encouraged early in the mechanics of art by her parents. She also studied with prominent artists as a child, further advancing her studies in later years at Washington University School of Fine Arts, St. Louis. She then did an "art tour" of Europe. Always interested in figure painting, she was able to visit all the various countries and meet the different nationalities that fascinated her so. Her study of the Great Masters made a lasting impression.

"I travelled in our country, also," she said. "Hawaii was a jewel. The beautiful faces and lovely bodies! I love movement and grace. I use it in many of my dolls, I've always been an opera fan, too. The costuming has always impressed me. My dolls are an expression of the many beautiful places and people I have met."

Her art work has enriched many facets of the trade—she designed and painted canvas for a needlecraft business she and her sister operated in St. Louis, and also whilst living there she designed a line of sweaters for a couturière in Tucson, Arizona. She enjoyed the latter especially as it gave her imagination a free reign.

The name "Dolly" was given her by her father, but the "Dufour" is her "art" name. It was bestowed upon her by her friends when she moved to Ste. Genevieve seven years ago. The Dufour house was originally owned by her great-grandparents, so when she took possession of the building, she became associated with the name to such an extent she legalized it. Her real name is Marie Jones or Mrs. Robert Surkamp.

"I was the girl next door married to a prominent St. Louis family," she remarked. "We were married 26 years—then divorced. The divorce could have destroyed me, so I turned to my art. My "wee" people made a whole new family and life. Living in a small town makes it hard to be known. My wee people have been ambassadors for me.

"I had a mail order to see if my 'wee sniffs' would sell (sachet dolls). They did, and it was more than I could handle at the time. A person does not have to collect dolls to buy the sachet dolls. They hang from a nylon cord and scent the room. I belong to an Angel Club, ACCA. Many of the sachet dolls are angels. I enjoy this national, non-profit group."

The Dufour art dolls are made mainly from clay and cloth and they average in height about 20 inches, although she makes miniatures and dolls that stand an imposing five feet. She dresses them in materials which represent years and generations of old laces, cloth, and trim. New cloth is carefully selected. She feels she'll never live long enough to use all the antique trunks filled with the old materials. One day a tourist espied the dolls and said she was closing an estate and would send Dolly a surprise box. The months passed and Dolly forgot about the box and the

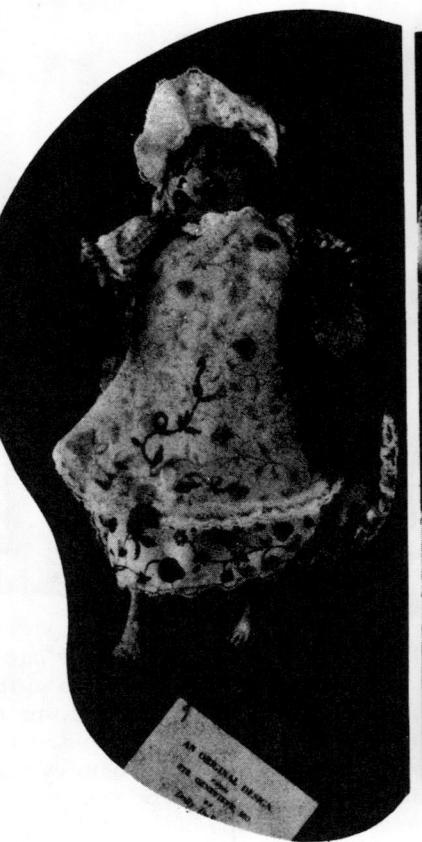

Wood and clay sachet doll—The Strawberry Doll.

Worlds Fair 1904 dolls (for 1981 U.F.D.C. Convention, St. Louis).

WHIMSICAL DOLLS

Dolly at work in her studio.

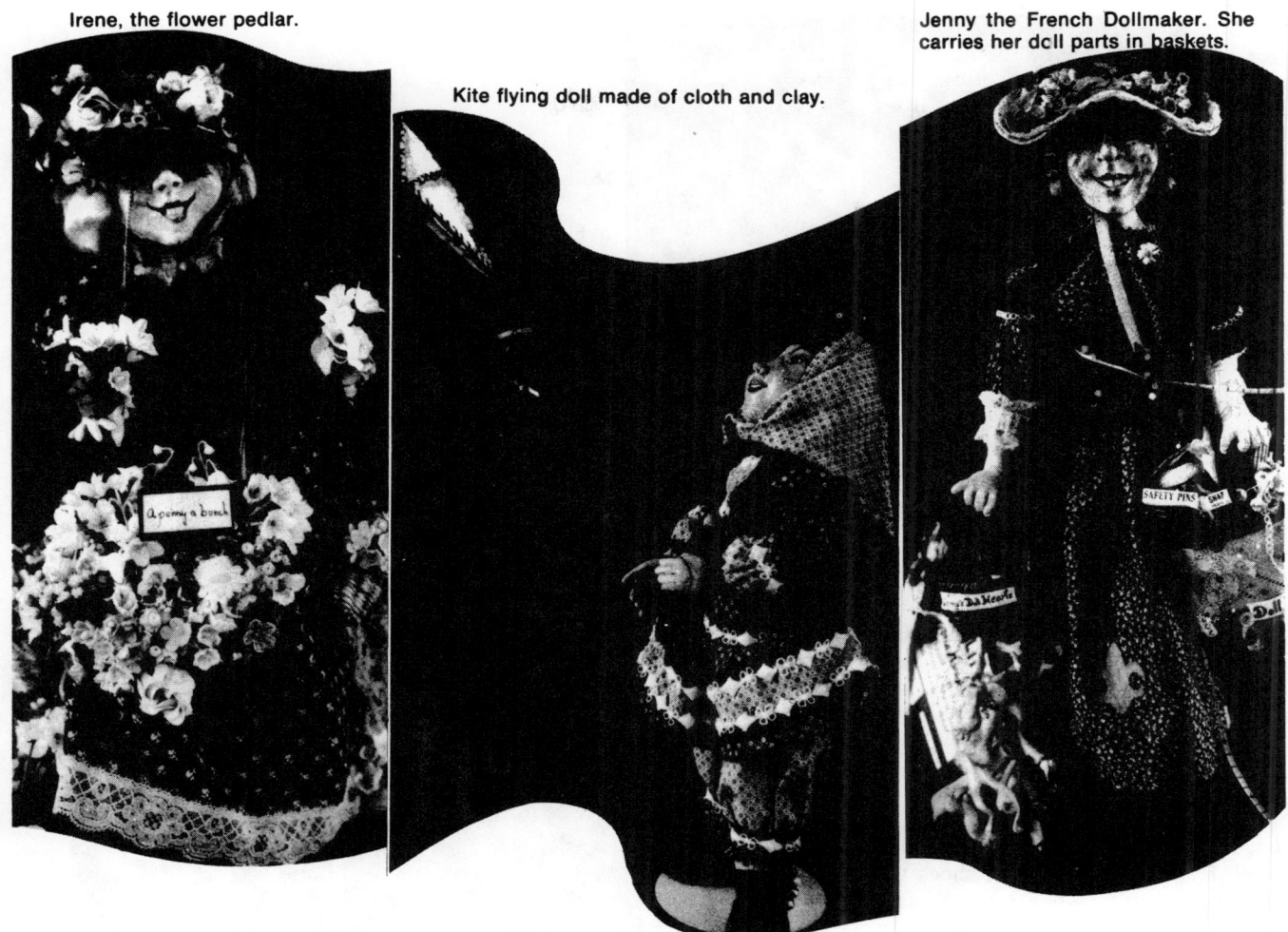

Irene, the flower pedlar.

Kite flying doll made of cloth and clay.

Jenny the French Dollmaker. She carries her doll parts in baskets.

incident. One day a large box arrived in the mail. It contained French Room hats, flowers, felt, and feathers of high antique quality. A note explained that the donor didn't wish to destroy them and knew Dolly would appreciate them. They were just what the doctor ordered. No doll ever lived to be more fancifully dressed than a Dufour creation. They are so sumptious you sense at once they belong atop an elaborate wedding cake.

"I guess you would call me a bedpan artist," Dolly muses with a wicked glint in her eye, "as all the dolls are made between chores. At this very moment, there is a path though the tiny, cluttered house. Dolls are everywhere I turn! I have a line of mice, too. I use antique pots, baskets, etc., for their homes. A chain of antique pots hang from the ceilings. All the windows and doors (in the pots) have been cut out by a tinsmith. They are waiting for me to let my imagination go wild."

Dolly is currently building a carrousel. A small motor and music box will turn and show the dolls she made from clay. It is all wood. Hopefully, it will be shown at an upcoming Doll Convention. A Victorian family (Lady of the House, Upstairs Maid, Cook, Gardener) are also being contemplated. Dolly is a member of the Spirit of St. Louis Doll Club.

Her antique doll collection is glorious to behold in that most of the dolls have been dressed personally by Dolly. The dolls are very special with her as the majority are "very personal gifts from childhood." She never actually sought dolls to be collected—they sought her. The Dufour family left generations of books and papers from which to glean ideas for costume and decoration, thus her work is authentic. "This town is full of retired people. I have only to walk down the street to capture a beautiful facial expression for my next doll.'

Dolly claims she has made dolls from any substance you can name. She never duplicated a doll via a mold—having too many fresh ideas from which to create. Besides, she didn't wish to make the same doll over and over again. "I will do any subject a person wants but I do not copy one doll. All are individual personalities. It's sometimes hard to see them go, but I often hear from people who have one of my dolls."

The dolls have an aluminum-wire armature covered with dacron. This outline is then contoured with white cloth for realism. The figure is then adhered to a heavy wood stand. Being rather heavy and awkward the dolls need a sturdy base for standing. Dolly doesn't like commercial stands, feeling that anything commercially made detracts from the original concept.

After the doll is completed to her satisfaction, so begins the chore of costume design. The Jenny Lind trunks are chock-full of vintage fabric and the old button boxes have an ample supply of buttons and ornaments. However, if something is amiss she'll scurry to a yardsale for a silk taffeta wedding dress, old formals, or a baby's smocked dress. As the doll wigs are handmade, she searches for discarded human hair

Mouse House by Dolly.

Flower Lady made of clay and cloth, 20 inches tall.

wigs previously worn by women or buys mohair by the yard. Wiglets are taken apart, washed, curled, and made to fit a doll. Some of her angel sachet dolls sport wigs made from horses' hair ... "I met a horse and left with a bit of his tail for my dolls."

She finds Polyform clay ideal for head and limb sculpture. If she makes cloth feet, she'll make real shoes to fit. She doesn't own a sewing machine, hence all sewing is done by hand. The wooden block on which the doll stands is covered with felt and trimmed. A few of the dolls have music boxes within the bodies.

"Anyone who really wants to make a doll can afford to if she or he uses what is around them," she said. "One winter I dried apples, made a body, and had a sweet doll. I dried the apples over a wood stove. A walk through the woods can provide dried flowers, twigs, nuts. A few of my mice dolls sleep in a turtle shell the old turtle left behind. Flea markets can come up with almost anything. I keep an eye out for handmade lace and tatting."

What impressed me most about Dolly Dufour is her unconscious kinship to the late Rose O'Neill of Missouri (the Mother of the Kewpies). Dolly's dolls are fey and whimsical—as were Rose's—and her fabulous paintings of children, animals, and fairies are every bit as good as Miss O'Neill's. Dolly has a great God-given talent and her art work alone could make her world famous. She attributes much of her success to her former art teachers, Charles Quest and Warren Ludwig. "If you have a good teacher like Mr. Ludwig (life drawing), making bodies for a doll is easy. He was not easy, but I learned to draw and sculpt the human body. Mrs. Jan McKinney was my 'color' teacher. If you never used your art again in your life, one thing a student learned was her course of color."

But life and learning continues to revitalize this fascinating artist. She went to an outdoor antiques auction not long ago, sat down to rest in an auction chair, and began to study people's feet, legs, and shoes. It was the best art school on earth—those people and their well-shod and busy feet. She went home with an antique desk and a new idea for "feet."

"These are the wonderful ways to get an idea," she concluded. "You cannot learn that at art school. My education will never stop. I enjoy people. Guess I am a 'people watcher.'" ■

Suzanne Marks - Doll Artist

R. Lane Herron

A DOLLMAKER'S most valuable asset is 'style.' Style identifies one's work instantaneously, and the better dollmakers always seem to have it. Suzanne Marks is amongst this elite group. Once you see her dolls you never forget them. And yet she is constantly seeking new ways to present her work. Not only do the movable parts move in the traditional sense, but, as she explains, the faces, the bodies themselves, suggest an inherent movement, playfulness, an animation rarely found in dolls. The dolls are total sculptures—as children are total children.

Suzanne's little Munchkins (my own term for them) seem to squirm, wiggle, and coo right before your eyes. Hold one in your palm though and you do not feel movement, they do not breathe. This aspect was part of Suzanne's original concept—to create dolls that were more then dolls—real children captured in lifelike porcelain.

It was only natural that Mrs. Marks of California chose children as her first dolls. She always enjoyed children, loved watching them at play—'They are such unique little beings, totally oblivious to the world, all wrapped up in whatever they are doing.' She marvelled at her own sons growing to young manhood and these 'growing up qualities' were so precious to her she wanted to capture them in a three-dimensional form. Her concept helps her share her innermost feelings and warmth with others.

Her second series of mini-dolls, which include two clowns, two little girls having a tea party, a mother with her children, are actually likenesses of Suzanne and her husband, Edward, when they were children, and she considers them even more expressive and animated than the first set of dolls.

Her most recent dolls are three black children. Her special favorites, no less, because she had such a struggle with them. She learnt to mix her own Negro flesh color in much the same way the black dolls of antiquity were done.

'It really helps to have the full support and love of one's family when one is trying something new and something that involved such risks,' Suzanne commented. 'Dollmaking not only takes lots of time and energy, but is an expensive venture to plunge into.'

It's indeed ironic that this obviously talented sculptor and artist ever embarked on a dollmaking career. Having three active older brothers as a child she never had time for dolls, let alone developing a need for them. She did have artistic leanings, however, and by the time she reached fifth grade she was chosen to paint a wall mural of the Amazon River for the classroom (with the aid of her girlfriend).

At ten, she entered a drawing contest on a local television show and was one of two winners selected out of hundreds of children. Being the top winner, she had first choice of prizes—a shiny new bicycle or an artist's drawing board. She wanted the bicycle desperately, but chose the board instead (still hoping for a future career as an artist). Months passed before she got her prize—the host's own battered board much

Suzanne Marks

worse for wear. The show had been cancelled. Alas. Needless to say, Suzanne was disappointed, so disappointed she shelved the board—and her plans for a career.

Suzanne was married shortly after she graduated from high school. She spent the next few years rearing children, running a household, and doing part-time typing to supplement their income—her husband had gone back to college to get a degree. Despite her frantic schedule and small children, a birthday gift from her mother-in-law encouraged her to splurge on a set of brushes and oil paints and enroll in an adult class in oil painting.

'For the next three years, I divided my time between home, children, and painting in the evenings when there were no little hands around to snatch a tube of paint and use it for a teething ring,' she confided in earnest. 'I'm sure that re-discovering art made me much better at mothering and homemaking.

Feeling she must delve further into the art realm, Suzanne enrolled in a sculpturing class and, much to her surprise, preferred it to painting. Sculpturing presented a challenge oil painting lacked—it offered an opportunity to work in all dimensions instead of merely one or two. She sold some of her paintings and a gallery accepted one of her sculptures. Still, she lacked the confidence to consider art as a career.

A few years ago, a friend asked her if she would be interested in earning extra money making miniature 'foods' for dolls' house collectors to be sold in shops. The work lasted only three weeks, but by the time Suzanne's apprenticeship was over, she found herself taken by things small and quaint. She began her own line of handmade, handsculpted miniatures in shops throughout the state of California.

Shows came next and with them the familiar chant: 'Do you make realistic miniature dolls?' With so many requests throbbing in her ears, Suzanne felt there must truly be a need for something 'different,' else the pleas wouldn't have been so persistent and plaintive. Dolls' house collectors were tired of Dumb Dora type dolls! (Princess Drina—Queen Victoria—realized this a century ago when she peopled her dolls' houses with jointed peg-woodens. At least they could assume positions, whereas the familiar china heads could not.)

After much research into the doll world she decided to try porcelain dollmaking in miniature. Much to her horror, all the firms she contacted who taught porcelain dollmaking, hadn't the slightest idea about how she should begin this phase of dolling. Or, if they did, they jolly well weren't ready to divulge any trade secrets!

'One lady referred to the prototypes of my first dolls as 'little junk.' Not being discouraged by her comment, and being faced with little

The girl doll (left) was among the first seven dolls made by Mrs. Marks. The boy doll (right) was a likeness of her eldest son, Eric. Neither doll is available today.

outside help and marked prejudice with regards to the size doll I had intended to design, I accepted the challenge..........

More determined than ever before Suzanne sought a friend who gave her four basic lessons in porcelain doll making—and then she was on her own. She quickly discovered that mini-dolls are not only very difficult to pour, clean, and paint, but dressing them proved almost impossible—unless one glued the clothes on, and Suzanne would not!

Suzanne continued to experiment and developed her own work methods which have proved successful. Unlike those who refused to help her in the beginning she has been generous with her advise.

She buys flesh-colored porcelain from a ceramics supplier. This is emptied into a large plastic bucket, stirred slowly for a least fifteen minutes, then poured through a nylon stocking to filter out pieces of lead and dried bits of slip, and emptied into another clean, plastic container.

It is thinned with bottled water until it is the consistency of skim milk and stirred slowly again to avoid any bubbling. The slip is poured into molds (secured with large rubber bands) through the pour holes. The flow must be kept steady and even to avoid air bubbles which produce a poor casting. Excess slip is poured off so that the walls of the casting will not be too thick. Twenty minutes later (or longer, depending on room temperature), the moulds are carefully separated and the casting gently removed. If it is satisfactory, Suzanne puts it aside to dry for 2 days. When Suzanne pours the moulds for head, torso, and limbs, she always makes extra pieces, allowing for breakage when cleaning and firing.

Cleaning the greenware comes next. Suzanne works with a facial mask, a full-length apron, Q-tips, X-acto knife, a small, stiff brush, nylon stocking, and cotton balls. Greenware has the consistency of an eggshell, thus cleaning the pieces is tedious and time-consuming. The x-acto knife is ideal for seam removal, the nylon stocking for sanding. A rounded toothpick is used to re-define facial features, nostrils, etc. The stiff brush cleans the areas around the nose and mouth. The hair strands are gently carved with the X-acto knife to give them a natural look. The final sanding is done with a Q-tip and cotton swab. Improper sanding renders a piece 'pitty' and of low quality.

Enough parts are cleaned for a kiln load of seven dolls. The first firing is to Cone 6. This takes over 8 hours in their kiln (Cress Kiln is a small kiln perfect for miniature dolls. It works on a regular household current.)

Suzanne Marks was elected to the Original Doll Artists Council of America in 1980.

Eight more hours pass before Suzanne gradually opens the kiln and peeks inside (too rapid cooling may cause cracking of some of the pieces). The parts are then inspected for first-firing splits in the bisque. Properly fired porcelain has a dewy, moist 'skin' look at this stage.

The fired pieces are again sanded with fine wet-dry sandpaper under hot water and finished with a ceramic scrubber, rinsed and set aside to completely dry.

China painting is difficult and requires patience and skill. This where Suzanne's years of art training come to her aid. Straying from the norm she used a soft, subtle approach to the painting. Face and body blushes are achieved with a special brush, leaving very little china to paint on, to create the natural look in lieu of the old-fashioned 'painted doll' effect. Now comes a two hour china firing. The eyes are painted—and another two hours of china firing. Pupils, hair color, shoes and socks, are painted after that firing. And, again, they, too, hit the oven for a good firing. Four firings complete each doll

Suzanne gathers her parts round her and with the aid of a doll compound, nichrome wire, kotter pins, and minute doll elastic she begins the stringing process. The fully-jointed bisque dolls are now ready to dress.

(please turn the page)

Top to bottom. 'The Tea Party' - dolls vary in height from 2" to 3¾". Black dolls - (left to right) 'Lizabeth is 4¼". 'Mahalia' is 5" and 'William' is 4". Five of the first seven dolls produced by Suzanne Marks in 1980 (no longer available.)

Wee's "Weedidit" Dolls

by R. LANE HERRON

Suzanne designs all the clothing and a friend, Joyce Yamagishi, helps with all the handsewn outfits. Materials for costumes always pose a problem for mini-dolls. Fabric must be lightweight and designs must be in keeping with the doll's size (tiny flower, birds, polkadots, etc.). Handsewing must be firm, neat and finished.

Suzanne Marks' hard work, patience, and perseverance has finally paid off and she has reached the point of no return. She has found her station in life; she is content. In 1980 she was elected to ODACA (Original Doll Artists Council of America). She enjoyed the comradship of the organization and viewing other people's dolls helps her own improve even more.

'It's an exciting profession!' she concluded. 'I'm glad I'm part of it!' ■

Fall Scene

Mother and children - the mother is 5½" and the children 3¼" each.

Clockwise from top left: 'La Comedie' is 5½", 'Sue' is 3½", 'La Tragedie' is 5½" and 'Ned' is 3½".

Red Loves Hattie

WHEN BETTY PAULSON was a baby, her older sister began calling her "Wee." The same sister's accusatory "Wee did it," whenever mischief was abroad, became a family catchword. Today, Mrs. Quentin S. Paulson, still known as Wee, is President of the National Institute of American Doll Artists, and her Weedidit dolls and doll scenes in "minutia miniatura" are Americana at its best.

Weedidits are subtle reminders—of a book, a childhood experience, a hobby, a dream—little doll people plagued

"Follow the Star"

Warm Feeling

Winter Scene

Happy Hanukkah!

with human faults and fancies. To some they are almost personal portraits. As Mrs. Paulson says, "It's the common thought or memory I attempt to achieve in a Weedidit creation—to call up in those who see them similar experiences and an 'I know exactly' recognition. There's just one rule I go by—that every doll I create must be happy and bring a smile to the beholder."

Wee Paulson's mania for detail is overpowering in its fulfillment. Authentic materials and accessories, down to the most minute detail, are incorporated in each reminiscent scene. In making a tiny tackle box for one of her fisherman dolls, her special jackknife will achieve a miniature box the spit replica of her husband's, complete with handle, hinges and lock. That jackknife, an Italian sewing machine, needles and thread, plus her clever fingers and agile imagination are Wee's only tools. She spurns the commercial and ready-made, she does everything herself.

The shoes, some with tiny hobnails in the soles, many with cobweb fine shoelaces threaded through miniscule eyelets and tied in neat bows, are made from scraps of leather; silk stockings from antique gloves; angel's sandals from a few strands from an old straw flowerpot. Hair is whatever substance is at hand—carded lamb's wool, fur, yarn, even combed string.

Summer Scene

Meet Wee Paulson with her "Convention Lady Scene", "Boy at Bat", and "Sunday Mornin' scene"—her "mascots" that attend every convention with her.

"Here"

for the original—to find a fresh way of saying the familiar."

Currently, she allows herself from one to two years for new doll orders. Each Weedidit takes from 30 to 200 or more hours to complete, depending on the number of characters, animals, scenery and accessories.

Weedidit note cards are her latest project. It took her some time to find a photographer who understood her little figures, but now Weedidit notes are on sale in various small galleries, museums, selective card shops, and at Doll Clubs. Her book, *What's It All About?*, illustrated with doll scenes with one line captions to a page, expressing her happy and positive outlook on life, is in the "coming soon" stage.

The sturdy felt bodies of all the dolls are built on wire armatures, padded with surgical cotton, enabling them to assume the desired poses. First the figures are cut from felt, wired with floral wire and pipe cleaners, and stuffed; then they are embroidered, painted, dressed, and finally posed and mounted on a wood base.

Mrs. Paulson received her basic art training at Iowa State University and the Minneapolis Art Institute. Over the years, she has experimented in many media—wood, clay, wax, papier-mâché, rags, and finally felt, her favorite. In her work with felt, she has captured many a happy moment in miniature.

"I've made around 500 scenes since 1965," Mrs. Paulson says. "At first I did many elves and foreign book interpretations. But now I concentrate on American scenes and American children, and since 1968, I have tried not to duplicate a scene. I have used a similar subject or situation maybe, but with all different characters, accessories, and surroundings. I try always

Spring Scene

MARTHA ARMSTRONG-HAND N.I.A.D.A.

by HELEN BULLARD

—Mattel Doll Designer

MARTHA ARMSTRONG-HAND, the daughter of a language professor and a psychiatrist, grew up in Berlin, Germany. Until World War Two started and drove she and her stepmother into the country, she studied at the Academy of Arts in Berlin. The war years were nightmares of hardship and fear for Martha. But in 1949, after the war was over, she and her Irish soldier husband and baby were able to go to California to join her mother. The struggle to raise a family of four little girls became even more difficult when, after a long illness, her husband died in 1967.

For nearly twenty years Martha had attended evening classes at several colleges in Los Angeles, majoring in art. One summer while working as a camp counselor she made a group of puppets. The father of one of the boys in the camp saw them and hired her to create costumes for Viewmaster, a company which produced miniature three-dimensional film slides and viewers. After designing the costumes for "20,000 Leagues Under the Sea," she made figures for Viewmaster's new productions. From Viewmaster she moved to Hagen-Renaker Ceramics, and from there to making puppets and then into "special effects" for movies which included making miniature people for falling off cliffs and riding dinosaurs. Sometimes she worked at three jobs at once.

After a fling at freelancing, she applied to Mattel, Incorporated, a family-owned toy business which had grown steadily since 1945 when the Handler family started their business in a converted Los Angeles garage. In 1960 this firm zoomed into international prominence with their introduction of the "Barbie" doll. This teenage miracle, the brainchild

"Baby First Step" modelled by Martha Armstrong-Hand for Mattel in 1964.

Facing Page: Martha Armstrong-Hand working in her studio near San Simeon in 1975. *Photo by Gil Rocha.*

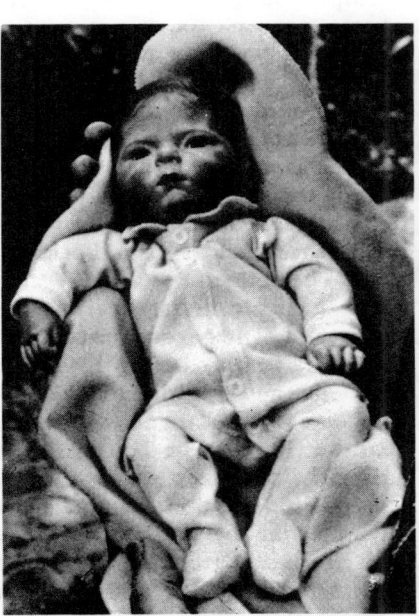

An original creation, "Baby Alex Paul," was made by Martha Armstrong-Hand to represent an infant just two weeks old. Length 11 inches.

"Baby Rosebud," a 7 inch doll modelled for Mattel by Martha Armstrong-Hand.

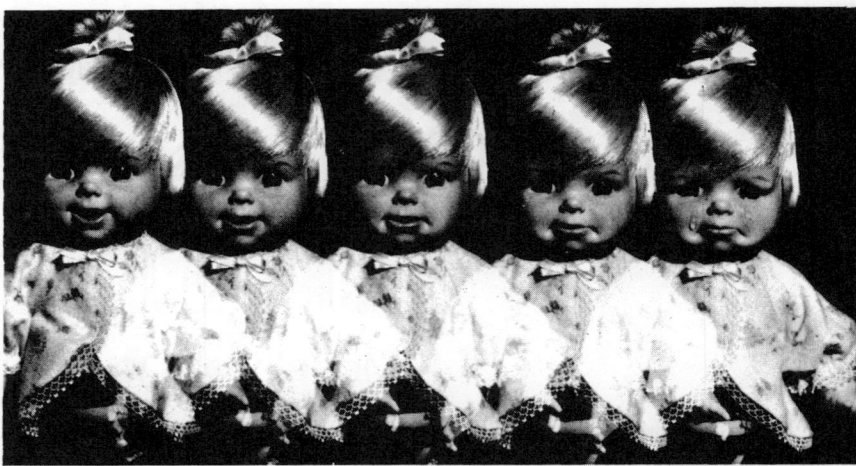

Left: "Cheerful-Tearful" sculpted by Martha Armstrong-Hand for Mattel in 1965. **Right:** The vinyl face of "Cheerful-Tearful" can be changed from smiling to crying by the movement of the left arm which is connected with a mechanism in the head of this doll.

The three "Baby Beans," shown left to right: Betsie, Bitty, and Booful, were designed by Martha Armstrong-Hand for Mattel.

 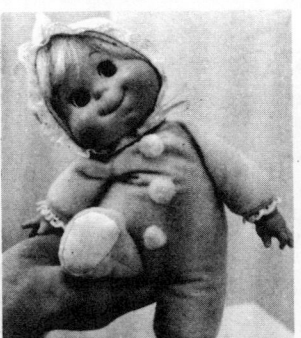 

of Ruth Handler, besides being purchased by the millions, was widely discussed by sociologists, psychiatrists, and endless self-appointed critics of current social mores. The doll's sexiness, clothes, and customs of her era were thoroughly explored. Mattel grew into the largest toy manufacturer and marketer in the world.

At Mattel, Martha Armstrong-Hand was assigned to paint master faces on dolls. The "Paint Master" is the pattern which must be designed for each new doll face in the production line and is used as the model for spraying on the features. (A far cry from the old days when long lines of girls sat at tables, each painting one eyebrow or the mouth of a doll.) The difficult part of this job is the need for three perfect duplicate copies of the head.

When Martha started at Mattel there were eight sculptors. That summer a baby's face was in the works and none of their designs seemed quite right. She was invited to try her hand at modelling a head and the one she completed was accepted for production. From that time forward Martha worked as a sculptor-designer (for ten years), and has for the past four years been a consultant working part-time for Mattel.

The procedure for making a million copies of a doll is complex. Once the idea is accepted—never an easy matter, the size, age of the doll, activity and age of the child for whom it is intended, and the retail price all have to be defined.

The graphic artist designs the complete doll on paper. The sculptor models it in clay, using his taste, knowledge and intuition to make the doll come to life; then he casts a wax head and paints the features. The hair girl dreams up a hair-do, the body attitude is decided upon, and any internal mechanism provided with its space. Last of all, fashion designers mock up the costume. The

"Marmi," who represents a three year old child, is another of Martha Armstrong-Hand's original dolls. Height 14 inches.

   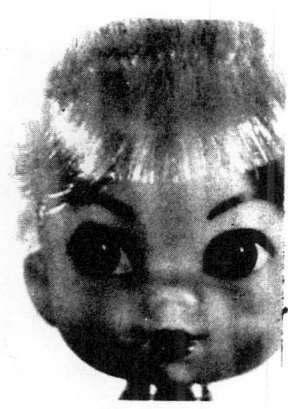

Left: The very first "Kiddles" designed by Martha Armstrong-Hand for Mattel in 1966. These dolls started the "Kiddle" empire for this firm. **Right:** The same "Kiddles" head with different eye painting can result in a total change of expression.

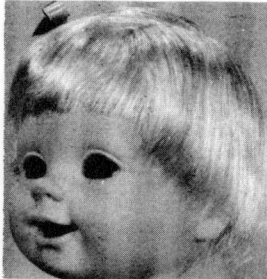 

Left: "Baby's Hungry" with monstrous mechanism in its head can be fed by her child-mother. **Right:** Unfinished "Baby's Hungry" head. This doll was modelled by Martha Armstrong-Hand for Mattel in 1966.

"Melissa" is an original creation by Martha Armstrong-Hand and represents a child just one year old. Height 14 inches.

The "Littlest Angel" created for Viewmaster by Martha Armstrong-Hand.

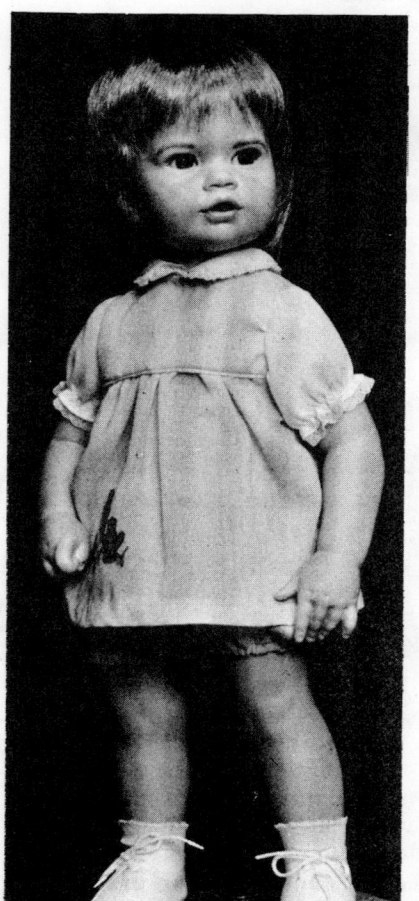

long process is a team effort, and often a doll goes through many changes before production. A graphic designer may suggest several appearances; a sculptor might model two or three heads for one doll; and the costume designers often make several choices of costume.

After the entire design is agreed upon, each part of the doll is carefully prepared for duplication. Sometimes the various parts are fabricated in different countries and brought together for assembly in Mattel's California plant. At times, the necessity of giving each of the elements in the product exactly the right form and treatment can be a demanding chore.

The resolute attitude which served Martha Armstrong-Hand well during the difficult times in war-torn Germany, throughout the struggle to raise her four children, and the ability to do whatever was necessary, served her equally well in her professional career. Her list of credits includes skills as a sculptor, moldmaker, costume designer and seamstress, arts and crafts teacher, graphic and lettering artist, and the painter of doll and toy masters for reproduction.

Presently, Martha works on her own original doll creations in a studio she found one day while exploring near San Simeon. She continues to work for Mattel, Incorporated, as a consultant, making regular trips from her home to the plant. She has achieved her dream with the help of her present husband, David Hand, who has also had a full career in art over the many years he has been working for the Walt Disney Studio as an animator, director and producer. ∎

Mme. Alexander Plastic Dolls

New Stars in the Doll World

by JUDITH WHORTON

"Polly Pigtails" was one of the very first hard plastic dolls produced by Madame Alexander, ca. 1949. Original clothes and hat, but wig has been replaced.

"Binnie" was a hard plastic doll made about 1954. She is dressed in her originial coat, dress, and fake leopard skin hat and muff.

Plastic dolls is one of the newest trends in doll collecting. The prices for these dolls are sometimes even higher than quoted for much older dolls. This has been a shock to many collectors who used to consider plastic dolls not worth collecting. Of all the examples produced by modern manufacturers, the discontinued dolls of the Alexander Company command the highest prices, and are among the most interesting of those produced in the 20th century.

Although Madame Alexander has been producing excellent dolls since 1923, the introduction of the Dionne Quintuplets established Madame Alexander's reputation all over the world. Even in countries on the continent of Africa, the Dionnes became the best selling doll. By 1937, more than a million had been sold. This figure is even more impressive considering that they were sold during a time of depression.

Imaginative promotions played a part in the success of the Dionne Quintuplet dolls. Yvonne Lerous, who had been a nurse to the Quintuplets, made public appearances for the Alexander Company. Stores advertised each birthday of the Quintuplets as a special event to feature the dolls.

Another of the continuing reasons for the popularity of the Alexander dolls is that many are inspired by themes that have a strong and lasting appeal with the public. For example, the Little Women dolls have been one of the most popular subjects. These dolls have been made in every material utilized by the Alexander Company. Beatrice Behrman, founder of the company, originally designed her dolls in cloth. In 1933 she created her first Little Women series. Since that time they have been made in composition, hard plastic and vinyl. In 1979, the eight inch hard plastic set of Little Women with the discontinued bending knees was advertised by dealers for $300. This was an increase of more than 500 per cent from the original retail price.

Scarlett O'Hara, another of Madame Alexander's popular creations, originally sold for $2.95 to $6.95. Today a collector would feel lucky to find one of these dolls for under $100. First made in 1936, these composition dolls ranged from 10 to 21 inches tall. The dolls were available in a variety of costumes, from a party dress before the Civil War to an outfit made of velvet curtains during reconstruction. Authentic details included a hoop skirt to accent the waist, and shoes without high heels. Scarlett O'Hara dolls have been made for many years and in various materials from hard plastic to vinyl. One

Composition "Scarlett O'Hara" doll.

The hard plastic version of "Scarlett O'Hara" was produced from Cissette molds. *Collection Winnie Gibson.*

of the interesting trends in doll collecting is the rising prices of many of the more recent dolls. The hard plastic Scarlett O'Hara of the Portrette series now often sells for as much as the original composition version which was made about 30 years earlier. Unlike the composition, the Portrette Scarlett was only dressed in green. A 1979 21-inch version of Scarlett was obviously made more for collectors than for a child, since it sells for $100 retail.

"Marta" and "Gretl" from the small size Sound of Music are 8 inches tall.

Three composition "Dionne Quintuplet" dolls with original clothes and name pins. *Formerly in the collection of the late Genevieve Angione.*

Madame Alexander was quick to recognize that the creations of Walt Disney would have a universal appeal. In 1937 she was licensed to make doll replicas of Snow White and the Seven Dwarfs. Through the years she has also designed a Disney inspired Alice in Wonderland, Sleeping Beauty, and a set of dolls from Peter Pan. The three hard plastic Sleeping Beauty dolls were produced in 1959 and 1960. The 16- and 21-inch size are of particular interest to collectors. The face for these dolls is one rarely used by Madame Alexander. Also, the body is jointed at the waist, knees and ankles. The 10-inch size was produced from the same mold as the Cissette doll.

The Cissette doll, produced from 1957 to 1963, was Madame Alexander's miniature fashion doll. Cissette had many clothes which could be purchased separately. The Queen's costume, made of brocade, originally sold for $9. Presently, a doll dressed in this outfit might bring as much as $150. Even the everyday clothes were made of quality materials such as taffeta, organdy, and velvet. The outfits ranged from sophisticated dresses with daring necklines to an old fashioned Gibson Girl costume. Accessories added much to the charm of the doll. Hats were made of real straw and decorated with flowers and veils of lace. Hose and high-heeled shoes could also be purchased separately.

When found undressed, the original Cissette and the slightly later Portrette series can be easily confused. The Portrette dolls have more elaborate make-up. These dolls wear eyeshadow and finger nail polish.

In 1960 Madame Alexander produced her tallest all plastic dolls, Janie and Joanie. They were 36 inches tall and had flirting eyes. These dolls are identified by the labels on their dresses. Since these dolls were made for one year only, and are so much larger than most Alexander dolls, when they are found undressed they are not always recognized as being made by Madame Alexander.

One of the most popular sets ever produced by Madame Alexander was inspired by the popular movie "Sound of Music." Recently NBC purchased the right to televise the "Sound of Music" for the next 20 years. Such national exposure is bound to increase the demand for these dolls. Marie and seven of the children were made in two sizes. The large size was available from 1964 to 1970. The smaller set was introduced in 1971 and discontinued in 1973.

Madame Doll was inspired by the book *The Secret of Madame Doll*, by Frances Cavanaugh. The story takes place during the American Revolution. Madame Doll's

"Fredrich" from the Sound of Music series is 8 inches tall. The illustration clearly shows the much desired jointed knees now considered so valuable. *Collection Ruby Woolley.*

Composition "Dopey" was one of the most popular of the dolls in Madame Alexander's Snow White and the Seven Dwarfs series.

"Maria," from the Sound of Music set, came in several costume variations. She was first made in 1965 and discontinued in 1970.

"Joanie" is Madame Alexander's most realistic hard plastic version of a little doll. She wears her originial dress and has flirting green eyes. This doll was made in 1960, and for one year only.

"Cissette" dressed in an elaborate Queen's gown with jewels (**left**) and in a lovely afternoon costume (**right**), was first produced in hard plastic in 1957.

Composition "School Girl" doll. This face was used by the Alexander Doll Company for many of their dolls.

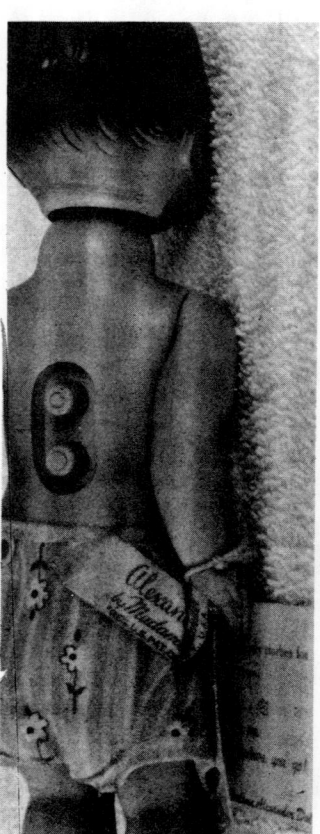

"Viet Nam" (**left**) and "Korea" (**right**) from the International series with the less common face and bending knee joints are difficult to find these days.

Hard plastic "Quizkin" was the only mechanical doll made by Madame Alexander, ca. 1933. **Above:** Dressed in its original sunsuit and with original tag. **Left:** "Quizkin" answered questions by nodding "yes" or "no" when the button on its back was pushed. *Collection Oneida Callaway.*

secret was a concealed pocket in her petticoats to hide the family's pearls. Production of the Madame Doll stopped in 1974.

The 8-inch International Dolls of Madame Alexander have been popular for more than 20 years. In 1972 a basic change was made in the International Series when the legs designed to bend at the knees were discontinued. When collectors realized this the prices of examples made before 1972 began to increase sharply. The International dolls that were made for a short time or had an unusual face increased even faster. Following are some of the International Series that were made for two years or less:

Argentine Boy (jointed knee)	one year
Belgian Girl (jointed knee)	one year
Czechoslovakian Girl (jointed knee)	one year
Vietnamese Girl (jointed knee)	two years
Peruvian Boy (jointed knee)	two years

The hard plastic "Sleeping Beauty" (crown is missing) in this 16-inch size is one of the more difficult to find today.

Madame Alexander's hard plastic "Southern Belle" doll.

The hard plastic "Madame Doll" was inspired by a delightful story book. This doll was produced from 1967 to 1974 and is 14 inches tall.

"India" (left) and "Hungary" (right) have the desirable jointed knees and most common face in the Madame Alexander International series.

The large size Sound of Music set ("Gretl" is 12 inches tall).

During the Bicentennial, Madame Alexander introduced her most recent set of dolls, the first six First Ladies. The idea of the series was so well received by collectors that some stores completely sold out their allotment before the dolls arrived. Unlike other Madame Alexander sets, most of these were sold as one unit. The price of approximately $260 for the set restricted the sales of the First Ladies primarily to collectors. Historians might question some of the costume details for accuracy, but the doll collectors don't seem to mind. Even while Madame Alexander continued to produce the set, ads appeared in antique magazines advertising the President Wives for more than the retail price. In 1979 the second set of First Ladies was introduced.

Madame Alexander is to be congratulated that her doll company survived the depression years and foreign competition. But she is even more fortunate that her dolls have begun to be judged as works of art in her own lifetime.

"Martha Washington" was the first doll in Madame Alexander's First Ladies series.

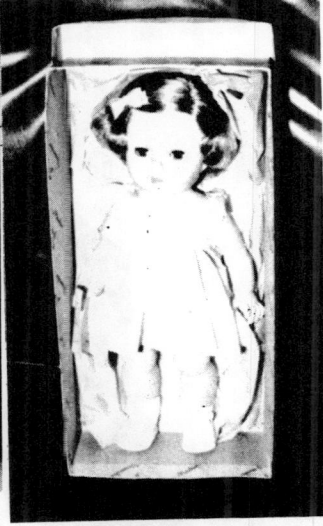

"Caroline" (Kennedy) in her original box. Original empty boxes have a resale value, too. Collection Myron Briley.

DOLLS

THERE WOULD APPEAR to be little connection between eggs and dolls, but in Emma Clear's life there was a definite link. Emma C. Clear, the first American doll artist to make china, Parian, and blonde bisque dolls, was the chief nurse and doctor at the Humpty Dumpty Doll Hospital in Redondo Beach, California.

Emma was born in St. Louis, Missouri, the daughter of a cattle dealer. The family was in comfortable, middle-class circumstances and she enjoyed travel and a good education. Emma received a commerical law degree and went on to Vanderbilt University in Nashville, Tennessee, for advanced study. At the Chicago

■ All dolls are from the collection of Lorna Love.

CREATED by EMMA CLEAR

by ANN S. BLAND

World's Fair, 1893, she became fascinated by the sculptures and decided she wanted to study sculpturing.

Shortly after college Emma married, had a son, and was soon divorced. The need for a remunerative career became immediate and in 1908 she and her sister decided to open a doll hospital in downtown Buffalo, New York, where her family had moved years earlier. As a child, Emma had repaired and operated on broken dolls for neighborhood children and loved doing it. The hospital was a huge success, but in 1914 Emma left the Buffalo operation to her sister and moved west. For a while she operated on a wholesale basis in Cleveland, Ohio. Then, in 1917, she moved to California and opened the Humpty Dumpty Doll Hospital in Los Angeles.

In California Emma met and married a farmer, Wallace C. Clear, a native of Tennessee. After twenty years Emma's doll shop was closed and the dolls packed away. Mr. Clear owned a poultry ranch at Redondo Beach, twenty miles from Los Angeles.

The poultry ranch kept the pair busy through several years and then came the 1929 Depression. Hard times followed with eventual failure of the ranch. The chickens were disposed of, the equipment sold at a loss, life insurance cashed in, the ranch mortgaged, city property sold and the final ignominy—the family was forced to apply for welfare. At about this time Emma fell so ill that doctors and relatives gave her up. But a country doctor saved her life, and as she lay too weak to move, she thought about what she could do to make some money. "Back to the dolls," she decided.

Emma still had the molds, equipment and know-how to make doll parts. Dolls could not be obtained from Europe, and she still had a supply of pre-World War II imported dolls. The doll collecting hobby was growing in America. The problem was money and location. There was not even a dollar bill in the house, and the farm seemed too far in the country to attract much business.

With some misgivings, Mr. Clear cooperated in the venture. The two

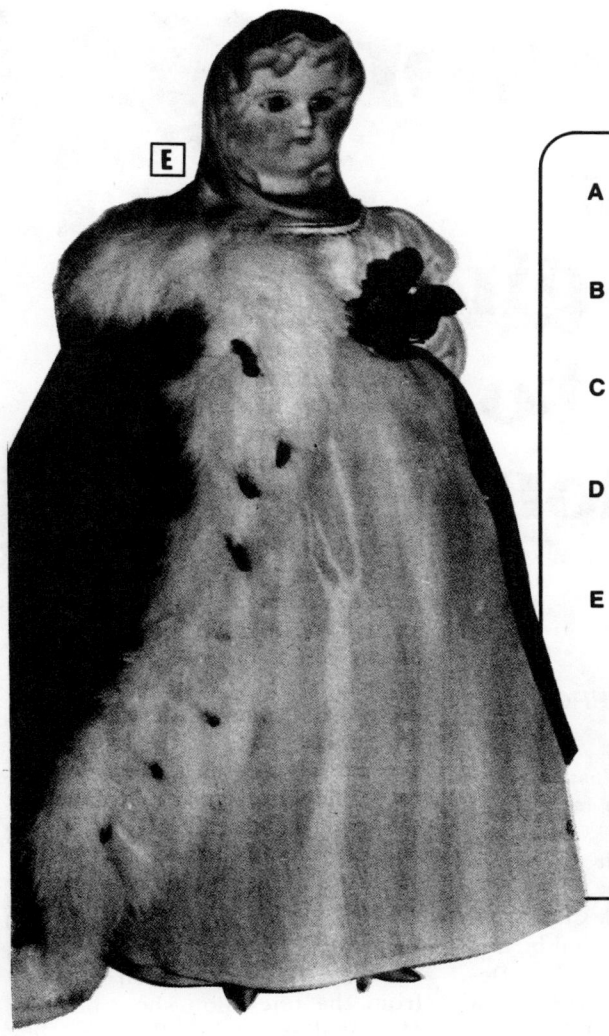

A Parthonea bisque came with gold intertwined in her hair and earrings. She is wearing pink lawn with white cape trimmed in gold lace and blue ribbons.

B "China Lady" with stippled curls. Most dolls were made with vertical curls and this is a hard-to-find china with a different hair-do. Worth about $250 today. Made in 1940.

C A Parian bisque with a Dresden rose in her hair, blue-gray glass eyes and pierced ears with earrings, all original. Modelled after an original of the late 1800s.

D The Gibson Girl has a wonderfully serene expression on her face. Note the lustre feather in her hat which has been omitted on dolls made by Emma's daughter. The hat and band are unglazed. She is bisque, dressed in silk crepe with lace and flowers in her hair. Made in 1941.

E The original "blue scarf doll" was a bisque made about 1870 in the likeness of Louise of Mecklenburg-Strelitz, Empress of Prussia from 1797 until 1810. Her husband was Emperor Frederick William III. She was very popular with her subjects because of her courage, grace and beauty. After the Prussian defeats of Jena and Friedland she made a personal appeal to Napoleon to spare Prussia, but was unsuccessful. The doll pictures Empress Louise descending the stairs at Schoenbrun Palace to intercede with Napoleon on behalf of her country. The Clear "blue scarf doll" has blue glass eyes, long fair curls and a blue scarf on her head. She is a finely molded bisque with delicately tinted arms and legs, brown button shoes with high heels and toe caps. The white dress is of the Empire period and cape is red velvet trimmed in white fur.

painted signs, cleaned and painted dropping boards, cleaned and painted chicken houses, and set up shop. Three days after their signs were erected the first out-of-state car drove up. From then on the hospital was a huge success. From all over the country boxes of dolls poured in for repair. Even dolls' hospitals sent their most critical cases, knowing that no wreck of a doll was too much for the Clears.

Mr. Clear himself proved quite resourceful. He made a machine for filling doll bodies with sawdust and his packing ideas were ingenious. No doll was ever broken in shipment. He even learned to carve parts for some of the wooden dolls.

Before World War II, most china doll heads were made only in Germany. Emma solved this problem by making her own. Her first was a recreation of the Jennie Lind doll of the 1850s. It was made in three sizes in white, pink and rose lustre. Other china and blonde bisques followed, all so beautiful that Clear dolls are today avidly sought by connoisseurs. Few new dolls were made during the War, only copies of old ones.

Emma's finest dolls are considered to be Martha and George Washington, in blonde bisque, copies of designs made for her by Martha Oathout Ayres. Historically correct and dignified, they are declared to be as finely done as old Dresdens. While designing the Washington dolls, Mrs. Ayres visited the Metropolitan Museum and studied the John Ward Dunmore portrait of Washington.

Lorna Love of Carney's Point, New Jersey, has a fine collection of Emma Clear dolls. She says, "I find all my dolls undressed and have them dressed in authentic period costumes by Agnes Detrich of Altoona, Pennsylvania. She uses all old material and does a beautiful job."

According to Lorna, "All Clear originals are different. Prices range from about $200 to $300 today, with the Martha and George Washington dolls going for about $1,000 a pair. The first dolls that Emma made were styled after those made in the late 1800s. You can always tell a Clear doll because they are signed and dated on the back shoulder plate. All Clear dolls were cloth bodied with bisque or china arms and legs. Emma's daughter is now making dolls from the original molds, but her work isn't as yet on a par with her mother's." ■

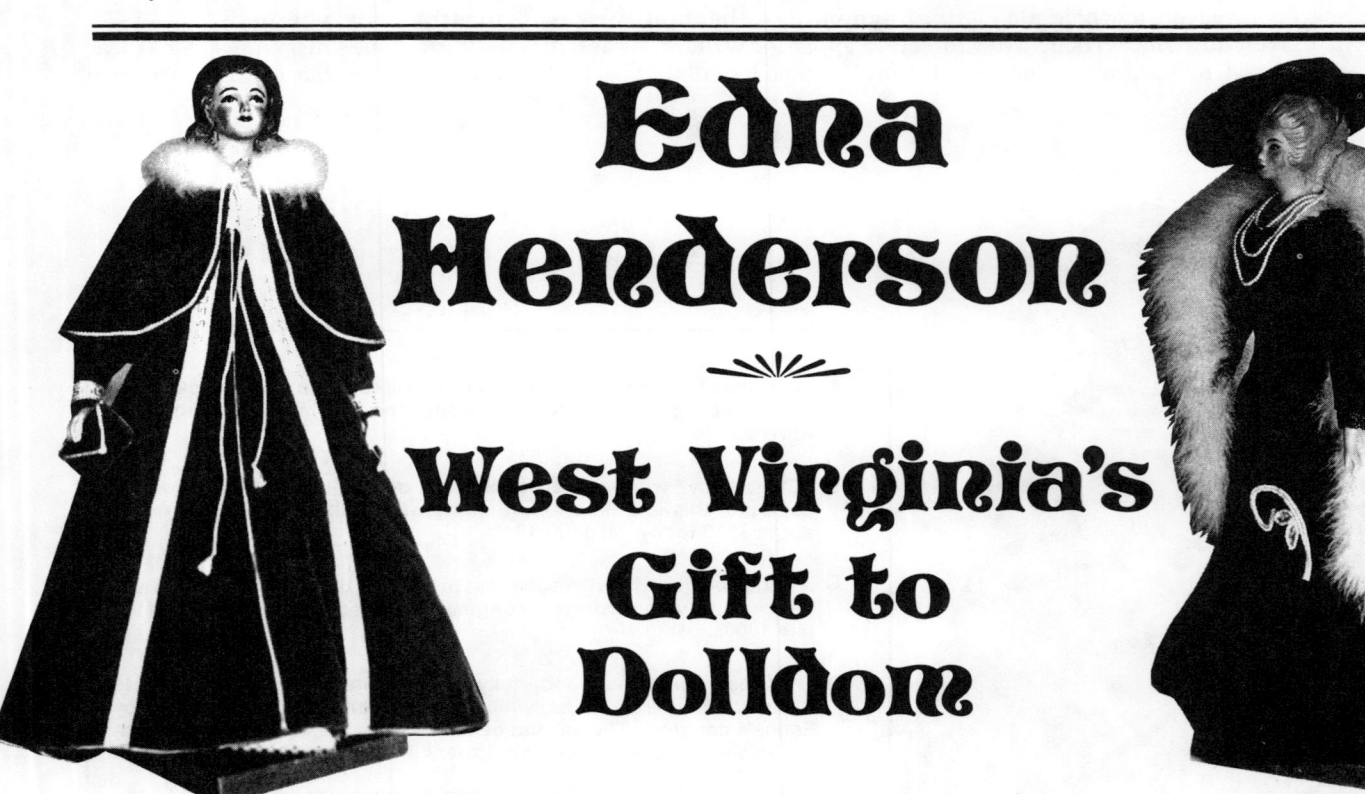

Barbara Walters doll.

Mae West doll.

Edna Henderson
West Virginia's Gift to Dolldom

by R. LANE HERRON

EDNA HENDERSON of Charleston, West Virginia, began working with clay in 1959 when her husband had the foresight to build a kiln and vat for her. Her first doll was a character study of television personality, Barbara Walters. Later, when she was exhibiting a group of her dolls at the Cedar Lakes Crafts Festival, the Department of Commerce invited her to enter the doll in a West Virginia promotional scheme for tourism.

Subsequently, the entire exhibit of West Virginia crafts was set up and displayed in a New York City hotel, inviting gift shop owners and buyers from all over the world. The Department of Commerce arranged a trip to New York City for the Hendersons. Edna was invited to appear on Johnny Carson's "Tonight" show to present the Barbara Walters doll to Barbara herself.

Edna arrived in New York at 5:30 p.m. At precisely 8:30 p.m. she was informed that she had been cancelled from the television show because Miss Walters had to fly from New

Edna Henderson with her doll of Pearl S. Buck.

York to Alaska to join the Nixons on their trip to China. "Oh, well," quipped Edna, "I suppose the President does come first!"

But the trip to New York was not a total disaster; far from it! Edna pulled several doll-kits out of her luggage and sold them to the Museum of the City of New York. An auspicious beginning for a novice dollmaker. And, today, after 17 fruitful years of dollmaking, Mrs. Henderson remains as eager and enthusiastic as ever. Enthusiasm is proof of the pudding, in doll lingo, as I've known cases where dollmaking has driven some people to despair!

Edna switched from Barbara Walters to many other famous faces—Martha Mitchell, Angela Davis, Mae West, Jacqueline Kennedy Onassis, Pearl Buck, Margaret Blennerhassett, and others. A score of other Henderson classics followed in rapid succession—Nita, Nena, Nettie, Nina, Mary, Dainty, Bobby, Lynn, Lou, etc. These stock pet names are sold to collectors in "kits" (head, arms, legs, body pattern) to be made-up and dressed on a cozy winter's day. These "pet" name dolls are originals—not repros—are signed by Edna, and named after a member of her family or even a friend or storybook character.

"Mary" doll turned out to be Edna's "good luck" talisman doll. She was created from the familiar Mary Poppins era and named after Mrs. Henderson's favorite Auntie, Mary. Her fetching hairstyle is patterned after that of blonde Judy Dunnavant. Mary was first shown in the National Arts and Crafts Festival in Madison Square Garden.

After this memorable debut, Mary was sold to Gimbel's department store in New York for window display. From Gimbel's, Mary was shuttled to Pogue's in Cincinnati for further honors and display, and, finally, to the Smithsonian Institution.

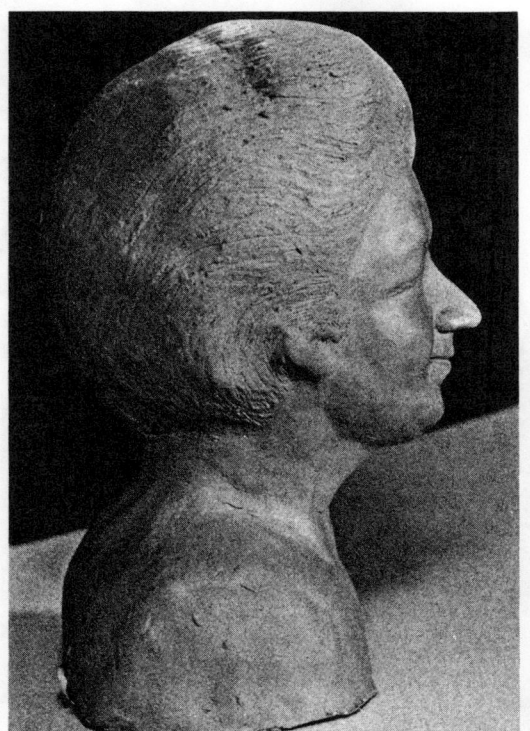

Sculpted head of Mrs. Arch A. Moore made in 1976.

Sculpted head of Mrs. William A. MacCorkle modelled from an old photograph.

Then, in 1970, she spent her days traveling throughout the United States with an exhibit sponsored by the Travel Division of the West Virginia Chamber of Commerce. However, the "original" Mary was spared all these public exhibitions—she remained at home in West Virginia—while her stand-ins, the repros cast in her faithful image, did all the showing-off.

Edna's fourth doll "Lynn Lou" (named after her two married daughters) also wound up at Pogue's, but her distinguished position of honor in the front window was short-lived. The window-dresser fell in love with her and purchased her on the spot. So ended her tale ... happily, of course.

The Franciscan nun doll, named for Sister Irene at St. Francis Hospital was dressed by Mrs. Dorothy Goffaux. Mrs. Goffaux dressed this doll in the official habit of the order, circa 1835. Each detail was astutely mastered, even the rosary and the three knots in the white cord belt which represents vows of poverty, chastity, and obedience.

Once, when Edna needed a special pan for her potter's wheel, she had the opportunity to make a trade with a man who had been an industrial arts teacher before he became vice-principal of a junior high school. He made the pan for her; she in turn made striking portrait dolls of his little daughters, Rhonda Kay and Brenda Sue.

A most interesting Henderson doll is the unusual portrait doll of Margaret Blennerhassett. Margaret was a cultured, aristocratic Irish beauty whose father was lieutenant-governor of the Isle of Man. Her mother was a direct descendant of King Edward III of England. When

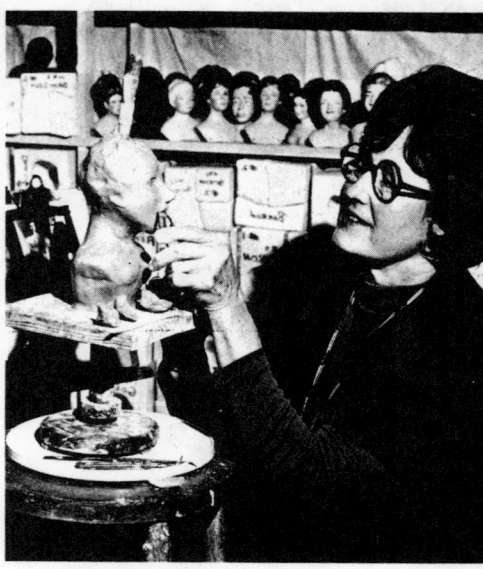

Edna Henderson sculpting a West Virginia Governor's wife; other Governors' wives shoulder heads are in the background.

Sculpted head of Mrs. Hatfield, wife of former West Virginia Governor Henry D. Hatfield (1895).

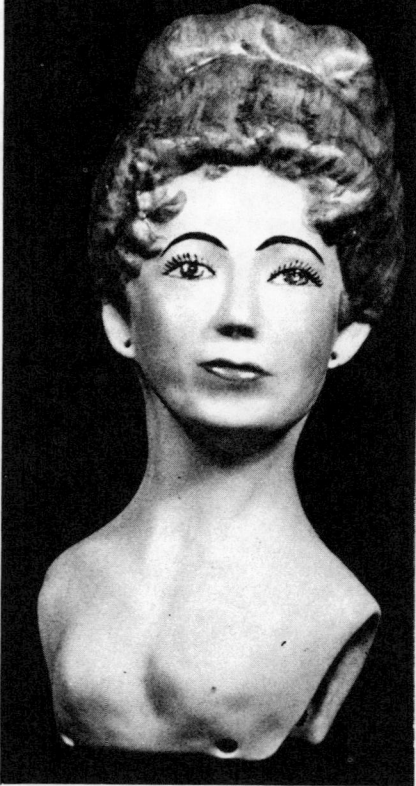

Henderson dolls. **Top, left to right:** Jed Clampett, Aunt Harriet, Freda, Barbara Walters. **Center row, left to right:** 1828 lady, Angela Davis, Gibson Girl, Martha Mitchell. **Bottom row, left to right:** Diane Carrol, Mary, Elsie.

Margaret was 18, she scandalized her family by marrying her Uncle Harman Blennerhassett (her mother's brother). Margaret was disinherited, and to escape further abuse the Blennerhassetts fled to America.

They lived in New York, Philadelphia, and Pittsburgh, before sailing down the Ohio River to an island near Parkersburg, West Virginia. Mr. Blennerhassett purchased the secluded island and built a mansion for his lovely young bride. But their Paradise was short-lived. Eight years later Harman was sent to prison for treason and his slaves accidentally burned down the impressive mansion which had already been plundered by drunken soldiers. Their fortune gone, Margaret fled the mansion with her two sons and escaped to New Orleans on a raft to join her disgraced husband.

Margaret was forever remembered by the townsfolk of Marietta, Ohio, not only for her wild Irish rose beauty, but for her shoulder-length earrings, her white beaver hat with wide brim and ostrich plume, elbow-length gloves, scarlet gown and white stallion, Robin. Mrs. Henderson's doll depicting this flamboyant woman was presented to the American daughters of Pioneers for the Cooper Cabin Museum in Parkersburg City Park in May, 1974. Plans are currently being formulated to rebuild the famous Blennerhassett mansion and convert it into a museum. Margaret, the doll, will eventually find her way back home to her "dear isle" at long last. (As she often lamented: "Oh why, dear isle, art thou not still my own?")

As for Edna Henderson's working methods:

"It would take at least four days of continuous work to make a hand-sculpted doll, if one worked at it full time," she says. "But dollmaking just doesn't work that way. There's quite a bit of waiting-time between processes. Hand-modeling the doll takes at least two days. But, I work awhile, then leave the doll and go back to take another look. I have to watch the personality grow. Casting the head takes an hour. The kiln firing takes about ten hours. The number of times the firing must be done depends upon the type of clay being used and whether the finish will be porcelain bisque or white glazed china. Then it has to be china painted. Many times there is a waiting period for one color to dry before the next color is added. Then the body must be cut-out, sewed, stuffed. I use sawdust for stuffing. Making the clothes takes at least another full day (unless I get too fancy!)"

Margaret Blennerhassett doll made in 1974.

Edna's dollmaking career was sparked several years ago, after she placed a small ad in an inner-circle doll collectors magazine. From this she had an order from a woman in Ireland who publishes an international doll collectors manual. Soon Edna was filling orders from around the world ... Wales, Holland, Rhodesia, Germany, England, Australia, Nigeria, France, etc.

The Bicentennial year has been a busy and lucrative one for Mrs. Henderson. She has completed a grouping of lady dolls representing the wives of West Virginia's 28 governors. They were presented to the State of West Virginia for placement in the new Science and Cultural Centre museum by Mrs. James A. Scarbro, president of the West Virginia Federation of Women's Clubs. Cost of the dolls to the federation will be between $3,000 and $4,000. The dolls are being copyrighted and are insured for a hefty $12,000.

The authentic antique materials and laces worn by the 28 dolls came from the estate of the late Mrs. Mary Wood, mother of Mrs. Nicholas Barth of Charleston. The materials originally came from 15 trunks of clothing and material which Mrs. Wood's mother-in-law brought to Charleston from Paris in the late 1880s. Edna purchased most of the materials from Mrs. Wood and received the rest as a gift when the internationally famous fashion stylist gave up her career.

Other antique materials were donated by ladies who helped dress the elaborate dolls. One doll was dressed in material from an old inaugural gown; another was dressed in materials and jewels found in an old trunk.

Mrs. Henderson was commissioned to sculpt the replicas after club women saw the likenesses of Mrs. Arch Moore and Mrs. Cecil Underwood. The sculpting began January 3, 1976 and had to be ready for the convention in March of 1976. Edna worked 18 hours a day to accomplish this major feat, and felt like a miracle worker when the incredible array of dolls was completed. She recruited volunteers to help costume the dolls properly for the period represented.

The federation had few fears or doubts about raising funds for the "First Ladies" project. Some years ago, when Mrs. Scarbro was state project chairman for restoration of the Pearl S. Buck birthplace at Hillsboro, the 16,000 federation members raised more than $32,000 in a brief two-year period!

Stephen Foster, modeled from a portrait of the composer.

DOLLS CREATED BY Xantos Kontis

*by JUDITH WHORTON
in collaboration with SHIRLEY BUCHOLZ*

XANTOS KONTIS, an artist from Smyrna, Turkey, began the American tradition of having a doll as a souvenir at a doll collectors' convention. His life story, which led to his career as a prominent American dollmaker, resembles an adventure drama. Perhaps this is why so many of Kontis' dolls strikingly illustrate the vitality of American history. The artist, as a three-time refugee, brings a special quality to the personalities important in a free land. Xantos' father was a prosperous merchant in Smyrna. The turmoil due to resentment of Greek nationals led to the internment and death of Kontis' father in a prison camp. In 1922 the nine-year old Kontis and the rest of his family were forced to flee to Athens.

When Kontis attended the Athens Polytechnic Institute to study sculpture, he met an instructor who worked for Lenci, the famous Italian doll company. The instructor helped inspire Xantos' interest in dolls. Later Xantos also taught sculpture at the institute. Then he started his own toy business. His shop soon became filled with his hobby horses and creations of stuffed animals covered with real fur. He developed his own formula for making composition dolls. "I was the first to make Greek dolls with movable eyes," says Xantos. Among his characters were Greek soldiers, cheese makers, wool spinners and the Queen of Greece. He also created puppets, including the characters in Snow White and the Seven Dwarfs, which sold by the hundreds.

His business was soon patronized by prominent customers, including members of the family of the Greek Prime Minister. His international clientele included Metro-Goldwyn-Mayer. In 1937 the movie studio ordered candy containers to resemble Laurel and Hardy as a promotion. Kontis also designed a Shirley Temple container.

During World War II, when German forces occupied Athens, Xantos

Father Junipero Serra, founder of the California missions, modeled from a portrait.

Benjamin Franklin; from a portrait.

Old Greek peasants. He carries a shepherd's staff and cheese pail; she has her "roka" and cotton to spin thread.

Women from Attiki, near Athens, wearing an authentic costume; made in Greece in 1938.

again became a refugee, this time because of his political caricature dolls of Axis personalities such as Hitler and Mussolini. The British ambassador had ordered a series of these dolls to be sent to King George. Xantos successfully escaped to Crete. Returning seven months later, he discovered much of his toy business had been looted. Fortunately though, the electric motors in his shop had not been disturbed. However, since so much equipment had been destroyed in Athens, Kontis used his motors to grind flour for his starving countrymen. When his own food supplies diminished, Xantos selected Persian rugs from his house and walked for three days in the countryside until he found a farmer willing to trade for food. Although many of his family heirlooms had to be bartered, Kontis managed to keep some of his dolls. In 1951, when Kontis joined relatives living in America, he brought some of these and also some of his puppets.

When he first came to America, he worked for a display company in Pittsburgh, making numerous designs for advertisements. One assignment he especially enjoyed was creating a life-size bust of Abraham Lincoln, which is on permanent display in Springfield, Illinois.

Kontis married Pauline, an American of Greek origin, who was also a doll collector and talented seamstress. Gradually he began to make a few dolls as a hobby, with Pauline designing the clothes. When Pauline displayed his creations at a doll club, collectors urged the couple to make dolls for sale.

Only two years after coming to this country, Kontis was commissioned to make the first doll given at the National United Federation Doll Club Convention in 1953. Pa Pitt represented a character symbolic of Pittsburgh, the site of the convention. Pauline designed and made the costume. A few Ma Pitt dolls were made as well. Before the creation of Pa Pitt, collectors received such souvenirs as commemorative plates, or doll albums, at conventions. Pa Pitt started a tradition. In the 23 years since then, 17 dolls have been given at national United Federation Doll Club conventions.

Kontis later designed two more souvenir dolls. In 1954, a portrait of Osceola, the undefeated Seminole Indian warrior, was created for the Miami convention. The artist designed a metal gun, chest decorations, and a powder horn as accessories for Osceola. Father Knickerbocker, complete with tiny spectacles with lens, was the symbol in

Peasant woman from Itirus, Greece; made in Greece in 1938.

1958 for the New York meeting. At the moment no other artist has made three complete dolls, fully clothed, as symbols of National U.F.D.C. conventions.

Many of Kontis' other dolls were inspired by Americans important in the history of his adopted land. Father Junipero Serra, a Franciscan monk, established many missions among the Indians of California. The costume for the portrait doll is authentic, including a tiny rosary.

Dolls representing revolutionary personalities included Paul Revere, Benjamin Franklin, and Richards, a black tavern owner. By 1968 Xantos Kontis had decided to retire, but he made one last doll. As his first major American commercial doll was designed for U.F.D.C., that last one, Stephen Foster, was created for a regional convention in Pennsylvania. ■

Charlie Richards, representing the first black tavern owner at Fort Pitt.

Old man from the Isle of Rhodes dressed in authentic costume and carrying his "worry beads"; 1938.

Osceola, chief of the Seminoles, dressed in authentic costume. Commissioned for a souvenir of the 5th Annual Convention of the United Federation of Doll Clubs in Miami, Florida, 1954.

Woman from Sarakatsanisa, Greece, in authentic costume; 1938.

the search for ALEXANDERS

RHODA SHOEMAKER

WHEN the national tour of The Search For Alexander, an exhibition of Greek artifacts from the Alexander the Great era, was announced locally, I received several telephone calls from doll collectors who mistook this publicity for an Alexander doll campaign. After clearing up the ensuing confusion, I was struck by the thought that, actually, those of us who are dedicated to the collecting of those very desirable little dolls created by Madame Alexander do spend a good deal of time in "the search for Alexanders."

Once an Alexander doll collector gets past the initial compulsion that says, "I must have them all!," most of us settle down to the pursuit of one category — i.e., babies, Portraits, the 8" series, etc. When a good-sized group of the chosen category is assembled, the collector may find that although she (he) has gathered together a nice little collection, it is indeed much like other people's collections. And it is *then* that the search begins — the search for the special issues, the limited editions, the special hair-dos — in other words, the doll that is "different!"

A case in point is Madame Alexander's ever-popular 8" Wendy, sold since 1953 under that name as well as Wendy-kin, Wendy Ann and Alexander-kins. Sometimes one doll carries two or even all three of those names. Illustration No. 1 shows a basic Wendy from the 1956 through 1964 period, a bending-knee walker with braids, original tagged panties, shoes and socks, and wrist tag. At the time she was sold, a complete line of clothing for her was also available and she could be provided with an enchanting wardrobe.

The doll in Illustration No. 2 qualifies as different, not necessarily because she is a Quiz Kin, but because she is a little girl as well. The Quiz Kin doll was issued in 1953 only, is a straight-legged non-walker, and is equipped with two small buttons at the back. Press one button and the doll nods "Yes"; press the other and the doll shakes its head "No." Most of the Quiz Kins seem to be of the boy type, with molded hair and wearing, in many cases, sunsuits which presumably make the buttons more accessible. This little Wendy has a wig and is completely outfitted as a girl.

Qualifying as both a special issue and a doll with a special hair-do is the Wendy shown in Illustration No. 3 and No. 4. From the same late 1950s-early 1960s period, she is delightfully dressed in rose-colored flocked organdy, with a straw headpiece. Under that headpiece, her hair is arranged in the regularly curly hair style, but with an added small braid, held in place by ribbon bows, across the top of her head. Additonally, she carries a tiny wooden toy.

In Illustration No. 5, Cherry Brunette seems to be saying, "Meet my sister, Cherry Blonde!" The Cherry Twins were issued for one year only — 1957 — and their claim to fame, in addition to their distinctive clothing, is that they are so difficult to find. Perhaps in 1957, most little girls were not lucky enough to receive two dolls at a time and so many of the sets were broken up and sold separately.

Another special issue from 1957 is Wendy Graduates (Illustration No. 6), in a gown of white dotted Swiss and carrying her rolled-up, ribbon-tied diploma. She also has a special hairdo, with a cluster of curls at the top of her head. Wendy's big sister Lissy (12") graduated that same year in a matching outfit.

Illustration 5.

Illustration 1.

Illustration 2.

Illustration 3.

Illustration 4.

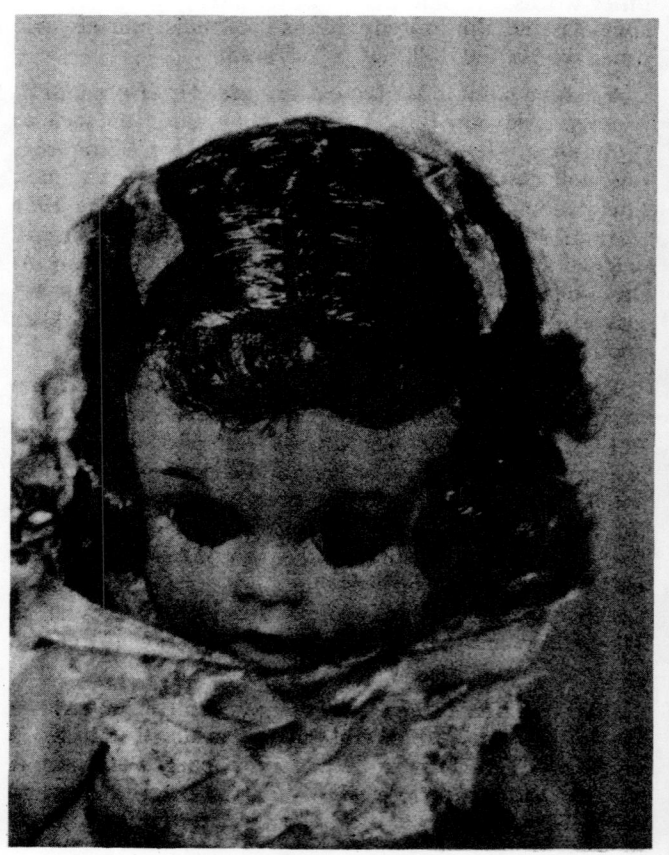

Illustration 6.

Illustration 8.

Illustration 7.

Wendy dressed as a Southern Belle was issued twice — in 1956 and 1963. The first time she was dressed in two different outfits, one of striped silk and the other of pink taffeta. In 1963 (Illustration No. 7) she was dressed in blue taffeta much trimmed in lace, a matching bonnet, and pantalettes. She also is a very scarce little doll.

The final illustration (No. 8) is of what is technically an off-shoot of the 8" Wendy. She is Maggie Mix-up, issued in 1960 and 1961. Her mouth is a soft smiling curve, rather than the typical rosebud; she has green eyes and a smattering of freckles; her hair is shiny, and straight and bright red, styled with bangs across her forehead. Occasionally she does turn up with a rosebud mouth, or with blue eyes, or even both. She came dressed in a variety of little girl outfits and is a much-sought-after Alexander doll.

One of the fascinating aspects of this search for different Alexanders is the chance of tracking down yet another variation of even the "special" issues. I have recently found a 1953 Quiz Kin that is wigged and dressed as an Angel, and a Maggie Mix-up with the only difference being that her red hair is pulled to side pony tails. What more can I say? Only "Good Hunting!"

Rhoda Shoemaker has been a Madame Alexander researcher and author for many years. She is the author of Compo Dolls Cute and Collectible *and* Rhoda Shoemaker's Price Guide for Madame Alexander Dolls. *Mrs. Shoemaker is an active appraiser and lecturer in her own state of California.*

"Parlor Meetings," by Betty Curtis, consists of eighteen figures, the adults 11 to 12 inches tall.

DOLL GROUPS
THAT EXPRESS AMERICAN CULTURE

by HELEN BULLARD

This early photograph inspired Helen Bullard to create "Afternoon in 1904—Appalachian Farm Family Portrait." The two brothers and sister, their spouses and children, and their grandparents, appear in an artistic set of rhythms worthy of a great artist.

Helen Bullard's hand-carved figures capture the feeling of an original old photograph in her "Appalachian Farm Family Portrait."

WHILE all of the people figures created by the artists of the National Institute of American Doll Artists are intended to "express American culture"—which is our objective, it is the groups of related figures built around a single idea which have the greatest impact. Gone are the days when Queen Elizabeth II in an elaborate gown was the acme of the American doll artist's skill. We are now free of that romantic preoccuation, having discovered great subjects in our own country.

These great subjects are everywhere. Take our western pioneers, for example, as created by Frances Bringloe of Seattle. She has built a series around the Lewis and Clark Expedition to the Northwest, and another around the early gold rush days in Alaska. Carefully authentic, her groups are intended mainly for museums and audio-visual school programs.

Ada Odenrider, also of Seattle, has created many pioneer groups for museums in the Northwest and has in recent years made convincing cowboys, woodsmen, trail men and lumberjacks.

Down in Utah, in the Capitol Building Museum in Salt Lake City, are Lewis Sorensen's "Mormon Pioneers," a serious work of art showing Brigham Young, three of his wives and other Mormon pioneer figures. It is worth a visit, especially since the handsome photograph used in *The American Doll Artist* and several other books has disappeared.

Of the East Coast immigrants of the 17th century and later, there are many individual figures, but the only large groups are Betty Curtis' "Maine Parlor Meeting" and my own "An American Family" consisting of nine generations of couples dating from 1630 to 1900.

Mirren Barrie's series on the American flag has been received with enthusiasm wherever she has shown the group, mainly in New England.

There have been many different (and some indifferent) interpretations of the Presidents and First Ladies, especially during the 1950s when Magge Head Kane and Lewis Sorensen each made many casts of complete sets of their original designs, hers in porcelain, his in composition. Of our other artists, Beverly Cerepak has made one set of Presidents, and Frances Ravca one set of First Ladies.

A body of work so nearly devoted to one type of American subject, such as Dewees Cochran's (*SW* May '72) upper class American children, can easily be arranged to illustrate a sector of our culture. The impact of such a group

Lewis Sorensen displays his "Presidents and First Ladies." **Left to right:** The Johnsons, the Nixons, the Carters, and the Fords. Earlier Presidents and First Ladies stand on the shelves behind Mr. Sorensen.

Ada Odenrider's "Trail Men" were made in 1974.

was accomplished at the Cochran Retrospective at the 15th NIADA Convention in Chicago, in 1977. Her group of six basic American little girls' heads, developed decades ago by Mrs. Cochran according to scientific principles of physiognomy, is the only such deep analysis of American faces.

In a romantic vein, Gertrude Florian in 1945, inspired by the individual stories of heroic actions of many nuns, created a group of 30 of them, of different orders and in authentic habits. The variation in dress was astonishing, as was the size of the figures—one and one-half inches! Only the early members of the Detroit Doll Collectors' Club have ever seen this significant group, which has since disappeared. How we wish Gertrude had photographed them!

Perhaps nothing is more American than our famous movie and stage stars. Fawn Zeller, Jo Stafford, Lita Wilson, Frances Ravca and Gwen Flather have each fashioned stars in favorite roles, many of which are displayed in groups in famous collections.

In quite a different, down-to-earth *milieu*, Magge Head Kane conceived "Kane's Rebels," a group of twelve rollicking kids dressed in play clothes and cutting up for each other. Her "pickaninnies," which were no-nos in the 1960s, are now with the development of black *amour propre*, acceptable. Black and white alike enjoy them for their nostalgic appeal. The mammies and old men which are in a companion group are near-portraits of Magge's old friends and helpers.

When it comes to "groups," Magge's museums take top honors. Her Windy Acres (of Carlos, Indiana) Museum subjects are favorite characters from children's stories as well as several Presidents and First Ladies, all arranged in dioramas by Mrs. Kane. The Museum Dollorama, formerly in Cedar Rapids, Iowa, and now in Illinois, includes 138 Kane figures, many of them original models created for the museum. These scenes, too, are by Magge Head Kane.

Roberta Bell of Chicago has the field of "Famous Black

Three couples from Helen Bullard's "An American Family, 1639-1900."

"Kane's Rebels" (1963), by Magge Head Kane. All dolls are about 14 inches tall.

Americans" to herself. Ever since 1966 she has designed, produced and commemorated blacks of achievement, many of whom were unknown except to students of black history. Powerful groups of these figures are now in many museums.

Working with ethnic subjects familiar in her childhood in New York City, Rose Sullo has made many humorous groups, such as the "Mudgutter Band," the "Singing Waiters," and "Milano Wedding Party."

Fern Deutsch's leading American group is one of "Early American Children," consisting of five storybook characters with farm animals. Sharon Johnson's "Playmates of the Past" has pairs of children of various decades of the 20th century which form an interesting historical group.

Nowadays when nearly every modest town has a ballet class, ballet dancers can no longer be considered exotic. When they inspire all-porcelain figures so skillfully articulated as those of Suzanne Gibson's (*SW* Sept. '75) professional dancers and Judith Condon's (*SW* Oct. '75) little beginners, they are clearly an expression of our own people. Besides the dancers, the Condon group of teenagers is strictly today and packs a wistful appeal.

Obviously, I went overboard on the "group" idea with my recently completed "Sunday Afternoon in 1904—Appalachian Farm Family Portrait" with its 23 members of a mountain family. When I came upon the handsome photograph about a year ago I was so impressed that I carved replicas from horse chestnut and dressed them in old materials. The group shows two brothers and a sister, their spouses and children and three grandparents, all rhythmically arranged by an itinerant photographer. (The dog escaped from my group when the glass door was open.)

Even with all these groups we have scarcely begun to explore the possibilities of dramatic and significant American groups with different stories to tell. Because the groups already in existence are expressions of the individual artists' interests and not assigned subjects, they are works of art, convincing and genuine. ∎

Judith Condon's "The Ballet Class"; the intricately jointed figures stand 11 ½ to 12 inches tall.

"Pioneer Family in Every Day Dress," by Frances Bringloe.

Effanbee's First Limited Edition Doll

by JUDITH WHORTON

A DOLL manufactured in the 1860s by the French firm Bru appeared to eat—almost a hundred years later a doll that ate baby food was presented as an innovation. Many antique wax dolls of England had inset hair—the rooted hair dolls of our century were hailed as a new idea! Students of doll history may well say there is little that is completely original.

Yet a major American doll company has recently developed a new dimension in manufacturing dolls for collectors. The Effanbee Doll Corporation is making a series of numbered, limited edition dolls.

In August, 1974, the firm offered collectors through mail invitations a chance to become members of the Effanbee Limited Edition Doll Club. A two-page letter, written by the chairman of the board, Leroy Fadem, introduced the premiere edition:

". . .This beautiful doll has been part of the Effanbee family for many years. It has been selected as the Club Premiere choice as its fond farewell—never again will *Precious Baby* be made. When this edition is completed the molds will be destroyed and *Precious Baby* will become part of the treasure house of Effanbee beauties of the past, . . . This Premiere Selection will be restricted to only 2,800 dolls, . . . There will be no extra dolls of this edition available for later purchase at any price."

Charter membership was closed on January 31, 1975. Each doll is accompanied by the number in order of production. Also included is a certificate with the name of the purchaser, the number of the doll, and the statement signed by Mr. Fadem and attested by the Secretary of Effanbee that *Precious Baby* is the first edition.

Precious Baby, designed by Bernard Lipfert, first appeared in its mass produced version in 1962. It was withdrawn from the market in the 1970s. The unlimited examples were dressed either in pajamas or a dress and coat.

The outfit designed by Eugenia Dukas for the limited issue is a long tucked dress graced with rows of lace. A pink taffeta slip accentuates her white organdy gown. She wears a ruffled tucked cap and rests on an organdy ruffled taffeta pillow. A

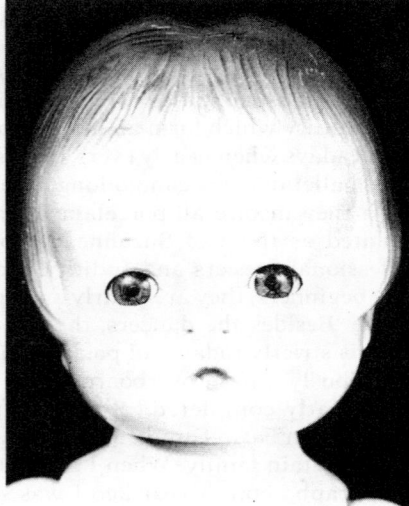

Fig. 2: Patsy.

label sewn in the dress and body verifies this is a limited edition Effanbee doll. Future collectors who consider purchasing a first edition from an individual should insist the doll has its original dress, verifying certificate, and both limited edition labels.

Collectors will appreciate the golden metal heart the doll wears as a locket. The tiny heart with the words "Effanbee Durable Dolls" in raised letters was first used in 1923. For a while girls could obtain a heart necklace for themselves from Effanbee for a few cents and a coupon. The use of the metal hearts began to be phased out in 1939, to be replaced by a paper heart. Mr. Raizen, President of the Effanbee Doll Corporation, who with his partner bought Effanbee in 1971, says:

"We found a number of these hearts . . . associated with Effanbee's past and as long as they last we do intend to use them on the Effanbee Limited Edition Dolls."

Precious Baby, 25 inches long, has blond hair with bangs and soft curls. The doll is made of vinyl, which may be an advantage in years to come. A

ILLUSTRATIONS

Figure 1: Perhaps Precious Baby, a limited edition, will start a new dimension in doll collection.

Figure 2: Effanbee's famous Patsy doll, designed by Mr. Lipfert in 1925, first had a stuffed body. When she was later given an all composition body and a separate wardrobe, she became a landmark in American doll history. She was so successful that eventually a series of Patsy's was created, including Patsy Ann, Patsy Lou, and others.

A Montgomery Ward catalog described Patsy as "the nation's most imitated doll." She made such an impact that the German firm Armand Marseille designed a similar doll in bisque, called "Just Me." In another innovation, Patsy had its own fan letter with more than 250,000 members.

Figure 3: Wee Patsy, another favorite with collectors, is 6 inches tall. At the moment Wee Patsy brings a higher price than many compositions of the same family. (*Both Patsy's from the collection of JoAnn Wynn, Homewood, Al.*)

Figure 4: Effanbee seems to have been interested in presenting new ideas. Charlie McCarthy, the dummy made a famous radio star by Edgar Bergen, was introduced in 1937. In March, 1938, *Playthings Magazine* reported that for the first time, thanks to Charlie McCarthy, dolls were bought for boys beyond infant age. Adults were not immune to the appeal of Charlie. Parties with a ventriloquist theme for gown-ups became popular. Charlie McCarthys were often given as favors. Many department stores set up ventriloquist classes. Although dummy dolls sold from 50 cents to $10, their popularity was so great it was hard to fill all the orders. Charlie McCarthy was sold in a choice of several different outfits. (*Eunie Collection of Birmingham, Al.*)

Fig. 3: Wee Patsy.

Fig. 4: Charlie McCarthy.

Figure 5: The Portrait Doll designed by Dewees Cochran for Effanbee were considered such an innovation that *Life* featured a cover story about them—the dolls resemble a real child. Between 1936 and 1939, Effanbee sold approximately 50,000 of them. (*Collection of the late Genevieve Angione.*)

modern bisque doll could be easily duplicated by any one who is talented and owns a kiln; the making of vinyl dolls requires more complicated equipment. The original price of the first edition doll was $40. It will be interesting to note its price in future years.

The Effanbee Doll Company has been making dolls for more than 65 years. Much of its history has been connected with Bernard Lipfert, designer of *Precious Baby*. In its early years the Effanbee Doll Company did not keep a collection of dolls, photos, or records that would help preserve its history. The dolls, themselves, provide the only records.

Although Mr. Lipfert made many dolls for Effanbee from the 1920s 'til the late 1960s or early 1970s, the exact number is impossible to estimate. According to Mr. Raizen, *Precious Baby* is one of the last dolls Mr. Lipfert designed for Effanbee.

An all vinyl *Patsy* made from new molds inspired by the original composition doll is the second choice in the series. The doll will be marked on the head and back "Patsy 1976 Limited Edition." The offer will be closed June 30, 1976 or when 2,880 dolls have been sold, whichever comes first. The book, *A Collector's Guide to the Patsy Doll*, will be accompanying the doll.

Fig. 5: Portrait Doll, designed by Dewees Cochran, with original box showing Effanbee's Heart Medal.

Half Dolls and Novelties

Purists argue about the definition of a doll. To some it must be an articulated figure primarily made for play. Others insist upon articulation, but allow other primary functions such as imagery, fashion, or theatre. For the generalist the scope is wider. The generalist includes related figures such as half-models designed as pin cushion decoration or candy container lids and novelty figures such as carnival dolls or historical memorabilia. To the generalist, half-dolls, and snow babies are as much a part of the doll collecting scene as more traditional style dolls. They reason that doll design is properly a representation of the human figure, however realistic or fantastic that design may be.

Also included in this chapter are fascinating articles on "The Wonderful Creeping Baby", a delightful predecessor to 20th century celluloid and composition examples. Simonelli explores our misconceptions about its designer, making us wish for more substantiated research of this kind. "The Snow Babies" by Jean Crowley also draws its conclusions from newly discovered primary material.

The diversity of the Gebruder Heubach firm is shown in this trio of dolls. Utilizing a basic facial mold, one of whimsy, somberness, or glee, the Heubach firm made a variety of dolls, figurines, or novelties. Shown are a typical doll, the traditional "piano baby", tiny sliding figures, and a skiing "candy container".

Marks on HALF FIGURES

by FRIEDA MARION

Fig. 1: Large bisque half-figure made by W. Goebel. *Collection Mr. & Mrs. Harry Tattersall.*

The Collector's fascination with marks found on half-figures is natural, for such symbols, trademarks or production numbers are one means of identification. They help us name the manufacturer of our treasures, know the country of their origin, or indicate the period when they were produced.

The bulk of half-figures were made of china, a general term covering the potters' wares, and some high quality pieces were produced in fine porcelain. Although often called "half-dolls," these little figurines which were terminated at the waistline were not dolls for children to play with, but were meant to be fastened to useful household objects. In this country they have been labeled "pincushion dolls," although in Europe they were first used to top tea-cosies. During the early part of the 20th century, half-figures were a popular decoration attached to small lamps, telephone screens, candy boxes, perfume bottles, hat-pin holders and cosmetic cases.

We're always pleased to see a half-figure with well-defined markings, especially if it confirms our earlier suppositions as to the model's origin. Such a half-figure is the bisque nude from an English collection, shown in *Figure 1*. Coded MW 207-701 in the *Collector's Encyclopedia of Half-Dolls* (Marion and Warner, Collector Books 1979), this model appeared to be a product of the W. Goebel Procellanfabrik yet we couldn't verify our guess until Mr. and Mrs. Tattersall sent us photos from London.

The author's example of the same model measures 6½ inches and is incised "406/6", while the one in the Tattersall collection is 8 inches and incised "406/7", with the W. Goebel trademark inside the base. (See marks, *Figure 2*). It's not uncommon for marks to be omitted on small half-figures although a company usually marked large items, but even tiny W. Goebel models often carry their distinctive trademark of entwined initials "W G" beneath a crown, so our 6½ inch unmarked speciman puzzled us.

Another familiar mark on quality half-dolls is the hand-painted blue symbol of the Dressel and Kister Company, easy to identify in spite of variations due to individual decorators. The model in *Figure 3* bearing this

Fig. 2: Marks found on half-figures: *A*—W. Goebel. The narrow crown (left) is an earlier mark and is found on the gold labels of their Historic Series of tea-cosie half-figures. *B*—Dressel and Kister symbols. *C*—Richard Eckert & Co., Volkstadt-Rudolstadt. *D*—Ernst Böhne Söhne, Rudolstadt. (Later known as Albert Stahl Company.) *E*—Pottery in Volkstedt-Rudolstadt founded by G. H. Macheleid (now in East Germany).

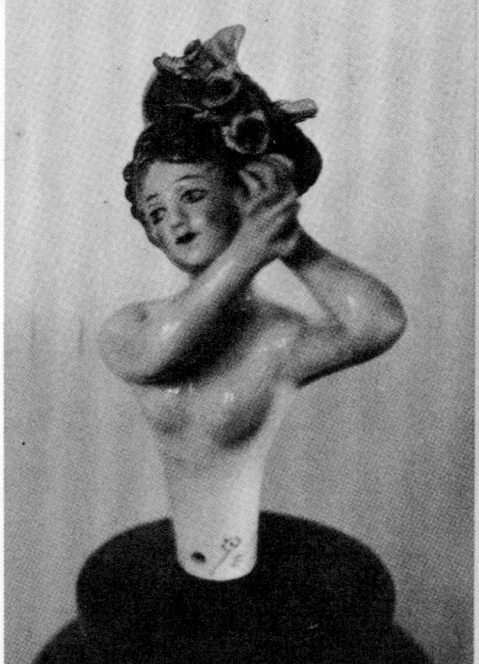

Fig. 3: Charming half-figure made by Dressel and Kister. *Collection Mr. & Mrs. Harry Tattersall.*

Figs. 4 & 5: Dressel and Kister half-figure from their Medieval Series, marked inside the Rear view shows added crossed-swords mark. *Collection Mr. & Mrs. Roy Pavitt.*

"reverse question mark" is also in the Tattersall collection. The fine modeling, delicately painted features, applied decoration, and unglazed, tapered base are all indicative of work produced in the Passau factory for over a hundred years (1840-1942). Having established familiarity with Dressel and Kister half-figures, we now encounter another puzzle—what can we make of the *two* different marks on the model in *Figures 4 and 5*, from the collection of Mr. and Mrs. Roy H. Pavitt of Surrey, England?

With her high hennin, flowing wimple, and flat gold necklace, this elegant half-figure is placed among the Dressel and Kister Medieval series depicting high-born ladies of the 15th century. The blue symbol inside the base verifies our opinion. What, then, can we make of the crossed swords mark on the outside of the base?

Most controversial of all marks on china are those resembling crossed-swords, as this symbol was used by the prestigious Königlich Porzellan Manufaktur (K.P.M.) in Meissen soon after porcelain production was introduced to Europe in the early 1700s.

Hugo Morley-Fletcher in *Antique Porcelain in Color–Meissen* (Doubleday & Company, Inc. 1971) writes about the "most enduring porcelain mark of all time, the crossed swords—derived from the arms of Saxony." He says that the job of marking the K.P.M. wares usually went to an apprentice called a "Schwerterer" or sword painter, and that the results varied considerably although by 1730 a fairly consistant style was developed. This mark has been copied by innumerable potteries so it takes a great deal of expertise to authenticate porcelain made in the Royal Meissen factory.

Knowledge about marks is helpful but obviously it's not enough to instantly place every item. For china lovers, the magic words "Meissen" and "Dresden" are coupled with the crossed-swords symbol, yet we've never

Fig. 6: Flapper model with incised heart mark. *Collection Mr. & Mrs. Roy Pavitt.*

Fig. 7: Although blurred, the painted symbol inside the base of this half-figure is undoubtedly one used by the Volkstedt-Rudolstadt factory of Richard Eckert and Company. *Collection Mr. & Mrs. Harry Tattersall.*

Fig. 8: A young woman of Krautgersheim, this half-figure apparently is one of a series modeled wearing European folk dress. *Collection Mr. & Mrs. Harry Tattersall.*

found evidence of early half-figures produced in these areas.

Now let's make another "educated guess" and assume that the crossed swords mark on the half-figure in *Figures 4 and 5* is not connected with the Royal Porcelain Factory but instead comes from one of the later potteries which were purchased by Dressel and Kister in 1903, along with permission to use their marks (*Handbuch des Europäischen Porzellans,* Ludwig Danckert, Prestel-Verlag München, 1974).

We don't have records of all the potteries the company acquired so at best this supposition only gives us clues for further research. By 1937 the Dressel and Kister factory was in the hands of one Philipp Dietrich, and by 1942 production ceased.

A heart-shaped mark has been found on half-figure models, and again we are not positive of the maker. The Coleman's *Collector's Encyclopedia of Dolls* (Crown Publishers, Inc., 1968) gives information on Bruno Schmidt of Waltershausen who used this on bisque heads for play dolls, and it is possible that the company also made half-figures. *Figure 6* illustrates a Flapper with a cigarette dangling from her lips, a model incised with a heart as well as the numerals "3853" and the word "Germany." This lively half-figure, in a tailored cloche and carrying a short-handled umbrella, is also in the Pavitt collection.

Sometimes the mark is so blurred as to be nearly undecipherable, as on the stylish lady shown in *Figure 7*. For what seemed an eternity, we stared at a photographic close-up beneath our magnifying glass, until suddenly we realized that we were seeing the Richard Eckert trademark. A wet glaze carelessly applied over the painted symbol before the latter was sufficiently dry had created a soft blur which at first we didn't recognize. Richard Eckert and Company of Volkstedt-Rudolstadt made "luxury articles" including figurines which were exported. This model, a splendid example of their wares, is now in the Tattersall collection.

Research uncovers groups of half-figures seemingly made by the same manufacturer, all belonging to a set. Most noteworthy are the Medieval Series by Dressel and Kister, or the well-documented Historic Series of tea-cosie half-figures by W. Goebel. *Figure 8*, another from the Tattersall collection, is one of a group of such models in European folk dress.

Marked with the incised numerals "14344", there is also the printed legend inside the base, "Fabrique en Allemagne," which tells us that the item was intended for export. The handsome head-dress simulating pleated linen is representative of a late 19th century Alsatian folk costume. Two similar half-figures are shown in the *Collector's Encyclopedia of Half-Dolls,* also in folk dress, and also falling into our Category A, i.e., those figures mod-

Fig. 9: One of a series of half-figures produced in the early 1920s dressed in contemporary fashion. *Collection Christina Alai Steenmeijer.*

Fig. 10: Marked only with numbers, this bisque half-figure by an unknown manufacturer has elastic-jointed arms and a silk floss wig. *Collection Mr. & Mrs. Harry Tattersall.*

Fig. 11: Though unmarked, this figure is attributed to an as yet unknown "Royal Rudolstadt" factory. *Collection Patricia Conn.*

eled with the arms as part of the main body and no protruding parts to necessitate a multi-mold production. All of these models are incised with five-digit numerals beginning with "14," (MW 361–441, page 174, and MW 361–410, page 169).

A more modern half-figure which may be one of a different series and by a different manufacturer is *Figure 9*, from the collection of Christina Alai Steenmeijer, Amsterdam, Holland. Again, several "sister models" were illustrated in the *Collector's Encyclopedia of Half-Dolls* (MW 537–405, page 377, and MW 537–544, page 383 are examples).

The similarities of this group include the general design and base construction, dress of the same period, and identical treatment of the eye painting. In these striking half-figures the colored iris is circled with a fine black line and the eyes themselves are heavily shadowed with painted make-up. Four digit numbers are incised on the bases of these models, all of which begin with "7" or "6."

From the Steenmeijer collection we have information about a mark so far unrecorded, at least, on a half-figure. Described as a crude crescent moon or a thickened letter "C," it is, like the crossed-swords, a symbol used by numerous old potteries so we can not hope to pin down the manufacturer without more information.

The opposite of this latter half-figure with an unknown mark is *Figure 11*, a model we have never known to be marked but one which collectors attribute to a "Royal Rudolstadt" factory. The illustration shows a half-figure in the collection of Patricia Conn, unusual because she is decorated in color although the same model more often is found decorated in black, white and gold. Other models are known, apparently by the same maker, nearly always decorated with the black, white and gold combination.

Danckert records a number of potteries in Rudolstadt but no "Royal" one. Ernst Böhne Söhne, later the Albert Stahl Company, used a crown-above-an-N symbol which has been seen on many fine half-figures, and this was a well-known Rudolstadt factory.

Volkstedt-Rudolstadt had its share of potteries, too, and collectors now can recognize the blue underglaze mark from the company founded there by G. H. Macheleid. Richard Eckert was another potter in the area, but we are not sure exactly where the "Royal Rudolstadt" factory was located. Unfortunately, Danckert's book is written in German and is not readily available in this country. However, while working on this article, we were privileged to see part of the manuscript of a new book on marks by Robert Roentgen, and were delighted to find that the work of this expert reinforces some of our own research on half-figures. We're looking forward to its publication and expect that serious collectors will welcome this authoritative source of information.

It is, of course, maddening to find no clue to the origin of half-figures of superior design and quality. Many half-figures compare with fine porcelain figurines both artistically and in careful craftsmanship, and we long to know where they were made and by whom. *Figure 11*, a 6½ inch nude bisque half-figure with elastic-jointed arms, was modeled and painted with skill and delicacy, yet we have nothing but the production numbers "1547" to guide us.

Marks are, after all, just a small part of the puzzle surrounding our half-figures. Only by continuous study can we add to our knowledge and thus to our appreciation of the pleasing little porcelain half-figures which long ago were made to charm and please us by gracing many of our mundane household objects. ∎

Fig. 12: One of the fine half-figures bearing the blue underglaze mark of a pottery founded in Volkstedt-Rudolstadt by G. H. Macheleid, now state-owned. See illustration of marks. *Author's collection.*

Fig. 13: Half-figures decorated with black and gold on white porcelain. These models are attributed by collectors to a "Royal Rudolstadt" factory, although the exact maker is as yet unknown. *Collection Sharon Smith. Photo by Norma Werner.*

Fig. 14: Half-figure lady in a truly fantastic hat is marked with the hand painted "crown-over-N" symbol which researchers Danckert and Roentgen say was used by Ernst Böhne Söhne. *Collection Linda Ballentine.*

This "pleasingly plump" matron clutches a bottle beneath her pink-striped shawl. She is 5 inches tall and very nicely made; we suspect she is a character from a novel by Charles Dickens, but have no documentation at present. *Collection Kathryn Orth. Photo by Bob Rozek.*

A charming model of a little girl wearing delicate porcelain flowers in her hair and on her gold-trimmed bodice. Inside the glazed base is a grey mark of a Crown and the letter "N" which we believe to be the one used by Ernst Sohne, Rudolstadt, Germany. *Collection Margaret Woodbury Strong Museum.*

A medley of fine PORCELAIN HALF-DOLLS
A PICTURE STORY
by FRIEDA MARION

Editor's Note: Earlier research in the field of half-dolls revealed that some of them represented famous portraits and historical persons, probably the best known of all being the elegant but ill-fated young Queen of France, Marie Antoinette.

Exploring further, it was discovered that some of these charming novelties made for the tops of tea-cosies were produced in series to represent the folk costumes of many lands. Several of the latter were actually modelled from costume prints, old engravings and Old World portraits.

In the late 19th century, porcelain half-dolls were imported from Europe in quantity to grace the tops of lamps, pincushions, cologne bottles, clothing brushes and other articles used by a lady. They reached their peak of popularity during the early years of the 20th century.

Since many of today's collectors have never seen some of the finer large portrait or character models, several from various collections represented in a new book, *A Collectors' Encyclopedia of Half-Dolls*, by Frieda Marion and Norma Werner, are being previewed here. Many of the half-dolls illustrated in this book are from the extensive collection of the Margaret Woodbury Strong Museum in Rochester, New York. Others are from private collections throughout the country. All of them and more are illustrated, described and coded in Mesdames Marion and Werner's book, soon to be released by Collector Books, Paducah, Kentucky.

Please turn the page for more illustrations of half-dolls.

Left to right: Miniature portrait of the Princess de Lamballe (Marie Therese Louise of Savoy), friend and confidante of Marie Antoinette. A popular subject with the modelers of half-figures, her likeness in porcelain was produced by several companies making half-dolls many years after her tragic death. *Collection of Mrs. Ralph Renwick. Photo by Norma Werner.* Half-doll depicting the Princess de Lamballe holding a gold snuff box in her hand and incised with the numbers "5105." The model was made in several sizes, from 3 to 5 inches. *Collection Mrs. Ralph Renwick.*

Photo by Norma Werner. A Dressel, Kister & Company model of the Princess de Lamballe. Here the full-blown roses topping her "pouf" were made with tiny, hand applied separate petal. Mounted on a frame, she wears her original gown of fine silk and lace, with garlands of silk rosebuds and "jewels" for trim. *Collection of Norma Werner. Photo by the owner.*

Less than 6 inches high, this Dressel, Kister & Company model shows many anatomical details typical of the beautiful half-dolls produced by this firm. Unlike play dolls, porcelain half-dolls were not toys and their value is much diminished by cracks or chips, so the loss of the tiny, separated fingers would be disastrous. *Collection Mable Oliphant. Photo by Darrel Oliphant.*

Outstanding, even among the finest half-figures, are the Dressel, Kister & Company models sculptured to represent Medieval ladies. Hunting with falcons was enjoyed by ladies of high rank in the Middle Ages. This model has elastic-jointed movable arms, and her authentic headdress is colored maroon and gold and lavishly trimmed with simulated sapphires. Height 5 inches. Susan Sirkis, doll artist and author of studies on costuming dolls, points out that the headdress and necklace on this model is shown in a book of hand-colored engraved plates published in France in the mid-19th century by Paquet Freres. *Collection Margaret Woodbury Strong Museum.*

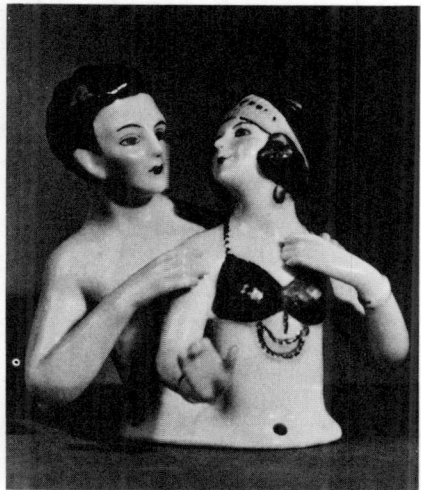

A pair of dancers modelled on one base, this rare group is only 3-1/2 inches high. The lady has a blue band in her striking auburn-colored hair, and wears a gold costume and jewelry. Obviously a delightful companion to her black-haired partner. Incised "10207" with no other clue as to its origin, this is an unusual half-figure. *Collection Ethel Strandberg. Photo by Arthur Johnson.*

Among the most exciting half-doll designs are those depicting the chic ladies of the late 1920s, known as "Flappers." These were produced during the last years of the craze to fasten miniature representations of the female figure to all sorts of household items. This delightful creature is actually reflected in the silver lustre mirror she holds. The model was made in several sizes from 4-1/2 to 6 inches. *Collection Mary Griffith. Photo by Norma Werner.*

This high fashion lady in a green hat follows the styles of the late 18th century, just prior to the French Revolution. Height 5-1/2 inches. A blue-grey stamp inside the base reads "Dresden/Made in Saxony." The Saxon porcelain factory owned by Carl Thieme used the word "Dresden" in several different trademarks. *Collection Margaret Woodbury Strong Museum.*

A string of beads around her neck, this brown-skinned beauty was purchased in the open market-place in Morocco in 1977. The large enamelled eyes, the black wig, and the movable arms make her an outstanding model. A special feature is the rolled-up piece of old Spanish newspaper stuffed into the open crown in place of a plaster pate to hold her wig. Incised "0/6 B." *Collection Frieda Marion. Photo by Christopher Fraser.*

Listed in an old catalog page sent to Mesdames Marion and Werner by the W. Goebel Porzellanfabrik, this model was one of their "Volkstrachtren" half-figures in national costume. Produced in several sizes, she was listed as "Nr. 31, Elsässerin," a woman from Alsace Lorraine. The enormous black headdress and cobalt blue laced bodice make her outstanding. *Courtesy Margaret Woodbury Strong Museum.*

Many models were inspired by the Liotard painting of "La Belle Chocolatiere" which hangs in the Dresden Art Gallery, and here we have the most famous of them all. In 1975, a 7-inch example of this model fetched an unprecedented $3800.00 at auction, the highest price to have been paid for a porcelain half-figure. Although there are at least two other models which are closer representations of the actual portrait, this one has the most beautiful face and is the most appealing to collectors. A century after the portrait was painted, it was adopted as the Walter Baker Company's trademark, now very familiar to every household in America. *Collection Margaret Woodbury Strong Museum.*

Inspired by a portrait of Marie Antoinette holding a rose, painted by Madame Vigée-Lebrun in 1779, this 5 inch tall porcelain half-figure has remarkable presence. The formal hair style and court fashions have been modelled in great detail, and the double ruff about her neck actually sculptured. Unmarked. *Collection Margaret Woodbury Strong Museum.*

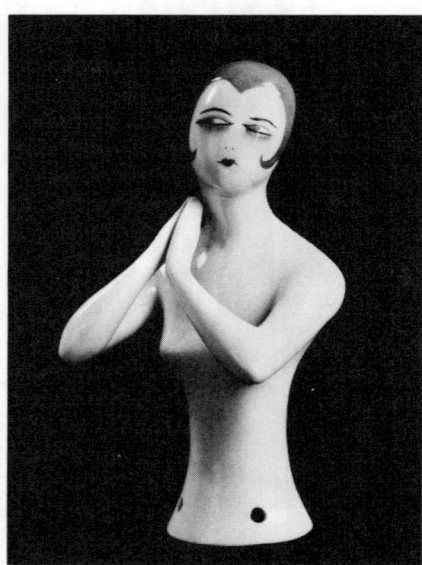

Incised with the mark of the W. Goebel Porzellanfabrik, this unusual Flapper half-doll has no modelling to her features. Orange hair is painted on the egg-shaped head, and the green eye shadow is enhanced by long, painted under-lashes. Stamped "Bavaria," she stands 5-1/4 inches tall. *Collection Charlotte Bill. Photo by Gene Tuck.*

"Spitzenfiguren" is the German potters' term for figurines with porcelain lace, a technique first introduced in Meissen in 1772. Cotton lace, dipped in liquid clay (slip) is draped around the modeled figure and then fired when dried, burning out the cotton fabric but leaving the porcelain. The fragile bisque lace must then be glazed and refired for strength. Half-dolls with this decoration are very rare. *Collection Joanlee Langone. Photo by Vince Langone.*

Her pretty face framed with hand-applied roses, this Old Fashioned Girl is wearing a flower-trimmed bodice and dainty lavender mitts. The most amazing ribbons and bows make her a charming fantasy of the modeler's imagination. A 7-inch tea-cosie doll, she is marked within the base with a crown above the letter "N." *Collection Elsie Meyer. Photo by Robertson.*

Pierrot and Pierrette Half-Dolls

by FRIEDA MARION

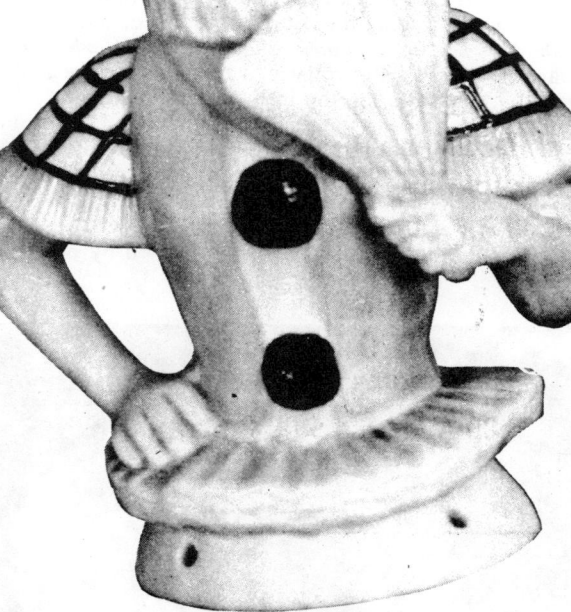

Carnival or Mardi Gras half-figure; sugar-loaf cap, black pompoms, and ruff borrowed from Pierrot's costume; a proper dress for a turn-of-the-century masquerade party. Collection Eleanor Lar Rieu.

COLLECTORS OF pincushion dolls, attention! New designations are in order for certain half-dolls now termed Clowns or Flappers. These are the representations of Pierrot and Pierrette, characters from the classic *Commedia dell Arte*. Easily identified, they should be recognized and given their correct billing.

In the 16th and 17th centuries, troupes of pantomime artists traveled throughout Europe giving performances in which stock characters, wearing traditional costumes, acted out stories handed down from generation to generation and from company to company. The actors had no script but developed the plot extemporaneously within a framework of tradition. *Commedia dell Arte*, developed most vigorously in Italy, was familiar in many lands as Italian Comedy. Its characters—Pantalone, Scaramouche, Il Capitano, Columbine, and the melancholy Pierrot—appeared again and again in literature, music, and the decorative arts as well as on the stage.

Pierrot, like the other basic actors in the drama, had his own distinctive costume—baggy white pantaloons and

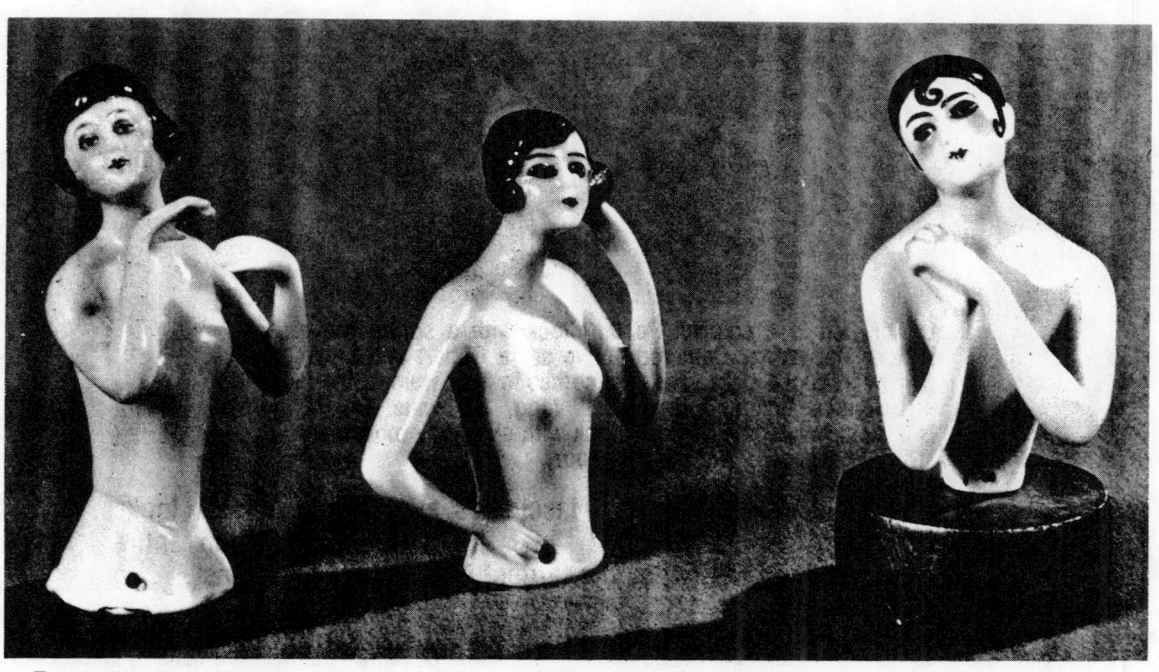

Two bobbed-hair Flappers, incised "Germany 15427" and "868" respectively, and porcelain Pierrette with painted mark of Dressel and Kister; all under 4" tall. Collection Helen Fagg.

long-sleeved, loose-fitting blouse with a wide neck ruff. A skull cap left his ears exposed and allowed locks of hair to curl on his forehead and cheeks.

Since the china half-figures were often modeled unclothed for the buyer to costume, Pierrot's headgear becomes his one sure mark of identification. If it is the ruff which has caused the pincushion Pierrot to be classed as a Clown, it is the skull cap and stray locks which collectors have mistaken for the Flapper's cloche and spit curls.

The original Pierrot was a clown, one Pedrolino, and played a rather obscure part. Though retaining some of his original features, he has undergone many alterations. Jean Gaspard Deburau, the French pantomimist, is credited with bringing him into prominence, but Thelma Nicklaus in her book, *Commedia dell arte (Harlequin)* declares Deburau's Pierrot was a terrifying figure and suggests it was through the influence of Watteau's paintings that the now familiar Pierot evolved. Certainly the Pierrot models found among pincushion dolls correspond to the later versions of the Pierrot which appear in the decorative arts and toys.

Pierrette, a late-comer to the theatrical scene, assumed the characteristics of Pierrot when modeled by pincushion

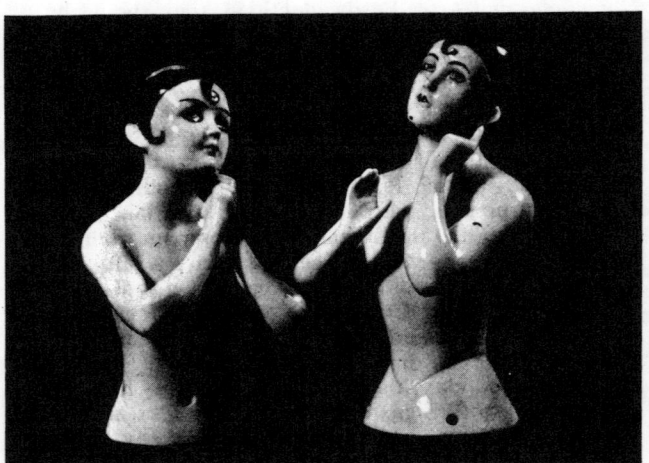
Pierrette and Pierrot posed together; note Pierrot's masculine shoulder breadth.

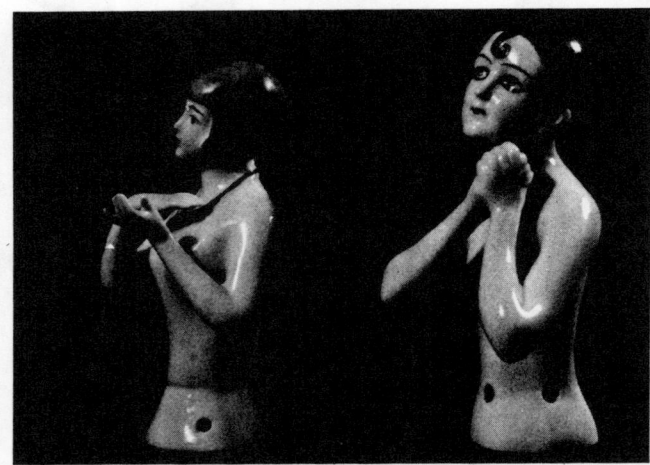
Bobbed-hair Flapper contrasts with melancholy Pierrette.

Large cloth Pierrette dressed in red taffeta, black cap, silk gauze ruff, purchased in Paris in 1912. China half-figures, left to right: black skull cap, red hair, 3½" tall; red-orange cap, black hair, 2" tall; head and shoulders only, black cap and hair, narrow base opening intended for use on brush handle.

Pierrots posed before a mirror—left to right: glazed porcelain, characteristic skull cap and face patch, incised mark, GH entwined, believed used by Gebruder Heubach, 5" tall; tiny bisque, modeled ruff; porcelain, black hair, white skull cap, brush marks delineate hair on nape of neck.

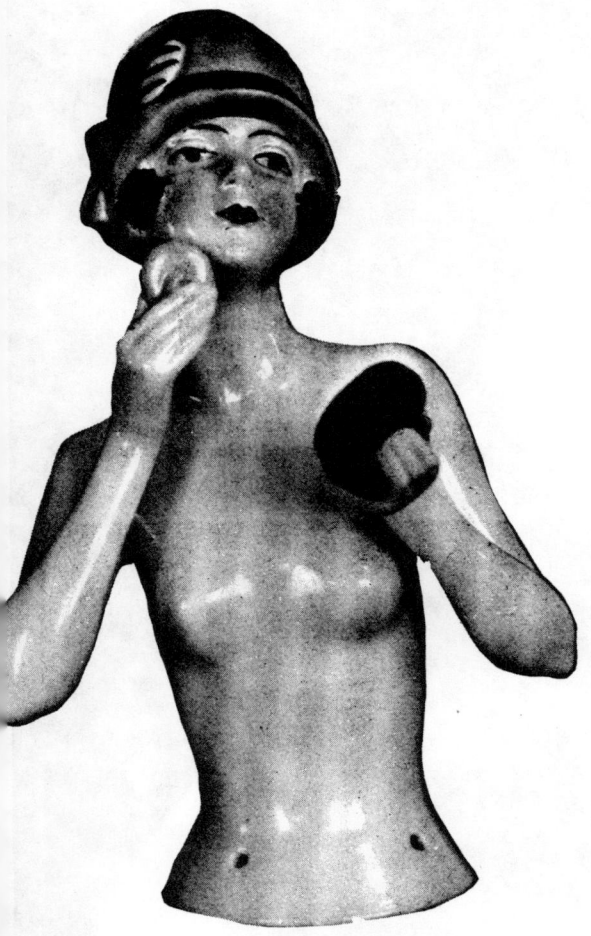

Flapper with compact and powder puff, wearing typical 1927 cloche. Collection Eleanor Lar Rieu.

Thelma Bateman in *Delightful Dolls* pictures a Pierrette doll similar to the large doll pictured here and says it was imported from France for sale in a music store where she was working in 1924. Numerous references in magazines, catalogs, and advertisements of the early 1900s indicate the popularity of the Pierrot and Pierrette characters. It is not surprising they were well-represented among half-dolls.

Pincushion models of Pierrot and Pierrette are to be found with skull caps painted in white, bright blue, red, and black. Their painted locks may be light brown, dark brown, black, or red. Pierrots have been modeled with musical instruments; with double ruffs; with black face patches; or wearing the unmistakable pompom-trimmed wide-sleeve blouse. Most of the figures are wistful of countenance with hands clasped or gesturing sadly. Like the traditional Italian Comedy actors, their faces are white, their eyes ringed with shadows. Frequently they wear expressions of distress.

Made of fired clay, these dainty half-figures have survived with little signs of wear, but the silks and laces of their original pincushion clothes have usually disappeared.

doll artists. Her immature figure, resembling the boyish shape popular in the 1920s, has contributed to the Flapper designation.

Numerous Flapper half-dolls were produced in the mid-1920s. Those modeled with the contemporary long waisted blouse, helmet-shaped tight-fitting cloche, and bobbed hair are easily identified. Despite spit curls Pierrette's cap, exposing her ears, separates her from the Flapper.

One of the finest half-dolls is the Pierrette model produced by Dressel and Kister. Without doubt, this delightful pose was copied by rival factories, sometimes with hand and head given a reverse tilt to avoid infringement suits.

Both clowns and Pierrots were made in doll and toy forms. An automated doll, ca. 1885, dressed as the traditional Pierrot is pictured in *The Golden Age of Toys*, by Remise and Fondin. Another early Pierrot doll, shown in *Wendy and Friends*, by Madaline Selfridge, is of composition, marked SFBJ-255-PARIS. Sears, Roebuck's 1920-21 catalog advertised a number of clown toys and dolls and at least one doll in Pierrot costume.

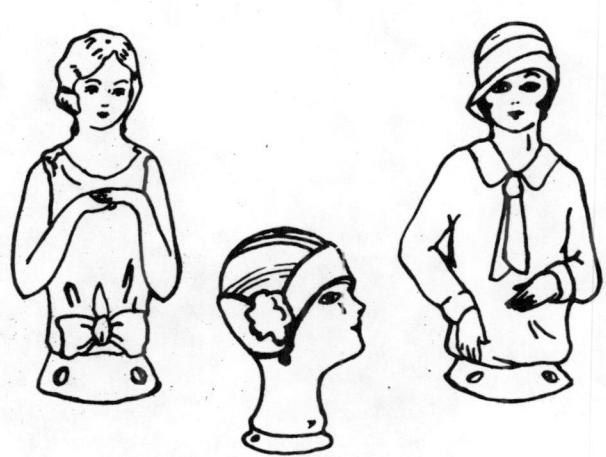

China pincushion dolls exemplify the Flapper of the 1920s with marcelled hair, long-waisted frocks, close-fitting cloches.

Parian shoulder head turned left and tilted downward, blonde molded hair in elaborate arrangement, tight curls framing the face and a large braided coil around the top of the head. Ca. 1880. *Photo Courtesy Theriaults' the dollmasters.*

Parian Ware And Parian-Type Dolls

YOLANDA M. SIMONELLI

DURING the early 1840s, a matte creamy white ceramic was formulated in England to imitate the fine white marble used by sculptors. Called statuary porcelain, it was used for production of figures and busts sold to middle-class Victorians who could not afford genuine marble. The ceramic statuary depicted many famous and royal personages, classical figures and animals. Since the new material could be molded in liquid state, works could be produced in large numbers. The Art-Union of London, who was pressing for a wider appreciation of the arts applauded the ceramic art forms, providing much publicity and awarding many statuettes as prizes to its members.

"Mary — Mother of Jesus" by Magee Head (Kane), a charter member of the Nat. Inst. of American Doll Artists, Inc. (NIADA). This ceramic bisque shoulder head has pale ivory skin tones, expressive painted eyes with molded eyelids. Comb marked molded hair is drawn back, extending to the shoulders in back. Round neck bodice is molded and painted a soft blue. This deep shoulder head is large and completed doll is about 24" tall. Expressive hands are of matching ceramic bisque as are the beautifully molded bare feet.

The new material caught the attention of many porcelain producers due to its popularity and excellent molding qualities. By the 1850s, it was in general use in the form of jugs, vases, candlesticks, table centerpieces, ornamental baskets, clock cases, breakfast sets, dessert services, and even chess pieces. The leading potters produced superb decorative items while lesser firms issued poorly made copies at cheap prices. Copeland and Minton called their products "Parian." Wedgewood used the term "Carrara," and other porcelain producers adopted the name "Stone China." Eventually "Parian" was the word most often used for wares made of the fine marble-like ceramic.

Popularity of parian wares extended into the 1870s. Records of porcelain producers show no evidence of parian doll heads produced in England or France. There are dolls called "parian" known to have been produced by German firms who, from the 1850s to the 1880s made beautfiul decorative shoulder heads of white bisque (unglazed porcelain). These apparently imitated the true parian ceramic formula. Such dolls were sometimes advertised as "parian dolls," and were seemingly directed toward adults rather than youngsters. Most depicted lovely females wearing many types of molded hair styles. Some of these were made from the same molds as the glazed procelains of the era. The parian models were often richly embellished with molded and applied hair ornaments, including combs, snoods, veils, ribbons, plumes, flowers, feathers and imitation jewels. Many had molded bodices with ruffles, collars, pleats and jewelry, as well as hand applied details such as flowers. Decorations were in many colors, sometimes with the addition of rich luster and gold paints. Hair was most often painted blonde. Some had glass rather than painted eyes. Males were not common, and swivel necks are perhaps hardest to find.

Many white bisque decorated heads are found minus bodies due to

(continued on next page)

Left: 19th century Parian shoulder head doll with molded light brown hair, ca. 1870. Right: Parian shoulder head doll with molded short brown hair, late 19th century. *Photo courtesy Theriaults' the dollmasters.*

the fact they were originally sold as luxury novelties in jewelry and gift shops where they were sometimes called "fancies." Bodies of completed dolls, therefore, vary. Ideally, they are most attractive mounted on well-stuffed cotton bodies with parian-type limbs.

Although good quality white ceramic doll heads have been called "parian" by collectors for many years, it is now generally accepted that none were produced by the originators and producers of the true parian bisque formula. Use of the word "parian" in connection with dolls has long been in contradiction. "Blonde Bisque" and "Dresden" were also debatable terms. In 1978, after study and consultation with many knowledgeable collectors, the Glossary Committee for the United Federation of Doll Clubs, Inc. (UFDC), adopted the following terminology:

"PARIAN-TYPE DOLL — Dolls made of fine white bisque (unglazed porcelain) without tinting. The features, hair and cheeks are painted (occasionally there are glass eyes). Eleanor St. George also used the terms "Blonde Bisque" and "Dresden"

Left to right: Parian head doll commonly known as the "Blue Scarf Lady." Parian shoulder head doll representing an adult woman with regal modelling of face and neck, ca. 1870. Parian shoulder head doll with oval face and slender neck, ca. 1865. *Photo courtesy Theriaults' the dollmasters.*

for these dolls. She also referred to early Jumeaus as being parian or blonde bisque. Her terms are rejected by the collectors."

The doll heads called "Blonde Bisque" by author St. George were pale tinted bisques. The dolls called "Dresden" had molded and applied decorations.

In spite of the Federation's attempt to clarify and standardize use of the word "parian," the other terms will undoubtedly continue to be used by some and, as a matter of fact, the Federation's current exhibit classifications for their 1982 National Convention competitive exhibit groups together "PARIAN AND TINTED BISQUE:

Class 56 — Undecorated with molded hair in any combination, with or without glass eyes.

Class 57 — Decorated on hair or chest, with or without glass eyes.

Class 58 — Wigged, with or without glass eyes (excluding Fashion Ladies).

Class 58 — Miniature 8" or under."

Like all ceramic wares of their era, so called parian dolls varied in quality, the finest being of satin smooth finish expertly painted and decorated. Value should therefore be determined by quality of workmanship and artistic details. Coarse grain bisques with gray white tones, better called "stone" or "sugar bisques," were cheap imitations not worthy of the title "parian."

Discussion of parian-type dolls would be incomplete without mention of fine works by modern dollmakers. Foremost was the late Emma Clear who made molds from many fine antique parian heads and limbs which were reproduced by expert artists and craftsmen. Mrs. Clear also commissioned artist Martha Oathout Ayers to sculpt original portraits of Martha and George Washington which were produced in a fine parian-type white bisque. The Emma Clear "parians" are desirable collector items as are the original art dolls in parian-type ceramics by three charter members of the National Institution of American Doll Artists, namely, the late Martha Thompson, Fawn Zeller and Magee Head Kane.

Collections of good quality pariantype dolls are admirable. The many variations of hair fashions and decorations demonstrate artistic sense and expert craftsmanship of makers. As minor works of art, such dolls are creditable offsprings of the fine art materials (marble and true parian) they imitate.■

Yolanda M. Simonelli has been researching and writing about dolls for more than a decade. Her articles have appeared over the years in **Spinning Wheel** *and other prestigeous magazines. Mrs. Simonelli is a Member At Large in the United Federation of Doll Clubs.*

BISQUE HALF-HEADS

by MAGDA BYFIELD

Fig 1: Parian-type bisque half-heads with painted features and blond molded hair, set in a padded fabric baby wrapper trimmed with ribbons. These heads terminate beneath the chin and are encircled with gathered lace to conceal the join. Possibly a Christening favor. Height of heads 1 cm (.3937").

Fig 2: Very fine quality half-head with elongated neck. Intaglio brown side-glancing eyes with black upper eyelines and red lower lines. Deeply molded eyelids give a dreamy expression. Mounted on the padded velvet opening in a walnut novelty pincushion. The nutshell is made of pressed leather and a gold braid loop at the top enabled it to be suspended. Applied millinery leaves and flowers conceal top of smooth head and base of throat. Height of head including neck 4 cm (1.5478").

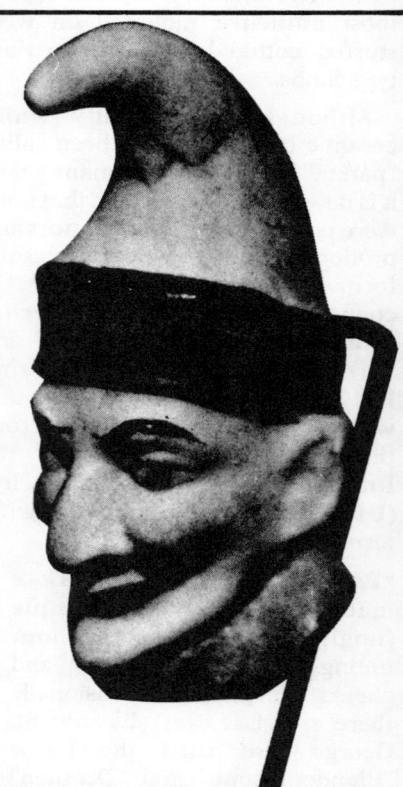

Fig 4: High grade bisque half-head of Punch mounted as a stickpin. Finely modelled features include well defined ears—an unusual feature in half-heads. Head is hollow and enclosed except for pouring hole in back. No marks. Height of head to top of molded cap 3.5cm (1.3779").

AS OUR knowledge of dolls and dollmakers increases, and the number of collectors multiplies, informative books and articles appear on the subject to meet the growing interest. Collectors are now able to familiarize themselves with the endless variety of dolls that were produced throughout the 19th and early 20th century. With this readily available information dolls become more rapidly absorbed into collections than ever before, and the enthusiast is increasingly hard pressed to find hitherto unplumbed areas in this field. As each new discovery is researched and recorded the type becomes sought after, and the prices rise. Partly because of this, collectors are extending their interests to the many by-products from the porcelain factories that produced the dolls. These side-lines are not toys in the

Fig 3: Bisque half-head with neck and shoulder section. Molded light brown curls with comb marks. Well painted features include blue eyes with black eyelines and red lid lines. Applied and fired to a pink glazed porcelain rose-and-leaf-posy, tied in back with a molded pink ribbon. Such items were used as card or letter holders. Height of shoulder head 2cm (.7874").

Fig 5: A coarse bisque half-head detached from the item it once adorned. The light blond hairstyle is topped with a blue molded bow. Black painted eyes are side-glancing. Cast in a very shallow mold with minimal profile relief. No marks. Height of head 6.5cm (2.5590").

true sense, and their intended use was prescribed and strictly decorative. In this group are the bisque figurines, piano babies, bathing belles, snow babies and half-dolls—the latter having been especially popular in the Art Deco period to furnish the top or handle of pincushions, tea cosies, lavendar bags, boxes, telephone and bottle covers.

But how many collectors are aware of the bisque half-head or plaque-head? This by product appears to have been freely adaptable and is found put to a variety of uses. Half-heads are found in solid bisque, as shallow plaques or most usually, hollow and enclosed except for an irregular opening on the flat back where the excess slip was poured from the one-piece mold. Some are literally just heads while others include the neck and sometimes a part of the shoulders. The heads rarely face forward but are turned slightly sideways often with side-glancing eyes. Where close examination of the back is possible an incised four digit number is sometimes found.

The purpose of half-heads was ornamental. They are found engagingly incorporated with novelty pincushions, needle cases, elaborate greeting cards and box lids. They are also found (sometimes in pairs) representing infants swaddled in fabric with lace and ribbon trim and one supposes these were Christening favors *(Fig 1)*. Most heads have molded hair but some are smooth, and this latter type has a head covering of paper, feathers, tightly curled or braided mohair, flocked hair or millinery flowers *(Fig 2)*. Half-heads were also incorporated into all-porcelain items applied together with a flower's petals in place of the stamen and fired in, as illustrated in the dainty card rack in which the rose and leaves are glazed porcelain and the applied head is bisque *(Fig 3)*. Many have turned up as stick-pin brooches *(Fig 4)*.

The majority of half-heads represent cherubic infants and girls. The quality of bisque and feature painting varies greatly from rough simplicity to high distinction. Sizes range from 1cm (.3937") to 7 cm (2.7559") and many are strikingly detailed. Molded hair is usually blond or light brown, often very elaborate and comb-marked. Fine specimens have well modelled upper and lower eyelids with black or red eyelines and red lidlines.

Strays are occasionally seen— usually puzzling the finder as to what this decapitated and bisected object was *(Fig 5)*! Not surprisingly heads remain, as they were generally the most durable component of the many products that incorporated them. There is no evidence that these heads were sold through retailers to be made up in the home, for all found intact on their cards, pincushions, box lids, etc., appear to be commercially assembled.

The writer has seen a saucy postcard of the 1890s which was a black and white print of a woman holding twins—one on each arm. The face area of the infants had been left blank and bisque half-heads had been glued in the spaces. Their long robes were applied pleated paper and the caption read: "Won't You Come Home Bill Bailey?" It says much for the tenacity of old glue and the care of the 19th century postal service that this card had come through stamped and delivered! It was, however, an unusual example as half-heads are traditionally incorporated into rather more romantic Christmas and Valentine cards.

A number of half-heads were used to make miniature wired dolls and the most frequently found appear to have been Christmas cracker toys or party favors, wearing outer garments of tinted cotton wool or crepe paper (Fig 6). Larger bisque *masks* are found on plush or fur-covered play dolls, but these have two or four sew holes for incorporation.

We really know very little about miniature half-heads. It is not known when they were first produced in their present form, and what other materials they were possibly cast in. The provenance of those found may be French or German or both, but they are not attributable to specific manufacturers. Their application was probably far more extensive than we know, for logically such mass-produced decorative miniatures must have had an almost limitless range. Quaint and enigmatic, half-heads are lingering little chronicles of departed tastes and obsolete traditions—remaining as miniature evidences of fashions long gone. ■

Fig 6: Wire and crepe paper doll with applied bisque half-head with flocked hair on forehead. Poorly painted features on coarse bisque. Height of doll 13cm (5.1181"). Height of head 2cm (.7874").

COLLECTING LITTLE CHINA HEADS

AMONG collectible items once overlooked, but now eagerly sought for both charm and novelty, are little china heads whose principle use were as handles for powder puffs. Manufactured by the many potteries which also made porcelain figurines and other knick-knacks, these heads were sometimes sold separately but more often assembled in the factories on swans-down puffs or small brushes, cosmetic cases, sewing aids and similar household accoutrements. Research indicates that most of them were made in Germay, but few have any markings to indicate their source.

Frieda Marion

A collector's dream, this dashing model was found with an old sales tag inscribed 'Prince of Wales Puff,' and stamped 'Made in England.' Incised on the base are the letters 'POW.' *Collection of Rose Hood.*

Opposite page: (1) This 2½ high shoulder head was probably originally attached to a down puff, creating the effect of a feathered boa around her shoulders. Such puffs were placed in china dishes on the fashionable dressing tables of the 1920s. No marks. *Collection of Shirley Pendergraph.* **(2)** Profile view of the Dressel, Kister & Co. two-faced lady made as a handle for a dresser-table brush. Coded MW 100-301 in the *Collector's Encyclopedia of Half-Dolls. Collection of Norma Werner.* **(3)** Is this a dog, or a clown? With the orange hat and painted spots, and the neatly defined eyebrows, it's hard to know what the modeler had in mind when this brush handle was designed. *Collection of Rose Hood.* **(4)** Pretty girls were a favorite design for porcelain powder-puff handles made during the first quarter of the century. This one is 2" high and marked "5800/Germany." *Collection of Shirley Pendergraph.*

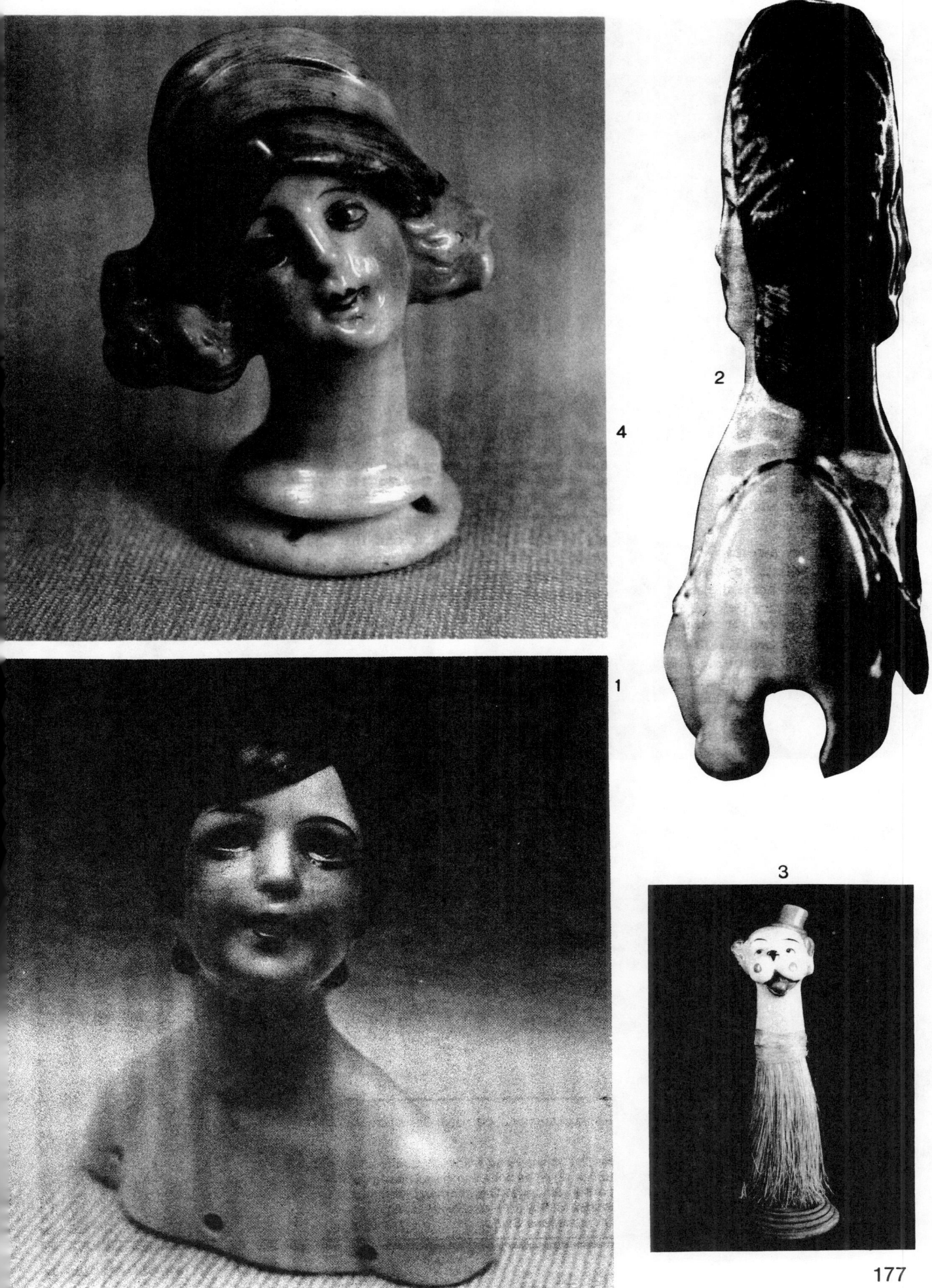

177

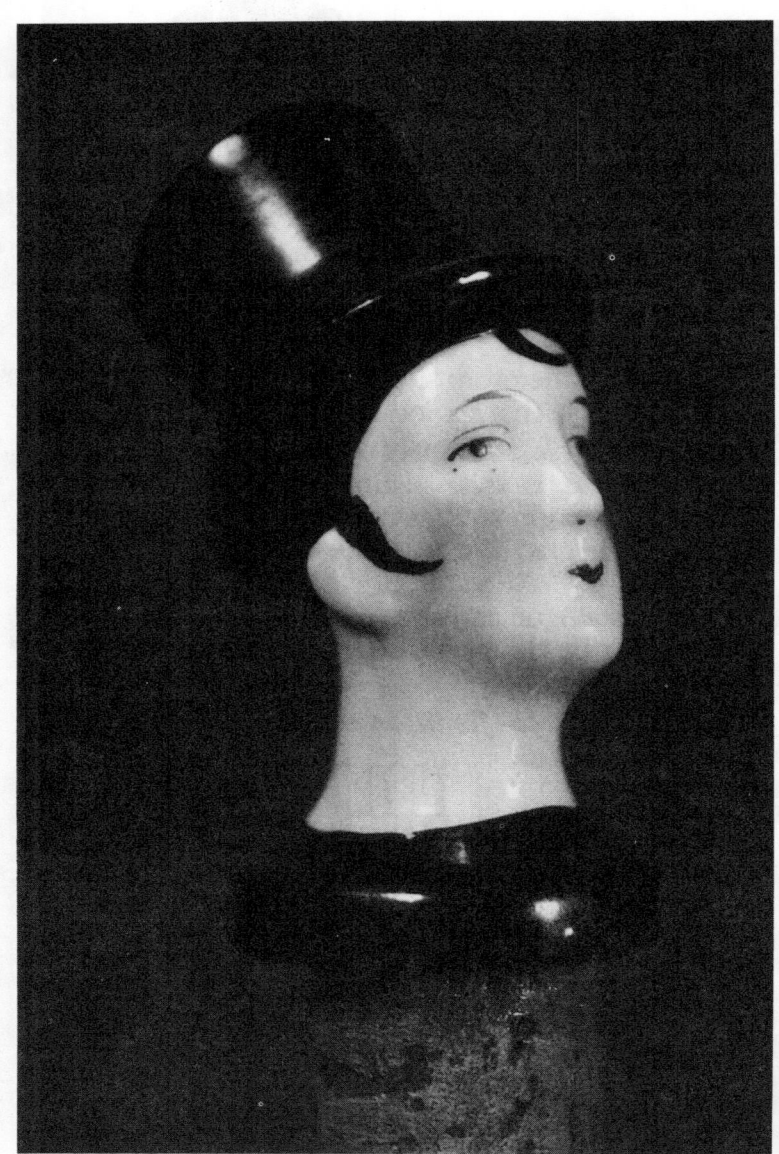

178

As with the china half-dolls attached to tea-cosies and pincushions, the most popular design for the little china heads was a pretty young lady, yet variety plays a large part in the appeal of these collectibles and many heads were modeled to represent little children, Pierrots, animals or even comic and grotesque faces.

W. Gobel Porzellanfabrik produced numerous examples of china heads, usually of good design and craftsmanship and consequently sought after today. Another maker was the Karl Schneider firm whose work generally carried an incised production number and sometimes their trademark or the word 'Germany.'

Manufacturers often used one model in many different ways. The head of a half-doll could easily be developed into a matching powder puff handle by eliminating the torso. The altering was done in the greenware stage, and separate casts were made from the original model so that the artist's sculptured design might yield a variety of forms.

In some cases the front of the model was used, resulting in a little bas-relief face. Called 'flat-heads,' these faces were sewn onto small pillows or bags, or sold in kits with instructions for the do-it-herself buyer whose goal was a decorated needle case, pen-wiper or guest towel rack. Heads depicting animals were frequently used on brushes, especially those of the coarser, whisk broom type. Since brushes of all kinds were deemed a necessity to the householder some seventy-five years ago, little china heads as well as half-dolls and full length figurines were often used as handles. The best-known porcelain head by Dressel, Kister and Company probably is their model of a two-faced lady (MW 100-103) made to top a narrow brush for hats or gloves, depending on the size. The same company made elegant shoulder heads which are sometimes found factory-assembled on padded tea cozy frames or, with delicate porcelain limbs, made into complete dolls.

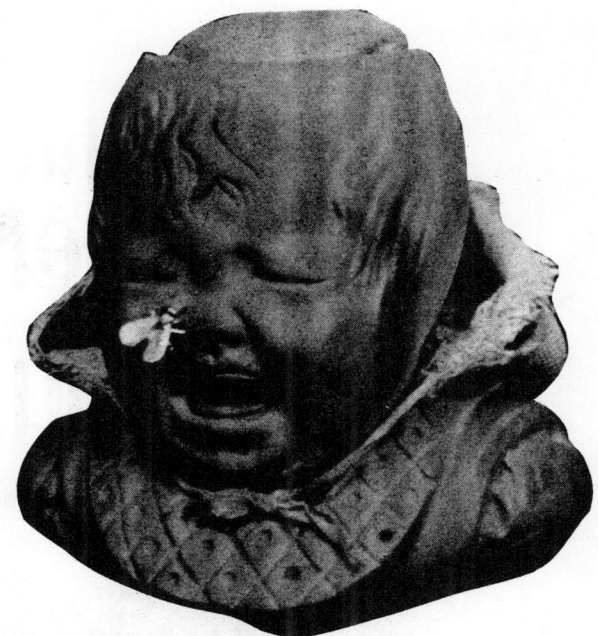

Terra-cotta head of a crying infant, 3¼" high, has a cloth bonnet to cover the pincushion stuffed in the open crown. Stamped '1184/G.D./Paris/depose,' and made by Monsieur Delcroix who manufactured heads at Montreuil, 1887. *Collection of Bess Goldfinger.*

A 3½ inch terra-cotta head of a crying infant with a tiny bee on his nose, shown here, bears the stamped mark of Monsieur Delcroix who manufactured heads at Montreuil from 1887. In *French Doll Trade Marks, 1885-1900 (Spinning Wheel,* September 1957), one of the Delcroix bisque-head play dolls is illustrated, but the head of the crying baby has an opening for a pincushion and obviously was made as a household item—not a toy. A cloth bonnet is made to cover the pincushion when not in use. The bee or fly is constructed to fit into a hole on the side of the child's nostril, and the whole effect is calculated to unsettle any sympathetic seamstress whenever she reaches for a needle or pin.

Little china heads were also attached to bottle corks, sometimes with ingenious pouring holes as part of their design. Birds were modeled for dainty powder puff handles, and butterflies, puppies and small animals were other motifs the modelers used to good effect. Most of the heads are under 2 inches high and some are as tiny as ½ inch. The painted decoration varies, as does the modeling detail but many of the tiny heads have surprising character and craftsmanship.

The period of their popularity extends roughly from the late 19th century through the first quarter of the present century, and while they have often been overlooked because of their size and seeming unimportance, today little china heads have caught the attention of many discriminating collectors thus saving them from historical oblivion.

■

Right: The Pied Piper of Hamlin, a very desirable little character china head. *Collection of Patricia Conn.*

Opposite page: (1) Top-hatted and debonair, this 2½" china head made an ideal bottle stopper in the Roaring Twenties. *Collection of the author.* (2) A fine porcelain Pierrot head for a swansdown powder-puff, by W. Goebel. *Collection of the author.* (3) This charming little head has a cork base and serves as a bottle stopper. *Collection of Roy & Phyliss Pavitt.* (4) A pair of tiny powder-puff handles, nicely detailed. *Collection of Marjorie Stark.*

The Wonderful Creeping Baby

by YOLANDE M. SIMONELLI

"The Wonderful Creeping Baby" with its original wooden packing case. *Author's collection.*

THE WONDERFUL Creeping Baby was a clockwork toy distributed by Ives Blakeslee & Company during the late 1800s. The doll pictured was purchased at the Philadelphia 1876 Centennial Exposition and is shown with its original wood packing box. Paper labels on the box illustrate the toy and explain its working instructions.

In mint condition, the creeping baby measures 11". A cardboard torso contains key wound brass clockworks in working condition. Arms, legs, and head are composition which was waxed over. Blue eyes, with a smiling mouth showing five teeth and feathered eyebrows exemplify quality artistry. A bit of blond hair escapes from beneath a lace bonnet. Cotton undergarments and dress are lace trimmed with original blue silk sash and bow intact. Blue knitted booties protect the feet.

Creeping babies sold for about $5.00 in their era. Rarely found, they exemplify toys of American ingenuity and craftsmanship.

America's early toy industry has not been well-documented. Early records were not carefully kept, or were sparse. Much information was lost in fires. Firms were sometimes absorbed or taken over and changed by other manufacturers, losing their original identity.

Europe is credited with providing American children with the bulk of their toys during the 1800s. However, in the mid-1800s, American toymaking emerged from homes and craftsmen's shops to develop into a strong industry, and although toy catalogs did not appear until around 1860, toys were being manufactured in some quantities before that time.

By the 1800s, the Ives, Blakeslee Company, Bridgport, Ct. had emerged as one of the most important and largest toy companies in the world, exporting great quantities to

Illustration from Ives, Blakeslee & Williams Co. catalog, ca. 1893.

Europe and South America. Ives clockwork toys were considered the finest and most ingenious on the market. At the 1876 Centennial Exhibition in Philadelphia, the firm occupied a prominent location.

Louis H. Hertz (*Messrs. Ives Of Bridgeport*—The Saga of America's Greatest Toymakers), reports, "The Ives catalogs of this period, veritable cyclopedias of toys and novelties, running to almost two hundred pages, give some idea of the size of the business and the extent of the line at this time. Each successive catalog was the largest and most comprehensive issued up to that date, for it was not an idle boast when they claimed to be "Leading Manufacturers of American Toys and Novelties."

Manufacturing began at Ives in 1868 with hot air toys. By 1887 there were three branch offices, two in New York and one in Philadelphia, and the company concentrated on absorbing or controlling lines of other toymakers. One such company, the Automatic Toy Works of New York, founded in 1870 by Robert J. Clay, a patent attorney, allowed Ives to gain control of the creeping baby as well as other mechanical toys which included "The Old Colored Fiddler", "The Famous Negro Preacher", "Womans Rights" (a Suffragette Speaker), and several fur mechanical bears, all of which developed into America's most popular mechanical toys of the era. Old catalogs fail to fully convey the fine quality and workmanship of these toys. Those toys that can still be found attest to the durability of the brass clockworks and other craftsmanship in details of painting and costuming.

The design of the creeping baby is sometimes attributed to Robert J. Clay, a patent having been issued to him in March 1871. However, on August 28, 1871, Patent #118435 (improvement patent having to do with head movement) was granted to George Pemberton Clark. Clark was listed as the inventor and Clay as witness. Here we have one of the questions clouded by sparse old records. Who invented the creeping baby, Clay or Clark? Or was it a combination of wits?

In any event, it was Ives, Blakeslee & Company who led the way in developing the creeping baby, an outstanding example of skilled American craftsmanship. ■

BIBLIOGRAPHY

Ives, Blakeslee & Williams Catalogue, circa 1893
Hertz, Louis H.—*Messrs. Ives of Bridgeport*—1950
Ruth and Larry Freeman—*Cavalcade of Toys*—1942
VICTORIANA—UFDC Souvenir Book—Omaha, Neb. 1974
UFDC Souvenir Book—Kansas City, Mo. 1959
UFDC Doll News—Feb. 1965

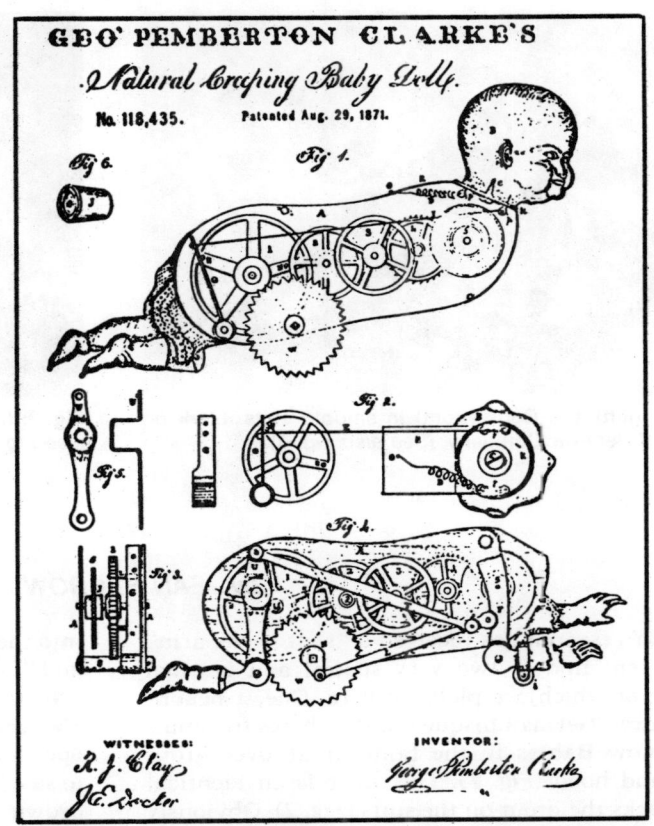

Illustrations for George Pemberton Clarke's "Natural Creeping Baby Doll" patent dated August 29, 1871.

Fig. 1: Peary (left) and Cook (right) Snow Baby figurine with grout representing snowsuits.

Continuing Research of...
THE SNOW BABIES

Illustrations from the collection of Mrs. R. C. Early.
Photos by Stephen H. Bradley.

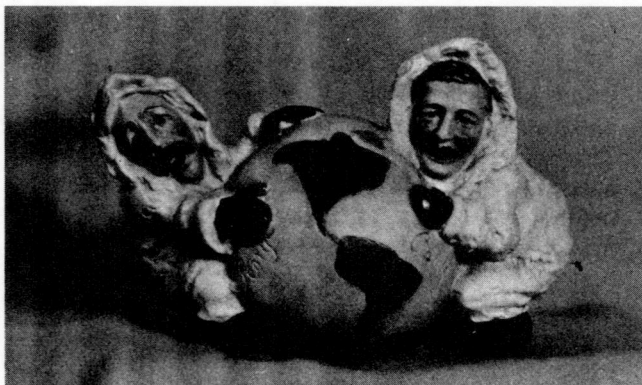

Fig. 2: Peary (left) and Cook (right) in smooth suits. Mark on base is that of Heber & Company. (*See also Fig. 3*).

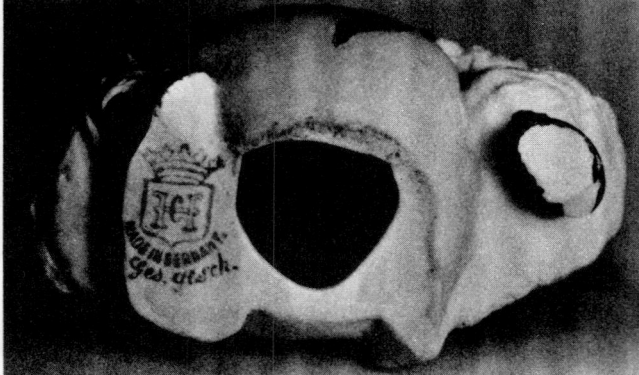

Fig. 3: Mark on base of smooth suited Peary and Cook figurine (*see Fig. 2*).

by JEAN H. CROWLEY

SNOW BABY research has received a "shot in the arm" with the recent find of two very special and unusual pieces, both of which are pictured here. One, a beautifully sculptured German bisque oddity, shows two mustachioed Snow Babies in the familiar all-over grout snowsuits and hood (*Fig. 1*). The other is an identical piece, but lacks the grout on the suits (*Fig. 2*). Obviously grown men, the figures are molded to a world globe (fired in light blue with continents of aqua-green), and incised into the globe beneath each figure are the names "Peary" and "Cook". At the top of the globe are the incised words "North Pole". The pieces, each measuring 3½" tall and 5¼" wide, show Peary on the left with furrowed brow, open-closed mouth with a very surprised expression, as if to say, "How could you?," a large nose, bulbous eyes and brown hair. Cook, on the right, also has a large nose, teeth exposed and brown hair.

The theory that Snow Baby production began after the

birth of Admiral Robert E. Peary's first child has long been conjecture in the minds of some Snow Baby collectors; but conjecture is one thing, proof another. Now, with the existence of these extraordinary figurines, the Peary theory certainly takes on increased validity. When one views all of the facts surrounding the Snow Baby, the pieces seem to fall into place. This author feels that, at last, the origin of the bisque Snow Baby has been established.

Let us examine the facts of the theory. In 1891-92, when Admiral Robert E. Peary returned from his first major expedition to northern Greenland, the venture was enthusiastically received all over the world. Lecture tours followed in the hope of raising enough money to finance a second trip, and Admiral Peary became universally known as the man who hoped, one day, to reach the North Pole, where no white man had ever been before. Consequently, when his first child, a daughter, was born the following year, her birth was widely publicized. Josephine Diebitsch Peary, Admiral Peary's wife, went with her husband as far north as 77° 40′N latitude in northern Greenland, where she camped in a tiny house to await the birth of their first child.

On September 12, 1893, Marie Ahnighito Peary was born—the first white child ever to be born at such a northern latitude, and the eskimos immediately nicknamed her "Ah-Poo Mickaninny," which translated means "Snow Baby." (Ahnighito, meaning "Snow Girl," was the name of the eskimo woman who made Marie's first suit of clothes.) The eskimos believed Marie to be made of snow at first, and whole eskimo families traveled great distances to see and feel this first white baby of the North. Even after their curiosity was satisfied, her nickname, the Snow Baby, remained.

Little Marie's mother wrote a charming book about her daughter which was published and copyrighted in 1901, and titled *The Snow Baby (Fig. 5)*. The accompanying photo of this book is a 10th edition, attesting to its popularity. The type is large and the book is of the kind often found in primary school libraries. A second book followed in 1903 (again proof of the popularity of the first) titled *Children of the Arctic, by the Snow Baby and her Mother*, and a third in 1904, titled, *Snowland Folk by Robert Peary*. All three books are profusely illustrated with photographs of Marie, her eskimo friends, and the animals indigenous to the north. In nearly every publication concerning Marie's birth and childhood (including many about, and/or by, her father, Admiral Peary), her nickname, the "Snow Baby" appears after her name. Even as late as 1934, a book titled *The Snowbaby's Own Story by Marie Ahnighito Peary* was published.

It would seem logical that somewhere in the period following Marie's birth, or the period following the publication of these early books, the bisque Snow Baby was born.

On April 6, 1909, after repeated Arctic expeditions, Robert Peary, the Snow Baby's father, at last reached his goal—the North Pole. Ecstatic over his success, he sent the good news back to America where it was received in September of that year. When he arrived home, however, a cloud had darkened his North Pole discovery news. Only then did he learn that Dr. Frederick A. Cook (a physician-explorer who had accompanied him on his 1891 expedition) had announced he had reached the Pole

Fig. 4 a & b: Clicquot Club Snow Baby in sitting and standing positions.

by another route in April 1908, one year earlier! For almost two years heated controversy plagued the two men, and much mudslinging took place (particularly by Dr. Cook). In fact, years later, Dr. Cook continued to attack Admiral Peary. However, in March of 1911 Congress, after lengthy investigations of both men, discredited Dr. Cook's claim and passed the Bates Bill honoring Admiral Peary as the discoverer of the North Pole, and retiring him from the U.S. Navy with the rank of Rear Admiral.

It is at some point in this 1909-1911 period that the pictured bisque pieces take on increased significance! It is highly doubtful that the Europeans, although eager to capitalize on American events, would produce such oddities as these figurines with both men shown in snowsuits of the type worn by a baby (and certainly not what an Arctic explorer would wear!) in recognition of such an awe-inspiring event such as the Peary-Cook discovery and ensuing dispute, unless those factories were already involved in Snow Baby production, and unless there was already some connection between them, such as Marie Ahnighito Peary, the Snow Baby.

The Peary-Cook figurines are beautifully defined, well-fired pieces with exquisite details. When comparing the figurines with early photos of Admiral Peary and Dr. Cook, it is obvious that the features were modeled after original photos of the men since they are exact likenesses. Although the pictured snow piece (*Fig. 1*) bears an aqua-green "Made In Germany" mark in a circle in the manner of some Heubach pieces, along with a four figure incised mold number 8447 under Cook's rear foot, the smooth-suited figurine (*Fig. 2*) clearly bears the mark of Heber & Co. (*Fig. 3*), which was a hard paste porcelain factory specializing in dolls' heads, and was in business in Neustadt (Gotha), Germany, from 1900 through 1925. Oddly, the four figure mold number is 1430 on the smooth figurine, indicating it may be the earlier of the two pieces.

Three companies are now known to have been involved in Snow Baby production. The earliest, Galluba & Hoffman, produced the large blue-grey snow children, but did not feature babies, and may not have had any connection with Marie Peary, although certainly they are considered to be in the Snow Baby category. Hertwig & Company, according to Mr. Keil, the Director of Deutches Spielzeug Museum in Sonneberg, Germany, produced the Snow Babies we're so familiar with. And now, authenticated Heber & Company pieces have come to light. No doubt a great many more companies will be found, which would account for the wide variety in the quality and style of known Snow Babies.

Although probably 99% of the Snow Babies produced would fall into the Peary category, the large-headed babies (*Fig. 4*) pictured here (in black face as well as white), seem to be in a category all their own. The back of their heads are open, leading one to believe they were originally containers of some sort, but not of the planter variety. The name "Clicquot Kid" comes to mind, with recollections of a small advertising bottle inside. The Clicquot Kid is pictured on two labels of the Clicquot Club Bottling Company's product, and has graced their advertising since that company's founding in 1881. The bottles bear a picture of a white child's head in eskimo parka on the neck label, and a full-figure child in eskimo clothes holding a miniature Clicquot Club bottle on the front label. Magazines of the 1930s (such as *Saturday Evening Post*) show the Clicquot Kid telling the readers of the virtues of the product he is representing, in the manner of the Old Dutch Cleanser Lady or the Campbell Kids. Although most helpful in trying to trace a connection, the Clicquot Club Company could find nothing in their files so, to date, this theory is unsupported. As study continues, these babies, too, will eventually find their niche in Snow Baby history.

It is only with continued research that we can ferret out all of the information still hidden about the charming Snow Babies, and, hopefully, one day their story will become as familiar and as beloved as that of Rose O'Neill's Kewpies. ∎

Fig. 5 a & b: Cover (left) and frontispiece (right) of Josephine Diebitsch Peary's book "The Snow Baby."

The Mysterious Nodding Head Doll

JURGEN AND MARIANNE CIESLIK

IN the past twenty years many books and articles have been published concerning the history of collectible dolls. Authors in the United States, England and Germany have tried to identify the makers of German dolls and the marks they used on their wares. Only a few of these authors used scientific investigation methods, and many questions are still left unanswered which are of importance to collectors and museums.

For the last ten years, the authors of this article have been researching the German doll industry. Thousands of records and historical photographs have been collected, all documenting the German doll industry and their products. They have journeyed to the major dollmaking center of Thuringen, East Germany, a dozen times, and obtained permission from that government to do research work in the Sonneberg Museum and in the library, studying old records and catalogs. The authors became acquainted with relatives and successors of the old dollmaking families in Sonneberg and Walterhausen. Their findings will soon be published in a new book printed in England for the benefit of American and English doll collectors. *(The authors have already written four books about dolls. Ed.)* They are now able to identify many heretofore unknown doll marks used by German doll manufacturers. We are now able to decipher the unknown number series used by such well-known makers as Simon & Halbig, Kammer & Reinhardt, Armand Marseilles, Baehr & Proeschild, and others, and can date them to the exact year, month, day and time of day of their registration.

Most of the German manufacturers of bisque doll heads began to register their design number series at the court around 1880. Doll heads

Doll described in "Portraits" catalog No.823, Auctions by Theriault, as **"FRENCH BISQUE CHILD DOLL**, 14" (35.5 cm). Bisque socket head, brown glass inset eyes, painted lashes, brush stroked and feathered brows, accent dots at nostrils, open mouth, shaded lips, four porcelain teeth, blonde human hair, French composition and wooden-jointed body, well costumed... **Marks:** 224 b 4 (head), D.E.P. 46 547 (stamp on torso)...**Comments:** Similar "Belton" style dolls have been found with this mold number. Maker unknown, ca. 1890. **Value Points:** Unusual pull-string mechanism in torso. When string alternately pulled, the doll turns its head from side to side."

with the number series or marked "Dep," (in German deponiert; in French depose; in English deposit) in conjunction with the initials of the manufacturer and the number series are now identifiable. To many collectors the letters "dep" indicate a French mark. But "deponiert" was also the term used in Germany 100 years ago.

In researching and deciphering these numbers series the authors depended greatly upon collectors all over the world who sent them marks

Nodding Head Continued

Patent! Neuheit!   Neuheit! Patent!
Josef Bergmann's patentirte
Nickende und verneinende Puppe.
Deutsches Reichs-Patent No. 46547.
Diese Puppe besitzt den bisher noch von **keiner anderen Puppe erreichten Vorzug**, dass sie an dem Gespräche, welches das Kind mit ihr führt, sichtbaren Antheil insofern nimmt, als sie mit dem Kopfe bejahend und zustimmend nickt oder denselben verneinend schüttelt, je nachdem das Kind den einen oder den anderen Mechanismus in Thätigkeit setzt. — Die Bewegungen sind vollkommen natürlich nachgeahmt. Die Puppen werden in verschiedenen Grössen und Ausstattungen geliefert. — Preise sind civil. — Bemusterung einzelner Exemplare an den Verkäufern nicht bekannte Firmen erfolgen unter Nachnahme. 288)
Alleinige Hauptbezugsquellen für Deutschland, Holland und Belgien sind
Fr. Müller & Strasburger,   **Josef Bergmann,**
Sonneberg S.-M.   Sonneberg S.-M.

Joseph Bergmann and Muller & Strasburger's 1888 advertisement for the nodding head doll.

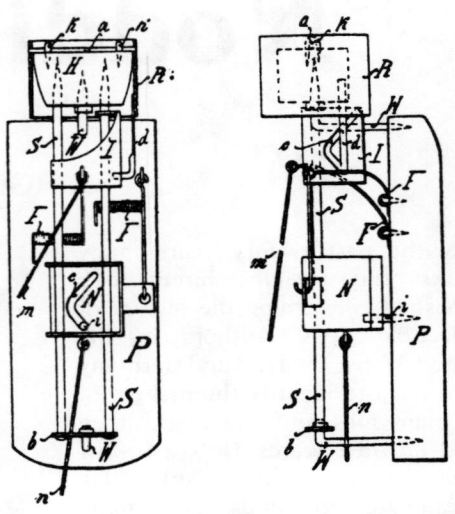

Patent drawings showing how Joseph Bergmann's nodding head doll operated. Patent D.R.P. 46 547, July 4, 1888.

found on their dolls. Auction catalogs from well-known auctioneers were also helpful. In Theriaults' "Portraits" catalog (May 8, 1982 sale), lot number 182 was an exciting find for the authors. The doll was described as "French bisque child doll, marked 224 b 4, stamped on torso D.E.P. 46 547, unusual pull-string, maker unknown, ca. 1890. Looking through their records the authors were thrilled to find such a rare doll was made in Thuringen, Germany. The bisque head with the number series 224 was registered and produced in 1888 by Baehr & Proeschild of Ohrdruff, Germany. This "French-type" doll is usually dated much earlier than 1888. The earlier heads bear only the registered number series, sometimes with the letters "DEP" or the initials "B & P." Around 1900 they used the crossed swords with their initials, and after 1919 the heart and their initials.

In 1918, Bruno Schmidt of Waltershausen purchased the factory; for a long time before the purchase, Bruno Schmidt used Baehr & Proeschild heads for their dolls.

The mark on the doll's body, D.E.P. 46547, referred to a patent registered by Josef Bergman, a doll manufacturer located in Sonneberg, Germany. The patent covered a special mechnism for the movement of the doll's head. It was Josef Bergman's intention to make the doll "talk" with children. An advertisement in an 1888 German toy magazine stated "...children now can ask questions and the doll will answer, nodding approval or shaking amazed the head."

A look at the patent drawings (illustrated) indicates how the mechinism worked. By pulling strings the doll was able to nod twice to the front, shake its head, nod to the right and to the left, bow the head forward and answer "No" or lay the head into the neck and say "No" again. The text of the patent read: "Pulling one of the strings very slowly the doll will nod Yes or No."

Josef Bergman made this doll in his factory in Sonneberg in several sizes and with different costumes. In 1891, Bergman advertised "leather dolls and jointed dolls with bisque heads, dressed and undressed dolls, bisque heads with wigs, papier-mache head. Specialty: patented leather and jointed dolls."

Later, an improvement on his 1888 patent was registered under D.R.P. 52573. Instead of pulling strings, pressing a metal button on the doll's shoulder activated the same head movements.

Bergman's patented "nodding and shaking head doll" was also distributed by Muller & Strassberger of Sonneberg, Germany. The founder of this old established doll factory and export house was Friederich Muller, who started in 1805 with the production of papier-mache toys and dolls.

The authors are hopeful that this bit of new information will give their readers an insight to the wealth of information that will be included in their forthcoming book. ■

Jurgen and Marianne Cieslik are German doll and toy collectors who have been doing extensive research in East Germany, where much of the German doll industry was located—a difficult task since they are citizens of West Germany. The material for this article has been excerpted from their soon-to-be-published book about German dolls. They are also the authors of **Lehman Toys, The History of E. P. Lehman, 1881-1981.**

Doll Houses and Furniture

We view the world of little things from a special perspective. The imperfections of everyday life are reduced to minutia, yet the form and color retain the strength of larger scale. Although miniatures date to earliest recorded civilization little research has been done on their makers and chronology. This is particularly strange since miniature collectors number in the hundreds of thousands, and their enthusiasm rivals their numbers.

Many collectors consequently limit their miniatures and dollhouse furnishings to contemporary models, commercial and handmade. Elizabeth Pullar in "American Furniture Made in the Orient" cites recent examples available to collectors and explores the incongruity of American colonial style furnishings reproduced in exactitude in the Far East while Marjorie Congram proposes models for making antique furniture in the home workshop.

For the connoisseur, however, the antique furnishings are most desired. Few examples earlier than the Victorian era are available, and even 19th century examples are rarities. In a series of articles on 19th century dollhouse furnishings Catherine Cook describes some of these rarities. They range from bathtubs to banquets, and provide in microcosm an overview of Victorian life. Of most value, Cook presents new facts on manufacturers and probable dates.

Sociologists suggest that the late 20th century will signal a return to a world of small villages. As our perspective of the world diminishes, the appreciation of all things small should increase.

The Oriental influence in miniaturia is well represented in this 8" x 11" sitting room. A pair of ebony setties with carved soapstone backs and matching sideboard, ivory carvings on the wall, brass lanterns, silk paintings, porcelain vases, a carved jade screen and an oriental rug have all been faithfully executed on a tiny scale.

Adjustable lithographed tin highchair in the lowered position forms a chair and table.

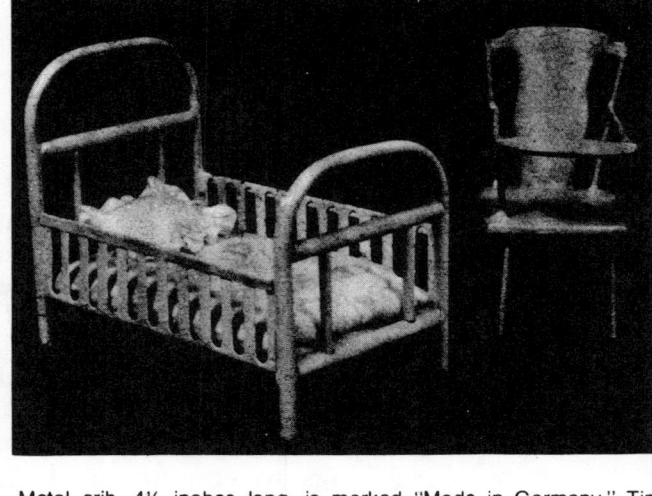

Metal crib, 4½ inches long, is marked "Made in Germany." Tin highchair is just 3½ inches high.

Tin baby carriage, 3½ by 4 inches.

Wooden baby's cradle, 4 inches long.

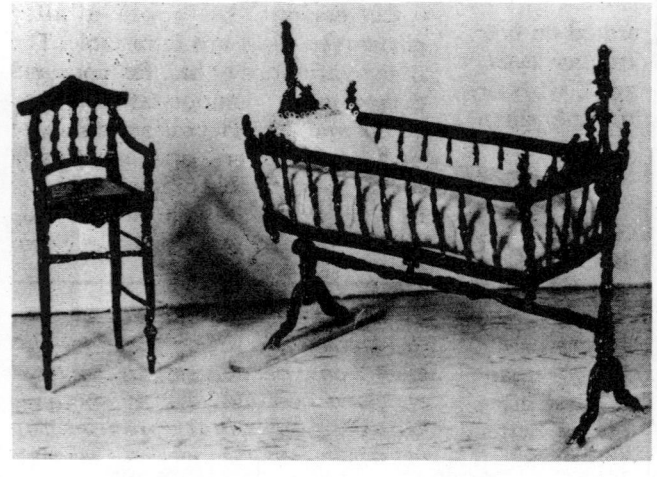

Metal cradle on stand, 3½ inches long, with matching highchair, 3 inches tall. Both have been painted with asphaltum.

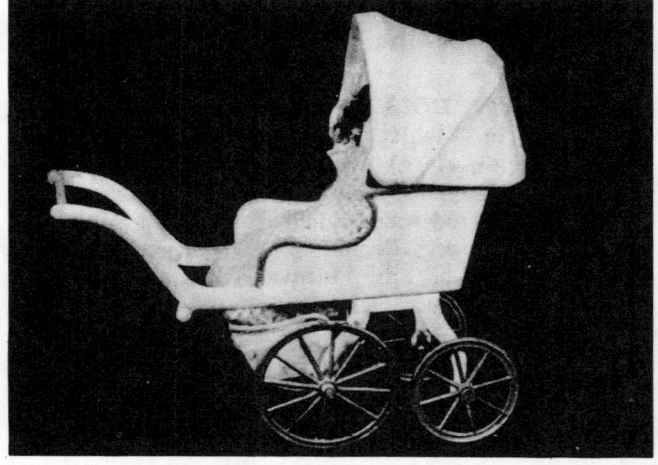

English-type tin baby carriage painted white and with fabric hood; measures 3½ by 4 inches.

Tin highchair on wheels; 3½ inches high.

Dolls' House Cradles, Cribs, Carriages, & HIGH CHAIRS

CATHERINE COOK
Photos by Charles I. Lennon

AMONG THE most intriguing of the miniatures made for dolls' houses are the cribs, cradles, carriages and highchairs made for the dolls' house baby. Although not made in large numbers as the other dolls' house furnishings, these baby furnishings show great ingenuity and craftsmanship.

Almost from infancy, the first toy given to a little girl is a doll, and in reviewing the history of dolls' houses, one of their original purposes was to train girls to be homemakers and mothers. One famous dolls' house, designed in 1631 by Anna Koferlen of Nuremburg, Germany, was built for the "instruction of young girls." although the house itself is gone, careful records and inventories have survived. "Toys," it has been said, "are an apprenticeship for life."

Cradle styles have varied little over the centuries; many

Illustations from the author's collection and the collection of the Hansel and Gretel Museum.

were made with a hood or bonnet at one end to ward off drafts from the baby's head. Some had pegs along the side rails so that the baby could be laced in place for safety. One of the earliest hooded wicker cradles known was that used by Peragrine White, the first English child born in New England, aboard the ship *Mayflower* at Provincetown, in 1620.

Toy cradles were first made in the 18th century, copying in miniature their larger counterparts. These included cradles made of oak, some with turned posts, others hooded, and still others raised up on stands. Like other early dolls' house furnishings, they would have been special orders made by skilled craftsmen for a fortunate child or adult collector, and only the best would have survived.

The cradle that appears most frequently in both early German and English dolls' houses, as well as later ones, is the little hooded wicker cradle. It is not surprising that few of these have survived unless safely ensconced in a dolls'

Hooded pine cradle, 3⅝ inches long, and a tiny cradle just 1¼ inches long.

the cradle. Athough not made as a miniature for a dolls' house, they are very suitable for this purpose.

Cribs appear less frequently than cradles. The early examples are made of wood and usually designed and constructed of continuous narrow slats, very similar to the present-day cribs. Some of the later ones were made with drop sides; others have springs and can be folded flat. In the early 20th century miniatures of iron beds and cribs were produced.

It is not certain exactly when the first baby carriages were made. However, from the middle of the 19th century, many American companies throughout the East and Midwest manufactured them. The first baby carriage is believed to have been made in Westerly, Rhode Island,

Adjustable lithographed tin highchair, 3 inches high.

Lithographed tin baby carriage with molded hood, pillow and carriage robe, marked "Made in Germany." Measures 3⅝ by 3⅝ inches.

house, for their construction makes them vulnerable to breakage.

Miniature cradles continued to be made in the 19th and early 20th centuries. With the introduction of metal toys in the 19th century, cradles were made of Filigree and Britannia metal. Still later, when the tin toy industry followed, painted and lithographed tin cradles were also produced.

In the 17th, 18th and 19th centuries, small pottery cradles were made in England as christening gifts and are known as "Christening Cradles." They were made in the Staffordshire District of England, but most found are not marked. The early examples were fashioned after the oak cradles of the period. Later productions were patterned to resemble wicker. In the early 19th century, some of these cradles were made with a dressed child represented inside

Bassinet-type "Christening Cradle," 4½ inches long, and a tiny wicker cradle, 2½ inches long.

Two lithographed tin cradles. **Left:** 3½ inches long, has permanently attached pillow and bedding. **Right:** 3⅞ inches long is marked "Made in Germany 1902."

in 1840. It was similar to today's strollers with two wheels and a wooden handle to draw it by, and had a support that balanced it when stationary. Made of wood, it had an upholstered seat and a folding canopy top. This company continued operations for years, and was one of the best known manufacturers of children's carriages and also of dolls' carriages.

After the Civil War, wicker and willow baby and dolls' carriages were produced by varous manufacturers throughout the East, and these were later followed by carriages made of metal and leather. Dolls' house baby carriages did not appear until Britannia metal and Filigree came into use for toys. It is known that Peter F. Pia of New York. a manufacturer of pewter toys ca. 1878, made miniature carriages of this type, but his toys are not always marked and cannot always be definitely attributed to him. The Adrian Cooke Metal Works, Chicago, Illinois, was another manufacturer of pewter toys. Many of these pewter toys were also imported from European sources, and some are still being reproduced there today. Dolls' house carriages made of tin quite naturally followed those made of pewter and Britannia metal.

Highchairs for babies were made as early as the 18th century, and in the same designs as other chairs of the period — Windsor, Spindle and crudely made country types. Later, highchairs were made of wicker and bentwood. Miniature highchairs are found in some early

Filigree metal baby carriage, ca. 1878, measures 5½ by 5¾ inches.

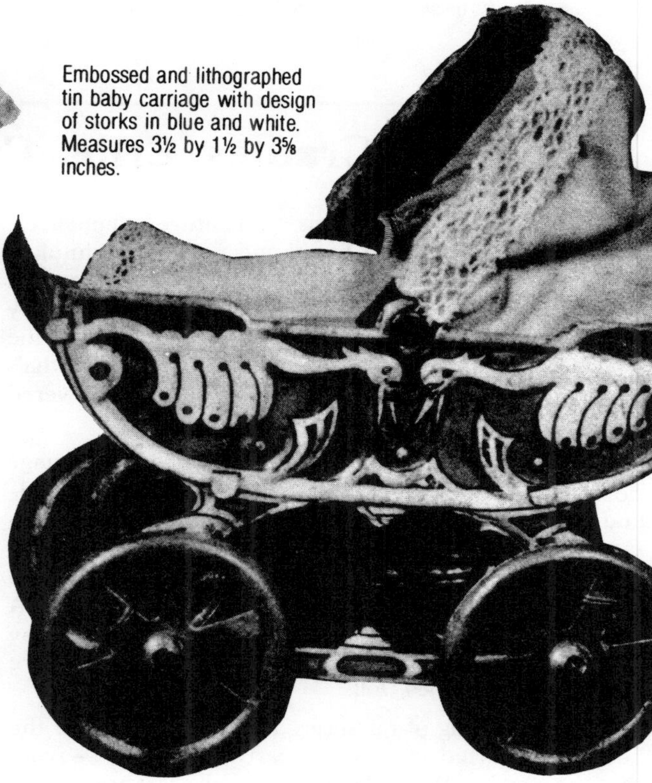

Embossed and lithographed tin baby carriage with design of storks in blue and white. Measures 3½ by 1½ by 3⅝ inches.

Forbes paper doll given by the **Boston Globe** with their Sunday edition, August 18, 1895.

Forbes paper doll given by the **Boston Globe** with their Sunday edition, September 22, 1895.

Doll House Cradles, Cribs, Carriages & High Chairs (cont'd)

of wood, and some have wheels. A miniature highchair, ca. 1878, made of Britannia metal and painted to simulate wood is shown in our illustrations with a matching cradle. Also included are two highchairs made of tin. A very unusual and colorful lithographed tin highchair from the collection of the Hansel and Gretel Museum, Martha's Vineyard, Massachusetts, is adjustable and when lowered forms a chair and table.

Two 1895 paper dolls with nursemaid, baby carriage and cradle are included in our illustrations. They were made as a novelty for the *Boston Globe*, which was first published on March 14, 1872. These were used in 1895 to promote the sale of the *Globe's* new color editon. A different paper doll was included with each Sunday edition. Printed on the bottom of the examples shown here is the legend "Forbes Doll."

The establishing of nurseries as a separate part of the household started surprisingly early in England — from the 16th century. By the 19th century, all great houses had a nursery under the dominion of a "Nanny." Nurseries are found in early English and German dolls' houses. In American dolls' houses, playrooms for the children usually superceded the nursery.

Sets of dolls' house dolls of the 1890 to 1910 period included not only members of the dolls' house family, but a very complete entourage of servants — one a nursemaid. These sets are being avidly collected by dolls' house collectors and doll collectors, and are being reproduced in a considerable number.

From the earliest times, dolls' house babies have been well provided for, having everything needed for their comfort. Little girls that played with them would have properly learned to take good care of their dolls' house babies. ∎

Catherine Cook *is co-author with Edith Morris of* Fascinating Tin Toys For Girls, 1820-1920. *Most of the dolls' house furnishings used to illustrate her articles are from her personal collection.*

One of the rarest French bebes a collector can acquire, the A.T., is shown here. This 15½" beauty has spectacular depth in her blue glass paperweight eyes and a delicate translucent porcelain face. A. Thuillier, a French dollmaker, only produced dolls for eleven years (1879-1890).

Although traditionally considered of English derivation, this Punch and Judy puppet theatre carries German documentation. From the late Victorian era, it boasts a colorful variety of players including a crocodile, monkey, skeleton and regimental guards. The French bebe by Ferdinand Gaultier, circa 1885, is a large 27", and like many of these larger French child dolls has remarkable artistry of facial decoration. Here the artist could demonstrate the full range of subtle complexion shades and highlight the feathered softness of each lash and brow.

Although the French bisque automata are most eagerly sought by most collectors, it is esoteric examples such as these two that excite the connoisseur. On the left, a papier mache lady sits at a rosewood piano, her hands resting lightly upon the keyboard. When wound, and the lever released, the figure turns her head from side to side while her fingers move across the keys and a delicate tune is played. The automaton was produced by Charles Ives of Connecticut about 1885 and is considered rare by collectors. Standing is a papier mache lady by Frenchman Alexandre Theroude made about 1850-60. A commanding presence, despite her somewhat homely face, she seems to sail through a room alternately touching a delicate lace handkerchief to her face, then sniffing the posies held in her right hand.

When Kewpies "do things" rather than simply stand, they are known as "action figures." The variations to be found are as imaginative as the mind of artist, Rose O'Neill, who created them. Rarities shown here include Blunderboo (lying on his belly), the Instructor, the Bellhop, the Street Cleaner, and the Bobby. All date about 1915-1925, and were made in German porcelain firms.

A large French bebe sits in the shadow of McLoughlin Bros. "New Folding Dollhouse." The New York firm produced this unique cardboard and paper lithographed dollhouse around the turn of the century; in 1911 it appeared in the Christmas catalogue of Woodward and Lothrop, a Washington D. C. department store with a $1.00 selling price. Although folding dollhouses were popular at the turn of the century few were made with the intricate detail, lavish decoration, and rich lithography of this example. The folding "garden" may be a singular invention of this house.

Early dolls in rare variations are assembled. On the left, a superb example of American folk art, a cloth doll by an unknown maker, with oil painted facial features, circa 1870. The two "china" dolls standing in the rear have brown eyes, a rarity for their type. The seated "china" doll is rarer yet; inset glass eyes and a charming piquant smile are its special features. Perhaps rarest is the bisque doll with molded hair (commonly called "parian"). Most have a stiff neck, painted eyes, and black or blonde hair. This example has a swivel neck, glass eyes, and brown hair adorned with a blue bow. The latter four were all made in mid 19th century.

An 18th French Parisienne stands alongside her wardrobe. The doll, circa 1870, has a totally wooden body with separately carved and curled fingers. With the doll are two antique doll trunks fitted with a complete wardrobe which includes: lace trimmed chemises, ivory handled parasols with fringed trim, leather music portfolios, leather boots and fitted leather gloves, an assortment of paper boxes and antique stationery, tiny jewelry, wooden and celluloid dresser articles, bonnets, quilted coverlet, and over 30 articles of clothing including silk dresses, coats, embroidered white nightdresses and lace trimmed blouses. One trunk, 18" x 12", has a domed top, is covered with leather and metal, and the interior, which contains numerous niches, is decorated in brightly lithographed Victorian decoupage. The other early domed trunk has an interior covered with lithographed wallpaper of the era. This valuable collection of trunks, wardrobe and antique French Parisiennes is seldom found in such a complete array.

A selection of cabinet size dolls in a fashionable array of antique costumes is shown here. The French dolls, circa 1880, to the left and center are examples of the so-called "Belton" style by an unknown maker. Both have a bisque socket head with a flattened solid dome and wig stringing holes rather than a hollow head with a cork pate. A beautifully rendered brown bisque complexion highlights the doll on the right. Simon & Halbig, a German firm, produced this doll about 1890.

A portrait doll of an aged man is here costumed as a farmer, more commonly as "Uncle Sam." The beaming smile, deeply incised frown wrinkles and over-sized ears are characteristic, although the larger than usual size of the doll, 18", makes this example unique. Produced about 1900, the maker was probably Simon & Halbig of Germany.

Flirtatious, worried, surprised—the many faces of Lenci dolls, made even more special by their brilliant and intricate costumes. Carmen, seated, has a unique suave complexion of a Spanish woman; not shown are details like the felt garter with petalled rose. On the left is "Oh, Il Mio Tresoro" pictured in the 1931 Lenci catalogue. The flirty eyed child on the right has a rare Lenci variation: glass "googly" eyes.

Humourous monkey faced automatons were popular in the last quarter of the 19th century. The magician was a particular favorite of firms such as Vichy et Fils and Leopold and Lambert of Paris. This example was located in an Austin, Texas saloon and was evidently used by the local clientele for boisterous fun. When keywound the monkey moves his head from side to side and his eyes blink open and close while he grins satanically. Meanwhile, the brass dome raises and lowers above the gambling table exposing the dice which are "thrown" by an internal mechanism. The garland of leaves and richly colored costume fabrics are entirely original and indigenous to this luxury toy.

Four French bisque bebes, represent the artistry of different dollmakers. Standing left to right are two examples by Emile Jumeau, a Rabery and Delphieu bebe, and an early portrait doll by Ferdinand Gaultier. All are 1875-1890. Seated is a German bisque "cousin", circa 1900, rarer than all the others. It is "Wendy" by Bruno Schmidt of Walterhausen.

Contemporary artist doll, a poured wax portrait of Marie Antoinette, stands 28" tall, and was one of only three made by American artist, Lewis Sorensen, about 1977. The intricate costume which includes ten lace trimmed petticoats and an ornate hair piece of ostrich feathers and silver birds was also designed by Sorensen.

The five dolls posing here are all examples of twentieth century dollmakers. Moving clockwise: a 40" Armand Marseille with lovely quality bisque and artistically rendered facial features, a 20" JDK character baby from Kestner with a dimpled chin and "stuck out" ears, a 38" Simon & Halbig with a perfectly matched Heinrich Handwerck torso, a hard-to-find 26" Kley & Hahn mold and a delightful 15" American composition character doll with dimpled cheeks and smiling eyes marked "American Beauty Doll." All were produced about 1915.

A MINIATURE MARYLAND MANSION

by SUSAN B. HOWARD

Built for the five little Dibb sisters of Bel Air, Maryland, in the 1880s. the elaborate dolls' house, part of a sizeable Christmas garden, was the fourth anniversary exhibit of the Washington Dolls' House and Toy Museum, where it will be on permanent display.

A GINGERBREAD DOLLS' HOUSE from Bel Air, Maryland, embellished to a fare-thee-well with spindles and balconies and other gim-crackeries has just been acquired for the Washington Dolls' House and Toy Museum. It was built in the 1880s for five little sisters—Lottie, Annie, Naomi, Margaret and Etta Inez Dibb, and acquired from the latter sister, Mrs. James Martz of Bel Air.

For many years the dolls' house was part of an elaborate Christmas garden, placed beneath a fourteen-foot tree, to which neighboring school children were brought for an annual visit during the holidays. An early photograph (*illustrated*) reveals an elaborate fenced garden beneath house and tree consisting of gazebo, dolls and other accoutrements. A painted tin cupola perched on the roof of the house in the early picture was made by Mr. Dibb, a Bel Air tinsmith. A wooden fountain and a pair of matching urns accompanied the house to its new home located at 5236 - 44th Street, N.W., Washington, D.C. 20015.

Although all but a few pieces of the original furniture are gone, the small mansion has been refurnished with antique pieces of the period. (No reproductions are used in the museum's dolls' houses.)

According to family tradition, two identical houses were built by a Baltimore carpenter, but the whereabouts of the twin house are unknown. It's hoped that information about the second house or its history will surface when the Dibb house is viewed by visitors to the museum.

Thousands of visitors from every state in the union, and from all over the world, have visited the museum since its opening four years ago. Its founder, Flora Gill Jacobs, internationally recognized author of books about dolls' houses and toys, has used more than half of her sizeable collection in the exhibits, and it is hoped that eventually there will be sufficient space to put more of this on display. There are many rare toys on view along with the numerous dolls' houses, shops, stables and other related buildings. All are antique, and with the exception of an 18th century Nuremburg kitchen, two early 19th century shops, and a house from the 1920s, almost the entire collection is Victorian.

The museum is open daily except Monday from 11 A.M. to 5 P.M., and Sundays from noon to 5 P.M. It's one block southwest of Western and Wisconsin Avenues in Chevy Chase.

Fig. 1: The facade of the Farie dolls' house stands 7 feet high and 4 feet, 8 inches wide.

Fig. 2: Interior view of the Farie dolls' house showing the arrangement of its thirteen rooms.

THE FARIE DOLLS' HOUSE AT AUCTION

by DOROTHY S. and EVELYN J. COLEMAN

THE FARIE DOLLS' HOUSE is well-known to dolls' house and miniature collectors all over the world. It has been featured in books by Flora Gill Jacobs and Vivien Greene. It was the subject of an article in the magazine *Homes and Gardens*. According to experts, this house boasts a history of about two hundred years; some of the furnishings were allegedly given to Miss Sarita Farie by the Empress Eugénie.

The original six-room house was made in Scotland and in the course of its history an attic, a basement and bay windows were added. The furnishings were accumulated through the years, but none of them are known to date back to the 18th century when the house was new. (Figs. 1 & 2).

At one time this house was displayed at the Rotunda Museum in Oxford, England, by Vivien Greene. Later it came to the United States and remained in the possession of Fanchon Canfield for many years. In October 1979, the house and its concents went up at a Richard Withington Auction in Concord, New Hampshire. Unfortunately the house and its contents were thought too valuble for a single purchaser to afford, and everything had to be sold separately or in small lots.

Through the years many of the furnishings had been added, and many of them lost, so that the dispersal in this fashion was not quite as tragic as it might seem to be. The clover-shaped sociable seat and inlaid spinet reportedly given by the Empress Eugénie and shown in Flora Gill Jacobs' *History of Dolls' Houses* (1965 edition) has disappeared. Long ago nearly all of the doll inhabitants had left the house. Nevertheless, many fabulous antique furnishings remained and collectors from all over the United States, and even from England, came to the auction.

The house without furnishings sold for $5,000, and the aggregate contents sold for $22,000, making a total of $27,000. For only $10 some lucky collectors bought a miniature cast iron stove or a lot containing an upholstered chair and a plain wooden table. A wood-framed standing mirror and two wooden chairs fetched $20 for the lot. Other single pieces of wooden furniture were among the highest priced lots in the sale. These pieces were made of "rosewood" with gold stencil decorations and included an upright piano 5½ inches tall and 5 inches wide for $630 (Fig. 6); a game table with tiny checkers in the drawer, 3½ inches tall, 3½ inches square, for $340; and a four-shelf what-not cabinet containing Oriental accessories standing 5½ inches tall fetched $300 (Fig. 6). It is believed that the piano and what-not were some of the pieces shown in *English Dolls' Houses* (plate 146) which was written by Mrs. Vivien Greene and published in 1955. The caption for plate 146 reads: "The furniture given by the Empress Eugénie." This suggests that many of the bidders had studied their books carefully before coming to the auction.

A considerable amount of the furniture was made of a gold colored metal and, as expected, these pieces realized sizable sums:

Gold colored metal cupboard with mirrored back, 6½ inches tall and 3 inches wide, $400 (Fig. 4).

Standing gold colored metal swinging baby cradle outfitted in pink and white, 3 inches tall by 3 inches long, $300 (Fig. 3).

Gold colored metal oval table, 2½ inches tall and 4¾ inches at its widest

Fig. 7: Diamond-shaped mark on gold colored metal chair indicates the design was registered on February 3, 1876.

Fig. 9: "Sparrow House," an English dolls' house, sold at Withington's September 1979 auction for $850.

point, $200.

Gold colored metal birdcage, 2¾ inches tall, 2½ inches wide, 2¼ inches deep, $220 (Fig. 4).

Gold colored metal standing mirror, 8 inches tal, $200 (Fig. 2, second floor room on the left).

gold colored metal desk with three drawers, 4¼ inches tall, 4 inches wide, $180 (Fig. 2 second floor room on the left.

A light wood wall cabinet (hutch) with its contents, 14 inches high and 10 inches wide, brought $350 (Fig. 5).

Lighting fixtures brought fairly high prices: A six-candle gold colored metal chandelier sold for $210 (Fig. 4); and a brass and glass hanging lamp 3½ inches tall brought $330 (Fig. 5).

Many of the furnishings were sold in lots or sets. An eight-piece bedroom set of gold-trim med dark wood with rose satin upholstery sold for $520. The set consisted of a canopied bed, dressing table, wash stand, towel rack and four chairs. (See room on second floor, left, Fig. 2).

Non-collectors of dolls' house furniture may be surprised to learn that these miniature masterpieces cost almost as much—and at times more—than full-size furniture. One reason for this is the fact that genuine reason for this is the fact that genuine antique dolls' house furniture such as this is seldom seen for sale, and is extremely rare. This sale was historically important because one almost never sees early pieces of this calibre with their original accessories. Full-size furniture has often been altered through the years, a fate

Fig. 3: The attic bedroom of the Farie dolls' house boasts a gold colored metal swinging cradle.

Fig. 5: A well-equipped kitchen is located on the first floor of the Farie house. The maid doll standing in back of the table in the center of this illustration sold for $180.

Fig. 8: Registry mark on a miniature Whitby jet clock translates to read May 3, 1878.

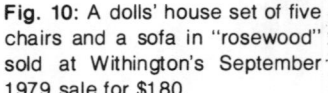

Fig. 10: A dolls' house set of five chairs and a sofa in "rosewood" sold at Withington's September 1979 sale for $180.

Fig. 4: The second floor parlor of the Farie house contains gold colored metal furnishings—a birdcage, cupboard with mirrored back, and a three-fold screen.

Fig. 6: The music room is located in the basement of the Farie house; some of the furniture includes a tiny upright piano, game table, and a what-not with Oriental miniatures on each shelf.

miniatures have escaped. This house, with its monogrammed linens, definitely had "class."

It cannot be said with certainty that some of the Lilliputian furnishings in the Farie dolls' house were made in England during the time that the diamond-shaped registration mark system was in use (1843-1883), but it is likely that this was the case. Several pieces of gold colored metal dolls' house furniture in the authors' possession bear such marks with a letter code designating the exact day, month and year the design was registered at the Patent Office in London. These codes can be found in books about English porcelain, such as Geoffrey Godden's *Encyclopaedia of British Pottery and Porcelain Marks*.

The registry mark on the authors' gold colored metal chairs (Fig. 7) reads: Roman numeral I, indicating the class as metal; the number 3 beneath Roman numeral I is the day of the registration; Roman numeral V is for the year of registration (1876); the letter G represents the month of registration (February); the number 3 on the left side of the mark stands for the parcel number.

A gold colored metal picture frame similarly marked indicates that the design was registered on June 5th, 1880.

A miniature clock made of Whitby jet (SW Sep. '72) also has a registry mark dating the design to May 3, 1878 (Fig. 8). In this case the Roman numeral IV indicated that the classification was porcelain, pottery or glass.

These marks, either incised or embossed, also identify W. Avery & Son of Redditch, England, as the manufacturer of these miniatures, a bit of information not mentioned in the books written by Flora Gill Jacobs or Vivien Greene as far as the authors can determine. All three of these pieces of dolls' house furniture once belonged to a littel girl born in Cornwall, England, in 1867.

Collector interest in miniatures was obvious at a previous Withington auction held September 1979 when a much smaller dolls' house, known as "Sparrow House," sold for $850 (Fig. 9), and a lot consisting of four tiny chairs and a sofa fetched $180 (Fig. 10). As such choice items disappear into private or public collections, similar or lesser pieces are expected to fetch even higher prices in future sales. ■

Mr. & Mrs. J.W. Elders - MINIATURE FURNITURE MAKERS

by SUSAN B. HOWARD

Kitchen "Master" cabinet and hanging spice cabinet.

MR. J. W. ELDERS, a retired painting contractor of Rogers, Arkansas, and his wife are meticulously and imaginatively constructing dolls' house furniture and furnishings. Each piece is exquisite in detail, creating an heirloom for the future as well as preserving the past in miniature. Every piece is copied after a life-size antique in the scale of one inch to one foot. All proportions, sweeps and curves are accurate to 1/64 of an inch, even to the little spindles that are only 1/32 of an inch in diameter. The chair rounds, legs, bed posts and spindles are all hand turned on a jewelers' lathe.

Every part that works on the life-size model works on the miniature. The flour bin in the tiny kitchen "Master" cabinet (illustrated) tilts forward for putting in the flour and has the sifter in the bottom with the handle that turns for sifting the flour. The miniature ice box has its tiny drain pipe and a Lilliputian gate-leg table works to perfection. A wall hanging spice cabinet has drawers only 5/16 of an inch wide which open and close, and all slightly larger drawers in dressers and washstands have glides.

Although every tiny piece looks fragile, quite the contrary is true. Each joint is pinned, tenoned and glued making them, for their size, as strong or stronger than their life-size models.

While Mr. Elders works on the furniture his wife, "Honey," makes the lamps and other accessories, such as miniature coffee grinders, and upholsters the tiny Victorian sofas and chairs.

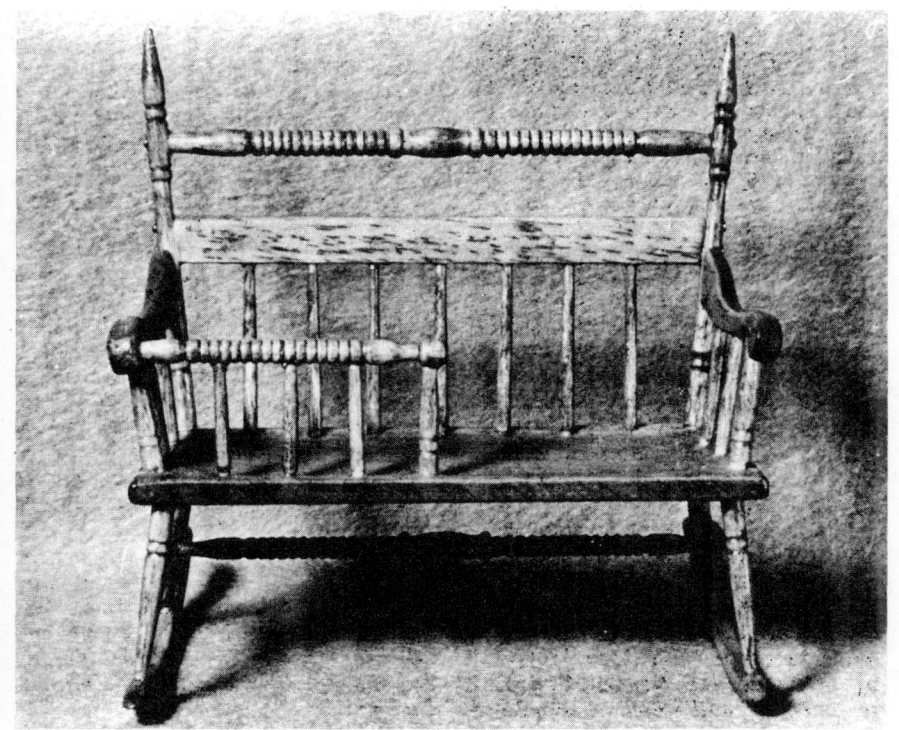

Mammy rocking bench with superbly turned crest, guard rail and stretcher; turnings were done on a jeweler's lathe.

Fig. 9.

Advertising dolls' houses and miniatures

by JUDITH WHORTON

In 1978, Hamleys offered a miniature version of its six-story toy store in London, England. Details in this miniature store included the wooden Noah's Ark that hung outside the original 1760 store. *Collection Judith Spaulding.*

AFTER four years of work, Queen Mary's doll house was described by its designers as the most perfect dolls' house created. It is not surprising that this elegant work of art has become so famous and remains on display at Windsor Castle. But less known is the fact that the Queen authorized models of the royal house to be made for advertising purposes.

Thus, the diverse range of discovered advertising doll items continues to grow from houses of royalty to humble cottages. To qualify as an advertising dolls' house item, the object must be used as a premium, or be used as a container for a product, or bear the name of a company or product.

The miniature model of Queen Mary's dolls' house qualifies in two ways. The original price of one shilling benefitted the Queen's charities, thus serving as a premium. Chubb & Sons Lock & Safe Co., Ltd. appears on the bottom of the model, along with the following words: "A diminutive Chubb safe protects the Queen's Doll's Jewells."

Figs. 1, 2, 3 and 4. Made of metal, the model is four inches tall as compared to the 39 inch height of the original house. The windows are re-

Fig. 10.

Fig. 1.

Fig. 3.

Photos by the Author.

cessed to give a three dimensional look. The exterior is illustrated on three sides. The main front is known as the north elevation (*Fig. 1*). The east front not only shows the house but details of the garden, including the iron gate (*Fig. 4*). The exterior of the original house was made of carved wood to resemble portland stone. Instead of walls opening as a hinged door, an elevator was designed. This raised the walls so that the internal part of the house could appear unencumbered. Perhaps the most interesting view in the model is the west end which shows the inside (*Fig. 2*). Although the rooms appear postage stamp size, details can be recognized on all five levels. The rooms with their furnishings include the nursery, two servants' bedrooms, the king's wardrobe, the library, and in the basement, the garage. The library has been considered the highlight, as it contains 200 miniature volumes of the works of then contemporary authors of 1924. A book, now a collector's item, was published describing only the library. The garage houses six "motor cars" including a Rolls Royce, a Lancaster, and a Sunbeam.

Figs. 5, 6 and *7*. Also English in ori-

Fig. 2.

Fig. 4.

Fig. 5.

Fig. 6.

Fig. 7.

Fig. 8. *Collection Myron Briley.*

Fig. 11.

Fig. 9. In 1911 the Lettie Lane dolls' house was used by the *Ladies Home Journal* as a premium to increase their circulation. For four subscriptions the reader received not only the 18 by 16 inch cardboard house, but paper furniture and an all bisque doll.

Fig. 10. Another magazine, *Needlecraft*, in Augusta, Maine, offered 120 pieces of dolls' house furniture for three subscriptions of fifty cents each. The 1918 furniture was made of heavy cardboard which had to be cut and pasted together. Included in the offer were "a sanitary refrigerator," cut glass candlelabra, and a 25-piece set of paper dishes.

Fig. 11. A cigar company in Pennsylvania was another surprising maker of dolls' houses. The cedar container, five inches tall and eight inches long, is designed to represent a log cabin. On the bottom is a State of Pennsylvania stamp about regulations concerning cigars.

Advertising dolls' houses as premiums began tapering off after the affluent 1920s, but in the 1970s companies are beginning to return to advertising miniatures. A few years ago, Rich's department store sold a reproduction of its first store built in Atlanta, Georgia. The wooden two-floor store contained shelves filled with bolts of old-fashioned prints and laces. The name, "M. Rich Dry Goods" and the date "1867" appeared on the front. The cost was over $100.00. Advertising dolls' houses have come a long way from the time they were worth only a shilling—even if they were royalty. ■

gin, but less elaborate, this cottage was also a candy container. Printed on the cardboard are the words "This doll house is issued solely by the Don Confectionery Co., Ltd., Sheffield" (*Fig. 7*). The eight-inch tall house is topped by a dark red roof. The cream colored walls are contrasted with a light red brick base. Other details include a bay window accented with stained glass. "Don" is printed over the front door.

Fig. 8. A 19th century tin doll house made in Austria has all the advertising printed in German. The royal factory made sausages, cakes and chocolates. On the back are copies of the medals won in competition; the latest, dating 1887, gives a clue as to its issue. It does not necessarily mean the house was made in 1887, but the award was current enough that the factory used it in advertising. The house is decorated in grays and greens, a somber contrast to the lively colors the English and Americans used. A woman giving cookies to children is another unusual feature, as people rarely populated these houses. A bell that actually rings hangs over one of the eves. The chimney and two attic windows are three dimensional. The shingles are also raised.

Advertising Dolls' Houses

by JUDITH WHORTON

Dunham Cocoanut Dolls' House.

THOUGH ADVERTISING DOLLS like Aunt Jemima, Kaptin Kiddo, and Campbell Kids are enthusiastically added to doll collections, advertising dolls' houses produced at the same period are often ignored. Indeed, these delightful sales ambassadors for all kinds of products, from varnish to foods, are not even well known.

Such advertising dolls' houses fell into two categories—those used for containers and those intended as premiums. They ranged in height from less than a foot to more than two and one-half feet. Many of them, made of cardboard with simple one-room designs, weighed less than an ounce and could be folded flat and shipped by mail. A wooden example with several rooms might weigh as much as seven pounds. From the 1900s to the 1920s, magazines such as *American Woman*, *Ladies' Home Journal* and *Youth's Companion* offered dolls' houses for new subscriptions and a fee, sometimes as much as $4.

The three advertising dolls' houses pictured and described here are from the Author's collection.

The Dunham Cocoanut Dolls' House

An elaborate example from the first decade of the 1900s was a specially designed wooden crate, 29 × 11¾ inches, filled with packages of Dunham cocoanut. Burned into the outside of the crate are the windows and brick siding of a doll house. Instructions on the back of the box warned to open front lid only, so as not to disturb the interior. The inside of the box is partitioned into four rooms, seven inches high, one above the other, each room appropriately decorated with lithograph paper to indicate kitchen, dining room, parlor, and bedroom.

The printed kitchen boasts red and white linoleum flooring, tongue-and-groove wall paneling, hanging pots and pans, and a dish cabinet in which three boxes of Dunham's cocoanut are displayed among the chinaware. A moose head and an aquarium are focal points in the dining room; the rug has an oriental design; the curtains represent scrim. Wallpaper for the parlor includes a piano with an opened song book on it, six paintings, four vases of cut flowers, and two potted plants. The bedroom at the top of the house has a printed stained glass bay window.

Three-dimensional furniture made of heavy paper could be ordered by number and a "cake" trademark from a one-half pound package of cocoanut, or two trademarks from a one-fourth pound package. Each piece of furniture has printed instructions on the back for obtaining additional pieces—some 15 different items. The amount of cocoanut required to complete the set of furniture, following a recipe in a contemporary cookbook, would make between 60 and 70 cakes.

Available for the kitchen were a wood-burning stove with eggs frying in a skillet and a table showing a pie in the process of preparation. For the dining room, the buffet was the only dark piece of furniture in the house; all others were printed to resemble

Edison Mazda Lamp Dolls' House.

A.P.W. Paper Co. Dolls' House.

oak. Parlor furniture featured a pink upholstered love seat with needlepoint pillow and a spindle-back rocker. Bedroom furniture comprised dresser, washstand, and bed. The dolls' house pictured contains a dresser and washstand, but no bed. Perhaps the family of the child who was furnishing it rebelled at 70 cocoanut cakes!

A.P.W. Paper Co. Dolls' House

The A.P.W. Paper Co. of Albany, N.Y., used the dolls' house as both premium and container. It was offered for five cents and a wrapper from a roll of A.W.P. toilet paper or, according to a full page advertisement in *Hearst International Magazine*, February 1925, it could be obtained free when four rolls of toilet paper, considered a year's supply, were purchased for $2. The rolls were packaged in the house.

Topped by a bright red roof, the cardboard house is 10 inches tall, nine inches deep. Printed on the outside are "cute dollies" in checkered dresses (a company trademark), playing ball, rolling hoops, or riding tricycles. On the bottom of the house is an offer for a muslin doll, in checkered dress, which could be purchased for 10 cents and a wrapper.

Edison Mazda Lamp Dolls' House

In 1928, General Electric produced a two-story cardboard dolls' house as

A.P.W. toilet paper was recognized by the checkered doll on the wrapper. This ad offering a rag dollie of the same design appeared in *Hearst International Magazine*, February 1925.

a carton to hold Edison Mazda Lamps. The charming house with its green and gray roof has two ivy covered red brick chimneys. Overlooking no opportunity to encourage the use of electricity, General Electric printed the following instructions on the bottom of the house:

> "The windows of this house have been scored. They may be pushed open and orange or yellow tissue or crepe paper pasted behind them. A Christmas tree string or a toy train lamp may be used inside the house to light it up."

Besides the 11 windows, the three doors also open. ∎

MAKING ANTIQUE FURNITURE IN MINIATURE

Part I by MARJORIE CONGRAM

FANCIERS OF antique furniture can now possess examples beyond their dreams through miniature models. Limitations of money and space disappear when the world of the miniature replica is entered. Ready-made items are available in a range of quality from simple dolls' house furniture to works of art, and are priced accordingly. When one makes the miniature furniture himself, satisfaction goes far beyond the pride of possession.

Corner washstand with drawer, walnut, 3½" high. Copper pitcher and ceramic basin.

Techniques of miniature furniture making lie somewhere between the complexities of full-scale construction and the simplicity of dolls' house pieces. Not every detail of a full-scale piece is necessary in a miniature. Dovetailing, for instance, is possible but structurally unnecessary. Yet it is not desirable to eliminate too much, because in reproducing the lines and joints in miniature, the craftsman gets a deep appreciation of the original.

Choosing a scale and working consistently in it enables the craftsman to relate his miniature pieces to each other. One-fifteenth or ¾ inch to the foot is about the smallest scale feasible; below that, parts become too small to manage without a magnifying glass. A one-twelfth scale (1"=1') is good to work in and easy to calculate; it is an accepted scale for dolls' house accessories in pewter, silver, pottery and glass. Larger doll and salemen's sample furniture might be in one-sixth scale; here hardware and trim are easier to fit. This larger size takes more space to display and store: a 9 by 12 foot rug, for instance, would scale down to 18 by 24 inches.

Good illustrated books on antique furniture provide models to copy. Measured drawings are helpful; personal examination and measurement of full-scale pieces are even better. After looking and measuring, a set of general standards can be made—chair seats are about 17 inches from the floor; bedsteads are about 6½ feet long; bureaus commonly have four drawers; preferred Windsor chairs have an odd number of spindles.

Where to begin? Properly fabricated chairs are among the more difficult items to make, and so should perhaps be a third or courth project. A piece with no moving parts, a bookcase or bedstead, makes a good beginning. An Empire-style sleigh bed is an example.

If it is not possible to examine and measure a full-size bed, photographs and measured drawings will supply necessary information. The Newark (N.J.) Museum's book, *Classical America 1815-1845*, has a photograph of a handsome sleigh bed, with good detail visible. Ormsbee's *Field Guide to American Victorian Furniture* gives the needed dimensions—36 to 44 inches high, 6'4" to 6'8" long, 4'6" to 4'10" wide.

With these figures, a scale drawing of the sleigh bed can be made on graph paper. Usually just two views, front and side, are enough. More complicated pieces will require more sketches of detail. Each part should be drawn on paper, and the direction of wood grain indicated. Also it is important to indicate how the piece joins the piece next to it—if the pieces lap, which goes over the other; if they are tongue and groove, which

Clothes cupboard or "Kas," painted yellow with gray, blue and green trim. Made of various woods; doors and drawers open and close. 6⅝" high.

Two-drawer table, 5¼" long, undetermined wood stained brown.

Settee, walnut, 6" long.

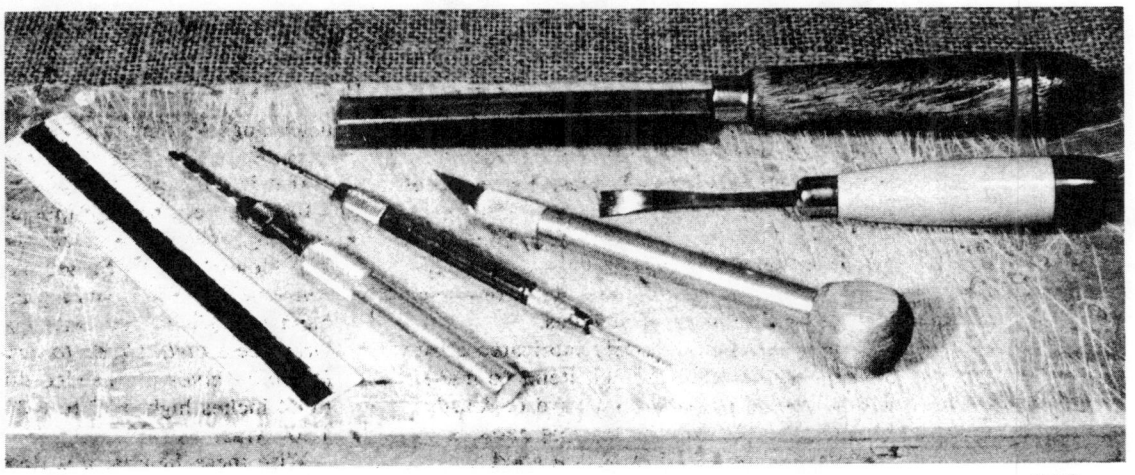

Tools needed to produce rustic miniature furniture: ruler, hand drills, knife, wood carving tool and saw resting on board 5½ by 14½" long.

goes into which, and so forth.

When all the pieces are measured, drawn, and the assembly thought out, they can be drawn on the lumber. Sawing can be done by hand or by electric jigsaw. Straight lines and proper angles are as important in miniature as in full scale models.

An adequate wood supply is needed with which to make miniatures. Suitably thin boards are hard to come by. Different kinds of wood, properly seasoned, are a pleasure to work and a challenge to pair up with suitable designs. Generally, ⅛" thick boards are the basic stock. Wood that will be turned, carved, or contoured can be thicker. To build an adequate supply of furniture wood, one has to look at old resources with a fresh eye. Drawer bottoms of discarded bureaus make fine mini lumber. A high Victorian bedstead contains many good boards. Rummage sales and auctions yield wood as well as lumber yards. Constantine's Lumber Company in the Bronx, N.Y. carries rare and fancy cabinet woods and veneers.

All sorts of odds and ends can go into a basic lumber supply. Here are the contents of one lumber box:
  Toothpicks, round
  Caramel apple sticks
  Slats from a wooden Venetian blind
  ⅛" thick walnut, maple, and ash boards
  ¼" pine board
  ⅜" walnut panel
  ⅞" walnut, pieced, a table leaf?
  2x2" block of mahogany
  Broom handle
  Cedar boards from hobby pack
  Cedar shingles
  Veneered back of discarded guitar
  Dowel sticks from ⅛" diameter up
  Veneer samples

It may be surprising how different woods handle. One of the first pieces made by this author was a settee out of black walnut. Nobody had told her that old seasoned walnut was a tough material to work with hand tools. A block of mahogany, on the other hand, accepted a carving tool willingly.

Fourposter bed, walnut, 7" long.

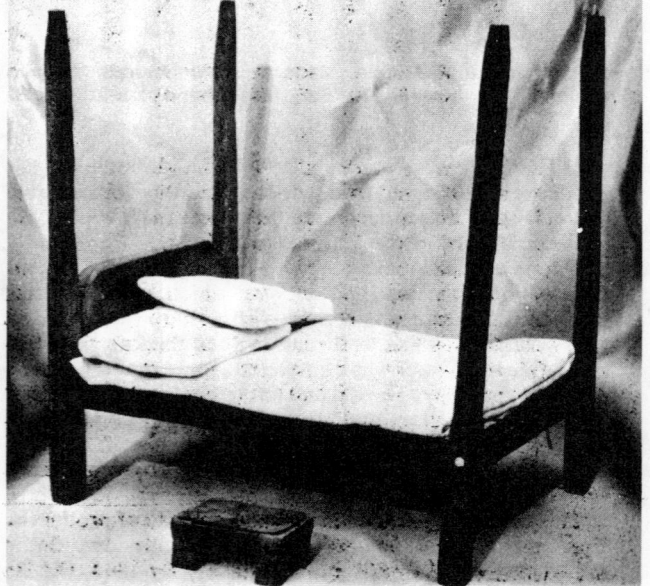

Skilled woodworkers will be able to join the pieces of their miniature furniture with rabbet, mortise and tenon, and dovetail joints. A simple but satisfactory joint is a lap, held with white glue and wooden pins. For the pins, either round toothpicks or 1/16" doweling works well.

Finding hardware for 1/12" scale furniture is not easy. Knobs and handles can be made of wood and painted with gilt to simulate metal. A blind hinge can be made by tapping a brad into the frame and door t top and bottom, thus avoiding the visible hinge problem. Escutcheons can be painted on.

Just about everything made in a 1/12" scale can be held in the palm of one hand. The tools should match the scale. Some tools which have been found useful are:
  Dremel hobby jogsaw for roughing out
  Millers Falls carving set, 6 pieces
  Atlas snap saw
  Exacto hobby knife
  Brace and several bits, hand drills with changeable bits, to match dowel sizes
  Tire tread depth gauge
  Fingernail emery boards (for sanding)

Some hobbyists may wish to go into miniature turning on a lathe. The examples shown, however, were carved on an old bread board. After the first blocking out on the Dremel saw, the work was done on the lap in the living room. Much of the pleasure is being able to work in comfortable, social surroundings; wood chips are clean and easily swept up. Of course, those who wish to do so can equip a shop for working miniatures in the basement.

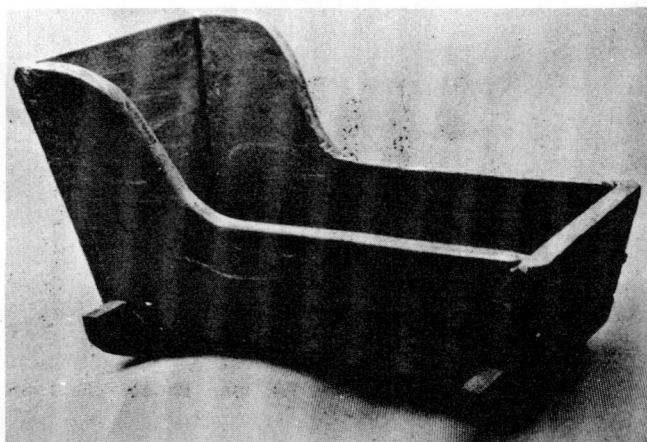

Cradle, painted blue, 3½" long.

Sleigh bed, walnut with taffy apple stick slats, 7¼" long.

MAKING ANTIQUE FURNITURE IN MINIATURE

Part II by MARJORIE CONGRAM

A WHOLE miniature furniture hobby could be built on the creation of chairs, so many varieties have existed. There are thrones, Brewster chairs, Windsor chairs, rocking chairs, wing and other upholstered chairs, high chairs, ladderbacks, bentwoods, woven splint chairs, and many others. They are all more complicated to build than beds or bookcases. The work takes a steady hand and a large dose of patience.

More than one kind of wood generally goes into a chair; pine is needed for a shaped seat, hardwood dowel sticks for legs and rungs. Toothpicks make good back spindles. A wood that can be bent is necessary for rockers, hoops, and shaped backs on "captain's" chairs.

One method of bending is to boil the cut-out pieces of wood in a pan of water for 20 minutes or so. Then, while the pieces are still hot and wet, they can be wrapped around forms (empty round spice bottles, for instance), and secured with several rubber bands. In making a set of captain's chairs, it is prudent to cut out a few extra backs, since even with the boiling, some pieces may crack on being bent.

Chair seats can be treated in the same manner as full scale seats. Slip seats can be upholstered and glued in place. A "rush" seat can be woven with string in the rush pattern. Fine cane can be used for splint-weave effects.

The vitality of a good chair is often in the turning and splay of its legs. This is where factory miniatures and dollhouse chairs are skimped. A good chair is a subtle balance of shaping, and will take a certain amount of trial and diddling to get it right.

Those who wish to show several of their handcrafted miniature pieces together in a display room can make one from ¼ inch thick plywood. The rooms shown are each 12 by 16 by 9½ inches high, but any dimensions can be used. The 12 by 16 inch size allows space for all the parts of a room in reality — windows, doors in and out, fireplaces, and such. A room in one's own house might be interesting. The measuring and rendering in scale teaches in a way no other method can.

It is possible in a display room to have windows and doors that work, but if the objective is a showcase for the miniature furniture, this is not necessary. The details on each wall should be measured off, drawn in, applied and painted before the walls are joined together.

Wallpaper can be created from shelf lining paper, from cloth, or from that especially made for dolls' houses. The important thing is the scale of the design and its suitability to the period and type of room.

With the walls completed, the floor and sides can be brought together with glue and screws. The ceilings can be affixed or used unattached so that it rests on the three upright walls. A removable ceiling is convenient for adjusting the room contents,

Highchair, painted ochre, ⅜".

General store interior with food, dry goods and hardware sections. 16" long.

Piano and stool, various woods, varnished, 5" long.

attaching chandeliers, and photographing the display room.

Accessories for miniature rooms are acquired or created with imagination. Scale is everything. If a believable scale of size and pattern is maintained, much crudity and lack of detail will be psychologically forgiven.

Some beautiful miniature pottery is now being made and sold through museum shops. Copper pots and pans come from Portugal and Germany. Beautiful mirrors, chandeliers, hollow-ware and other pieces in pewter and silver are offered for sale. Miniature glassware is on the market also. It is easy to spend a considerable amount of money on accessories.

The poor man's challenge is to find some at-hand solutions to miniature accessory needs. Rugs can be made from low-pile fabric or hand-crafted in needlepoint. A full size rug can be copied, a good color illustration of a rug reproduced, or an original design can be created. Excellent rugs can be made by braiding worsted weight yarn. Variegated yarn gives a simulation of the multiple flecks of color of a large rug and the braid can be laced together with a fourth strand of yarn in the same manner as a large rug.

Pictures for the walls can be cut from magazine illustrations, and portraits cut from photographs. A skilled hand might make silhouettes with India ink on white paper. Original oil paintings can be made on a canvas covered board that is available in a 1½ by 2 inch size.

A set of manikins to occupy the miniature rooms can be made on a pipecleaner base with lingerie tricot knit fabric and a little thread and yarn. Pipecleaner figures are more workable than rigid dolls' house dolls because they can be bent to sit, lean, and hold objects. They can be crafted in any age-size desired. Again, proportion is everything in creating believable figures.

A general rule for size would make an adult man 6" high, a woman 5½", and children 4" and 3". A baby would be 2", more or less. The pipecleaner frames can be adjusted to fit these lengths. One or two cotton balls can fill

1840s kitchen with early style of stove, 16" long.

Manikins and pipe cleaner frames. 3" to 6" high.

Wool needlepoint rug, gray and blues, 9" x 12".

Late 1920s kitchen. Stove is metal and old, all other furniture is wooden.

Manikin and cello on "roundabout" sofa of purple velvet.

Music room with harp, piano, and cello, 16" long

Cupboard with two chairs. Cupboard painted green with wood stain interior, 7" tall. Hoop-back chair 3½" high. Armchair 3¾" high.

Rush seat chair, mahogany, 3⅝" high.

in the head; then head and hands are covered with beige nylon tricot and wound with thread at the neck and wrists to secure the fabric. The torso can be padded or wound around with worsted weight yarn to plump it out.

A thin, skeletal doll dresses easier than a fat one. Clothes can be draped and sewn right onto the doll. Shoes can be fashioned out of adhesive tape and colored with ink. Features on the head can be drawn with a ball point pen. Hair can be made from strands of cotton embroidery thread, affixed with white glue in any style.

Perhaps the ultimate in the miniature antiques field is the work of Mrs. James Ward Thorne, whose 67 rooms in 1/12 scale may be seen at the Art Institute of Chicago. Two books of photographs were published by the Art Institute: *Handbook to the European Rooms in Miniature* (1943) and *American Rooms in Miniature* (1962).

These photographs are an inspiration and source of ideas as to what can be done in varieties of interior, ceiling treatments, indirect lighting, and the like. They show such perfection of scale that it is difficult to believe they are miniature.

Some of the rooms are reproductions of specific places, such as Theodore Roosevelt's New York City Victorian parlor, George Washington's West Parlor in Mount Vernon, Virginia, and Andrew Jackson's entrance hall from the Hermitage near Nashville, Tennessee. Other rooms represent an average of a prevailing period style, such as a contemporary New Mexico dining room, and the "Middletown" parlor in the last quarter of the nineteenth century. The European rooms are grandiose, being modeled after rooms in the palaces and great houses of England and France.

This author has discovered no really good books on the crafting of antique model miniature furniture, but books concerned with the construction of full-scale furniture are helpful, and measured drawings may be scaled to desired proportions. The person who gets into the creation of miniature replicas will soon develop his own technique, style, and area of specialization. What is offered here is essentially the encouragement to start.

Among helpful books, showing construction details and measured drawings of full-sized antique furniture are:

Amateur Furniture Construction, by Vernon M. Albers (Barnes, 1970). By Franklin H. Gottshall, *Heirloom Furniture* (Bruce, 1957); *Reproducing Antique Furniture* (Crown, 1971); *Simple Colonial Furniture* (Rev. ed. Bonanza, 1935); *How to Make Colonial Furniture* (Bruce, 1971). *Furniture Antiques Found in Virginia — A Book of Measured Drawings*, by Ernest Carlyle Lynch, Jr. (Bruce, 1954). *Construction of American Furniture Treasures*, by Lester Margon (Home Craftsman, 1949; Dover, 1973). *Masterpieces of Furniture in Photographs and Measured Drawings*, by Verna C. Salomonsky (Dover, 1953). *Colonial Furniture Making for Everybody*, by John G. Shea (Van Nostrand, Reinhold, 1964). *Early American Furniture You Can Build*, by Ralph Treves (Arco, 1965). *Antique Reproductions for the Home Craftsman*, by Raymond F. Yates (Whittlesey, 1950).

Biedermeier DOLLS' HOUSE FURNITURE

by CATHERINE COOK

Bedroom of an 1870 cabinet-type dolls' house with a set of gilt stenciled Biedermeier furniture, including a French-type bed, an armoire, and a marble top commode.

An 1870 dolls' house parlor furnished with a set of "ebony" Biedermeier furniture, including a sofa and chairs upholstered in rose China silk, an oval center table, and a console. Two tiny holes in the top of the latter indicate that originally there was a pier mirror. Also included are a piano and a bookcase in imitation rosewood with gilt stenciling.

Biedermeier, often referred to as the "Tiffany" of antique dolls' house furniture, is the ultimate choice of many collectors.

Biedermeier dolls' house furniture was made from 1830-1870 in the Waltershausen section of Germany, an early center for the manufacture of dolls' house furniture as well as other toys. The variations in the furniture, both in design and construction, indicate that it was made by more than one manufacturer. Few records of this period have survived, making research difficult.

One firm, the Gobraeder Schomiegias Company, established in 1845 in that Thuringia town, is believed to have made this furniture. This company continued to make dolls' house furniture until 1920, which undoubtedly accounts for the similarity to Biedermeier in some of the later dolls' house furniture.

Research also indicates that Biedermeier dolls' house furniture may have been made in France, another country to early manufacture toys.

Great quantities of Biedermeier furniture was made and shipped to England and the United States and is found in early dolls' houses of both countries.

The original name for this style of furniture is not known, and different ones have been given to it. Vivian Green, the English authority, calls it "imitation Duncan Phyfe" because of the similarity of one of the chairs and some of the other pieces. Flora Gill Jacobs, the American

Miniature German room furnished with "ebony" Biedermeier furniture in one of the larger scales. Included are a secretary-type desk 6 inches high, chest of drawers with bone embellishments, a chess table with gilt stenciled chessboard on the top, and three styles of chairs. A recent discovery of a Manufacturer's Agents catalog indicates that the room was also made in the Waltershausen area of Germany during the same period as the furniture.

authority, prefers to call it "Biedermeier," and this is the name most frequently used in this country. It is also sometimes referred to as "Waltershausen," the name of the area where is was manufactured.

The Dictionary of Antiques and the Decorated Arts (Scribners, 1957), describes Biedermeier as a potpourri of some of the features, but not the best ones, of Sheraton, Regency, Directoire, and especially French Empire, and they define it as an incongruous assortment of several styles. As the definition indicates, the styles and taste of many periods influenced Biedermeier furniture. And since dolls' house furniture copies that of the adult world of the era in which it is made, Biedermeier miniature furniture, too, transversed many periods.

Many of the early dolls' houses were quite large requiring larger scale furniture than is being made today. Unlike present-day miniature furniture which adheres so rigidly to the one inch to one foot scale, Biedermeier furniture was made in five different sizes.

For the larger scale Biedermeier furniture, heavier wood was used in the construction—7/16 inch in thickness for bases and supporting sides—giving the furniture an appearance of solidity not found in the smaller scale and those of more fanciful design.

In design and decoration there are two distinct types of Biedermeier furniture, one known as "imitation rosewood" with delicately stenciled gilt patterns on

Commode with mirror and marble top, and an armoire. Both are beautifully grained and have elaborate gilt stenciling, the armoire with an unusual design of shields and swords.

"grained" and polished wood. These stenciled designs are usually conventional scrolls, borders, and medallions. Occasionally a variation is found, as in one piece with a bird alighting on a naturalistic branch. Two pieces are known to have stenciled designs in silver rather than in gold. On the earlier pieces of furniture these designs were painted by hand, later lithographed designs on ebony paper were used. It is believed that this decoration may, in some instances, have been used as a substitute for ormolu.

The second type, described in early periodicals as "ebony," does not usually have the gilt decoration. When it does, it is referred to as "black and gold lacquer."

Real marble was sometimes used for the tops of bureaus, commodes, tables and sideboards of both types of furniture. And on the earlier pieces, turned posts of bone were used as decoration. Colored paper in both blue and green was used as a lining for glass-fronted cabinets.

Further indication of the infinite care and detail used in making this furniture is shown in the selection of upholstery fabric for the sofas and chairs. Cotton, silk, wool, and cut velvet were all used with some of the fabrics especially designed in the same small scale as the furniture, one with a design of birds and flowers centered in a formal arrangement for the back and seat of the sofa and chairs, another in a tiny overall "chintz" pattern on cotton, or wool challie.

China silk in shades of rose, mauve, and green was used for the more formal pieces, as was cut velvet in an especially designed small scale pattern.

Narrow gilt paper braid and a tiny "rickrack" type of braid were used as a finish for the upholstered seats and backs.

Biedermeier dolls' house furniture was made and sold in sets of seven or more pieces for parlor, dining room, and bedroom. The parlor sets included a sofa, center table, console—often with a pier mirror, and chairs, one usually an armchair. Dining room sets included an extension-type table, sideboard, china cabinet, and chairs. Seven or more pieces were included in the sets of bedroom furniture. In addition to the bed, chairs, a bureau or chest of drawers, a commode or dressing table were included; and since this was the closet-less era, a wardrobe or armoire.

Pianos, desks, bookcases, display tables, and cabinets are also found in antique doll's houses, as are sewing and chess tables. These may have been included in the larger

Duncan Phyfe chairs in four sizes. The smallest chair is 2¾ inches high, the largest is 4 inches.

Rare desk, 5¾ inches high, believed to have been made in France. It has a beautifully grained finish with fine stenciled border around the top edge. Tiny turned finials connected with wire trim the ends of both top and writing area. The recessed compartment between the small drawers is lined with green paper.

Piano, 4½ inches high, in imitation rosewood with gilt stenciling. The keys sound when played.

and more expensive sets of furniture, and may also have been sold as individual pieces.

The furniture shown in the parlor and bedroom illustrations for this article were purchased as complete sets; the other pieces illustrated here were collected one, or two at a time.

A great variety of styles were found in the individual pieces of Biedermeier furniture due to the long period that is was manufactured. Five different styles of sofas were made; the Victorian is the most frequently seen. Others include Gothic Revival and the open back type. Most rare is the French Empire style and, because of its "elegant" appearance, it may have been made in France. Chairs, too, are found in a variety of styles to match and go with the sofas.

Tables include both the center table for the parlor, usually oval in shape and with a pedestal base, and the dining room table. The latter was made in both types; the one in ebony finish is oval and has a heavy pedestal base; the other, of imitation rosewood with gilt stenciling, has a shaped oblong top and tapered legs. Both are extension-type tables.

A variety of sideboards and china cabinets are also found. One in the larger scale is very much like the Victorian sideboard, but with gilt stenciling in place of the usual carved fruit and game. A smaller scale, more of a serving table, was also made. Both styles often have marble tops.

Two very distinct types of china cabinets were made, the one in ebony is of the heavy, solid type with glass enclosed shelves above and drawers below. The one of imitation rosewood is of the fanciful style with shaped cut-out legs and has a mirrored door.

Other tables include the chess table with the chessboard in gold stencil on top, and the sewing table with a lift top and sectional compartments below.

Desks, too, were made in several styles. The one most frequently seen is the secretary-type desk in ebony finish. It has the drop front with drawers above and below the writing area, and was made in all five different scales. One of the loveliest desks seen is believed to be French because of the detail. A similar type of desk was also made in a number of scales in the imitation rosewood with gilt stencil; both types are illustrated. The Davenport desk, well-known in adult size, was also made.

Beds, too, were made in several styles including the French type. Commodes, bureaus, and dressing tables of

Center and Right: Two Victorian sofas in two scales, the small one only 4 inches wide and 1⅞ inches high. Both are upholstered in the same "chintz" pattern fabric and have gilt stenciling. **Left:** Sofa in the open-back style has been reupholstered; originally, China silk was used.

Secretary desk, 6 inches high, in ebony. The compartment between the small drawers has a mirrored back.

Chess table, 3⅜ inches high with gilt stenciled chessboard on top of table and gilt paper braid on base. The chair, one of the fancy cut-out types, also has gilt stenciling.

both types are found, many with marble tops and attached mirrors.

A recently discovered combination coat rack and umbrella stand adds to the Biedermeier dolls' house furnishings for still another room, the hall.

A second oval table in the writer's collection has a beautifully grained finish and a scroll design in gold. Stenciled in the center in silver is a building and the words "Islsberg Haus." It is believed that this piece of Beidermeier miniature furniture was made as a souvenir.

With the overwhelming profusion of modern miniatures to choose from, present day collectors of dolls' house furniture feel that Biedermeier is too difficult to find. This has always been true, but the delight when one finds a piece more than compensates for the time spent in searching. The only unfortunate thing, as one collector has said, is that Biedermeier, like many other antiques, is being "auctioned off and priced out of existence." ∎

Illustrations include pieces from the author's collection and the collection of the Hansel and Gretal Museum, Martha's Vineyard, MA.

China cabinet, 7½ inches high, and "extension-type" dining room table. The original mirror in the cabinet door has been replaced with glass to display silver miniatures against the old blue background.

Gothic Revival sofa and armchair in rosewood with gilt stenciling upholstered with printed material in a tapestry design. The chair is 5½ inches high, the sofa, 7 inches wide and 4¾ inches high.

Small desk, 3½ inches high, and bookcase in imitation rosewood with gilt stenciling.

by CATHERINE COOK

BANQUETS IN MINIATURE

Christmas dinner in an 1860s dolls' house. The dining table is set with turned and decorated wooden dishes (Bavaria, 1830-1860) and supplemented with a miniature blown glass wine decanter and stemmed glasses, and pewter and Britannia metal flatware and serving pieces.

Practically everything made for use in adult life has at some time been made in miniature. Nowhere is this more apparent than with the miniatures made as table settings and accessories for antique dolls' houses. One may find a china fish set complete with platter and plates, silver lustre candlesticks, or a tantalus of Britannia metal replete with blown glass bottles.

The miniatures found in antique dolls' houses came from the four corners of the globe, and many countries have made their contributions. Wood, ceramics, glass, silver and pewter were all used to make these tiny replicas.

Among the rarest and most acceptable for table use are the turned wood tea and dinner sets made in Bavaria, Germany, from 1830 to 1880. Like so many early toys, they were made in several sizes and, because they were unbreakable, have survived. The dinner sets came with three types of plates—dinner, soup and dessert size. Serving pieces included a soup tureen, pedestal cake stand, candlesticks and a tray. A complete dinner service would consist of twenty-five or more pieces. In addition, tea and coffee sets, sets of goblets and egg cups, complete with trays, were also made. The dishes were usually painted white, cream color or yellow, and many were decorated with tiny sprays of flowers; others were bordered or banded with colored stripes.

Also made, but in a limited number, were complete toilet sets con-

213

sisting of a wash bowl and pitcher, chamber stick, jars and bottles for cold cream, toilet water and powder, and a ring tree. A toilet set of this type was included among the accessories in a doll's house owned by the late Queen Mary of England, and now on display in a London museum.

China was used to make the greatest number of table settings for dolls' houses and, from 1850 on, miniature china tea and dinner services were made in England and Germany. Already known for her beautiful china, England became a leader in this field with many 19th century potteries as the producers. Sets of dishes were often made in three sizes—adult, child and doll, and frequently in the same designs—in the Tea Leaf pattern, some transfer-printed designs, or copies of Oriental patterns.

Tea and dinner services in doll size, often with as many as fifty-five pieces, are found in antique dolls' houses, though they are usually too large in scale. More of these were made by Spode and other Staffordshire potteries than by other companies. Even today, many Staffordshire potteries continue to make these miniature wares.

At the end of the 18th century, Staffordshire potteries were making miniature dinner sets of china with attached food. These are among the most colorful and intriguing of the miniature dishes. Since many are from two to three inches in size, they are much too large for most dolls' houses. A reference to these dishes can be found in Beatrix Potter's book, *The Tale of Two Bad Mice*. Specifically mentioned are "two lobsters, a ham, a fish, and a pudding and some pears and oranges."

France, also noted for its beautiful china, made miniature dishes, but in a more limited number. The French miniature dishes included those in dolls' house size. One Limoge firm specialized in miniature pieces for many years. It is now owned by Haviland & Company, and continues to produce these wares. In addition to tea sets, vases, baskets and inkstands, they also make complete toilet sets. Many of the miniature pieces are decorated with a reproduction of an early pattern that has since become their trademark; still others are decorated with floral designs. The Limoge miniatures have always been among the most perfect in scale for dolls' houses.

Prior to World War One, Germany was the main source of many of the miniature sets of dishes sold in the United States. These dishes were

Breakfast in a country kitchen. The table is set with ironstone dishes and Britannia accessories. The plate of bacon and eggs is of embossed paper with gesso food. China plate with coffee bread (marzipan) is from Vienna.

made in both ironstone china and porcelain. Designs and decorations varied and included, in dolls' house size, the popular Meissen Onion Pattern. Also made in porcelain and ironstone china were miniature toilet sets and sets of "banquet food" similar to those made in England. Later sets of dishes made of embossed cardboard with attached food of gesso were made. Two pieces in the author's collection represent a platter of salmon and green peas and a plate of bacon and eggs.

Japan replaced Germany when their supply of toys was curtailed at the outbreak of World War One. And Japan continued to expand their toy market when Germany later re-entered the market. Tea sets in dolls' house size are among the miniatures produced in Japan. A partial set of jade green in the author's collection is believed to have been produced for the Japanese "Doll Festival." Another and later set in its original box is labelled "Made in occupied Japan."

Among the Oriental miniatures to be found are vases, figurines and other decorative accessories. Two very interesting signed pieces in the author's collection are a plate, one and three-eighths inches in diameter, set into a folding easel stand; the other is an oval dish with rolled edge in one of the Japanese blue and white designs.

Miniature pottery is frequently found among the accessories of early dolls' houses and, like the china, was made in several different countries. Among the earliest and choicest pieces are the English tan and brown wares which include jugs, pitchers and mugs—all in perfect scale.

Miniature pieces of pottery were

Photos by Charles J. Lennon.

made in the United States at a number of early potteries in New England, Pennsylvania and Ohio. To be found are jugs, pitchers and crocks of stoneware, slipware and Rockingham. From 1821 to 1892, in Bennington, Vermont, Rockingham-type jugs ranging in size from one-half to one and one-half inches, and three to four inches were being produced. Unfortunately, these pieces were not marked and cannot be attributed to any particular Bennington pottery. Another potter, John C. Crotens, working in about 1820, made stoneware pitchers in the one-half to one and one-half inch sizes.

With today's interest in old crafts, miniatures of all kinds are again being made in the United States as well as other countries. Some years ago, Mexican potteries began making miniature tea sets in colorfully glazed pottery and unglazed redware. The glazed sets were produced in green and deep blue, the former resembling majolica in color. Other pieces were made with a mottled cream, blue and green glaze. The colors and simple shapes of this Mexican pottery make it very suitable for use in early American dolls' house kitchens.

In more recent years, Portugal has been making miniatures in dolls' house sizes. These include jugs, pitchers and baskets in variegated colors.

Miniature examples of glassware can be found in almost every technique and category from simple mold-blown bottles to various types of art glass. While many of these miniature pieces of glass were not originally meant for use in dolls' houses, they are nevertheless very compatible in these surroundings.

Miniature pieces of blown glass proved to be a very satisfactory accessory for dolls' houses, and in the 18th and 19th centuries such wares

Toilet set of turned and painted wood (Bavaria, 1830 to 1880); a duplicate of this set is in a dolls' house once owned by the late Queen Mary of England.

Pewter and Britannia metal serving pieces including plates, vegetable dishes, tea kettle on stand, cups and saucers, and small trays.

were produced—some only one-half inch high, and consisting of tea sets, dinner services, and decanters with matching wine glasses.

In Germany, mold-blown, enamelled, and Nailsea- and Bristol-type glass in imitation of Venetian wares were made in miniature. In the 18th century, all types of glassware in miniature were being made in England; by the end of the century the centers of production were Birmingham and Bristol. These centers became famous for the so-called "Bris-

Left Above: Top row: Miniature pottery pieces from England. **Bottom row:** Pottery miniatures made in Portugal, Mexico and the United States.

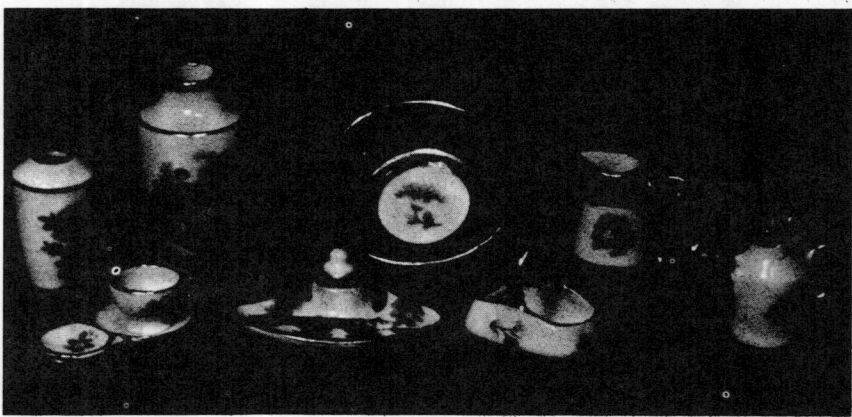

Bottom Left: A selection of Limoge miniatures including vases, wash bowl and pitcher, watering can, flower basket and inkstand.

Below: Miniatures for serving wine and other beverages. The tantalus has mold-blown glass bottles, and the wine pitcher of glass is encased in Britannia metal with matching Britannia glasses. The punch bowl and ladle are also made of Britannia metal.

tol" and "Nailsea" glass miniatures, including tea sets of opaque glass with floral decorations, as well as pieces with opaque stripes and spirals. In the 19th century, colored waves became very popular and many lovely little blown glass miniatures were made in blue, green, amethyst and striped glass. During the 1870s and 1880s, blown glass miniatures were being sold at fairs all over England.

Among the delightful pieces of miniature blown glass are those that came in combination with Britannia metal and a soft metal known as "trifle." Collectors can find glass wine pitchers encased in metal, a tantalus with blown glass bottles, and beverage sets, the latter often made of Nailsea striped glass. A very charming beverage set seen recently consisted of a metal holder with six tiny Nailsea striped glasses. Handles at each end of the holder crossed above the glasses to form a small shelf on which were six little Britannia plates, then continued upward to form a loop handle.

From 1835 to 1853, miniature glassware was produced in a variety of pressed glass patterns by the Boston and Sandwich Glass Works in Massachusetts. Miniature pieces in clear and colored glass were made, but only in doll size and therefore too large for use in a dolls' house. The Westmoreland Glass Company of Ohio also made miniature sets of glassware from 1890 to 1958, but only in child and doll sizes. Very few pressed glass miniatures in dolls' house size were made, as pressed glass was not too satisfactory a method for producing miniatures. Those made tend to have a heavy, and sometimes clumsy, appearance.

Metal alloys, including heavily leaded pewter, was used to fashion little tea and dinner sets and kitchenwares early in the 18th century. By 1820, Britannia metal, a mixture of tin and antimony, replaced the earlier pewter. Tea and dinner sets in several sizes were produced and included appropriate flatware. Also made in a variety of designs were caster and condiment sets with two or more blown glass bottles. Spoon holders, toast racks, knife rests and other pieces for a dolls' house were also produced.

Later filigree, a lighter and more fragile alloy sometimes referred to as "white metal," was used to make miniatures, and is still being used for reproductions of earlier pieces. Sets of flatware in several sizes were also made in filigree and Britannia metal. Although often called "pewter," most of the metal miniatures are made of filigree and Britannia.

The Netherlands is credited with making the first silver miniatures during the 15th to the 17th centuries. Germany soon followed making copies of the Dutch pieces. The making of silver miniatures spread from the Netherlands to England where they were produced in London from 1684 to 1746 by "Toy Silversmiths."

At first, these silver miniatures were made to please adults who displayed them in cabinets and miniature room settings. Tea sets complete with trays and cake baskets, as well

Left: Turned wooden dishes made in Bavaria (1830-1880). Plates show designs of five different dinner services, soup tureen, pedestal cake stand, a tea set and miniature goblets on a tray.

Center: Silver miniatures including a bowl with handles, a two-handled cup, meat platters, a pair of pepper shakers, compote, pitcher, and two coin silver spoons (2 inches in length).

Bottom: Two Japanese tea sets. The set on the left came in its original box marked "Made in Occupied Japan." Teapot is ⅞ inches high. The other tea set is believed to be from a "Dolls' Festival" set.

as miniature pieces of furniture, were among the items made. In America the best known silversmiths, including Paul Revere, made miniature pieces of silver. Unfortunately, these were too large in scale for use in dolls' houses.

Research has disclosed that tiny coin silver tea spoons were made by Roswell Bailey of Woodstock, Vermont, in 1839. He made the first one for his daughter, then went on to produce four thousand dozen—the work of his apprentices—as "an exercise in training the eye to exactness and nicety of line." None of these spoons were marked, and since they were widely disseminated by tin peddlers of the period, they have been scattered all over New England. One of two in the author's collection is inscribed with the name "Ellen" on the front of the handle.

Copies of early silver miniatures have been reproduced many times in the ensuing centuries. Those made in the late 19th and early 20th centuries are now being sold as "antiques." Currently, they are being made in Holland, England, Japan and Portugal.

Scale, which is more and more being emphasized by today's collectors, has not yet been discussed. It is true that one finds discrepancies in scale in antique dolls' houses, but strangely enough this only seems to enhance their charm. Perhaps, as one author so aptly said, "Perfection lies not in slavish imitation, but rather in the imperfections themselves." It is this feature that gives them their charm.

For the purist, only the old miniatures are acceptable. Other collectors will compromise and accept what is available. Today's dolls' houses may contain a *pot pourri* of miniatures from different periods. But many years will pass, and many miles will be covered before a dolls' house can be completely furnished.

A History of Bathing in the Dolls' House

CATHERINE COOK

Photos by Charles J. Lennon

EVERY SOCIAL change, once accepted and adopted in the adult world, invariably finds its way into the miniature world. To understand the acceptance and adoption of bathing as portrayed in the dolls'house, and the changes and additions it has brought, one needs to examine the history of bathing in the adult world.

An early proverb, "Cleanliness is next to Godliness," attributed to John Wesley (1672-1719), is believed to have influenced and promoted the acceptance of cleanliness and the development of means and ways to attain it.

The present generation, with an abundant supply of hot and cold running water and private baths, little realizes what has transpired to make this possible. In the 18th century, the only source of water for the household was a well from which pails of water had to be drawn and carried into the house. If hot water was needed, it was heated in kettles in the fireplace or in small tanks attached to a stove. A special container, known as the "hot water can," was used to transport the hot water to where it was needed. These containers, resembling the watering pot in shape but with a hinged cover, were made of tin and other metals in several sizes.

Miniature bathroom, circa 1900, with varnished wainscoted walls and early style fixtures and water tank of painted wood, the washstand is 4 inches high. Note the shaving mirror.

Above & Below: Exterior and interior of a bathing house; water for the shower was poured down the "chimney." (*For more information, please refer to the text.*)

Later, water was piped into the house using hand pumps and stored in small tanks. Not until the advent of electricity was it possible to store large quantities of water in a home as we have today.

The washstand on the wall, now called a "lavabo," is the ancestor of all other washstands and dates from 1390 to 1890. These were made of tin, pewter, silverplate, copper and ceramics, the material used connoting the social status of the owner. Most examples had cisterns for either hot or cold water, and some had divided cisterns with two taps, one for each. Many have survived, indicating their almost universal use.

Washstands came into use in 1740 and ten years later shaving mirrors appeared. The latter fitted into little stands, often a former wig stand. At first the washstands were slender affairs with three legs and three supports that held a slender circular basin ring, and were used primarily for finger washing. Later, in the 18th century, with the demand for more washing and less powdering of wigs, washstands became larger and more square in design.

English cabinetmakers combined elegance with utilitarian purposes to make washstands popular. Chippendale, Hepplewhite and Sheraton considered the piece important enough to repeat the same carving of the bed posts on the legs and suppports of the washstand. Sheraton developed the washstand into a thing of distinction and beauty, especially the corner washstand.

In America, cabinetmakers simplified and modified the English models. When Empire furniture was fashionable in this country, about 1810-1830, washstands were made in a heavy, square design, usually in mahogany. Later in the 19th century, as they became more common, washstands were made of pine and oak and in plainer and more simple designs.

(continued on next page)

Left: Rare miniature lavabo made of painted metal. *Collection Hansel & Gretel Museum.* **Right:** Bathtub on legs complete with bathing baby. **Below:** Early unpainted tin "Bathing Room" with water tank on back wall; the room measures 7⅜" x 5" x 6".

Toilet sets of tin, china, pewter, brass and copper were made and included a washbasin, water pitcher or ewer, soap dish, toothbrush holder and shaving mug.

In the larger and more affluent homes, which frequently included a small dressing room adjacent to the bedroom, the addition of a movable tub transformed the latter into a bathing room.

In rural areas and more modest homes, a portable tub would be brought into the bedroom and, in some instances, the tub would be placed in front of the kitchen stove for a warm Saturday night bath. These portable bathtubs, usually made of tin or copper, were made in several shapes and sizes, including a round tub, the hip bath, or one made in a shoe shape.

Bathing was available in early inns using portable tubs brought into the guest's room. One can imagine the commotion when an important guest arrived demanding a hot bath.

One ingenious idea of the Victorian period was the invention of a tin trunk which could be used for the traveler's clothes and when emptied turned into a hip bath.

The first English public bath was built in Liverpool in 1843. It was not until the late 19th century that complete bathrooms as we know them today became an integral part of the home. One such early bathroom in a mansion in Maine has the fixtures encased in beautiful mahogany to match the furniture in the room.

Early toys for children were not made just for amusement, but also as learning aids and for the devlopment of good habits and behavior. Dolls' houses provided an excellent opportunity for teaching the importance of cleanliness.

In determining the age of miniatures for bathing, they should be dated later than those of adult size for they would not have been made in miniature until they had been long accepted and used in the real world.

Miniatures for bathing were made in great quanity and variety for dolls' houses and, beginning with the lavabo followed closely those made for adult bathing. Although miniature lavabos were made in tin, pewter and ceramics for dolls' houses, few, because of their size, have survived and are therefor very rare. One of painted metal from the Hansel & Gretel Museum, Martha's Vineyard, Massachusetts, is illustrated here.

Manufacturers of early dolls' house furniture emulating those of the adult world included washstands and commodes in their sets of bedroom furniture. Consequently one finds Biedermeier, Red and Yellow Cherry, etc. washstands and commodes. Washstands were also made as individual pieces in a variety of designs and materials. There are tin stands, pewter stands, wooden stands and even stands made of papier mache. Some have mirrors, others rods and hooks for towels, and some are made with one, and sometimes two, attached basins. Five washstands in the author's collection indicate the wide variety made. A reproduction of an early type made of Britannia metal (ca.1878) has three legs, a small shelf for the sponge and a circular basin ring. It is painted with asphaltum and decorated with gold.

A wooden washstand from the R. D. Cook collection (1940) is in a style very popular in America. Made of pine, it has a shelf and drawer below and is painted black with gold powder stenciling.

The third washstand is an English table type with shelf below. It is painted and "grained" with yellow ochre and burnt sienna and shaped to simulate carving.

The fourth stand, also made of tin, is a type made with many variations and in large numbers. Painted green, it has a mirror and attached washbasin.

The fifth washstand, with three legs, is quite unusual; painted gold, it has a water tank and faucet and a permanently attached washbowl.

Individual commodes were not made in as great quantity in miniature. The three examples in the author's collection were all made as part of bedroom sets and include a painted stand of tin with mirror, and one each of Beidermeier and Yellow Cherry. The Beidermeier stand has a marble top and mirror, the Yellow Cherry is an enclosed cabinet type with lift top and recessesd area for washbowl and pitcher.

A commode in the collection of the Hansel & Gretel Museum was undoubtedly made by the same manufacturer as one of the washstands in the author's collection. The mirrored tops of the two pieces are identical, including the decoration. But the lower sections differ in that one is enclosed and the other is open.

Miniature toilet sets were as complete as those made for adults and included soap dishes, basins and ewers of tin, pewter, silver and ceramics. Pieces from a lithographed set were appropriately decorated with ducks and swans.

Miniature portable tin tubs were made in different shapes and sizes, including the early round tub and the hip bath, as well as later types. Some also stand on legs and were especially made for bathing the dolls' house baby.

Painted and stenciled pine washstand, 5 inches high.

An interesting innovation of the 19th century bathing toys were miniature "bathing rooms." Made of unpainted tin, they have three walls and a floor, similar to the tin kitchens, and a removable bathtub. Some also have tanks for water on the back of the center wall with a faucet on the inside. Others have mirrors and rods for towels.

An unusual bathing room in the author's collection is a complete building, 8¼ x 6¼ x 9 inches painted light green, with frosted glass windows and a painted "tile" floor. it has a shower head and faucet for the water which can be poured down the "chimney" and came complete with tub and little "bathing doll."

Complete boxed sets of bathroom fixtures made of wood, metal and porcelain were made. Some of the earlier sets with water tanks and exposed piping were made with fixtures attached to sections of the wall and floor; the pieces were made so they could be set into a room in a dolls' house. A wooden set of this type is shown in our illustrations.

(continued on next page)

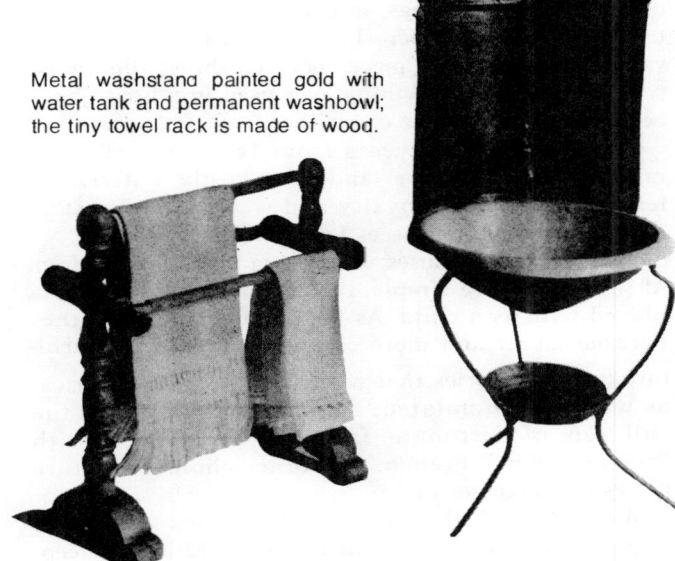

Metal washstand painted gold with water tank and permanent washbowl; the tiny towel rack is made of wood.

Catherine Cook *is a longtime collector of miniatures and dolls' house furnishings. She is the co-author with Edith Morris of* Fascinating Tin Toys For Girls, 1820-1920.

Left: Washstand and commode, obviously made by the same manufacturer, have identical decorated tops; the lower sections are entirely different. **Above:** Toilet sets of ironstone. **Below:** Toilet sets of decorated porcelain.

Just as today's children are given plastic toys to play with in their baths, so "bathing dolls" were provided for children of an earlier period. Made of china, bisque and rubber, these bathing dolls have stationary limbs and were made in both standing and sitting positions.

The social changes of bathing in the adult world so permeated the miniature world that in today's dolls' houses of any size one will find a bathroom, or even two, emulating the modern homes of our time. ■

Dolls' House Miniatures in Metal

by CATHERINE COOK

FOR THE COLLECTOR of antique dolls' houses and dolls' house furnishings, miniatures of metal—pewter, trifle, brass, and copper—have special fascination. The variety of such metal pieces is astonishing; tiny metal replicas of almost anything ever used in a house have been made at one time or another.

Miniatures in the years from 1680 to 1780 were made in gold and silver and other costly materials, a few for children of royalty and wealth, but most as trinkets and cabinet pieces for adults.

By 1800, dolls' houses were being made for children. At first they were simple, like the one Queen Victoria played with as a child. As the century advanced they became larger and more elaborate, as did the furniture and accessories that went into them. In America, as wealth accumulated, dolls' houses made for the children of fortunate families were filled with "Biedermeier," French, and other choice furniture pieces and accessories.

Many of the 19th century dolls' houses were quite large; some had rooms 24 inches wide, 22 inches deep, and 20 inches high. Dolls' house furniture was made on a proportionate scale; some pieces were offered in as many as four different sizes to accommodate large and smaller dolls' houses. Very little was made in today's preferred scale of 1 inch to 1 foot; accessories were also made in larger size and with less attention to scale.

Few pewter miniatures from the 18th century have survived. By 1820 Britannia, a white alloy of tin, cop-

Pewter (Britannia) unpainted: Wine decanter stand with glass bottles; two caster stands, one with bottles; amber blown glass pitcher encased in filigree.

Brass: Table with inset wooden top; table lamp with Bristol glass shade; standing dinner gong, marked "Germany"; umbrella stand.

Pewter (Britannia): candelabra; ice water tank; crumber.

per, and antimony, had replaced the earlier pewter and nearly all so-called "pewter" dolls' house pieces found today are of Britannia. Though miniatures in silver were still made, as were pieces in copper and brass, the increased demand favored less expensive materials. Dolls' house items in Britannia and what was known as "trifle" (a combination of tin, lead, and pewter) which were easily molded and inexpensive to produce were made in quantity. Trifle varies in strength and durability depending on the proportions of the ingredients in the mix.

A variety of finishes were used on the Britannia and trifle pieces. Some were left in original silver or pewter color; some were gilded in imitation of brass; and some, especially of the earlier pieces, were painted with asphaltum to imitate wood.

Accessories made of unpainted Britannia included sets of dishes as well as individual pieces such as Queen Anne and Georgian teapots on stands, copied from earlier silver examples, gravy boats, goblets, steins, candle snuffers on trays, and such 20th century pieces as coffee urns and chafing dishes. Through every period candlesticks and lighting fixtures were made in keeping with current styles; early chandeliers held candles, later ones were furnished with tiny light bulbs.

Britannia and trifle pieces painted gold included lamps and candlesticks and chandeliers; those painted with asphaltum ran to fireplace accessories and furniture, extending to light brown iceboxes and washtubs with wringers.

Filigree furniture, believed to have been copied from miniature silver furniture made in Holland in the 16th and 17th centuries, was made of both Britannia and trifle. Some of the pieces were extremely fragile, bending with the slightest pressure; others were quite sturdy.

An early toymaker in New York City who made filigree dolls' house furniture and accessories was Peter Pia. The business he started in 1848 continued for more than 100 years. Best known of his toys today are the sets of filigree parlor furniture which came in four designs and three sizes, the set most frequently found is one made at the time of the Columbian Exposition in 1893—a relief design showing Columbus setting foot in the New World.

The other three designs, all worked in filigree, show horse shoe, heart, and lattice patterns. Chair seats of

Dolls' house study: On the table with pewter student lamp and brass picture frame is Art Nouveau style writing set with two inkwells and attached block of paper labeled "Notizen"; pewter plates and candlesticks on mantel; brass framed picture above mantel; chandelier of brass.

heavy cardboard were covered with velvet to represent upholstery. These boxed sets included a sofa, rocking chair, and one or two side chairs; a table was sometimes included in sets of the larger sizes.

In her *Dolls' Houses in America*, Flora Gill Jacobs writes of another set of filigree furniture made by Pia, this one of simple scroll design with bits of the scroll painted gold for decoration; the seats were of colored cardboard. Mrs. Jacobs also verified that Peter Pia

Brass vase; Art Nouveau design clock, painted gold; brass table lamp; candelabra; unusual footed brass cakestand.

Brass: fireplace equipment; plant stand; sewing basket, with bamboo turned legs, lined with pink crepe paper, contains thimble 5/16" high; umbrella stand. Furnishings in Oriental design, like sewing basket here, and birdcage with parrot, were popular in the 1820s, came to favor again about 1870. These are probably of the later period.

Pewter (Britannia): dustpan and brush; teapot on stand; chafing dish from the early 1900s; toastrack, probably English.

Antique miniature room showing fireplace with brass and copper grill; brass umbrella stand; rare wall newspaper rack in brass; brass clock and wall light.

made other pieces of filigree furniture, including a baby carriage.

Manufacturers in other countries also made dolls' house furniture in filigree. A Bavarian firm, Schweizer of Dissen, produced some fine pieces about 1880. Furnishings marked "Germany" are occasionally found. Examples of a sturdily made French type, marked "France", painted in gold or bronze, sometimes in blue, have been found in chairs, tables, clocks, and standing hall trees.

Often it can be noted that an economy-minded manufacturer used the same part in different furniture pieces as, for instance, when the framework for a butler's table served for a standing sewing bag, or a plant stand with the top removed became a washstand.

Many miniatures were made of brass; today they are sometimes referred to as "ormolu." Among old brass accessories are to be found candlesticks, chandeliers, mirror and picture frames, desk fittings, such as elaborate inkstands and roll-on blotters, umbrella stands, fireplace equipment, and a smattering of vases and table pieces.

Little dolls' house furniture was made of brass, though brass tables, some with inset wooden tops, and rocking chairs with mesh backs and seats will reward the determined seeker.

Copper was not used for miniature furniture, but copper accessories appeared early on the scene. How-

Brass dressing table mirror was originally attached to a mauve colored velvet shelf; brass jars are replacement for original brass vases; rare brass man's watchholder on wall holds pocket watch 5/16" in diameter; hand mirror and single candlestick of brass.

Brass: crumber and brush; pricket candlestick. Pewter: teapot, candle snuffers and tray.

Dolls' house living room set for tea. Pewter teaset and fireplace equipment; brass Vases, candelabra and clock. By the window a filigree birdcage in Chinese Chippendale design holds a parrot. The chandelier has sprays of leaves between its three arms.

ever, few are found in dolls' house size since they were made for ornaments and cabinet pieces rather than toys. Lovely pieces are still being made and sold in England, Holland, and the Scandinavian countries as souvenirs for tourists, not as dolls' house items.

Except for the early silver miniatures which were hallmarked, it is almost impossible to date dolls' house furnishings exactly. Early toy catalogs may show examples, but they do not name the maker, and though they give a date the toys were in production, it must be remembered that the same designs and patterns were made over a long span of time. Miniatures found in an old dolls' house are not necessarily the same age as the house; many may have been added by later generations of children who played with it.

The age of a miniature may be deduced if it represents an object used at a particular time but is no longer needed as, for instance, a Britannia ice water tank. Again, the design or decoration of a miniature may indicate its age. Art Nouveau designs (1890-1910) are examples of this, though they would not have appeared in dolls' house furnishings until they had proved popular in adult usage. Traditional designs, like a Queen Anne teapot, continued in use for generations and were reproduced over and over again. It is always best to say a piece was made "about" such and such a date.

If a dolls' house item is scarce or rare, it is usually original. On the other hand, if an accessory in an old design begins to appear in quantity, beware! It is no doubt being reproduced. As with all metal pieces, miniatures are usually shiny when new, but darken with age. Comparison of a known old piece with a reproduction will help one to distinguish and "get the feel" of antique miniatures.

Since old dolls' houses pieces were never made to a set scale, those who love and collect them are not concerned with discrepancies in size of accessories, but count them part of the charm of age.

Most of the dolls' house miniatures pictured here date between 1850 and 1900; a few are from the early 20th century.

Pewter ice water tank.

Filigree furniture: fireplace with attached overmantel mirror; wall display cabinet with mirrored back; desk; birdcage with canary inside. Cabinet and desk believed to be by Schweizer of Dissen, Bavaria, ca. 1880.

Editor's note: Catherine Cook is the co-author, with Edith Morris, of *Fascinating Tin Toys For Girls, 1820–1920*.

Folding Dolls' Houses and Rooms

Made by McLaughlin Bros.

by CATHERINE COOK

Front view of the "Garden House" (ca. 1911).

THE McLAUGHLIN BROS. COMPANY of New York City is well-known among collectors for its lithographed paper toys, games, blocks, books and folding dolls' houses. It was one of several companies that manufactured lithographed toys in the late 19th century. Others included R. Bliss of Pawtucket, Rhode Island, and Converse of Winchendon, Massachusetts.

Among the best known of McLaughlin's lithographed paper toys are their folding dolls' houses. These include the "Book House" (1884), "Dolly's Play House" (ca. 1884-1903), and the "Garden House" (ca. 1911). A fourth dolls' house advertised in the 1911 McLaughlin catalog but not yet seen by the author, is a "Bungalow-Type" house.

The ingenuity shown in the design and construction of these folding dolls' houses is unique. They require no additional fasteners, as do most other folding houses. The houses are made of strawboard and wood, and the number that have survived years of use attest to their durability. The lithographed paper, too, is heavier than that used by other manufacturers and the cloth hinges are nearly indestructible.

The lithographing itself is very colorful and the designs present a contemporary picture of the periods

Living and dining rooms of the "Book House" (1884). In the dining room (right) is a set of lithographed paper furniture also made by McLaughlin.

Kitchen and bedroom of the "Book House."

Top: Interior view of the "Garden House."
Bottom: "Garden House" with front down showing garden on the left.

represented—that is, in architecture, decoration, and taste—and mix enough reality with fantasy to give the atmosphere of the era.

The folding "Book House" (1884), originally designed by a Baltimore woman, was patented by McLaughlin in 1896. It is made up of a series of partitions radiating from a center hinge with floor sections attached to the bottom of the walls that drop down. The house folds into a twelve-inch square and came in a box measuring thirteen inches square by two inches deep. The four rooms, each with two walls and a twelve-inch square floor consist of a parlor, dining room, bedroom and kitchen. Fireplaces are included in the lithographed wall designs in three of the rooms, and the kitchen boasts a cooking stove and wall cupboards.

The most attractive of McLaughlin's dolls' houses is the two-room, two-story "Dolly's Play House" (1884). Assembled and set up, the house is 17½ inches high, 12 inches wide and 9 inches deep. Three hinged walls form the back and sides of the house and the front is open. The attached floors swing down with the upper floor resting on a strip of wood. A curved cornice fits into the upper ends of the side walls holding the house securely in place. The outside of the house is covered with "brick" lithographed paper and there is a "tile" roof, with removable chimney, that rests on top. The upstairs bedroom is relatively simple, but the drawing room below is elegantly furnished with gold leaf cornices at the windows and gold leaf frames for the mirror and pictures.

The third house, known as the "Garden House" (ca. 1911), is a town house with red brick exterior and has many windows and three doors. When open, the four walls form a square. Closed, the two end walls with center hinges turn inward so that the house folds flat. The two attached floors fold down and the roof rests on top of the house. To make the garden and provide access to the interior, the front of the house drops down.

The lithographed paper on the inside walls indicate a later period than that of the other two houses mentioned here. There are fireplaces with over-mantels, one with a mirror, the other with display shelves, and both have window seats on either side. A plate rail in the lower room indicates it was planned as a dining room, and the upper room as a living room. There is much red used in the color scheme for draperies and rugs, and the floors are paraquet. The garden is of a formal design with a small center pond.

A fourth folding dolls' house, advertised as a "Bungalow-Type" in the 1911 McLaughlin catalog, was described as being 16½ inches wide, 6½ inches deep, and 8 inches high.

(please turn the page)

Exterior of a German-made folding dolls' room.

Interior of a German-made folding dolls' room.

There were four rooms and the front of the house dropped down to form a garden.

A book of paper dolls' house furniture entitled "The Model Book of Furniture," copyrighted in 1904, was made by McLaughlin Bros. to be used in the folding dolls' houses. Included were six sheets of furniture for two bedrooms, kitchen, parlor, drawing room, and dining room. The furniture is the correct scale for the houses; a cut set of the dining room furniture is shown in our illustrations of the "Book House."

Also made by this inventive company was a set of four "Folding Rooms" with furniture and accessories. An uncut set of these is in the author's collection. The rooms, when cut out and set up, measure 5 inches wide, 3½ inches deep, and 5¼ inches high, and have a back wall, floor, and side walls similar to a "tin kitchen."

The four rooms in this set of "Folding Rooms" are dining room, kitchen, bedroom and nursery. Printed on separate pieces of cardboard are the furnishings, with six pieces of furniture for each room. Interestingly, the furniture for the dining room includes a sofa and a piano, indicating it was also planned for use as the living room.

The writer knows of no other McLaughlin Bros. folding rooms, although folding rooms were made by other manufacturers during the same period. Peter Pia of New York City, known for his set of metal furniture designed for the Columbian Exposition, made a series of four cardboard rooms.

Toy manufacturers in other countries also made folding lithographed dolls' rooms. An interesting one in the author's collection is illustrated here. It is a box type measuring, when folded, 10½ inches long, 6½ inches wide and 2½ inches high. It

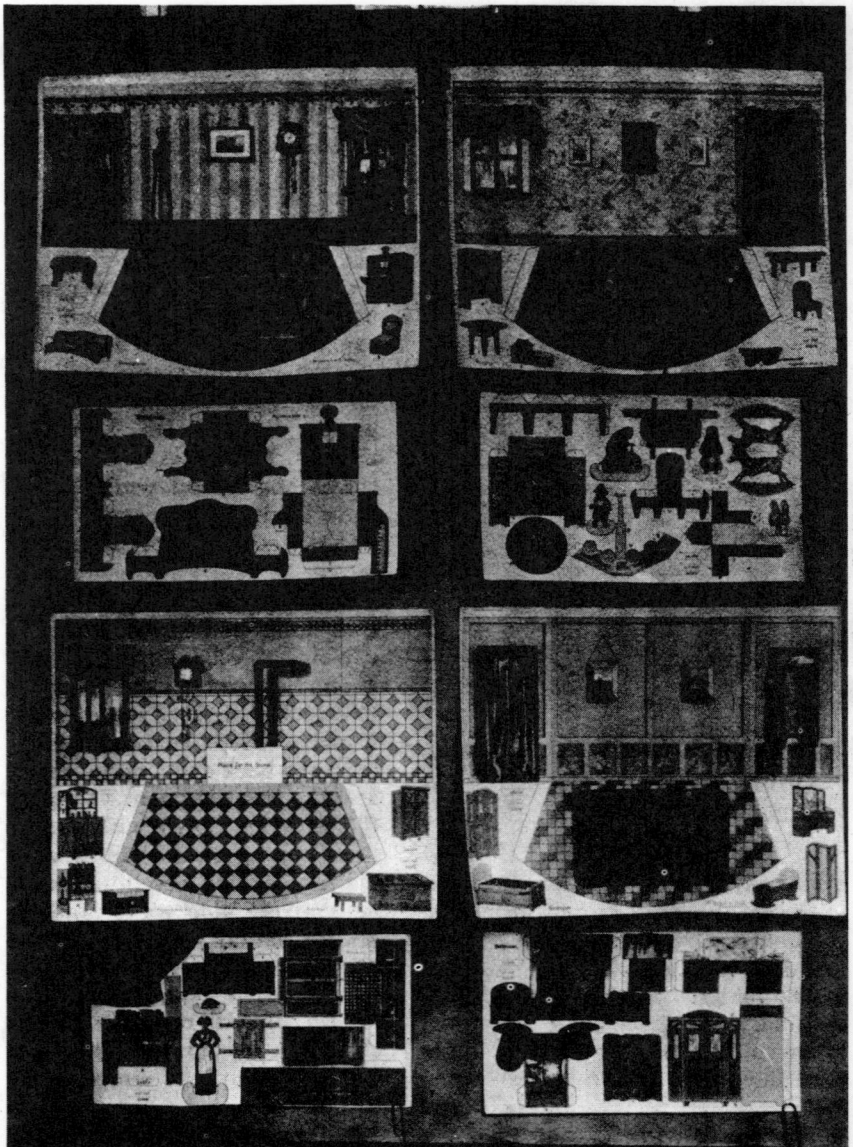

Four uncut McLaughlin lithographed folding dolls' rooms with furniture and accessories.

has lithographed paper simulating yellow brick on the outside and "Made in Germany" printed in English and German. The top of the house opens in two sections to form the side walls of the room, and a second flap folds down to form the floor. Set up, the room measures 11½ inches wide, 9 inches deep, and 6½ inches high. The interior is very colorful and has a doorway lithographed on the back wall which gives the illusion of looking into a second room.

A set of upholstered oak furniture came with this room and was purported to be "original" furniture. At first, there may have been some doubt about this assumption. However, some years later another such room was seen, a bit smaller in size, but identical in every other respect—including the set of furniture.

The McLaughlin Bros. list of lithographed toys also includes a folding set of buildings called "The Pretty Village," which was advertised in the 1892 Marshall Field & Company catalog. This set was made in two sizes, No. 547 being the larger, and No. 545 the smaller, and came packed in boxes with lids depicting them assembled and set up as a village.

This toy village consisted of nine or ten cardboard buildings, including a church, hotel, fire station, blacksmith's shop, combination post of-

Original box for "Dolly's Play House."

Front and interior view of "Dolly's Play House" (1875).

"The Pretty Village" (1892), McLaughlin's folding village.

fice and general store, a boat club, and a barn. The buildings are approximately 6 inches wide, 3 inches deep, and 6 inches high, and are hinged to fold flat when the roof is lifted off.

Some figures of the village residents are also included, as well as cut-outs of horses and teams, boats with people fishing on the pond, etc. A large panoramic map of the village area showing the roads, pond and other features came with each set. A complete set was seen at a private museum. Eight buildings from the author's collection are shown in the illustrations.

In 1903, Montgomery Ward & Company illustrated another set in their catalog, now called "The New Pretty Village," with eight buildings and twenty-four figures. There were changes in this later set, such as the updating of the villagers' clothing and other features. This toy was apparently very popular and was copied by other manufacturers. The author has pieces from a later set, much smaller in scale, in which an early gasoline station has replaced the blacksmith's shop and an automobile the horse-drawn vehicle. Although the cover of the box came with the set, no manufacturer's name was in evidence.

Dining room in folding dolls' house furnished with yellow cherry includes an extension table, marble topped console with pier mirror and cane-seated chairs. The sideboard (right foreground) is not yellow cherry, although it is German-made and stained to simulate bird's eye maple.

DOLLS' HOUSE FURNITURE
in Red and Yellow Cherry

by CATHERINE COOK

RED AND YELLOW CHERRY dolls' house furniture, manufactured from 1845 to 1914 in the Walterhausen section of Germany, has been attributed to the Gebruder Schneegass Company and is sometimes referred to as "Schneegass."

In design and construction, the furniture is the same, only the color of the finish varies—one finished in a cherry red stain, the other in a light stain resembling maple. Some pieces made for bedrooms were also painted white.

During the period that this furniture was made, tastes were changing and people were selecting furniture of lighter colored woods to replace their heavy dark furniture. And since dolls' house furniture follows the trend and style of the adult world of its era, yellow cherry was the choice for dolls' houses.

Some of its later popularity may be attributed to the revival in the 1930s of the early maple and pine furniture which it resembles in color. Because of this similarity, the name "Honey Maple" was attached to it. Later the name appropriately was changed to yellow cherry to coincide with its counterpart finished in red stain and known as red cherry.

The quantity of yellow cherry furniture that has survived both here and abroad testifies to its early popularity; and its continued popularity can be ascertained in its selection by present day collectors.

Bureau and bed in larger scale in yellow cherry. Bed is 5⅝ inches long and 3¾ inches high; bureau is 3½ inches high and 4½ inches wide, and has turned posts.

Bedroom in an antique dolls' house furnished in yellow cherry. The furnishings include a bed, wardrobe, commode and bureau, the latter two pieces having marble tops. *Collection Hansel and Gretal Museum, Martha's Vineyard, Massachusetts.*

Very little of the red cherry furniture is found in early dolls' houses or appears for sale, indicating that much less was made.

Both red and yellow cherry dolls' house furniture, made in at least four sizes, is quite simple in both design and decoration. The decoration includes "turned" legs for chairs and tables and as posts for decoration on other pieces. Real marble was used for the tops of sideboards, bureaus and tables, and knobs of molded pewter for pulls on drawers and cupboard doors.

Upholstery, when used for sofas and chairs, was of velvet—mauve for the yellow cherry pieces and maroon for the red cherry.

A yellow cherry commode with lift top in the writer's collection has a divider of dark wood between sections similar to the white dividers found on Biedermeier furniture; figured paper was used as lining for the recessed area.

Chairs were made in several styles, some with plain wooden seats, and included a rocking chair; others have woven "cane" seats, a unique and one of the nicest features of this furniture, and was used for both arm and side chairs. Some of the chairs have backs of vertical strips of wood, on others a shaped splat was used.

The armchairs with the upholstered seats of velvet used in the parlor sets are very like the Biedermeier armchair sometimes referred to as the "Duncan Phyfe" chair. Another type of chair, with velvet upholstered seat and back and used with a bench-type sofa for parlor sets, has turned posts extending up each side of the back.

Red and yellow cherry furniture was made and sold in sets for parlor, dining room, and bedroom. Since partial

Cane-seated armchair and Davenport desk in red cherry.

Chest-of-drawers flanked by two tables in small scale red cherry. Chest-of-drawers is 2¼ inches high.

Tall case clock and side chair in large scale yellow cherry. Clock stands 8½ inches high.

Commode in small scale (2¾ inches wide by 1¾ inches high) with figured paper showing on the uplifted lid.

Sofa and armchair in yellow cherry upholstered in mauve velvet.

Sewing table with fitted drawer for equipment, an armchair with cane seat and a wall clock in yellow cherry.

Left: Sideboard in red cherry with stencil design in silver; believed to be a "transitional" piece. **Right:** Sideboard in yellow cherry with marble top.

sets are so frequently found in antique dolls' houses, it no doubt was also sold as individual pieces.

The bedroom set, the one most frequently found, came both with a double bed and with twin beds. Two designs for beds are known—one with a plain headboard and square posts, and the other has a shaped headboard with a circular cut out piece at the top.

Bureaus, often with marble tops, have turned posts much like the "spool" bureaus and attached swivel mirrors, very often with small shelves on either side. One quite different bureau-dressing table, seen in both red and yellow cherry, has a long pier mirror between two small attached cabinets, each with two drawers at the top and a cupboard below and resembles in style the adult oak furniture of the early 1900s.

Commodes, often with marble tops, came in two styles—one a table-type with splash board, the other is cabinet-type with lift top.

Wardrobes were included in some sets. And a small table with shaped marble top and pedestal base was used as part of the bedroom sets and was also used with both the parlor and dining room sets.

The dining room set included an extension-type table with turned legs and a sideboard similar to the bureau. One seen had a shaped mirror with small compartments and shelves.

The small oval table with shaped marble top was used with this set and sometimes a glass-fronted china closet was included. Usually the cane seated chairs, one an armchair, are found in the dining room sets of furniture.

In the writer's collection is a sideboard in the red cherry glossy finish with black dividers, legs, etc. and with a stenciled design in silver. This is believed to be a "transitional" piece.

The parlor sets included a sofa, usually reclining type, and armchairs upholstered in velvet. Also a console with pier mirror and marble top and, as "center" table, one of the little marble top tables.

A second style of sofa—the settee type—with upholstered back and seat was also made and came with matching chairs.

One of the most charming of the individual pieces of furniture is a sewing table. It has a four-splay pedestal base and a drawer divided into sections for the sewing equipment.

Among the individual pieces, once again, is found the popular Davenport desk. One of these seen in the larger scale had the back extended and included pigeonholes and shelves for books.

Clocks, too, were made and in two styles—the wall clock and the grandfather (tall case) clock.

Antique dolls' houses on exhibit in museums and shown in photographs in books indicate that red and yellow cherry furniture was used intermittently with Biedermeier. While the parlor and dining rooms were furnished with Biedermeier, the bedrooms are with yellow cherry. This may, of course, be a later addition when lighter colored bedroom furniture became popular.

Dolls' house furniture in red and yellow cherry is quite difficult to find and, when found, duplicate pieces of the two were usually offered for sale.

Much of the history of this early German dolls' house furniture is still shrouded in mystery. One would like to know more about the people who made these charming toys that have long outlived them. Mainly we know them only by their skillful and intricate work. ∎

Miniature copies of early American furniture include a hutch, corner cupboard, drop-leaf table, slant top desk and several types of chairs.

EARLY AMERICAN MINIATURES
MADE IN THE ORIENT

by ELIZABETH PULLAR

Photos by T. Budney.

INCONGRUOUS as it may seem, Japanese and Korean craftsmen have been making miniature replicas of early American furniture and household furnishings. Scaled to doll house size, many of them are authentic copies of pieces found in American museums. They are not made to sell in the Orient but are imported to the United States by B. Shackman & Co.

This unique company was founded in 1898 as a small business in Wilkes Barre, Pennsylvania. Bertha Shackman and her four sons Harry, Alfred, Edgar and Monte, ran the family business which later moved to New York City. Today the firm is still owned and managed by descendants of the original founders. They feature handmade miniature replicas of old American articles and accessories. These reproductions are adaptable for dolls' houses, shadow boxes, general display and as parts of miniature collections. The Federal Smallwares Corporation in New York City is an affiliate mail order firm of B. Shackman and carries a most extensive selection of these hand-crafted models. They also are available in limited assortment from some mail order catalogs and many antiques stores and gift shops.

During the 1960s, this early American miniature furniture was produced largely in Japan. Individual pieces were copied exactly from museum originals in this country and carefully made from cherry or other fine hard woods. The wood was given a natural stain and a hand rubbed finish so that its quality is very good. Within ten years the value of some of the early articles purchased by the writer has increased five times. Now Korea is exporting miniature replicas of American antiques identical to those made in Japan. All of them are appropriate additions to dolls' house furnishings and make charming display material for wall boxes or shelves.

Anyone who owns antique furniture and accessories more than likely will be able to find duplicates of some of his possessions made up as miniature replicas. It is entirely possible to reproduce a mini-scene of a portion of one's own home. Chairs, tables, desks, candle stands, beds and small articles such as clocks, mirrors, books, and old kitchenware are imported from the Orient in great variety to afford a wide choice of styles. Even old dolls have been copied and dressed in clothing suitable to the period of their origin.

Among the many period chairs—

These 8-inch "penny wooden" dolls are in proportion to the small copies of early American furniture.

A Windsor chair and stand with wash bowl and pitcher.

miniatures of revered antiques—are Boston rockers, ladderbacks, Windsors, Federals with upholstered seats, bentwood rockers, the traditional captain's chairs and even old porch rocking chairs. Some have hard seats, others are of hand-woven rush. There are upholstered wing chairs, platform and Lincoln rockers, several styles of sofas and love seats, plus all kinds of stools, including a copy of a Shaker original and a cobbler's bench.

Drop–leaf tables with straight or rounded leaves, block tables, drum and Duncan Phyfe tables are among many that appeal to collectors. Bedside stands with a drawer that opens are reproduced with tapered legs to resemble in detail an original early American stand. Circular candle stands with tripod legs are sold complete with wooden candlestick. Even tilt-top tables may be had.

The reproduction in miniature of a classic slant top cherry desk has four drawers that open and compartments in the upper section. Schoolmaster's desks, roll-tops and an antique lap desk are among many to be chosen. There are cabinets galore, all more or less patterned on original old American models. A hutch cabinet has three display shelves behind a pair of doors that open—a delightful piece of miniature furniture. China cabinets, an apothecary hutch with twelve drawers that open, corner cupboards, chests-on-chest, highboys and blanket chests are some of the irresistible items in the cupboard category.

For dolls' house bedrooms, there are several different styles of beds that are authentic replicas of museum pieces. There are doubles and singles, most of them come equipped with a mattress. Extra special are beautiful little beds with canopies—either lace trimmed or ruffled—and four tall posts. These copies are made of hand-rubbed cherry and the bedding is included. Amusing is a miniature of a trundle bed with rope springs, mattress, pillows and flowered coverlet. Brass beds, not easy to find, are available for more modern dolls' house bedrooms. Cradles for baby-sized dolls may be had with or without a hood or in the swinging pendulum style.

Fascinating miniature antique accessories are numerous and made to complement furniture displays as truly as original larger items. Clock styles are tall-case, cathedral, banjo, school, cuckoo or glass-domed. Picture frames are criss-cross, baroque, embossed, gold, Victorian or bey-

A Boston rocker, dry sink and stool.

eled. The pictures themselves might be Kate Greenaway prints, dried strawflowers, mottoes, embroidered flowers or reproductions of masterpieces and other oil paintings. Mirrors, too, duplicate old American looking-glasses such as the ogee and Federal. Even realistic looking tintypes ready for framing are obtainable in miniature size.

Books and newspapers are made in tiny sizes proportionate to the furniture. Newspapers are reproductions of 1865 editions of both the *New York Times* and *Tribune* and actually can be read with the aid of a magnifying glass. Classic books, too many to list fully, include *Alice in Wonderland*, *Gulliver's Travels*, *Peter Rabbit* and Dickens' *Christmas Carol*. And very choice are the minute replicas of the die-cut originals of *Only a Doll* and *Little Flower Girl*. Old magazines such as *Harper's Weekly*, *Leslie's*, etc. are dated between 1899 and 1902. There is also a family album, a miniature of the velvet covered antique albums, that has 24 pages to hold tintypes or mini-sized pictures.

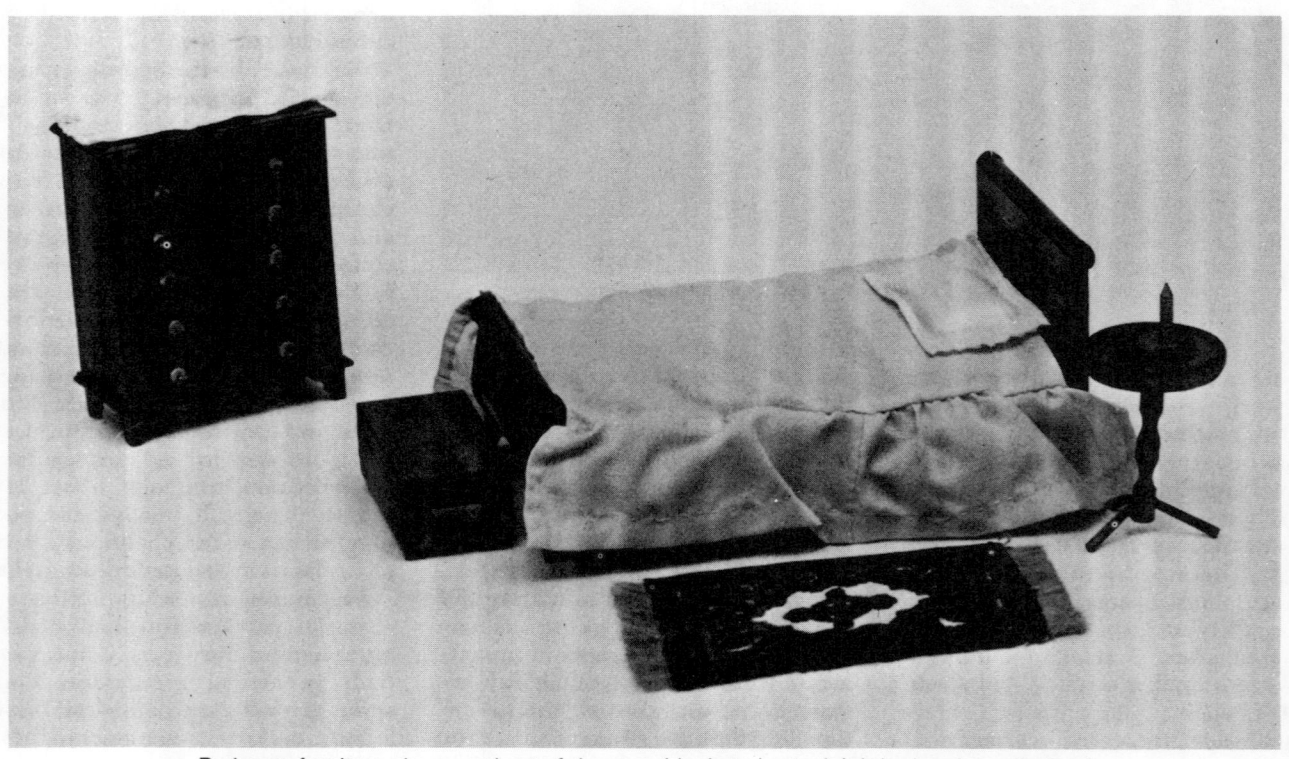

Bedroom furniture shows a chest of drawers, blanket chest, sleigh bed and candlestand.

Irresistible copies of early Americana in the odds-and-ends group might be a wooden bucket, ironstone pitcher and bowl, chamber pot, old funnel, spinning wheel, C. & C. thread cabinet, fireplace, baskets, iron cooking pot, rugs, lamps and a flat iron. Tea sets with trays in a size befitting a dolls' house are reproductions of Limoges and Dresden china or of a metal to resemble silver or pewter.

A doll or two is essential to vitalize the appearance of the furniture. Small bisque dolls dressed in old-fashioned clothes and made in a size suitable to the furniture, are imported from Japan. Another Americana copy is a wooden doll dressed in mid-19th century clothing. This 8-inch doll is taller than dolls' house size and is imported from Korea. A Boston rocker, Windsor chair and a deacon's bench are made especially for this copy of a "penny wooden" doll. The calico dresses are of various colors so that a set of four dolls does not appear as an identical quartet. ∎

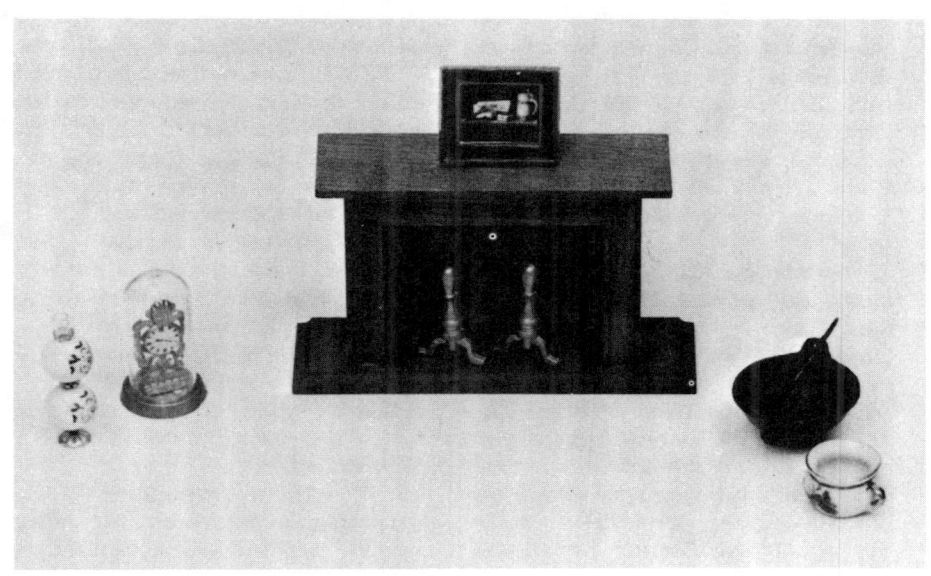

A lamp, dome-clock, fireplace, iron fireplace utensils, and a chamber pot are miniature accessories.

Tiny replicas standing in front of three old books are sized to fit doll house furniture.

237

CAST IRON RANGES
Child Size

by EMMA STILES

"Triumph" range, complete in all its working parts, and trimmed with nickel silver. One of the larger toy stoves, its name appears on both the oven door and the side hearth.

JUST LIKE MOM'S—that's what the kids wanted. Manufacturers agreed, and produced toy ranges that in mechanical construction embraced all the practical features found in mom-size ranges, complete in all their working parts.

Cast iron working models, coal and wood burning mini-cook stoves were produced in large quantities during the latter part of the Victorian era. They contained every useful invention known to stove manufacturers—duplex dumping and shaking grates, adjustable quick draft dampers, swinging detachable oven doors, hinged removable side doors, workable doors on high back elevated warming ovens, side shelves beneath the warming oven, detachable reservoir with two-part removable cover, four to six burning holes with lids, removable extension front, and detachable hearth.

Such special features made the heavy first class toy ranges oh, so grand! So serviceable! What could offer Mother's Little Helper more fun and education than a real stove big enough to cook on with a real fire burning in it!

A boon to housewives of that day were the reservoirs at the end of their stoves which held gallons of conveniently heated wash water. Child-size range reservoirs also held water heated by the stove.

All sorts of accessories were included with the purchase of the finer, more expensive toy ranges: length of metal pipe, coal hod and shovel, lifter, poker and shaker, pressing iron and stand, a wide assortment of cast iron and copper cooking utensils, skillets and spiders, kettles, pots and pans, and a cast iron footed kettle, white enameled inside.

Prevailing taste during the Victorian era demanded the elaborate and ornate. Manufacturers of toy stoves put their best foot forward and produced ranges handsomely ornamented. On some of the finer models the decorative detail graced the entire stove; others bore massive designs, burnished edges with polished nickel trimmings. Some ranges were nickelplated all over; others were ornamented with heavy castings decorated with gilt lines. Naturally, the most popular models were those most attractive in appearance and most complete in all their working parts.

One of the most handsome ranges ever put on the market was the JEWEL RANGE, child-size, made in Detroit about 1880 as a publicity feature. It sold for $7.50 at Marshall Field's in 1892.

The famous Ives Toy Company, of Bridgeport, Conn., featured several perfect working iron toy ranges complete with utensils in their 1893 "Ives Blakslee & Williams" manufacturers' catalogue:

Left: Range made by Kenton Toy Company; the name "Oak" is on the front oven door which is finished in nickel. **Center:** Nickel-plated range with the name "Eagle" on the oven door. **Right:** Toy range made by Ives Toy Company; the word "Baby" is embossed on the oven door; missing is the reservoir lid and shelf.

Name	Size	Price Per Dozen
"O.K." No. 2	5-¼ x 3-⅞ x 5	$ 6.00
"O.K." No. 1	6-⅝ x 3-⅞ x 5	9.00
"I.X.L."	8-¼ x 5-¼ x 5-⅛	12.00
"PET"	11-½ x 7 x 7	24.00
"BABY"	16 x 9-¼ x 8-¾	36.00

The J. & E. Stevens Company, of Cromwell, Conn., one of the largest United States manufacturers of iron toys advertised some fine ranges in their 1906 catalogue. The STAR, the IVY, the RUBY, the GEM, the QUEEN, the PRIZE, the ROYAL, and the ACME, ranged in size from 5 to 12-½ inches in length (without hearth); 4-½ to 7 inches in width; and 3-¼ x 12-½ inches in height (without pipe). They were priced at retail, complete in every way, from 25 cents to $2.

Among other names used were SUNSHINE, GRAND JEWEL, OAK, IDEAL, AMERICAN, TRIUMPH. Generally the names were molded into the oven door. The IDEAL toy range must have been extraordinarily fine in workmanship; it wholesaled at $2.75 in the 1895 Butler Brothers catalog and was retailed at $5.

The Arcade Manufacturing Company, Freeport, Ill., advertised the ROYAL range in their 1926-27-28 toy pamphlet, stressing: "They look real" and that all their toys "are exact miniature reproductions of the real items they represent."

The GRAND JEWEL, the RIVAL, the PRIZE, and the ECLIPSE were extra large size ranges. The elaborate E-CLIPSE range, which weighed 32 pounds was offered for $3.90 in the 1903 Montgomery Ward catalog. ■

Left: Cast iron range with all-over embossed decoration and the name "Queen" on the side hearth; 9" tall without the high-back warming oven, 13" long, and 7" wide; fine detailed polished nickel medallion is fastened to the oven door. **Right:** Black cast iron range with the letters "A.F.T." embossed on a shield-shaped cartouche and the word "American" on the oven door; maker as yet unidentified.

Potpourri

The following section is a catch-all for some interesting articles that could not be categorized previously or are hot-off-the-press selections from *Spinning Wheel's* 1983 season.

Read about the origins of Mother Goose and delight in some early book illustrations that accompanied her rhymes. More children's cloth books—and their illustrators and publishers—are covered in another story. McLoughlin Brothers, noted for their doll houses, also published children's books and are covered in their own story.

Rose O'Neill and her ever-popular Kewpies are the subject of Inez McClintock's article. Lastly, Mary Hillier explores the fascinating history of automatons, the whimsical inventions of the Industrial Revolution.

An irresistible trio of collectibles! Rose O'Neill's whimsical creation, the Kewpie, is guarded by two plush teddy bears. Collections built around stuffed animals, such as Stieffs, and comical bisque characters can still be started with a modest amount of money.

The Polemic Mother Goose

by ELIZABETH PULLAR

THERE IS NO DENYING that the subject of Mother Goose is controversial. Who she was, where she lived and when, are matters of conjecture that vary with different authorities. In fact, there are some who think of her as only an imaginary figure that became associated with a collection of assorted nursery rhymes over a period of many years. Others, depending upon their nationalities, think that Mother Goose must have been French, British or Amerian.

Historically, it is noted that the name Mother Goose was connected with a group of stories that appeared in France in the mid-1600s. Her curious name became attached positively to writings for children when a scholarly architect named Charles Perrault wrote a collection of legends for French children that eventually were adopted by young people everywhere. The book appeared in 1697 and was called *Histoires ou contes du temp passe.* The illustration on the title page of this book showed several children listening to a storytelling goose above which was written "Contes de ma mere l'oye" (Tales of Mother Goose). The stories written by Perrault included the classic favorites "Little Red Riding Hood," "Hop O' My Thumb," "Cinderella," "Sleeping Beauty," and "Puss in Boots."

Charles Perrault was born in Paris and was a most versatile individual. It was difficult for him to pursue only one profession. He did become a lawyer, but shortly abandoned the bar. He then became a successful architect and was put in charge of completing Versailles. In addition, he designed tapestries and helped found the Academy of Science.

Except as noted, photos by Budney.

The amusing cover of "Mother Goose's Melodies Set To Music" is undated, but from the late 1800s.

A page from "Mother Goose's Melodies Set To Music." Note the ferris wheel in the background of the "Simple Simon" illustration.

This "Hey Diddle Diddle" was the frontispiece to an 1878 edition of "Mother Goose Melodies."

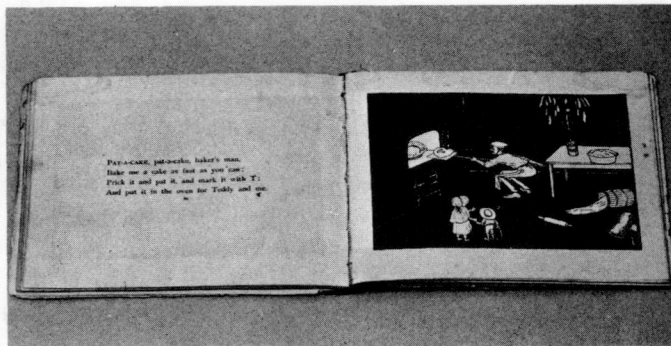

"Pat-a-cake" from a 19th century Mother Goose book illustrated with full-page sketches "in white" by J. F. Goodridge.

Poetry, too, was one of his accomplishments, but the world remembers him as the originator of famous children's stories. Perrault's fairy tales with the sub-title *Tales of my Mother Goose* were published under the name of his infant son, Perrault d'Armancourt.

William A. Wheeler, in 1869, tells us that the French Mother Goose reference had no connection whatever with the American Mother Goose with whom he identified the well-known nursery rhymes. The explanation is that King Robert II (970-1031 A.D.) of France married a close relative, Bertha. Their only child was deformed and, reportedly, resembled a goose. Since one of Bertha's feet was shaped like that of a goose, the King's wife became known as Queen Goose. The French soon began to associate any odd or incredible tale with the expression "one of Queen Goose's or Mother Goose's stories." So it happened that in Perrault's French story book, Mother Goose is shown with children listening to her tales of fascination.

It was not long before Perrault's beloved stories crossed the channel from France into England. An English translation of the tales was published in 1729, and others followed as the popularity of the stories and their web-footed narrator grew. But these were stories in prose. Presumably it was in England that rhymes, existing perhaps centuries before, became grouped as attributes to Mother Goose and soon any writings for children under the heading of Mother Goose became rhymes or verses.

Some authorities testify that the melodies or rhymes of Mother Goose have hidden meanings that refer to Britain's political or cultural history. If so, unless one is a dedicated historian, the connotations are so obscure as to be unrecognizable. Certainly to children the rhymes, absurd as they may be, are only amusing jingles appropriate for lullabies, singing, counting out, or memorizing. One of the earliest editions of Mother Goose that is accompanied with pages of explanatory notes is one edited by the William A. Wheeler, mentioned earlier. The basis for his historical information is the 19th century Halliwell's Nursery Rhymes of England.

For example, the familiar rhyme "Bobby Shafto's Gone to Sea" is supposed to be a shadowy reference to the real Robert Shafto who stood for Parliament in the election of 1761. In "Baa Baa Black Sheep," the division of bags alluded to the export tax on wool imposed in 1275. The sources and the occasions for many of the so-called Mother Goose verses are unrelated to the many thousands of children who have grown up with them. But it is interesting to note that the British version of *Mother Goose Rhymes* is compiled from ancient songs and references to people, places, and things that existed years before Mother Goose was ever mentioned.

Among the English settlers of early Massachusetts was a Peter Goose, or Vergoose as it was sometimes spelled, who arrived in Boston and soon became respectably wealthy. His son was Isaac Goose, an enterprising man who accumulated a large property of his own. Isaac's first wife was Mary Balston, who he married in 1667. They had ten children before she died in 1690, at the age of 42.

Isaac's second wife, who in America is reputed to be the real Mother Goose, was Elizabeth Foster (1665-1757). She became the mother of at least six children, and stepmother to Mary's ten children. It is recorded that with at least sixteen children around, the second Mrs.

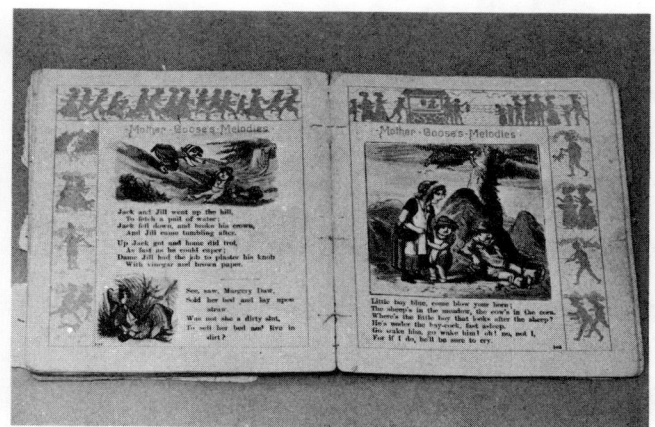

A ragged Mother Goose book from 1881 that has delighted four generations of children.

Pages from the 1886 "Mother Goose Complete Melodies," published by M. A. Donahue & Company.

Goose was want to croon old lullabies she had heard as a child. Possibly it was she who first sang of . . . *the old woman who lived in a shoe. She had so many children she didn't know what to do!* One of her own six children was Elizabeth Goose who married Thomas Fleet, a printer who had come from England. Their first child was grandson to Elizabeth Goose, the widow of Isaac. Mrs. Goose reacted as any normal grandmother would—she cared for the baby and sang to it the old rhymes she remembered from her own childhood which, quite naturally, were British in origin.

But apparently this grandmother, Mrs. Elizabeth Goose, had a loud, raucous voice and the constant chanting of her queer little verses became annoying to her son-in-law Tom Fleet. He had no alternative but to submit to the infliction of hearing her endless strains as she sang so boisterously to first one baby and then the next. In a sort of revenge, the resourceful Mr. Fleet decided to turn his irritation into a profit. He wrote down her somewhat silly ditties, added more verses from other sources, and published all as a book called *"Songs for the Nursery or Mother Goose's Melodies for Children. Printed by T. Fleet at his printinghouse Pudding Lane 1719. Price two coppers."* No copy of the booklet has been found to date.

This Mother Goose, widow of Isaac

The back cover of a 1922 "Mother Goose Nursery Rhymes," illustrated by Lois Lenski.

Goose, died about 1757, aged 92, and was probably buried in Granary cemetery in the heart of Boston. Although no headstone exists for her gravesite, there is in that cemetery the ancient decorative stone that marked the grave of her predecessor, Isaac's first wife, Mary Balston Goose, who died in 1690. This stone mistakenly is believed by some cemetery visitors to be that of Mother Goose, Isaac's second wife, Elizabeth Foster Goose.

Bautiful contemporary Mother Goose books are familiar to us all. Old copies dating back to the late 1800s are collector's items, and may still be found with patient searching.

The old gravestone marking the burial site of Mary Goose, the first wife of Isaac Goose, in the Granary cemetery in Boston is dated 1690. *Photo by Richard Merrill.*

Some of them have a complete set of Mother Goose verses, while others concentrate on only the most popular rhymes. In all probability they will be illustrated with original prints, yet some are copies of old engravings from earlier books. Well-known illustrators of long-ago Mother Goose books include Edward Lear, John Tenniel, John Gilbert, Henry L. Stephens, Kate Greenaway, Walter Crane, and J. B. Zwenger. A facsimile of the 1833 *True Mother Goose* published by Monroe & Francis is worth a place in a collection for both its engaging illustrations and large number of popular nursery rhymes. ∎

Children's Old Cloth Books

by ELIZABETH PULLAR

Photos by Budney.

Cloth books from Sam'l Gabriel & Sons, 1911-1923.

Ever Wear — Never Tear.
They may be washed
And the colors will not run.
A child can chew them
And have a lot of fun.

WITH SUCH JINGLES, Saalfield Publishing Co., in the early 1900s, touted the cloth books they produced for children. Cloth books had been charming at least two generations of children and their Mammas before Saalfield came on the scene, and some are still on the market. They were especially popular in the first half of this century. Cloth books, published before 1925, are more and more often turning up in antiques shops; most of them in surprisingly good condition.

The pages of linen or muslin could not be torn; the books were usually small and pliant, comfortable for little hands to hold, and if not always entirely washable, at least amenable to a damp cloth. Their illustrations were colorful, with subject matter ranging from Mother Goose rhymes and fairy tales to ABC instruction and lessons in conduct.

The pages of the cotton muslin books were double, open at top and bottom. Linen books often had stiff board covers lined with strong linen, making them practically indestructible. The inside

244

pages were of linen, heavily sized, upon which the words and pictures were lithographed in color. Some linen books of eight to sixteen pages had softer covers of a sized fabric. A publisher's catalog of the early 1920s quoted the wholesale price of linen books in gross lots at from 15 to 20 cents, depending on size and number of pages.

Among prominent producers of these oldtime children's cloth books were McLoughlin Bros., New York; Dean's Rag Book Co. Ltd., London; Saalfield Publishing Company, Akron, Ohio; Sam'l Gabriel Sons & Co., New York; M. A. Donahue & Co., Chicago; Graham & Matlock, New York; and Raphael Tuck & Sons Co. Ltd., London, Paris, New York.

McLoughlin Bros., who had been publishing children's cloth books for some years, began to produce them in great numbers after 1880. Linen, rather than muslin, was their most commonly used fabric. *Bright Thoughts For Little Ones,* dated 1867, is a story book with full-page colored illustrations by Cogger. The distinguished artist, R. Andre, did the full-page color illustrations for their *Red Riding Hood,* published in 1888. McLoughlin Bros. became a subsidiary of Milton Bradley in 1933, this connection being discontinued in 1948.

Dean's rag books are delightfully humorous. An *Odd ABC* portrays letters of the alphabet as people and positions each one most imaginatively. Their *Benny and Bunny* uses equally entertaining colored illustrations of H. G. C. Marsh to accompany a four-line verse on each page. Dean's cloth books have pinked edges which keeps them nicely intact while being laundered. As a rule, they bear no copyright date, but each is numbered. Copies in this writer's collection are known to be from the first decade of 1900.

The Saalfield Publishing Company was founded in 1900 by Arthur J. Saalfield; his grandson, Henry R. Saalfield, is now president of the company. Saalfield's first rag books came out in 1906. Both linen and muslin were used for their early books which usually carried a copyright date from the early 1900s. ABC's, fairy tales, and stories of foreign children were popular subjects in their line. Harrison Cady illustrated their Thornton W. Burgess' *Animal Pictures* in 1925.

Sam's Gabriel Sons & Co. featured Mother Goose rhymes, ABCs, and animal books, most of them in the 1910 to 1925 period. A. E. Kennedy was the artist for some of their earlier books; Mary L. Russell illustrated some in the 1920s. Pictures in these children's stories are often informative as to contemporary clothing styles for boys and girls.

M. A. Donahue & Co. published comparatively few children's cloth

Early McLoughlin Bros. cloth books — 1884, 1888, 1890, and 1867.

M. A. Donahue & Co.'s *Jack in the Beanstalk,* 1912; Graham & Matlock's *Animal ABC,* undated; and *Where are you going to, my Pretty Maid,* 1895, from Father Tuck's Dolly Dear Series.

Saalfield cloth children's books dating from 1910 to 1912.

Dean's Rag Books, from about 1913, with pinked edges to prevent fraying.

books. *Jack in the Beanstalk,* put out in 1912, is one of their early productions. This house purchased the cloth book line of the Hampton Publishing Company in the 1950s. M. A. Donahue & Co. was itself acquired by the Hubbard Press of Northbrook, Ill., in 1970. Cloth books still published there are advertised as machine washable, printed with colorfast, non-toxic inks.

The ABCs of Graham & Matlock are not always dated but they do carry a series number. Linen books published by Raphael Tuck & Sons Co. Ltd., of paper doll fame, likewise seldom bear a date, but usually carry a series number. Tuck's title *Where are you going to, My Pretty Maid* has one word too many, perhaps, but it is a whimsical little linen booklet from "Father Tuck's Dolly Dear Series."

Colored centerfold illustration by Richard Andre, in a cloth *Red Riding Hood,* published by McLoughlin Bros., in 1888.

To Make A Cloth Book for A Favorite Child

by ELIZABETH PULLAR

(1) Materials needed for a 12-page cloth book, 6 × 8 inches:
For the pages, 3 pieces of firmly woven white material — sheeting is excellent — each 5″ by 15″.
For the cover, 1 piece slightly heavier material, neutral color, 6″ by 16″.
Bias tape binding, assorted colors.
Carpet needle.
Heavy white "button" thread.
Wax color crayons.
Indelible ink pen.

(2) Fold white material lengthwise through the center, then sidewise, so that 4 double pages will result from each piece. (This allows space for 4 drawings back to back on double pages.) Some sides will be open, others closed. Cut subject of drawing from construction paper. Position it on single fold of the fabric and trace around it with a pencil onto the cloth. Space simple drawings slightly off center to allow an inch at the center fold for book binding. Leave room at bottom of page for caption, if desired. Mark outline with black indelible ink pen. Fill in colors with ordinary wax crayons.

(3) Place each colored drawing singly between two paper towels and press (not iron) with heat from an iron. Some of the wax color will be absorbed into the toweling, leaving the design on the cloth permanently colored.

(4) While book cover is still in a single piece, embroider the title of the book or print it with indelible ink. It's a happy thought to write the child's name, your name, and the date on the bottom of the back cover.

(5) Stitch bias binding, in colors of your choice, around each of the four pieces of material, covering the folded as well as the raw edges. Start at the centerfold, so that the raw edge of the bias tape will be later hidden in the book binding.

(6) Assemble the three white pages with the cover on the bottom. With a heavy carpet needle and strong thread, stitch a center seam through all four cloths, dividing the book into separate pages.

(7) Close the book and stitch down on the outside about 3/4 inch from the fold. Cover stitching with wide bias tape matching in color the cover edging, thus concealing the white stitching.

(8) More elaborate details can be added to books as the child advances in age and interests, and the bookmaker, in experience. A one-a-year birthday book for a child from one to six is truly a handcrafted "heirloom of the future."

Cloth books made by the author include: "Water Craft of Our World"; "Buildings of Our World"; "Creatures of Our World"; "Plants of Our World"; "Wild Flowers"; "Les Chapeaux Du Monde (Pour Les Hommes)"; "Les Chapeaux Du Monde (Pour Les Dames)"; "Birds"; "Pierre's Very Own Book"; "Cybele's Own Book." **Photo by Budney.**

McLOUGHLIN BROS.
The Prolific Publishing House for Children's Books

by ELIZABETH PULLAR

One of the few known portraits of John McLoughlin, founder of the firm that later became known as McLoughlin Bros.

BACK IN 1819, a youth by the name of John McLoughlin came to America to seek his fortune in the land of opportunity. He was a coachmaker by trade, but work in this line was not available. He did find employment, however, with the Sterling Iron Company in New York. This occupation unwittingly led to his eventually founding a fabulously successful publishing company, largely for children's books. It is a far cry from coachmaker to publisher, but this is how the change occurred.

Robert Hoe was a New Yorker who specialized in making presses for various printers during the 1820s. Since he was experimenting with iron for the framework of his presses, he was in close contact with the Sterling Iron Company. Here he made the acquaintance of young John McLoughlin who, in turn, apparently often visited Hoe's shop. The inevitable result was that McLoughlin developed an unexpected interest in presses and printing.

The young man, being of an industrious nature, began to study the art of printing, both from personal observation and from books on the subject. By 1827, the erstwhile coachmaker found himself unexpectedly employed in the office of the original *New York Times*.

The following year that prestigious newspaper temporarily suspended publication and John McLoughlin was without a job. This circumstance proved to be a blessing in disguise for it prompted him to organize a printshop of his own.

Obtaining space in a building on Tryon Road in New York City, McLoughlin installed a second hand press, an assortment of various type and other bare necessities that composed the equipment of a job printshop in 1828. As a matter of interest, Tryon Road was the short exposure that now forms one side of the New York Municipal Building. Here McLoughlin both wrote and published pamphlets of a semi-religious nature geared to the perception of children. After a number of these tracts had been published, he bound them together within a colored paper cover and lo, there was the first of a great number of McLoughlin books for children that were to follow.

In 1840 McLoughlin and a competitive publishing house owned by a John Elton joined forces. The new firm briefly took the name of John Elton and Company. There do exist today some of these children's books published under the name "Elton and Company" but they are more

A group of Children's books published by McLoughlin Bros. in the late 19th century.

All Photos by T. Budney

Richard Andre was one of the distinguished artists whose names appeared on the covers of McLoughlin books. This "Red Riding Hood" cover by Andre was copyrighted in 1883.

than extremely rare and exist probably only in private collections. By 1848, both McLoughlin and Elton had retired.

A junior John McLoughlin together with his brother Edmund, who retired in 1885, took over the firm that then became known as the familiar "McLoughlin Bros." The business of publishing children's books reached such a peak that in 1869 McLoughlin Bros. built and moved into a factory in Brooklyn. Often it became necessary to add to the buildings until eventually an impressive plant resulted, the largest of its kind in the country.

There were several reasons for the phenomenal success of this early publishing house for children's books. First, it had few if any real competitors. Then, it was the first company to feature colored illustrations. In addition, photo-engraving was adopted in its infancy to reproduce the work of famous artists who provided covers for many of the McLoughlin books. It is said that as many as seventy-five lesser artists were staffed in the Brooklyn plant to design illustrations for books and for children's games that McLoughlin Bros. also initiated. In 1894 it became necessary to build a complete lithographic division due to the great increase in the McLoughlin publishing business.

It is interesting to note that the early color illustrations in McLoughlin books were done by hand. A stencil was printed from the given engraving with a section cut-out for one color. This pigment was applied with a paint brush. By making as many stencils as needed, each with its own cut-out, the completed picture boasted a variety of colors.

Well-known artists whose works were reproduced by photoengraving for McLoughlin books are said to include Thomas Nast, G. A. Davis, Helena Maguire, the animal painter, Josephine Pollard, Palmer Cox of Brownie fame, Howard Pyle and Gordon Grant. Very few illustrations in any of the books are signed by the artists. Richard Andre, a popular illustrator of children's books during the late 1800s, was an exception. His name was prominently featured on the covers of a number of McLoughlin books. Another artist who signed his covers was J. H. Howard, whose work is seen in McLoughlin books from 1867 until 1887 or beyond.

The second John McLoughlin died about 1907. His sons James and Charles ran the organization for a while, but neither one was dedicated to the publishing industry. In 1920, the business was sold to the Milton Bradley Company and moved from Brooklyn to Springfield, Massachusetts. Children's books continued to be published under the McLoughlin Bros. name until 1944 when the Milton Bradley association was dissolved.

Collectors of early McLoughlin Bros. children's books will find a fertile field since there were so many of them

Novel die-cut books were popular presentations of favorite stories. The center of the book opened to reveal box seats filled with people viewing the scene on stage. This is the grand finale to Red Riding Hood, so the central picture is not cut to fold back for further episodes.

ABC books were the subject of many McLoughlin Bros. publications. This is a typical ABC book printed on linen.

In addition to books, McLoughlin Bros. produced games and instructive activities for children, including this box of drawing stencils dated 1897.

published in the first place. Early games are not as plentiful as books, for wear and tear has worn away the name identifications, or the boxes bearing the McLoughlin Bros. label have been discarded with time. Books dated between the years 1885 and 1910 are not hard to acquire, but will become scarce as their number diminishes. Variations of ABC books, Mother Goose stories and animal tales are prominent subjects for the McLoughlin publications.

Anyone seriously interested in assembling children's books published by McLoughlin Bros. may wish to complete sets of the little volumes, for some of them were put out in that form. Among others, there were the series designated as *Cock Robin, Little Pig, Red Riding Hood, Pleasewell, Little Linen, Ding Dong Bell* and *Bible*. The number of books published in one series varies so that it is a matter of conjecture as to when a set becomes complete. Presumably there were at least six in each series.

Covers for old McLoughlin books may be board, paper, linen or cotton. Novelty books included die-cuts representing a stage as covers within which half pages might be turned from the center to reveal the unfolding drama. Stories of Red Riding Hood, Cinderella, etc. were presented in this form. If original die-cut books from the 1890s cannot be found, reproductions are available to add interest to a collection.

In the first decade of 1900, Saalfield and Company was founded and published books for children similar to those produced by McLoughlin Bros. Early Saalfield books are collector's items today. The firm is still very active in Akron, Ohio. Other early 20th century American publishing houses for children's books include Graham & Matlock, Sam'l Gabriel Sons, M. A. Donahue & Co., and Jesse H. Leonard. These companies eventually were taken over by others or have been discontinued altogether so that their books, too, are collectible as supplements to the many that are to be found published by the very prolific and most admirable McLoughlin Bros. ■

KEWPIES

INEZ B. McCLINTOCK

ON a recent cold, gray, mid-June New Hampshire day, grateful for the long johns, wool knee socks and extra sweater I had sheepishly put on, and wrapped in the car emergency blanket, I sat on an auctioneer's folding chair watching the sale of the effects of a woman who had died in her late nineties and who had obviously been a saver.

The auctioneer is popular, has a good following and has developed a kind of obvious but low-key homespun country humor. His crew has worked together for some years. They often indulge in byplay, particularly if things are a little dull, or if they're going very well, or if the weather is against them, or...The weather was no help and, despite the good-sized crowd, things were dragging a bit. One runner hurried out with an old piece of cardboard in hand. "Here's something for you collectors—a 1922 calendar taken right off the wall!" He got the laugh he expected; the few old-time knitters kept their needles clicking.

"Hold it! Hold it!" cried the auctioneer. "That's a good item you've got there!" And he held up a fly-specked, curled-edged, 1922 calendar, the month of December still attached. There stood a beaming Kewpie, clad in pink ribbons. The opening bid was five dollars. In short order the remains of the Kewpie calendar went for $35! There was a general murmur as buyers turned to each other. Natives commented, "These summer folk really are crazy!" Others reminisced, "I had a little Kewpie...I wonder what ever happened to my Kewpie paper dolls?"

The adorable Kewpie by Rose O'Neill was produced in Germany, circa 1915. This one was an unusually large (8 inches) version with its original box still intact.

ROSE O'NEILL, the creator of Kewpies, was born June 25, 1874. She spent her early childhood in a sod house in Nebraska. The O'Neills were poor but they had carried their culture with them on the westward trek. Rose probably heard nursery rhymes and Mother Goose; she also heard Shakespeare and pored over picture books of Greek and Roman art. By the time she was 10, at school in Omaha, no one was surprised that she was writing poetry and winning prizes for her drawings. All the O'Neills were talented, but Rose also had drive.

Educated in Catholic schools, she studied violin, piano and dramatics as well as the three R's. At 16 she had good local notices for her acting, was earning her own living and helping to support the family with the sale of illustrations to local papers and magazines. Then, as now, New York City was the mecca for young artists. Rose O'Neill's sweet-sixteen venture (1890) was moving to New York. She lived at a convent on Riverside Drive where she financed her own

By 1913, the Kewpies has so captured the imaginations of young and old that Miss O'Neill created the "Action Kewpies." These all-bisque figures recreated the antics of the characters introduced in **Woman's Home Companion**. Featured are "The Guitar Player", the "Bobby", the "Blunderboo", "Huggers", the "Bellboy", the "Street Cleaner", "Traveler" and the "Instructor."

education for three years by selling illustrations to *Collier's Weekly* and *Harper's Bazaar*. Her first marriage was to Gary (or Gray) Latham, the man who developed the peepshow arcades along Broadway, and from whom she was divorced five years later. In 1902 she married Harry Leon Wilson, author of *Ruggles of Red Gap*, later made into the great movie starring Charles Laughton as the English butler, transplanted to Pennsylvania, having been won in a crap game by an American tycoon.

The Wilsons were part of the New York literary set of the day. In 1905 they sailed for Capri, Italy, together with the Booth Tarkingtons, the two men planning to collaborate on a play. Rose, too, had become a serious artist and published writer as well as a commercial illustrator. And it was she who had won instant success, and whose works were hung in Paris at the Salon des Beaux Arts and the Luxembourg Gallery. Trouble was soon brewing on paradise island. For whatever reasons, Rose had never completely abandoned a kind of baby talk which many people found amusing. It also added a naive dimension, and perhaps even provided a cover up for the talents of this resourceful and independent woman. Whether Harry tired of the literary and artistic competition or of her whimsical chatter, the second marriage also ended in divorce. Rose O'Neill lived out her years single, devoted to her family, surrounded and loved by many friends.

In the late 19th century and well into the 20th, letter writing was the major means of communication, an art to be cultivated especially by young ladies. Rose often doodled in the margins of her letters: tiny fat babies, fairies, elves, cherubs. A close friend maintained that they were

This set of Kewpies wears original crepe paper costumes. The heavy eye decoration was overpainted, yet original as sold. Together the seven piece set represent a scarce party favor set, circa 1915.

modeled after a baby brother who had died in infancy. Rose herself wrote: "His body was plump and round, his starfish hands stretched out to reach your heart. He was a shy little cherub, with tiny wings just sprouting"—a good description of a Kewpie.

In 1905 Rose contracted to illustrate an Eastman Kodak ad for a "Folding Brownie" that children could use. The illustration showed a girl taking a snapshot of a baby's first steps. The baby is plump and round with the characteristic starfish hands and the top-knot which O'Neill herself referred to as the "turnip-knot." This ad marked the public debut of the Kewpie.

Kewpies were soon featured in the women's magazines. The September, 1910 issue, of *The Woman's Home Companion* carried an O'Neill story about the Darling family. Dotty, the youngest, was unable to keep up with the older children, causing a problem for the whole family. So O'Neill supplied Kewpies to "act as her guardian angels and to entertain her." The "Kewps," "respectful, grave, yet light and free," made such good progress that by the February, 1911,

(continued on page 52)

In its 1931-32 catalogue, B. Shackman & Co. of New York advertised 3 pages of Kewpies in sizes from 2¾" to 8". Rose O'Neill's name is not mentioned in the catalog. The three models shown ranged in price, wholesale, from $5.40 to $9.00 the dozen.

86/76

86/1½

86/1

86/88

253

KEWPIES Cont.

issue, not only the three older Darlings, but their stern father and their mother went sledding together, taking Dotty and her Kewpies with them! The "Kewps" were definately on the side of little children. By their goodness and unfailing cheerfulness they resolved or circumvented many such problems.

The resourceful Rose was quick to capitalize on the Kewpies' popularity. Each of the women's journals carried a page of paper dolls, an excellent promotional item. Then Rose O'Neill dreamt up *Kewpie Kutouts!* All other paper dolls were printed front view only; *Kewpie Kutouts* were printed front and back. If one cut and pasted carefully, and bent the little base provided at their feet, one had a standing doll! There were also directions for cutting the neck opening of the clothes which could then be slipped over the head of the doll, a real novelty! Subsequently, *Kewpie Kutouts* appeared in the *Ladies Home Journal*, the *Delineator* and the *Pictorial Review*. Kewpies took an active part in each holiday issue. They worked independently, i.e., not as Santa's helpers, but dispensing their own Christmas cheer, and bringing their own messages of love for St. Valentine's Day. During World War I they helped the Red Cross Drive to gather Christmas presents for the orphaned children of war-torn France.

Next came the hands-on Kewpie, patent applied for December 12, 1912, and granted the following year. The first Kewpies were manufactured in Germany, imported into the United States and sold by George Borgfeldt, one of the biggest jobbers of the day. Others were manufactured in Pennsylvania by Cameo Doll Products whose president, Joseph Kallus, was O'Neill's friend and fan. The traditional Kewpie was made of bisque, an unjointed, standing figure; a movable shoulder joint was the first improvement. Cameo Kewpies were made of a wood-pulp composition and painted. These were subject to surface cracking over the years. Of course, many of the bisques lost their tiny arms when the elastic snapped. Perfect Kewpies are not so easy to find!

Sears, Roebuck sold the Cameo Kewpies. Their post-war catalogue description reads:

> "Aren't they sweet? See their plump bodies, roguish eyes and smiling faces! Everybody loves a Kewpie. Made of light but durable composition, beautifully tinted. Movable arms, rigid body. Splendid for Christmas gifts, favors and home decorating."

The bare Kewpie cost 98 cents. Others had a "neat bonnet and apron," a "flowered pattern dress and bonnet to match." One, ready for winter, had a "cute knitted sweater and cap." There were two deluxe items at $1.98: the choice, "a splendidly made dress and fancy hat" or "a charming dress and hat of point d'esprit net with a large silk ribbon sash."

On the very same page, for $1.29, stands Peterkin, also bare, plump and rigid, but with a baby's painted hair, no top-knot. A small inset photo shows him dressed "in a yard of 4-inch satin ribbon," looking like a small Cupid. Peterkin was only one of many imitations, not nearly so flagrant as the copies done by the Japanese. Current market reports claimed that the copies were "easily recognizable even to the amateur" and "never perfect."

One-piece action Kewpies followed, in every imaginable cute pose—sliding on their little bare bottoms or bellies, sailing with arms and wings outstretched, on tiptoe, all looking innocently heavenward or archly sideways obviously confident that their antics were appreciated.

How many kinds of Kewpies are there to collect? The numbers must be almost countless. They were made of bisque, composition wood-pulp, celluloid, plastic, rubber, vinyl, zylonite, silver and gold. Kewpie charms were carved not only in silver and gold, but in bone and ivory as well. They came singly and as twins; there were Kewpie soldiers, sailors and marines; a Kewpie Uncle Sam and little black Hottentots. Kewpies decorated children's and dolls' dishes. Some were made in jasperware, looking for all the world like Wedgewood! Kewpies adorned clocks, wall plaques, sterling silver picture frames. They curled themselves around napkin rings, toothpick holders, inkwells and stood guard over small glass candy jars that served as banks once the candy had been eaten. They perched coyly on

Joseph Kallus, Cameo Products, produced Kewpies in many materials and sizes. This 25" size in vinyl was marketed as "The Big Kewpie Doll" about 1965 and is considered scarce.

dressing table powder jars, also on radiator caps or as hood decorations for cars of the roaring twenties. They decorated candle sticks and electric lamps. Boxed Kewpie soap was a pleasant gift. Ice cream Kewpies were served as dessert for special celebrations, which means that the heavy Kewpie metal ice cream molds do exist.

Kewpies were printed on postal cards; they decorated place cards held, in turn, by Kewpie place card holders. There were Kewpie playing cards, coloring books, handkerchiefs, yard goods—from daintiest dimities to serviceable flannelette. One could buy Kewpie wallpaper for the nursery, writing paper, stamped kits of Kewpies to embroider. Kewpies were made with holes in their heads—dispensers of salt, pepper, bath salts, talcum powder. Two Kewpie books were published in 1910 and 1911. As late as 1936 Kewpies were cavorting in a *New York Journal* comic strip.

To promote tobacco sales, premiums were included in the package: Kewpies printed on flannel rectangles, coveted as doll-house rugs. They were printed on tin trays for ice cream parlors, also on cardboard, the latter intended for re-use as Christmas tree ornaments. Kewpies were not partial and advertised several different kinds of ice cream! They enlivened the covers of menus and were made as decals. They were sold two or three for a penny in chewy chocolate or hard jelly candies.

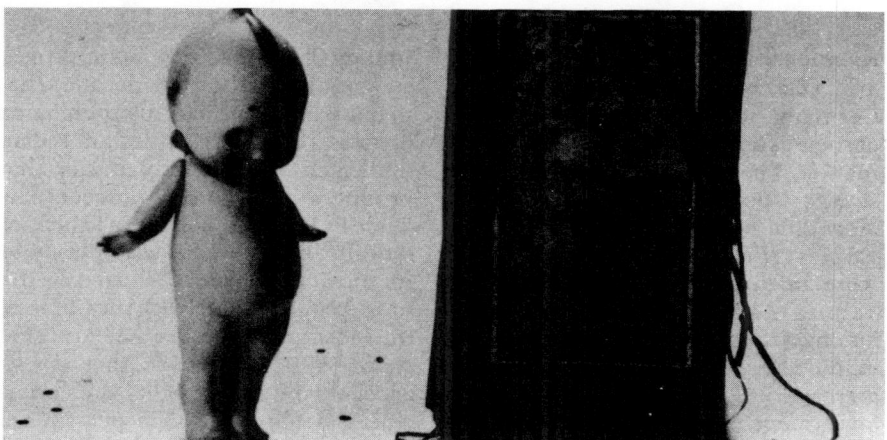

O'Neill's protection of her copyrights extended to judicious labelling of dolls *and* their boxes. This early bisque version is found in its original box.

Rose O'Neill seems to have cornered the market on subsidiary rights. Many of her Kewpie verses now seem saccharine, too precious, too whimsical for children of the space age. However, there is not the slightest doubt about her Kewpies: they made her a wealthy woman, they have staged a most successful comeback. They are highly collectible, growing in popularity and in monetary value. ∎

A wide variety of sizes can be found of O'Neill's bisque Kewpies. This group ranges from 5½" and 8"

The Automa...

MARY HILLIER

Mary Hillier has collected and studied old dolls most of her life. Her research ventures often take her to France and Germany to search through dusty archives and interview people who made dolls and automata. Mrs. Hillier lives in Surrey, England.

"Musical Monkey," by Theroude, ca. 1860. The elaborate costume, gray wig and tricorne hat are all original to this automaton.

GHOSTS abound in London. Echoes of those early years when the city was full of entertainment, peopled by gay dandies and their colorful ladies travelling by foot or carriage in pursuit of pleasure, are everywhere. At the end of the 18th century especially, the society flourished on every sort of show whether it was theatre, magic or the introduction of some new scientific marvel.

Near the hub of London, Picadilly Circus, a very small street called Spring Gardens still marks the site of one such show. Housed in a large gallery which had once been a Huguenot chapel, the crowds thronged to gaze at a collection of automata — marvelous working toys and figures publicly exhibited.

In 1772, a London watchmaker called James Cox had established his museum of treasures here, including clockwork animals richly jewelled, beautiful singing birds and moving tableaux. He had made a fortune designing precious toys for the Rajahs and other Eastern Potentates, employing famous sculptors and artists, but finally he became bankrupt and was forced to sell his exhibits by lottery, so they were dispersed all over Europe. After his death in 1788, his son joined with some other famous makers of automata from Geneva, Switzerland, such as Jaquet-Droz and Maillardet, and once again a fine spectacle was staged in Spring Gardens. The most popular automata were those of lifesize moving figures. Very authentic in detail, they performed in miraculous style — playing the harpsichord with moving jointed fingers (illustrated), writing actual words and poems, drawing pictures, or in some cases playing musical instruments such as a trumpet or drum. They were the talk of the town, and many people crowded to see them. Obviously their reaction to these toys was very different to our present-day one, since we are surfeited with all sorts of musical and theatrical performances available at the touch of a switch. To the less educated of that time it seemed almost too amazing, and they often suspected magic or witchcraft. To the scientists it forecast the shape of things to come. In automata they could envisage future inventions with a practical purpose — factory machinery, recorders of music and voice. Spring Gardens was pulled down in 1820, and ten years later in a letter to Sir Walter Scott the eminent scientist David Brewster wrote:

"The same combination of the mechanical powers which made the spider crawl or which waved the tiny rod of the magician (referring to two

Future of Automatons

PART ONE

inventions of Maillardet) contributed in future years to purposes of higher import... those automatic toys which once amused the vulgar are now employed in extending the power and promoting the civilization of our species...."

By this period the public exhibition was less popular, or had become something more aimed at children. In a little volume entitled *Girl's Own Book*, by Mrs. Child, published in London in 1842, the author describes the exhibition of Maelzel's automata she had once seen. This included a carousel with wooden horses, a marksman who fired a tiny pistol, a famous vaulter, a doll dancing a Wreath-dance and, best of all, the Rope Dancers who "performed all manner of feats on a rope suspended across the room. Sometimes they were seated firmly, with arms outstretched; sometimes they turned heels over head; sometimes they hung with head downward and sometimes suspended by only one foot. By moving the limbs of these figures, they could be made to utter quite distinctly 'Mamma!' 'Papa!' and 'La, La.' Later a rather similar performing figure was used by the conjuror Robert-Houdin (illustrated).

The Maelzel mentioned by Mrs. Child was a German, a large phlegmatic figure by all accounts but kindly and a born showman. It was he who appropriated the very famous automaton Chess Player of von Kempelen when the inventor died, and showed it throughout Europe and later in the United States where it was finally destroyed in a fire. (A full account of this machine is given by Charles Michael Carroll in *The Great Chess Automaton*, Dover Publications, 1975.) The chess player in the guise of a Turkish figure mystified the world for years but was eventually proved to be a deception and worked by a man inside, not by machinery. "A thinking machine: Was the chess player such a creation? Was such a thing really conceivable?"

"The Snake Charmer," a later version of Roullet's "Snake Dance," by Ernest Decamps. *Courtesy Christie's, London.*

The original "Snake Dance," by Jean Roullet; 19th century. *Courtesy Sotheby's, London.*

asked a correspondent in 1889. Now, almost a century later, we have electronic chess but still there is a sense of "a man inside" for such machines play and appear to think but are of course programmed.

Maelzel showed his exhibition in many American towns during the the period 1826-1837, complete with tableaux, rope-dancers, etc., but he died on board a ship returning to Europe and his effects were auctioned in America to pay debts. Other famous European automata reached America in travelling shows, and one which has survived is the famous *Writing Child* (illustrated) now in the Franklin Institute of Philadelphia. When first presented there it was in a ruined state and dressed as a French soldier, but now it is beautifully restored and depicts a girl. In action the eyes follow the hand as it sketches, or writes beautiful copperplate script. An old print of 1826 showed this same mechanical doll dressed as a little boy. The mechanical cams working the apparatus were most skillfully designed and still perform. *cont'd*

By the first half of the 19th century the fashion for these prestigious exhibition mechanicals was vanishing, but a new novelty was introduced in smaller working automata which people performed in their own salons. One of the prettiest and well-loved was the cage of brightly-plumed singing birds motivated by a system of hidden valves and bellow-movement. Based on those earlier serinettes (musical boxes imitating bird song which were used to teach canary birds to sing) these had the additional attraction of artistic foliage and blossoms of artificial flowers. The Parisian family of Bontems who had also been involved in the making of large-size automata specialized in these singing birds and took out a patent in 1861 which involved the movement of the mechanical birds — flitting their tails and opening their bills. Examples of this work are highly sought after now and far exceed in expertise any of the modern imitations.

Performing birds with real feathers were followed by performing animals with real fur and skin, and quite often fancy costumes to emphasize their elegance. One ingenious Parisian mechanic, Alexandre Theroude, took out many patents and was obviously an originator of some of the most delightful automata. Slightly in bad taste was the *Lapin mal eleve* (Badly brought up rabbit); a life-sized papier mache animal, fur-covered, which walked around and left a trail of droppings in the form of chocolate dragees! Similarly he invented a chicken which laid golden eggs. This was in 1844, and ten years later he won an award with a life-sized goat at the Paris Exhibition. It amused the Emperor of France as it, too, provided chocolate drops in the same inelegant manner.

Best of all, and for pure charm among automata everyone's favorite, Theroude introduced the musical monkey. Perhaps he was inspired by the famous monkey orchestra made by the German porcelain factories, but these animals were life-like in their grimacing, the roll of their eyes and curl of their lips. The patent, taken out in 1862, shows how cleverly the inventor linked his strands of wire working all the various limbs and features to a central drum turned by

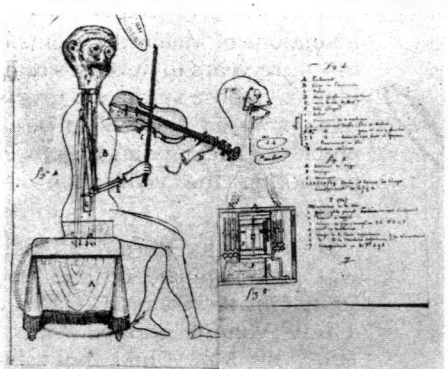

Top photo: Patent drawing for Alexandre Theroude's mechanical monkey playing a violin with musical accompaniment, dated 1862. **Left photo:** The original version of the "Little Bugler," by Vichy. **Bottom photo:** "Mustachioed Monkey Sculptor" with monocle. He chisels away to the accompaniment of music. The winding key bears the initials "D.J." for Durand & Jacob of Paris; ca. 1870. Height 26 inches.

clockwork and accompanied by a pin-cylinder musical movement. (The musical boxes invariably came from Switzerland and were often ordered to render the most popular airs of the day in Paris.) The bare body of the monkey sketched in the patent (illustrated) was of course decked out with Parisian finery and often with a grey wig and tricorne hat. I have seen many skeletons of these automata, relics of some luxury toy, and the mechanism is most intricate and finely wrought.

Soon the monkey was used in character parts other than as a musician and, in addition, other characters were used in place of the monkey. Theroude was in league

"Writing Child," now dressed as a little girl, was originally dressed as a boy. *Collection The Franklin Institute, Philadelphia, Penn.*

"La Musicienne," by Jaquet-Droz, plays the harpsichord with moving jointed fingers. *Musee d'art et d'histoire, Neuchatel.*

Top left: "The Trick Chess Player" made by Von Kempelen about 1770, and later exhibited by Maelzel. From an early 19th century engraving. **Top right:** "Le Voltigeur au Trapeze," Robert-Houdin's mechanical trapeze artist. **Bottom left:** The later version of the "Little Bugler," by Vichy, has a phonograph in the base.

with some of the finest of Parisian dollmakers of the 1860 period. He had provided patents for walking dolls with clockwork platforms on wheels, and for talking dolls with the insertion of mechanisms worked by pull strings. During the 1860 period two specialist automata makers were founded in Paris — Vichy of Rue Montmorency and Roulet of Parc Royale, both situated in the famous Marais district, the toy-making area of Paris. The specialty at first was for life-size musical automata often representing some favorite performer of stage or circus — Harlequin acrobats, negro mandolin players, clowns and ballerinas. They must have been immediately recognizable to the theatre-going public. Sometimes several different versions exist. For instance, the *Serpent Dance* by Roullet (illustrated) was followed some years later by a version made by his talented son-in-law Ernest Decamps (illustrated). The original version of the *Little Bugler* by Vichy (illustrated) was eventually produced with a phonograph adaption (illustrated) but the modelling and clothing was very similar. Tradition was everything with these great firms and we are told in Pierre Calmettes' *Jouets* that each craftsman specialized in a particular section.

To be continued.

The early automata of the 18th century were often featured in travelling exhibitions, fashioned and handled by trained experts. The 19th century saw the rise of smaller "mechanicals", expensive toys for the luxury classes. In the January-February issue of *Spinning Wheel*, the development of noted firms—Theroude, Bontems, Vichy, Roullet—was detailed. Here, their story is continued.

OBVIOUSLY the most skilled worker in each of the great firms was the designer who created each scene and performer. One of our illustrations shows Vichy's workroom and a Pierrot head being given the finishing touch by a worker whilst other items of various size are drying off. One of his most famous automata "Pierrot at his writing desk" (illustrated) incorporated this head. In action the figure dozes, but as the light of the lamp dims he wakes up, turns up the wick, and begins to write. He is magically realistic. Another version of this rare character is in the Museum of Automata at Monaco. Pierrot is in an original costume of white and black bobbles and wields a long quill pen.

After a century or so, obviously it is often necessary to restore the automata and perhaps completely redress them as near as possible to the original. They are so valuable that work is deserved. Illustrated here are two relics both of which may be recognized to have originated with Vichy. One day they will perform again; the bust will have new arms and the standing figure a musical instrument. There is a famous restorer who served his apprenticeship in the workroom of Vichy, and who can create a complete automaton or restore most of these earlier ones. His chief concern is to acquire original parts, so he has drawers full of different size eyes, teeth, wires, fragments of material to

The Autor

MARY HILLIER

match, ribbons and rosettes—all of the paraphernalia necessary, and best of all his own recollection of techniques and old examples. He also possesses some of the original molds for mask-making. He was responsible for a lot of the work done on the

The workroom at Vichy's, Paris, about 1900. The artist is seen painting a head for one of their Pierrots. **Photo courtesy Jacques Boyer.**

Pierrot at his writing desk, by Vichy; late 19th century. Height 25 inches.

ure of atons

PART TWO

Monaco collection. This was based on a much earlier collection assembled by a Parisian lady named Madame Galea. Just as a child in playing pretends it is an adult and is "mother" to her dolls, or "general" to his soldiers, so for Madame Galea her collection returned the nostalgia of a very happy childhood of a little girl spoiled with these luxury Parisian dolls.

Most automata in present-day collections date from the last quarter of the 19th century. After the war with Germany (1871) there followed a period when Paris was the entertainment center of the world and a byword for frivolity and gaiety. Sometimes the term *fin-de-siecle* is used to describe the last decades of the 19th century with a sense of decadence. A page from a French book of 1893 shows some Vichy automata, including the world wearing a top hat and monacle and waving his cane as he smokes a jaunty cigarette in imitation of a *roue* of the period. He is accompanied by La Japonaise (a Japanese dance performed by the American artist Loie Fuller) and a Musical Clown with an expression of mock despair.

These obviously were automata for adults and a very popular, if luxurious, tourist attraction. They were also sold in the best stores of London and America, and there was a long range of popular tunes provided in their musical accompaniments. Before the days of the gramaphone or radio, they must have been notable drawing room entertainment. But the children also were catered to and the very beautiful porcelain dolls of Jumeau and other Parisian dollmakers were used in great variety by such firms as Roullet & Decamps, Phalibois, Durand & Jacob and Lambert (who also served apprenticeship with Vichy). Their mechanism was relatively simple compared with earlier automata, but their greatest charm lay in their costume and their droll performance. Nowadays in the sales rooms these toys are eagerly sought and there are fine private collections world-wide. Recently the enchanting clockwork walking doll with carriage (illustrated) sold for L5,000 at Sotheby's in

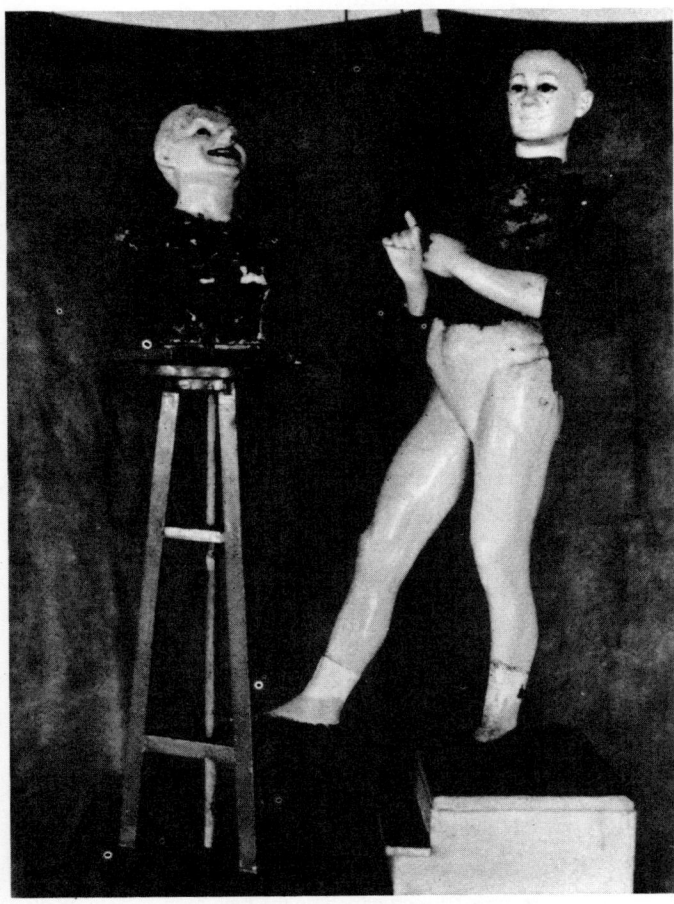

Two relics of automata from the Vichy factory, ready for restoration.

A page from a sales catalog issued by Decamps, ca. 1912, shows their Sentinel with Bear (top), piano-playing doll (bottom, left) and "Japonaise" (bottom, right) automata.

Walking doll with baby carriage, probably by Decamps who used this motif as a trademark.

London, and a Lambert piano player with Jumeau doll for L3,200. A similar model is shown in an old sales catalog page issued by Decamps about 1912 (illustrated), and there was no doubt considerable competition and piracy between the rival firms.

The original art of making automata is almost dead, though there are still skilled craftsmen who can imitate the old technique. The son of Ernest Decamp, Gaston, died only a few years back. When I last met him, a pleasant old man in his eighties, he was chuckling over a model he had just finished—a working giraffe peering into a nest of birds, one of whom popped out and cried "Mama." Perhaps the joke was old fashioned and outdated for our sophisticated society. As he showed me around his workshop containing relics of enormous old automata, he agreed sadly that it was no longer possible to obtain suitable materials. In the window a little bear with nylon fur nodded his head as he drained a plastic bottle. ∎

"The Pretty Barber," a musical scene by Durand & Jacob; Paris, ca. 1870. **Photo courtesy Sotheby's, London.**

This pair of Musical Clowns dance as they strum their instruments, and their eyes roll as they move their heads. Black and yellow costumes are trimmed with spangles. Late 19th century. Height 27 inches.

Index

—A—

Adrian Cooke Metal Works 191
Advertising Dolls 53-55, 184
Alexander Doll Co. 97-99,
136-139, 149-151
- Cissette 137, 138
- Dionne Quintuplets 136
- Little Women Dolls 136
- Madame Doll 137-138
- Maggie Mix-Up 151
- President's Wives 139
- Quiz-Kin Doll 136, 149
- Scarlett Doll 137
- Sound of Music 137-139
- Southern Belle 139, 151
- Wendy 149-151

All bisque dolls 38-39, 66, 68-71, 182-184
Amberg, Louis 68, 70
American Dolls 20-21, 40-43, 53-55, 64-65, 67-68, 97-99, 100-104, 105-108, 114-115, 116-119, 120-124, 125-129, 132-135, 136-139, 140-142, 142-145, 146-148, 149-151, 152-155, 180-181
A.P.W. Paper Co. Dollhouse 202
Artists, Comtemporary
- Ayers, Martha Oathout 142, 173
- Barrie, Mirren 153
- Bell, Roberta 154-155
- Bringloe, Francis 119, 153, 155
- Bullard, Helen 116-118, 153, 154
- Clear, Emma 140-142, 173
- Cochran, DeWees 153, 157
- Condon, Judith 155
- Curtis, Betti 152-153
- Deutsch, Fern 155
- Dufour, Dolly 120-124
- Florian, Gertrude 154
- Goodnow, June 100-104
- Hand, Martha Armstrong 133-135
- Henderson, Emma 142-145
- Hirato, Goyo 110
- Kane, Magge Head 105-108, 153, 154, 170
- Kontis, Xantos 146-148
- Lee, Avis 119
- Marks, Suzanne 125-128
- Odenrider, Ada 153, 154
- Paulson, Wee 129-131
- Serikawa, Eiko 111
- Sorensen, Lewis 153
- Sullo, Rose 155
- Thompson, Martha 171
- Zeller, Fawn 171
Au Bon Marche 50, 51
Automatons 64-65, 169, 180-181, 256-259, 260-263
Avery, W. & Son 196
Ayers, Martha Oathout 142, 173

—B—

Baby, Alex Paul 133
"Baby Beans" 134
Baby First Step 133
Baby's Hungry 135
Baby Rosebud 133
Bailey, Roswell 217
Barbie 133, 134
Barrie, Mirren 153
Bebe, Articule 49, 50
Bebe Louvre 50
Bell, Ceramics 106, 107, 108
Bell, Roberta 154-155
"La Belle Chocolatiere" 166
Belton 45
Biedermeier 208-212
Bisque dolls 2-4, 36, 44-48, 49-50, 51-52, 63, 66, 67, 68, 78, 91, 92, 95, 101-104, 109, 111, 125-129, 134, 135, 140-142, 174-176, 251-255, 256-259, 260-263
Bliss Co. 226
"Blonde bisque" 173
Bontems 258
Borgfeldt, George 69-71, 254
Bradley, Milton 249
Bringloe, Frances 119, 153, 155
Bullard, Helen 116-118, 153, 154
Butler Brothers 67, 68

—C—

Cameo Doll Products 254
Candy container 66
Carrier-Belleuse 46
Carte de visite 61-63
China dolls 67, 93, 94, 164-166, 176-179
Christianing doll 66
Chubb & Sons, Lock & Safe Co .. 198-199
Cissette 137, 138
Clarke, George Pemberton 181
Clay, Robert J. 181
Clear, Emma 140-142, 173
"Cliquot Kid" 184
Cloth dolls 22-24, 25-27, 28-30, 31-35, 40-43, 55, 97-99, 129-131
Cochran, Dewees 153, 157
Composition dolls ... 67, 120-124, 136-138
Condon, Judith 155
Converse Company (Dollhouse) 226
Costumes 2-4, 8, 9, 12, 19, 46, 47, 48, 49-50, 51, 52, 59, 63, 77-78, 79-82, 83-86, 87-88, 89-90, 91-95, 137, 142
Corn dolls 43
Cox, James 256
Crib figures 56-61
Crotens, John C. 215
Curtis, Betty 152, 153

—D—

Dean's Rag Book 28, 29
Delcroix 179
Delineator 87, 88, 89, 90
Descamps, Roullet 257-259, 261-262
Designers (Dolls) (see also Artists, Dolls)
- Carrier-Belleuse 46
- Cochran, Dewees 153. 157

Disney, Walt 137
Jordan, Kate 69, 70
Kruse, Kathe 25-27, 29, 31-35
Lenci 22-24, 30
Lipfert, Bernard 156
Deutsch, Fern 155
Dionne Quintuplets 136
Disney, Walt 137
Dollhouse Furniture See Miniature Furniture
Dollhouses 193, 194-196, 198-200, 201-202, 207, 226-229
Dolls of Wonderland Museum 109
Donahue, M.A. & Co. 245-246, 250
Don Contectionary Co. Dollhouse 200
"Dresden" dolls 173
Dressel, Kister & Co. 159-161, 164, 165, 167, 169, 179
Dufour, Dolly 120-124
Dunham Coconut Dollhouse 201
Durand & Jacob 258, 261-262

—E—

Eckert, Richard & Co. 160, 161, 162
Edison, Mazda Lamp Dollhouse 202
Effanbee 156-157
Egrefeuil, Felix 66, 67
Elders, J.W. 197
Ellis, Joel 20-21
Elton, John & Co. 248
Enchanted World Doll Museum 71-73
English dolls 14-19, 28, 30, 75, 115

—F—

Farie Dollhouse 194-196
F.G. 2-4
Flapper dolls 161, 165, 166, 167-169
Florian, Gertrude 154
Forbes paperdolls 192
French dolls 2-4, 44-48, 49-50, 51-52, 63, 66, 178, 179, 256-259, 260-263
French Fashion 2-4, 45, 46
Friendship Dolls 5-9

—G—

Galluba & Hoffman 184
Gabriel, Sam'l & Sons 244-245, 250
Garment Samplers 83-86
German dolls 25-27, 29, 31-35, 36, 66-68, 69-71, 91, 92, 95, 159-163, 165-169, 174-175, 176-179, 182-184, 251-255
Gesland, A. 51, 52, 53
Goebel 159, 161, 166, 179
Goodnow, June 100-104
Goodwin, William 64-65
Goose, Mother 241-244
Graham & Matlock 245-246, 250

—H—

"Half" dolls 159-163, 164-166, 167-169, 174-175, 176-179
Hand, Martha Armstrong 133-135
Happifats 69-71
Hawkins, George 64, 65
Heber & Company 184
Henderson, Emma 142-145

Index

Hertwig & Company 184
Heubach, Gebruder 168
Hieulle, Edmond 66, 67
Hirato, Goyo 110
Holly Dolls 116

—I—

Indian (American) dolls 42-43, 100-104, 115
Italian dolls 10-13, 22-24, 30, 56-61
Ives, Blakeslee & Co. 180-181

—J—

Japanese dolls 5-9, 110-113
Jaquet-Proz 256
Jordan, Kate 69, 70
Jumeau, Emile 38-39, 44-48, 49-50, 51, 173

—K—

Kane, Magge Head 105-108, 153, 154, 170
Kewpies 251-255
Koniglich Porzellan Manufaktur (K.P.M.) 160
Kontis, Xantos 146-148
Kruse, Kathe 25-27, 29, 31-35

—L—

Lambert 261-262
Lee, Avis 119
Lenci 22-24, 30
Lettie Lane Dollhouse 200
Limoges 214
Lipfert, Bernard 157
Little Women Dolls 136
"Littlest Angel" 135

—M—

Madame Doll 136-137
Maggie Mix-Up 151
Manufacturers (Dollhouses)
  Bliss 226
  Converse 226
  McLoughlin Bros. 226-229
Manufacturers (Dolls)
  Alexander Doll Co. 97-99, 136-139 149-151
  Amberg, Louis 68, 70
  Bell Ceramics 106, 107, 108
  Belton 45
  Bontems 258
  Borgfeldt, George 69-71, 254
  Cox, James 256
  Deans Rag Book 28-29
  Delcroix 179
  Descamps, Roullet 257, 259, 261-262
  Dressel & Kister Co. 159-161, 164 165, 167, 169, 179
  Durand & Jacob 258, 261-262
  Eckert, Richard & Co. 160, 161, 162
  Effanbee 156-157
  Egrefeuil, Felix 66, 67
  Ellis, Joel 20, 21
  F.G. 2-4
  Galluba & Hoffman 184

Gesland, A. 51, 52, 53
Goebel 159, 161, 166, 179
Heber & Co. 184
Hertwig & Co. 184
Heubach, Gebruder 168
Hieulle, Edmond 66, 67
Ives, Blakeslee & Co. 180-181
Jaquet-Proz 256
Jumeau, Emile 38-39, 44-48, 49-50, 51, 173
Koniglich, Porzellan Manufaktur (K.P.M.) 160
Kruse, Kathe 25-27, 29. 31-35
Lambert 261-262
Lenci 22-24, 30
Maelzel 257
Maillandet 256-257
Marque A. 109
Marseille, Armand 67, 68
Mattel 133-135
Royal Rudolstadt 162, 163
Schmidt, Bruno 161
Schoenhut, Albert 72, 74-75, 79-83
Simon & Halbig 38
Sohne, Ernest Bohne 164, 166
Vichy 258-259, 260-261
Volkstadt-Rudolstadt 160, 161, 163
Wellings, Norah 29-30
Manufacturers (Miniatures)
  Adrian Cook Metal Works 191
  Avery, W. & Son 196
  Bailey, Roswell 217
  Crotens, John C. 215
  Elder, J.W. 197
  Limoges 214
  Pia, Peter 191, 223, 224, 228
  Schneegras, Gebruder 230
  Schomiegias, Gobraeder 208
  Schweizer of Dissen, Bavaria 224
  Shackman, B & Co. 234
Marionettes 10-13
Marks, Suzanne 125-128
"Marmi" 134
Marque, A. 109
Marseille, Armand 67, 68
Mattel 133-135
  Baby Alex Paul 133
  Baby Beans 134
  Baby First Step 133
  Baby's Hungry 135
  Baby Rosebud 133
  Littlest Angel 135
  Marmi 134
  Melissa 135
  Cheerful-Tearful 134
  Kiddles 135
McLaughlin Bros. 226-229, 245-246
Melissa 135
Miniatures
  Furniture 188-191, 194-196, 197, 202-204, 205-207, 219-221, 222-225, 228, 230-233, 234-237, 238-239
  Books 236
  Dolls 192, 235, 237

Dishes 213-217, 237
  Accessories 213-217, 222-225
  Bathroom 218-221
Museums 71-73, 109, 193

—N—

Neapolitan figures 56-61
NIADA 100-104, 132-135, 152-155, 170, 173
Nut dolls 43

—O—

ODACA 123-126, 129
Odenrider, Ada 153-154
O'Neill, Rose 251-254

—P—

Paperdolls 43, 54-55, 192
Papier Mache dolls 5-9, 14-19, 53, 64-65, 67, 77, 180-181
Parian dolls 170-173
Patsy 156-157
Paulson, Wee 129-131
Peary, Admiral Robert E. 182-184
Peary, Marie Ahnighito 183-184
Pedlar dolls 14-18
Penny Wooden Dolls 114
Phalibois 201
Photographs, Antique 61-63
Pia, Peter 191, 223, 224, 228
Pierrot 167-169
Placque dolls 174-176
Plastic dolls ... 133-135, 136-139, 149-151
Political dolls 53-55
Portrait dolls 66, 67, 68, 100, 138, 139, 141, 142, 146-148, 164-166
Poupees du Littoral 2-4
Precious Baby 137
President's Wives 139

—Q—

"Queen Anne" dolls 112, 114, 115
Quiz-Kin doll 138, 149

—R—

R.R. 49, 50
Royal Rudolstadt 162, 163

—S—

Saalfield & Co. 244-245, 250
Scarlett 137
Schmidt, Bruno 161
Schneegass, Gebruder 230
Schoenhut, Albert 72, 74-75, 79-83
Schomiegias, Gobraeder 208
Schweizer of Dissen, Bavaria 224
Seri Kawa, Eiko 111
Shackman, B & Co. 234
Simon & Halbig 38
Snowbabies 182-184
Soap dolls 53-54
Sohne, Ernest Bohne 164, 166
Sorensen, Lewis 153

Index

Sounds of Music 137, 138, 139
Southern Belle 139, 151
"Spitzen figuren" 166
Stores
   Au Bon Marche 50, 51
   Bebe Louvre 50
Sullo, Rose 155

— T —

Techniques (Doll-making) 8, 10-11, 31-35, 102, 116-117, 126-127, 134-135, 142
Terra Cotta dolls 56-61, 179
Theroude, Alexandre 256, 258-259
Thieme, Carl 165
Thompson, Martha 173
Thorne, Mrs. James Ward (Rooms) ... 207
Tuck, Raphael & Sons, Co. 245-246

— V —

Vichy 258-261
Vinyl dolls (see "Plastic")
Volkstadt-Rudolstadt 160-161, 163

— W —

Wax dolls 77
Wee Patsy 157
Wellings, Norah 29. 30
Wendy 138, 149-151
Winkler, Friedrich E. 50
Wooden dolls 10-13, 14-18, 20-21, 42, 56-61, 72, 74-75, 110-113, 114-115, 116-119, 152, 154, 155

— Z —

Zeller, Fawn 173

Author Index

Bland, Ann 140-142
Bucholz, Shirley 146-148
Bullard, Helen 102-108, 110-113, 114-115, 116-119, 132-135, 152-155
Byfield, Magda 10-13, 25-27, 28-30, 31-35, 38-39, 49-50, 51-53, 56-60, 174-175
Child, Julie Masterson 69-70
Cieslik, Jurgen & Marianne 185-186
Clendenien, John W. 74-75
Coleman, Dorothy & Evelyn 2-4, 22-24, 61-63, 77-78, 83-86, 194-196
Congram, Marjorie 202-204, 205-207
Cook, Catherine 188-190, 208-212, 213-217, 218, 221, 222-225, 226-229, 230-233
Crowley, Jean 182-184
Hartlap, Diane 109
Herron, R. Lane 120-124, 125-128, 129-131, 142-145
Hillier, Mary 256-259, 260-262
Howard, Susan B. 191-193, 197
Hunter, Marsha Trentham 97-99
Lavitt, Wendy 40-43
Marion, Frieda 159-163, 164-166, 167-169, 176-179
McClintock, Inez B. 251-255
Mish, Eleanor J. 14-19
Narkiewicz, Beverly 20-21
Noell, Dorothy H. 91-95
Pullar, Elizabeth 79-82, 234-237, 241-244, 244-246, 247, 248-250
Shoemaker, Rhoca 149-151
Simonelli, Yolanda 5-9, 36-37, 44-48, 64-65, 100-104, 170-173, 180-181
Stiles, Emma 238-239
Whorton, Judith 53-55, 66-68, 87-88, 89-90, 136-139, 146-148, 156-157, 198-200, 201-202

265